The Civil War
A Narrative

ALL THESE WERE HONOURED IN THEIR GENERATIONS

AND WERE THE GLORY OF THEIR TIMES

THERE BE OF THEM

THAT HAVE LEFT A NAME BEHIND THEM

THAT THEIR PRAISES MIGHT BE REPORTED

AND SOME THERE BE WHICH HAVE NO MEMORIAL

WHO ARE PERISHED AS THOUGH THEY HAD NEVER BEEN

AND ARE BECOME AS THOUGH THEY HAD NEVER BEEN BORN

AND THEIR CHILDREN AFTER THEM

BUT THESE WERE MERCIFUL MEN

WHOSE RIGHTEOUSNESS HATH NOT BEEN FORGOTTEN

WITH THEIR SEED SHALL CONTINUALLY REMAIN

A GOOD INHERITANCE

AND THEIR CHILDREN ARE WITHIN THE COVENANT

THEIR SEED STANDETH FAST

AND THEIR CHILDREN FOR THEIR SAKES

THEIR SEED SHALL REMAIN FOR EVER

AND THEIR GLORY SHALL NOT BE BLOTTED OUT

THEIR BODIES ARE BURIED IN PEACE

BUT THEIR NAME LIVETH FOR EVERMORE

Ecclesiasticus xliv

THE
Civil War

A Narrative

★ ★

FIVE FORKS
to APPOMATTOX

★ ★

Victory and Defeat

By SHELBY FOOTE

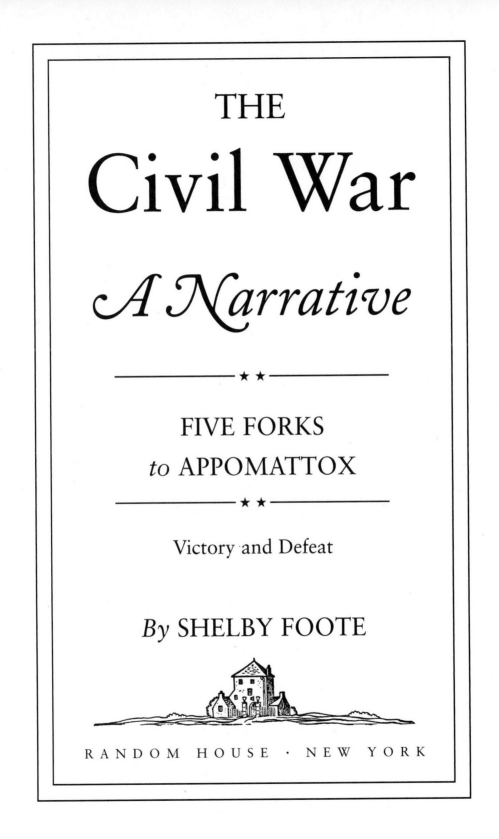

RANDOM HOUSE · NEW YORK

Library of Congress Cataloging in Publication Data
Foote, Shelby.
The Civil War.
CONTENTS.—1.   Fort Sumter to Perryville.—
2.   Fredericksburg to Meridian.—3.   Red River to
Appomattox.
1.   United States—History—Civil War.
E468.F7 973.7 58-988
ISBN 0-307-29031-X
Manufactured in the United States of America
10 9 8 7 6 5 4 3 2 1

CONTENTS

★ � ☆

☆

Five Forks
to
Appomattox

☆

Grant's Close-Out Plan
Early Spring 1865

Miles
0   200

Atlantic Ocean

Gulf of Mexico

MEADE AND ORD 120,000
Washington
Richmond
Petersburg
SHERIDAN 10,000
Winchester
Lynchburg
Danville
Greensboro
Raleigh
Goldsboro
New Bern
SCHOFIELD 24,000
Fayetteville
Cheraw
Wilmington
Charleston
Savannah
Jacksonville
SHERMAN 60,000
Columbia
Milledgeville
STONEMAN 4,000
Knoxville
Chattanooga
Charleston
Cincinnati
Frankfort
Bowling Green
Nashville
Louisville
Indianapolis
Atlanta
Macon
Columbus
Waycross
Tallahassee
WILSON 12,000
Tuscaloosa
Selma
Montgomery
20,000
Mobile
CANBY 45,000
Tupelo
Meridian
Jackson
Memphis
Cairo
St. Louis
Springfield
Jefferson City
Fayetteville
Little Rock
Vicksburg
Baton Rouge
New Orleans
Shreveport
Galveston
Topeka

CHAPTER

✗ **1** ✗

A Tightening Noose

★ ✗ ☆

TECUMSEH SHERMAN SHEATHED HIS CLAWS
for the occupation of Savannah. Not only did he retain the city's elected
officials at their posts, conducting business more or less as usual; he even
allowed Episcopal ministers to omit from their services the traditional
prayer for God to "behold and bless" the President of the United States.
"Jeff Davis and the devil both need it," he remarked, implying that
Abraham Lincoln didn't. Meantime he kept a restraining hand on the
veterans he had described, on the eve of their arrival, as "burning to
avenge the national wrong." Geary's division garrisoned the town —
milder-mannered Easterners for the most part, whose commander, ex-
ercising talents he had developed as mayor of San Francisco a decade
back, tempered discipline with compassion. He hauled in firewood to
warm the hearths and hearts of citizens, reopened markets for the sale
of farm goods, and encouraged public meetings at which, in time, a vote
of thanks was tendered "the noble Geary" and a resolution was adopted
urging Governor Brown to call a state convention for peace discussions.
Savannah's people knew that this was basically Sherman's doing, and all
in all the consensus was that the red-haired conqueror, whose coming
they had so greatly feared while he drew nearer mile by smoky mile,
had been maligned by editors whose views were printed in regions he
had not visited, so far. If not benign, he proved at any rate forbearing, and
certainly not the apocalyptic monster they had been told to expect before
he landed in their midst.

He himself was rather amused, seeing in all this a parallel to the
behavior in far-off Natchez, well over two years ago, of propertied
Confederates who found in coöperation a hope for the preservation, if
not of their treasured way of life, then in any case of their fine old
homes: an inducement altogether lacking, incidentally, in such new-
rich towns as Vicksburg and Atlanta, whose defiance was characterized
as an outgrowth of their war-boom attitude. He could chuckle over that,

referring to Savannah's mayor, Dr Richard D. Arnold, as "completely 'subjugated.'" But there was little of amusement in the reaction of those editors who had warned of his savage nature. "A dangerous bait to deaden the spirit of resistance in other places," the Richmond *Examiner* said of this pretended mildness down the coast, and the rival *Dispatch* was even more specific that same day, January 7, in exposing the duplicity being practiced. "Sherman seems to have changed his character as completely as the serpent changes his skin with the approach of spring," the Virginia editor observed, and then discerned a likeness in the general to an animal just as sneaky in its way, but considerably more voracious: "His repose, however, is the repose of the tiger. Let him taste blood once more and he will be as brutal as ever."

In point of fact, there were sounder grounds for this suppositional metaphor than anyone had any way of knowing without access to certain letters the Ohioan was sending and receiving through this period of rest and preparation. "Should you capture Charleston," Halleck wrote on learning that the Carolina march had been approved, "I hope that by *some accident* the place may be destroyed, and if a little salt should be sown upon its site it may prevent the growth of future crops of nullification and secession." Sherman's plan was not to move on Charleston, "a mere desolated wreck . . . hardly worth the time it would take to starve it out," but rather to feint simultaneously at that point and Augusta, respectively on the right and left of his true line of march, and strike instead at Columbia, the capital between. However, he told Halleck, "I will bear in mind your hint as to Charleston, and do not think 'salt' will be necessary. When I move, the XV Corps" — Logan's: the Illinois soldier-politician returned to duty January 8, bringing Lincoln's congratulatory thank-you note along — "will be on the right of the right wing, and their position will naturally bring them into Charleston first. . . . If you have watched the history of that corps, you will have remarked that they generally do their work pretty well."

Nor was that the worst of it, by far. For all the alarm rebel editors felt on contemplating the repose of the tiger in coastal Georgia, they would have been a great deal more disturbed, and with equal justification, if they had known what was in store for them throughout the rest of their country east of the Mississippi. Sherman's march to scourge the Carolinas on his way to gain Lee's rear, while altogether the heftiest, was by no means the only move Grant planned to make on the thousand-mile-wide chessboard he pored over in his tent at City Point. The time had come to close out the Confederacy entirely, he believed, and he proceeded accordingly. He did so, moreover, not without a measure of personal satisfaction, although this was incidental to his larger purpose. Benjamin Prentiss, John McClernand, Don Carlos Buell, William Rosecrans, all had incurred his displeasure in the course of his rise to the top of the military heap — with the result that, shelved or snubbed into retirement, they were all four out of the war. And so too now, to all effect, was George Thomas: or soon would be, so far at least as a share in the final victory was concerned. Idle since its mid-December triumph over Hood, his army was quite the largest force available for carrying out the peripheral work Grant had in mind, but the general-in-chief had no intention of exposing himself to another nerve-wracking span of trying to prod Old Slow Trot into motion. Instead he proposed to do to the Virginian, in the wake of the botched pursuit that followed Nashville, what Halleck had done to Grant himself after Shiloh and Vicksburg; to wit, dismember him. This he would do by dispersing his troops — some 46,000 of them, all told — leaving Thomas with barely a third of his present command to garrison Middle and East Tennessee and north-ern Alabama: a thankless assignment, unlikely to call for much fighting, if any, unless Lee somehow managed to get away westward, in which case Thomas would be expected to stand in his path while Meade and Sherman came up in his rear to accomplish his destruction.

Schofield was the first to be subtracted. In early January, expect-ing Fort Fisher to fall under renewed pressure from Porter and units already on the way back there from the Army of the James, Grant ordered the XXIII Corps detached from Thomas and hurried north and east, by boat and rail, to a point near Washington. There Schofield would put his 14,000 men aboard transports for a trip down the coast and a share in the follow-up drive on Wilmington, which then would be converted from a haven for blockade-runners to an intermediary refuge and supply base for Sherman, in case he ran into trouble slogging north. Otherwise, reinforced to a strength of 24,000 by troops from Foster and the Army of the James, Schofield was to move up the North Carolina littoral to occupied New Bern, where he would turn inland for a meeting with Sherman at Goldsboro, and from there the two columns would go on together — better than 80,000 strong — for the rest of the march, by way of Raleigh, into Virginia. Meade by then would have been joined by Sheridan from the Shenandoah Valley, and Grant would have well over 200,000 seasoned fighting men around Petersburg and Richmond: surely enough, and more than enough, as he put it, to "wipe out Lee." However, by way of encouraging further confusion in the region to be traversed, he also instructed Thomas to send Stoneman and 4000 troopers pounding eastward from Knoxville into North Carolina, where they would serve to distract the state's defenders while Sherman and Schofield were moving northward through it near the coast. This done, Stoneman too would cross into Virginia, where he would not only rip up Lee's supply lines west of Lynchburg, but would also perhaps be in position, when the time came, to get in on the kill.

That so much concerted havoc was about to be visited on the Carolinas and the Old Dominion did not mean that the Deep South was to be neglected or spared. No; Grant had plans for its disruption, too. In addition to Schofield's corps, shifted eastward in mid-January, he also ordered A. J. Smith's detached, along with a division of cavalry under Brigadier General Joseph Knipe, and sent by steamer down the Mississippi to New Orleans, where Edward Canby had gathered the survivors of last year's expedition up and down Red River. Smith's 16,000 veterans, most of whom had also had a share in that unfortunate adventure, would lift Canby's available strike force to a strength of 45,000 of all arms: enough, Grant thought, for him to undertake the long-deferred reduction of Mobile, which continued defiant, behind its outlying fortifications, despite the loss of its Bay and access to the Gulf. Moreover, that was only to be the first step in the campaign Grant proposed. Once the city fell (if not before; haste was to be the governing factor) Canby would move with a flying column of 20,000, mainly composed of Smith's free-swinging gorilla-guerillas, north and east into the heart of Alabama. Specifically he would proceed against Selma, the principal center for the production of munitions in that part of the country, where he would make contact — much as Sherman was to do with Schofield, six hundred miles to the northeast — with still another detachment from Thomas's fast-dwindling army up in Tennessee. In the weeks that followed the pursuit of Hood from Nashville, James Wilson had continued to mount, arm, and train incoming cavalry units at so rapid a rate that by the end of January he had no less than 22,000 troopers under his command. Knipe took 5000 of these to New Orleans with Smith, and Wilson presently was instructed to strike southward with 12,000 of the rest, sturdily mounted and armed to a man with repeaters that gave them more firepower than a corps of infantry. Forrest would no doubt attempt to interfere, as he had done before in such cases; Grant was willing to leave it to Wilson whether to avoid or run right over him, which he should be able to do rather easily, considering his advantage in numbers and equipment. In any case, his immediate objective would be Selma, where he would combine with Canby's flying column, after wrecking the manufactory installations there, to continue the heartland penetration eastward: first to Montgomery, the Confederacy's original capital, and then across the Georgia line to Columbus and Macon, all three of which had been spared till now the iron hand of war.

Such then was Grant's close-out plan. As he saw it, the Confederacy was already whipped and clinging groggily to the ring ropes; all that remained was for him to land what boxers called a one-two punch, delivered in rapid sequence to belly and jaw, except that this was to be thrown with both hands simultaneously. In broad outline, the design resembled the one he had worked out nearly a year ago, on taking command of all the armies of the Union, but this time he was not obliged to include any unwanted elements, such as the Red River venture, or any unwanted subordinates, such as Banks. For example, aside from maintaining garrisons within it to preserve the status quo, and gunboats on patrol along its watery flank to keep it cut off from all contact eastward, the Transmississippi had no share in his calculations; either it would wither on its own, from sheer neglect or folly such as Price's recent raid, or else he would attend to it in a similar undistracted fashion when the time came. Not only would this affordable neglect represent a considerable savings in troops who could be used where they were wanted, but the fact was he now had more of them than he had had when he began his forward movement, back in May. Despite heavy losses incurred in the past nine months — 100,000 in eastern Virginia alone, and about that number elsewhere — his total combat force, East and West, had grown to better than 600,000 effectives, exclusive of reserves amounting to half as many more; whereas the enemy's had dwindled to barely 160,000 of all arms. That too was part of his calculations, and part of his hope for an early end to the conflict which by now had cost the country — the two countries, Confederates insisted — close to a million casualties, on and off the field of battle, North and South.

Nowhere in all this was there any mention of an assignment for Ben Butler, and the reason was quite simple. He was no longer around. Grant had fired him; or at any rate — now that the election was safely over — had persuaded Lincoln to fire him. The one-time Democratic senator was out of the war for good.

Fort Fisher had been the final straw. Though Grant said nothing of the ineffectual powder-boat explosion or even of the precipitate withdrawal, when he had determined the facts in the case he wrote to Stanton requesting the Massachusetts general's removal. "I do this with reluctance," he declared, "but the good of the service requires it. In my absence General Butler necessarily commands, and there is a lack of confidence felt in his military ability, making him an unsafe commander for a large army. His administration of the affairs in his department is also objectionable." This was put aboard a fast packet at City Point on January 5, and when Grant found out next morning that Stanton was on his way to Savannah to visit Sherman, he followed it up with a telegram directly to the Commander in Chief. "I wrote a letter to the Secretary of War, which was mailed yesterday, asking to have General Butler removed from command. Learning that the Secretary left Washington yesterday, I telegraph asking you that prompt action may be taken in the matter."

Lincoln's response was prompt indeed. General Order Number 1, issued "by direction of the President of the United States," arrived by wire the following day. "Maj. Gen. B. F. Butler is relieved from command of the Department of North Carolina and Virginia.... [He] will repair to Lowell, Mass., and report by letter to the Adjutant General of the Army."

Grant passed the word to Butler next morning, January 8, and named Ord the new commander of the Army of the James, some 8000 of whose members had embarked — or reëmbarked for the most part, having only just returned from the fiasco down the coast — at Bermuda Hundred four days ago, under Brigadier General Alfred Terry, for another go at Fort Fisher. Butler, however, did not "repair to Lowell" as ordered; at least not yet. He went instead to Washington, where political connections assured him a sympathetic hearing before the Joint Congressional Committee on the Conduct of the War, which assembled just under ten days later to hear his complaint of unjust treatment by the Administration and its three-starred creature down at City Point. Grant had left the charges vague, presumably on grounds that they would be harder to refute that way, but Butler at once got down to specifics. He had been relieved, he said, for his failure to take Fort Fisher, and he brought along charts and duplicates of reports by subordinates to prove he had been right to call off the attack in mid-career, not only because Porter had failed to give him adequate support, but also because a close-up study of the thick-walled fort and its outlying torpedo fields had shown it to be impregnable in the first place, both to naval bombardment and to infantry assault. While he spoke, referring assiduously to the documents at hand, a hubbub rose outside the room — cheers in the street, the muffled crump of shotless guns discharging a salute, and newsboys crying, "Extra! Extra! Read all about it!" Fort Fisher, it seemed, had fallen. "Impossible!" Butler protested, clutching his papers. "It's a mistake, Sir." But it turned out to be more than possible; it was a fact, confirmed by dispatches on hand from Porter. Laughter rippled, then roared through the room. After a moment of shock adjustment, the cock-eyed general joined in as heartily as anyone. Adjournment followed, and as the members and spectators began filing out, still laughing, Butler raised his hand and called pontifically for silence. "Thank God for victory," he intoned.

In time, the committee not only voted unanimously to exonerate the former Bay State senator — referred to affectionately by a colleague as "the smartest damned rascal that ever lived" — from all blame in connection with the failure of the earlier expedition; its members also commended him for having had the nerve, the presence of mind under pressure, to call off the assault at the last minute, thereby saving many lives. Such action, they ruled, "was clearly justified by the facts then known," including Porter's ragged gunnery, which had done little damage to the fort, and his inadequate support of the troops ashore. Not that their judgment affected either officer's future war career; Butler had none, and the admiral even now was receiving congratulations for his share in one of the best-conducted operations of the war, by land or sea or both.

Terry and his 8000 — Butler's force, plus two brigades of Negro troops for added heft — reached Beaufort on schedule, January 8, for the rendezvous with Porter and his sixty warships. Delayed there by another three-day blow, they planned carefully for this second amphibious strike at Fort Fisher, then set out down the coast and dropped anchor before nightfall, January 12, within sight of the objective. Porter was altogether pleased with his new partner, whom he pronounced "my beau ideal of a soldier and a general," adding: "Our coöperation has been most cordial." Partly this was the result of Grant's instructions, which were for Terry to get along harmoniously with his sea-going associate, and partly it was because of Terry's natural tact and training, in and out of the army, where, as the phrase went, he had "found a home." A thirty-seven-year-old former clerk of the New Haven County superior court, admitted to the Connecticut bar while still at Yale, he had fought as a militia colonel at First Bull Run and then stayed on to pick up much experience in coastal operations, including the expedition against Port Royal, the reduction of Fort Pulaski, and the siege of Battery Wagner, after which he was made a brigadier and put in charge of a division in the Army of the James. Now that he had command of a provisional corps, with a promotion to major general in the works, he was determined to justify the added star by disproving Butler's contention that Fort Fisher could not be taken by assault. Once ashore, he told Porter, he intended to stay there until Confederate Point was Federal Point again, by right of exclusive occupation, and blockade runners would no longer find a haven up Cape Fear River for the discharge of their cargoes.

Just how important those cargoes were to continued resistance by the rebels was shown by the fact that R. E. Lee himself had sent word to the fort commander, William Lamb, that he could not subsist his army without the supplies brought in there. More specifically, a government report of goods run into Wilmington and Charleston during the last nine weeks of the year — practically all into the North Carolina port, for Charleston was tightly blockaded — amounted to "8,632,000 pounds of meat, 1,507,000 pounds of lead, 1,933,000 pounds of saltpeter, 546,000 pairs of shoes, 316,000 pairs of blankets, 520,000 pounds of coffee, 69,000 rifles, 97 packages of revolvers, 2639 packages of medicine, 43 cannon," and much else. Lamb was back down to a garrison of 800 men, the Junior Reservists having departed, and though he had appealed to both the district and department commanders, W. H. C. Whiting and Braxton Bragg, no reinforcements had arrived by the time the outsized Union armada returned and dropped anchor, just out of range of his biggest guns, on the evening of January 12.

Two hours before dawn, Porter opened the action by committing all five ironclads at short range, his object being to provoke the defenders into disclosing the location of their guns by muzzle flashes. It worked, and he followed this up after sunrise by bringing the rest of his 627 pieces to bear on targets the lookouts had spotted. The result, according to one Confederate crouched beneath this deluge of better than a hundred shells a minute, was "beyond description. No language can describe that terrific bombardment." Moreover, the fire was not only heavy; it was highly accurate. Butler's complaint that the navy's gunnery had been ragged throughout the previous attempt was in large part true, and Porter, amid his denials, had taken pains to correct it. For one thing, his marksmen then had fired at the rebel flag, high on its staff above the fort, so that many of their shots plunged harmlessly into the river beyond the narrow sand peninsula. This time, he cautioned in his preliminary directive, "the object is to lodge the shell in the parapets, and tear away the traverses under which the bombproofs are located. A shell now and then exploding over a gun en barbette may have good effect, but there is nothing like lodging the shell before it explodes. . . . Commanders are directed to strictly enjoin their officers and men never to fire at the flag or pole, but to pick out the guns; the stray shots will knock the flagstaff down." And so it was. He saw through the smoke and flying debris that his instructions were being followed to the letter. One by one, sometimes two by two, rebel pieces winked out and fell silent in the boil of dust and flame. "Traverses began to disappear," he would report, "and the southern angle of Fort Fisher commenced to look very dilapidated."

Since 8 o'clock that morning, four hours into the bombardment, Terry had been landing troops on the stretch of beach Weitzel had selected in December. By 3 o'clock all 8000 were ashore. This time, in addition to the accustomed "forty rounds," each man carried three days' rations on his person, backed by a six-day reserve of hard bread and a 300,000-round bulk supply of rifle ammunition. He had come to stay, and he emphasized this by digging a stout defensive line across the peninsula, facing north in case Hoke's division, known to be camped this side of Wilmington, tried an attack from that direction. Out on the water all this time the fleet kept up its smothering fire on the fort two miles below. Porter was clearly having the better of the exchange, yet a number of his ships had taken cruel punishment; *Canonicus*, for example, a monitor from the James River squadron, took 36 hits in the course of the day, and though none of them pierced her armor she was badly cut up about her deck and wore out several relays of gunners, stunned by the jar of solids against their turret and unnerved by the ping and spatter of bullets aimed at their sight-slits by sharpshooters in the fort. Porter cared little or nothing for any of this, however. He kept banging away past sunset, using every gun that could be brought to bear, and only retired his wooden vessels after twilight. Even so, he held the ironclads on station all night long, with instructions to continue lobbing their 11- and 15-inch shells into the shoreward darkness and thus discourage the rebel repair crews from doing much about the damage the place had suffered from the unrelenting daylong pounding, much of it heavy caliber and most of it point-blank.

Friday the 13th had indeed been an unlucky day for Lamb and the fort in his charge. More than a hundred of its defenders had fallen, and less than half the guns on its seaward face were still in operation. Despite his pleas, no reinforcements had come downriver: only the district commander and his staff, who arrived at the height of the bombardment. Whiting had come unglued at Petersburg last spring, victim of a too vivid imagination, but he seemed resolute now, even jaunty, in contrast to the gloomy news he brought. "Lamb, my boy," he announced as he entered the works, "I have come to share your fate. You and your garrison are to be sacrificed." Startled, the young colonel replied: "Don't say so, General. We shall certainly whip the enemy again." But the Mississippian explained that when he left Wilmington that morning, the department commander — Bragg had returned by now from his failed attempt to intercept Sherman down in Georgia — "was hastily removing his stores and ammunition, and was looking for a place to fall back upon." In other words, so far as the survival of Fort Fisher was concerned, Hoke and his 6000 veterans might as well have remained with Lee in Virginia; Bragg was unlikely to order them within range of Porter's big-gunned warships for a fight with the superior force Terry had landed and intrenched just north of the doomed fort. Lamb hoped against hope that Whiting was wrong in this assessment, yet as the day wore on he came more and more to see that, under the rain of all that metal, there was little he could do about it, even in the way of repairing damages. Nightfall brought a slackening though by no means a cessation of the fire. Still at work beyond the surf, the five ironclads bowled their big projectiles "along the parapets, scattering shrapnel in the darkness" with such effect, Lamb said later, that "we could scarcely gather up and bury our dead without fresh casualties."

Dawn brought a resumption of the full-scale bombardment, with all the Federal warships back on station. In the December effort Porter had fired 20,271 projectiles weighing 1,275,000 pounds. This time, having called for a more deliberate rate of fire, he would expend several hundred fewer rounds — 19,682 all told — but greater reliance on his heavier weapons resulted in a total weight of 1,652,638 pounds, a new record for the amount of metal thrown in a single naval engagement. Lamb's casualties rose above two hundred before this second day was over, and though some 700 North Carolina soldiers and a detachment of 50 sailors arrived to lift the strength of the garrison to about 1550 — minus, of course, the sick and wounded and the dead — there was little the defenders could do but huddle in their bombproofs, awaiting word from lookouts that the land assault was under way, at which point they were to turn out and contest it, hand-to-hand if necessary.

It did not come today, as Lamb expected, but it would tomorrow. Porter and Terry met that evening aboard the flagship *Malvern*, and while the ironclads kept up their nightlong harassment, holding the rebel gunners in their burrows, the two commanders planned the timing for next day's climax to their joint effort. The fleet would resume its all-out pounding of the objective until 3 o'clock, then suddenly cease fire for the assault, which would be made by two separate columns driving down opposite sides of the peninsula, thus avoiding the field of torpedoes north of the fort. On the river flank, half of Terry's troops would attack the land face near its western end, leaving the other 4000 to hold the in-trenchments against a possible attempt by Hoke to interfere at this critical moment. Simultaneously, a 2000-man all-navy column, recruited piecemeal from most of the vessels of the fleet — 1600 sailors, armed with cutlasses and revolvers, and 400 marines armed with rifles — would advance down the beach to strike the northeast salient of the fort, where the land and seaward faces joined. Both forces were to press the issue until Fort Fisher was secured.

Sunday, January 15, went much as Porter and Terry had planned it aboard the *Malvern*. A calm sea, after two days of intensive target practice, so improved the fleet's marksmanship that by noon only one gun remained in service on the seaward face and none at all on the other, whose palisade was swept away by the longitudinal fire. Around 2 o'clock a steamer put in at the wharf in rear and began unloading a brigade of South Carolinians sent downriver by Bragg in response to Whiting's telegraphic pleas. Only about a third of them made it ashore, however, before the boat was driven off by a storm of shells from the warships on the far side of the fort. These 350, exposed without pre-amble to this holocaust of screaming metal, barely replaced the casualties Lamb had suffered over the past three days, and by the time he got them into bombproofs, he said later, "they were out of breath, disor-ganized, and more or less demoralized." Just then a lookout shouted, "Colonel, the enemy are about to charge!" A heavy blue column was working its way down the beach, apparently with the intention of gaining a close-up position from which to launch an assault. While Lamb called out the garrison to meet the threat, Whiting got off a frantic wire to Bragg: "Enemy on the beach in front of us in very heavy force. ... Attack! Attack! It is all I can say and all you can do." By now the time was straight-up 3 o'clock, and the roar of guns hushed abruptly beyond the surf. There was a moment of eerie stillness, broken in turn by all the steam whistles of the fleet, shrieking and moaning in concert. Lamb wondered at this, then realized they were sounding the charge for the troops ashore. "A soul-stirring signal," he called it, "both to besiegers and besieged."

Cutlasses flashing in the wintry sunlight, the bluejackets made their dash along the beach, only to be stopped within 300 yards of the objective by well-aimed volleys of musketry. There they held on for a time, their losses mounting while they dug frantically in the loose sand for cover, then turned, despite the pleas of their officers — who "in their anxiety to be the first into the fort," a wounded ensign later said, "had advanced to the heads of the columns, leaving no one to steady the men behind" — and fled back up the low-tide-widened beach. One who did what he could to stop them was William Cushing, recently promoted for having sunk the *Albemarle*. He was weeping over the loss of a friend, shot down along with some 300 others in the course of the attack, and swearing at the retreaters in his frustration; to no avail. "We witnessed what we had never seen before," Lamb would report, "a disorderly rout of American sailors and marines."

Exultant, he looked down the line of blasted works and saw, to his dismay, three Federal battle flags atop the ramparts near its western end. Concealed by trees and brush along the river, the army column had made its way up close to the fortifications undetected, then mounted them in a rush.

Whiting too had seen the enemy flags, and while Lamb prepared to follow with the rest of the main body, which had repulsed and been distracted by the attack on this end of the land face, the Mississippian led a countercharge against the other. He retook one of two lost gun chambers, but was wounded twice in quick succession. By the time Lamb arrived with reinforcements, the general had been carried rearward on a stretcher and a fierce struggle was raging for possession of the connecting traverse. With the penetration thus contained (though only by the hardest; "The contestants were savagely firing into each other's faces, and in some cases clubbing their guns, being too close to load and fire") the attackers seemed to falter; Lamb believed that if he could hold on until nightfall he would be able to drive them out. Just then, however, the fleet steamed back into action, shelling the Confederates massed in rear of the lost segment of their line. The result, combined with all that had gone before, was "indescribably horrible," he said. "Great cannon were broken in two, and over their ruins were lying the dead; others were partly buried in graves dug by the shells which had slain them." Up near the occupied portion of the works, where the warships could not intervene for fear of hitting their own men, the fighting continued at close quarters. "If there has ever been a longer or more stubborn hand-to-hand encounter," Lamb declared, "I have failed to meet with it in history."

Knocked sprawling by a bullet in the hip, he was put in a cot alongside Whiting's in the hospital bombproof. Outside, the fighting and shelling continued past sundown, on into darkness. At 8 o'clock an aide reported the land face lost from end to end; the contest now was for the interior, and he suggested that further resistance would be a useless sacrifice of life. Lamb replied that so long as he lived he would never surrender. Whiting approved. "Lamb," he assured him from the adjoining cot, "when you die I will assume command, and I will not surrender the fort."

By now, however, Terry had four brigades inside the place. They did their work well, as indeed they had done from the outset, pressing the defenders southward down the sea face, traverse by traverse, until there was nothing left to fall back on. At 10 o'clock that night the flag came down. Something over 500 men had fallen in its defense, and now the survivors were prisoners, including Lamb and Whiting. (The former would survive his wound and a doleful stretch as a captive in Fort Columbus, New York Harbor, but Chase Whiting would die there in March, after nearly eight weeks of suffering from his wounds, complaining bitterly all the while of Bragg's failure to support the beleaguered garrison during a three-day resistance "unparalleled in the history of the war.") Terry lost 955 killed and wounded, Porter 386, ashore and afloat. "If hell is what it is said to be," a weary sailor wrote home next day, "then the interior of Fort Fisher is a fair comparison. Here and there you see great heaps of human beings laying just as they fell, one upon the other. Some groaning piteously, and asking for water. Others whose mortal career is over, still grasping the weapon they used to so good an effect in life."

For all the compacted horror of the scene, and despite the even steeper price the victors paid in blood for its creation, nothing deterred the gaudy all-night celebration that followed the announcement of surrender. "Cheer after cheer came from the fort," a Federal officer would recall, "and was answered by the ships with cheers, rockets, lights of all colors, ringing of bells, steam whistles, and all sorts of unearthly noises." To a watching sailor, "The rockets seemed to shoot higher and sparkle more brilliantly than usual," and even the shrieking whistles, whose shrillness had always hurt his ears, "seemed to discourse a sweet melody." Ashore, the informal distribution of whiskey found among the captured medical stores livened the rout for the jubilant soldiers, sailors, and marines, for whom the end of the fighting meant the end of discipline. Fort Fisher had been a hard go, and officers tended to overlook excesses, including the rapid-fire discharge of revolvers and a good deal of rowdy prowling after souvenirs in the wreckage. In the end, this resulted in tragedy. Guards had been posted at the entrances of some thirty underground powder magazines, but somehow the largest of these — a 20 by 60 foot chamber, roofed over with 18 feet of sand piled in a flat-topped mound sodded with grass to keep the rain from washing it away — was missed. Apparently no one suspected there were between six and seven tons of powder under the springy turf: certainly not the wearier members of a New York regiment, who found it too inviting a bed to be resisted this mild January night, and certainly not two drunken seamen who entered the magazine with lighted torches, shortly after dawn, in search of loot. The resultant explosion added 104 killed and wounded and missing to the Union casualty list, which thus was increased to just under 1500, or roughly three times the number the garrison suffered before it surrendered.

Confederates might find grim satisfaction in such a mishap, just as they did when news arrived that off Charleston this same day, 150 miles to the south, the monitor *Patapsco* struck a torpedo while searching for obstructions in the harbor channel. She went down fast, with the loss of more than half her crew of just over a hundred. Porter, however, was no more inclined to be daunted by this than he was by the explosion of the powder magazine. "Our success is so great that we should not complain," he informed Welles in the dispatch that broke up Butler's hearing before the Joint Committee. "Men, it seems, must die that this Union may live. . . . We regret our companions in arms and shed a tear over their remains, but if these rebels should succeed we would have nothing left us and our lives would be spent in terror and sorrow."

★   ★   ★

Fort Fisher's fall confirmed Butler's. Whatever his friends on the Washington committee might say as to his perspicacious conduct during the earlier attempt, he was gone for good. And so too now, to all effect, was Samuel Curtis; not at Grant's urging, but his own. Promoted to major general as a reward for his Pea Ridge victory nearly three years ago, he was disappointed to find little attention being paid to his recent Westport achievement or the rigorous follow-up southward, down the length of Missouri, into Arkansas and the Indian Territory. Apparently neither the newspapers nor the War Department had space or time for anything but Sherman's triumphal march across Georgia to the sea. Taken aback by this imbalance Curtis fell into a fit of pique. "Sherman's success was glorious," he wrote privately to his brother in early January, "but in justice to myself not equal to my pursuit of Price, in that I had a less force against a larger, won several victories, and had to go as far *through a desolate country*." Thinking it over, and finding it rankled, he applied to the War Department to be spared the strain of another campaign, and his request was promptly granted. Before the month was out he was transferred to command of the Department of the Northwest, with headquarters at Milwaukee, well removed from any possible clash of arms. Nor was there a commander appointed in his stead. As if to suggest that Curtis's role had been superfluous in the first place, Dodge's adjoining Department of the Missouri was simply enlarged to include Kansas and the Nebraska and Utah territories.

But this too went largely unnoticed. A peripheral shift having little to do with the close-out maneuver everyone could see was in the making on the seaboard, such a subtraction had no more bearing on the central issue than, say, the death of seventy-one-year-old Edward Everett, whose two-hour oration had preceded Lincoln's two-minute speech at Gettysburg just over a year ago. By now, with the end conceivably in sight, men looked beyond the cease-fire to insist with a new fervor that the victory be put to proper use. Slavery returned as the burning issue it had been at the outset.

Everett died on January 15, amid a congressional furor over the proposed adoption of a constitutional amendment — the first in more than sixty years — forbidding the existence of slavery "within the United States or any place subject to their jurisdiction." The Senate had approved it nine months earlier, but House proponents then had failed to secure the two-thirds vote required. Lincoln in his December message urged reconsideration during the present session, on grounds that approval would surely follow the seating of newly elected Republicans at the next. "As it is to so go, at all events, may we not agree that the sooner the better?" He asked that, yet he also did a good deal more than ask. He set out to get the necessary votes, mainly by logrolling. One opposed Democrat was promised a government job for his brother in New York; another was assured support in holding onto his contested seat; while a third, hired by a railroad to fight off adverse legislation, was guaranteed the threat would not mature. These three came over more or less gladly, and eight others, firmer in their resistance or more fearful of the home reaction to an outright shift, were similarly bargained into agreeing to abstain. Finally, on the last day of January — as soon as the Administration was reasonably certain of the outcome — House Speaker Schuyler Colfax put the resolution to a vote. Members and spectators alike followed the tally with mounting excitement. It came out 119 aye, 56 nay; passing thus with three switched votes to spare. Colfax's announcement of the result, according to the usually staid *Congressional Globe*, was greeted with an outburst of emotion. "The members on the Republican side of the House instantly sprang to their feet, and, regardless of parliamentary rules, applauded with cheers and clapping of hands. The example was followed by male spectators in the galleries, who waved their hats and cheered long and loud, while the ladies, hundreds of whom were present, rose in their seats and waved their handkerchiefs, participating in adding to the general excitement and intense interest of the scene. This lasted for several minutes."

Outside the chamber it lasted considerably longer. Three batteries of regular artillery, loaded and ready when the time came, began firing a hundred-gun salute from Capitol Hill, and men embraced on the streets in celebration. In addition to the realization that a goal had been reached, there was the feeling that a new road had been taken, even though by no means all were pleased to travel it, not being satisfied that they wanted to go where it led. All twelve amendments up to now, including the last in 1804, had dealt exclusively with governmental powers and functions; that is, they were "constitutional" in the strictest sense.

But this one — lucky or unlucky Thirteen — went beyond that to effect reform in an area recently considered outside the scope of the Constitution, overriding protests that no combination of parties to that contract, however sizeable their majority, could alter it to outlaw a domestic institution that existed before it was written. Pendleton of Ohio, McClellan's running mate in November, voiced his party's opposition in the debate leading up to the roll call. "Neither three-fourths of the states, nor all the states save one, can abolish slavery in that dissenting state," he told the House, "because it lies within the domain reserved entirely to each state for itself, and upon it the other states cannot enter." Such was the States Rights position, many of whose principal supporters had departed, just four years ago this month, to set up on their own. Then came the vote, and States Rights went by the board. Moreover, any last-ditch hope that the Supreme Court might overturn the measure was abandoned when it was noted, not only that five of the nine members — including Salmon Chase — were present for the vote, but also that their judicial gravity scarcely masked their satisfaction at the outcome.

Ironically, this Thirteenth Amendment abolished slavery, rather than assuring its continuance, as a direct result of secession. Six weeks before Sumter, both the Senate and the House had passed by a two-thirds vote a proposed Thirteenth Amendment stating flatly that Congress could never be given "the power to abolish or interfere within any State with the domestic institutions thereof, including that of persons held to labor or service by the laws of said State." Buchanan signed it on the eve of Lincoln's inauguration, but the measure was forgotten when the issue swung to war. On the other hand, if the departed Southerners had remained in Washington they and their northern friends, whose influence would have been for peace, could almost certainly have secured the requisite three-fourths ratification by their respective states. Charles Sumner, well aware of this, wasted no time in consolidating the victory he had worked so hard to win. He appeared before the Supreme Court next day, February 1, to move that a fellow lawyer, John S. Rock of Boston, be admitted to practice before it. Embraced by the Chief Justice, who had prepared his colleagues, the motion carried. Here indeed was a change; for Rock was a Negro, the first of his race to address that high tribunal, which less than a decade ago had denied that Dred Scott, a non-citizen, even had the right to be represented there.

Elated, a crowd with a brass band trooped onto the White House lawn that night and shouted for the President, who came out on a balcony to take the music and greet the serenaders. "Speech! Speech!" they called up, and he obliged them. He praised Congress's action yesterday as "the fitting if not indispensable adjunct to the consummation of the great game we are playing," and emphasized that his aim all along had been to root out this basic cause of national disturbance —

slavery — against the day when the states would be reunited. The Emancipation Proclamation had been issued with that in mind, he said, even though it freed only those slaves who came within the reach of blue-clad soldiers. Moreover, once the war had ended, it might be held invalid by the courts, leaving much of the evil uncorrected and still a subject for contention. "But this amendment is a King's cure for all the evils. It winds the whole thing up." Applauded, Lincoln paused and then remarked in closing that he could not but congratulate all present — himself, the country, and the world — "upon this great moral victory."

The victory claim was valid on other grounds as well, but only within problematical limitations. Ratification, once it came, would give the nation all that he maintained. Yet the dimensions of the victory depended altogether on the dimensions of the country when the amendment was adopted, and this in turn depended — more or less as had been the case, over the past two years, in the application of the Emancipation Proclamation — on the progress, between now and then, of Union arms. In short, it depended on whether Grant's close-out plan succeeded. Sherman's part was the critical one, at least in the early stages, and by coincidence he set out in earnest, this same February 1, on his march north through the Carolinas to gain Lee's rear.

Although he was thus some four weeks behind the schedule he had set for himself when he wrote Grant on Christmas Eve that he expected to start north "in about ten days," the delay was unavoidable. Heavy winter rains had swollen creeks and swamps along his projected route of march, while ice on the Potomac — their staging area, once they arrived from Nashville — prevented Schofield's men from steaming downriver aboard transports on their way to Wilmington. This last did not disturb the red-haired general, any more than had Butler's failure to clear the way by reducing Fort Fisher. "Fizzle; great fizzle!" he snorted when he heard of that yuletide fiasco. "I shall have to go up there and do that job myself. Eat 'em up as I go, and take 'em backside." In this connection he requested Dahlgren to keep up the scare along the South Carolina coast, maneuvering his warships as if to cover a series of landings by Foster, whose troops would go along. That would confuse the rebels throughout Sherman's period of preparation at Savannah. Later, when his march had pulled the defenders inland and cut the seaports off from reinforcements and supplies, such feints could be converted to actual landings, probably against nothing worse than token opposition, and possibly not even that. "I will shake the tree," he told Foster, "and you must be quick to pick up the apples."

He was feeling good, despite the delay, and he showed it. Pride in all his men had done was matched by pride in their conduct throughout the present span of comparative repose: as was demonstrated in a letter informing Grant that, "notwithstanding the habits begotten during our rather vandalic march," the behavior of his soldiers in Savannah had "excited the wonder and admiration of all." Not even a four-day visit by Stanton, January 11–15 — ostensibly for reasons of health, but actually to explore his fellow Ohioan's position on the Negro question — upset Sherman's feeling of well-being. He fancied he had set the Secretary straight as to his views on "Inevitable Sambo," alarming though they were to abolitionists up in Washington. "The South deserves all she has got for her injustice to the negro," he wrote Halleck at the time, "but that is no reason why we should go to the other extreme." Stanton heard him say such things, and seemed not to disapprove. As for the restoration of states now claiming to have departed from the Union, Sherman told Georgians who called on him in the course of the Secretary's visit: "My own opinion is that no negotiations are necessary, nor commissioners, nor conventions, nor anything of the kind.... Georgia is not out of the Union, and therefore talk of 'reconstruction' appears to me inappropriate." Meantime he kept busy, doing all he could to "make a good ready" for the expedition north. Dahlgren's loss of the *Patapsco* outside Charleston, along with 64 of her crew, was more than offset by the news that Porter and Terry had taken Fort Fisher that same day, preparing the way for Schofield, who wrote that he would be off down the coast as soon as the Potomac ice broke up. January was more than half gone by now, and Sherman stepped up the pace of his preparations.

His march would be due north in two columns, enabling him to feint simultaneously at Charleston and Augusta, on the right and left, while aiming in fact at Columbia, between and beyond them. North of the South Carolina capital he would feint again, this time at Chester and Charlotte, then turn east-northeast, through Cheraw and Fayette-ville, for Goldsboro — chosen because two rail lines ran from there to Wilmington and New Bern, up which Schofield would be marching with supplies from those two ports. Refitted and reinforced to a strength of better than 80,000 Sherman then could drive on Raleigh, the North Carolina capital, en route to Petersburg and the combination with Meade. Now as before, Slocum would lead the two-corps left wing, Howard the two-corps right, while Kilpatrick's horsemen shielded the western flank. This time, though, they would stay closer together, cutting a narrower swath for readier mutual support, since an attack was con-sidered far likelier here than in Georgia, where the outcome had been less obviously disastrous to the Confederate high command. "If Lee is a soldier of genius," the red-head explained to his staff, "he will seek to transfer his army from Richmond to Raleigh or Columbia. If he is a man simply of detail, he will remain where he is and his speedy defeat is sure. But I have little fear that he will be able to move; Grant holds him in a vise of iron."

In point of fact, so far as interference was concerned, there was

Shaded area indicates width of swath;
many outlying points were
struck as well.

more to fear from rebel terrain than there was from rebel armies. Not
only would the Carolinas march — 425 miles, all told, from Savannah to
Goldsboro — be nearly half again longer than the one from Atlanta to
the sea; the difference in natural obstacles he would encounter, both in
kind and number, made the earlier expedition appear in retrospect as
something of a lark, a holiday outing in pleasant weather, through a
region of rich crops, ripe for harvest, and livestock waiting only to be
rounded up and butchered. Here the crops had already been gathered,
such as they were, and the cattle were few and scrubby at best, having
little to graze on but muck and palmetto. Moreover, luck had exposed
him to almost no rain on his way through Georgia, and it would not
have mattered a lot in any case; whereas he would be marching now in
the dead of winter, the rainiest in years, and it mattered a great deal.
Many rivers lay ahead, all reportedly brim full. After the Savannah,
there would be the Salkehatchie and the Edisto, the Congaree and the
Wateree, the Pee Dee and the Lumber, the Cape Fear and finally the
Neuse, all nine of them major streams, with creeks and bayous webbing
the swampy ground between, wet with all the rain that had fallen and
was falling between the seaboard and the near slopes of the Appalachi-

ans. Yet here too Sherman could prepare for trouble, much as he had done when he drilled repair crews for work on the railroads north of Atlanta and Chattanooga. Michigan lumbermen and rail-splitters from Indiana and Illinois were organized into a pioneer corps, 6600 strong, armed with axes for cutting, splitting, and laying saplings flat-side-down to corduroy roads for the 2500 wagons and 600 ambulances rolling northward in the wake of his 60,000 marchers. He did not intend to get bogged down, nor did he intend to be slowed down in avoiding it: in token of which he had already selected a rangy half-thoroughbred bay named Old Sam to serve as his accustomed mount on the campaign. Sam, a staff major noted ominously, was "a horribly fast-walking horse."

Beginning the feint, Sherman sent Howard's wing by boat to Beaufort, forty miles up the coast beyond Port Royal Sound, with instructions to move inland and occupy Pocotaligo, on the railroad about midway between Savannah and Charleston. By January 20 this had been done, and Slocum began slogging in the opposite direction, thirty miles up the drowned west bank of the Savannah River to Sister's Ferry, as if about to close upon Augusta. Unrelenting rain made the march a roundabout nine-day affair, with much discomfort for the troops. For them, however, as for their chief, "city life had become dull and tame, and we were anxious to get into the pine woods again." Moreover, they were sustained by anticipation of another kind. Ahead lay South Carolina, and they had been promised a free hand in visiting upon her the destruction she deserved for having led the Confederate exodus from the Union. "Here is where treason began, and by God here is where it shall end," they vowed, pleased with their role as avenging instruments and eager to put into sterner practice the talents they had acquired on the march through Georgia, accounts of which had reached and frightened the people in their new path northward. Sherman approved of the fear aroused. "This was a power, and I intended to utilize it," he said later, explaining: "My aim then was to whip the rebels, to humble their pride, to follow them to their inmost recesses, and make them fear and dread us. 'Fear of the Lord is the beginning of wisdom.'"

Already there were signs that the two-pronged feint was working in both directions. Augusta was in ferment over Slocum's approach, and in Charleston, menaced from the landward side by Howard and by Dahlgren from the sea, clerks were busy packing and shipping official records and historical mementos to Columbia for safe-keeping, never suspecting that the inland capital was not only high on Sherman's list of prime objectives, but was also to be dealt with as harshly as Atlanta had been served two months ago. "I look upon Columbia as quite as bad as Charleston," he wrote Halleck while cooling his army's heels in Savannah, "and I doubt if we shall spare the public buildings there as we did in Milledgeville." What was more, subordinates from private to major general took this prediction a step further when the march began in earnest, February 1. Blair and Logan cleared Pocotaligo and Davis and Williams crossed the Savannah in force that day. On the far left, at Sister's Ferry, Kilpatrick's troopers led the way, hoofs drumming on the planks of a pontoon bridge thrown there the day before. Soldiers of a Michigan infantry regiment, waiting their turn to cross, had heard that the bandy-legged cavalry commander had instructed his men to fill their saddlebags with matches for the work ahead, and now they believed it; for as he rode out onto the bridge he called back over his shoulder, "There'll be damned little for you infantrymen to destroy after I've passed through that hell-hole of secession!"

Here indeed was an end to what the Richmond editor termed "the repose of the tiger," in the course of which Sherman had told Old Brains: "The truth is the whole army is burning with an insatiable desire to wreak vengeance upon South Carolina. I almost tremble for her fate, but feel that she deserves all that seems in store for her."

✕ 2 ✕

A proposal that the women of the South cut off their hair for sale in Europe, thereby bringing an estimated 40,000,000-dollar windfall to the cause, had gained widespread approval by the turn of the year, despite some protests — chiefly from men, who viewed the suggested disfigurement with less favor than did their wives and sweethearts — that the project was impractical. After the fall of Fort Fisher, however, the Confederacy's last port east of the Mississippi was no longer open to blockade runners, coming or going, and the plan was abandoned. Even if the women sheared their heads there was no way now for the bulky cargo to be shipped, either to Europe or anywhere else; or if it could somehow be gotten out — from Charleston, say, in a sudden dash by a high-speed flotilla — the odds were even longer against a return with whatever the money would buy in the way of necessities, all of which were running low and lower now that the war was about to enter its fifth spring. Like so many other proposals, farfetched but by no means impossible if they had been adopted sooner, this one came too late.

Another was a return to the suggestion advanced informally by Pat Cleburne the previous winter, soon after Missionary Ridge, that the South free its slaves and enlist them in its armies. Hastily suppressed at the time as "revolting to Southern sentiment, Southern pride, and Southern honor," the proposition seemed far less "monstrous" now than it had a year ago, when Grant was not at the gates of Richmond and Sherman had not made his march through Georgia. Seddon, for one, had been for it ever since the fall of Atlanta, except that he believed emancipation should follow, not precede, a term of military service. In early January, Governor William Smith — "Extra Billy" to Old

Dominion voters — proposed that Virginia and the other states, not the central government, carry out the plan for black recruitment. Appealed to, R. E. Lee replied that he favored such a measure. "We must decide whether slavery shall be extinguished by our enemies and the slaves used against us, or use them ourselves at the risk of the effects which may be produced upon our social institutions. My own opinion is that we should employ them without delay. I believe that with proper regulation they can be made efficient soldiers." This was powerful support. If Lee wanted Negro troops, a once-oppugnant Richmond editor wrote soon afterward, "by all means let him have them." Westward, Richard Taylor agreed. In Mobile, when he congratulated a group of impressed slaves on their skill in building fortifications, their leader told him: "If you will give us guns we will fight for these works, too. We would rather fight for our own white folks than for strangers." Down in South Carolina, however, Mary Boykin Chesnut had her doubts. "Freeing Negroes is the latest Confederate Government craze," the mistress of Mulberry Plantation wrote in her diary. "We are a little slow about it; that is all. . . . I remember when Mr Chesnut spoke to his Negroes about it, his head men were keen to go in the army, to be free and get a bounty after the war. Now they say coolly that they don't want freedom if they have to fight for it. That means they are pretty sure of having it anyway."

Opinions differed: not so much along economic lines, as might have been expected — large slave-holders versus the slaveless majority of small farmers, merchants, and wage earners — but rather as a result of opposition from die-hard political leaders who contended that no government, state or central, whatever its desperation under the threat of imminent extinction, had the right to interfere in matters involving social institutions: especially slavery, which Aleck Stephens had called the "cornerstone" of the Confederacy, insisting that it made the nation's citizens truly free, presumably to establish a universal white aristocracy, by keeping the Negro in the inferior position God and nature intended for him to occupy down through time. As a result, after intense discussion, Virginia's General Assembly voted to permit the arming of slaves but included no provision for their emancipation, either before or after military service. Little or nothing came of that, as Mrs Chesnut had foreseen, but even less seemed likely to proceed from a similar bill introduced in the Confederate House and Senate in early February, only to run into virulent Impossiblist opposition. Despite Lee's earlier warning "that whatever measures are to be adopted should be adopted at once. Every day's delay increases the difficulty. Much time will be required to organize and discipline the men, and action may be deferred until too late," debate dragged on, week in, week out, as the legislators wrangled. Meanwhile, Federal enlistment teams kept busy in the wake of blue advances, signing up and swearing in black volunteers, many of them substitutes to help fill the draft quotas of northern states. In the end, of the nearly 180,000 Negroes who served in the Union ranks — 20,000 more than the "aggregate present" in all the armies of the South on New Year's Day — 134,111 were recruited in states that had stars in the Confederate battle flag, and the latter figure in turn was several thousand greater than the total of 125,994 gray-clad soldiers "present for duty" that same day; when the North had 959,460 and 620,924 in those respective categories.

It was by no means as great, however, as the total of 198,494 listed that day as absent from Confederate ranks. Moreover, this invisible army of the missing grew with every passing week, its membership swollen even by veterans from the Army of Northern Virginia, whose morale was said to be high despite short rations and the bone-numbing chill of the Petersburg trenches. Adversity had given them a pinched and scarecrow look, hard to connect with the caterwauling victors of so many long-odds battles in the past. A Connecticut soldier, peering through a Fort Hell sight-slit one cold morning to watch a detail of them straggle out to relieve their picket line, wrote home that he "could not help comparing them with so many women with cloaks, shawls, double-bustles and hoops, as they had thrown over their shoulders blankets and tents which flapped in the wind." Many by now had reached their limit of endurance; they came over into the Union lines in increasing numbers, especially from units posted where the rival works were close together and a quick sprint meant an end to shivering misery and hunger. A New England private told how he and his comrades would speculate each day on how many were likely to come in that night, depending on the darkness of the moon. "The boys talk about the Johnnies as at home we talk about suckers and eels. The boys will look around in the evening and guess that there will be a good run of Johnnies." Lee of course felt the drain, and knew only too well what the consequences must be if it continued. Before the end of January he warned Davis that if Grant was appreciably reinforced, either by Thomas from the west or by Sherman from the south — or, for that matter, by Lincoln from the north — "I do not see how in the present position he can be prevented from enveloping Richmond."

If in Virginia a sort of numbness obtained because of the military stalemate and the long-term deprivation of troops confined to earthworks, something approaching chaos prevailed at this time in the Carolinas while the various commanders — Bragg at Wilmington, Hardee at Charleston, G. W. Smith at Augusta, who between them mustered fewer than 25,000 effectives, including militia — engaged in a flurry of guesses as to where Sherman would strike next, and when, and how best to go about parrying the thrust, outnumbered and divided as they were. Yet the region in which conditions were by far the worst in regard to the physical state and morale of its defenders, even though there was no immediate enemy pressure on them, was Northeast Mississippi: specifically in the vicinity of Tupelo, where the Army of Tennessee made camp at last, January 8–10, on returning from its disastrous five-week excursion into the state from which it took its name. Its strength was down to 17,700 infantry and artillery, barely half the number answering roll-call when the long files set out north in mid-November. Most of the foot soldiers had no shoes, having worn them out on the icy roads, and an equal proportion of batteries had no guns; 72 pieces had been lost, along with a score of brigade and division commanders. Edward Walthall, whose division had shared with Forrest's horsemen the rear-guard duty that saved what remained of the army in the course of its ten-day retreat across the Tennessee, ended his official report on a sad and bitter note: "The remnant of my command, after this campaign of unprecedented peril and hardship, reduced by battles and exposure, worn and weary with its travel and its toil, numbered less when it reached its rest near Tupelo than one of its brigades had done eight months before."

Aside from a raft of scarehead accounts in northern papers, which told of a great conflict outside Nashville, of rebel prisoners taken in their thousands, and of victory salutes being fired in celebration all across the North, the authorities in Richmond heard nothing of what had occurred until more than two weeks after the battle, when a wire Hood sent on Christmas Day, via Corinth, reached the War Department on January 3. Headed Bainbridge, Alabama, it merely informed Seddon: "I am laying a pontoon here to cross the Tennessee River." That was all it said. But another, addressed to Beauregard at Montgomery, repeated this jot of information, then added: "Please come to Tuscumbia or Bainbridge."

The Creole was already on his way in that direction, not from Montgomery but from Charleston, whose defenses he had been attempting to bolster against expected pressure from occupied Savannah. His purpose in returning West was two-fold: first, to see for himself the condition of Hood's army, widely rumored to be dire, and second to draw troops from it, if possible, to help resist Sherman's pending drive through the Carolinas. He set out on the last day of the year, armed with authority from Davis to replace Hood with Richard Taylor if in his judgment a change in commanders was required. At Macon, three days later, he received two dispatches from Hood, both encouraging. One was nearly three weeks old, having been sent from Spring Hill on December 17, the morrow of the two-day fight at the gates of the Tennessee capital. In it Hood admitted the loss of "fifty pieces of artillery, with several ordnance wagons," but added flatly: "Our loss in killed and wounded is very small." The other message, dated January 3 and wired from Corinth, was quite as welcome. "The army has recrossed the Tennessee River without material loss since the battle in front of Nashville. It will be assembled in a few days in the vicinity of Tupelo, to be supplied with shoes and clothing, and to obtain forage for the animals." A few days later, still pressing westward by a roundabout route on the crippled railroads, Beauregard received a more detailed report, dated January 9, in which Hood not only repeated his claim that his loss in killed and wounded had been light, but also declared that few were missing from other causes. "Our exact loss in prisoners I have not been able to ascertain," he wrote, "but do not think it great."

Considerably reassured by what he had heard from Hood in the course of his balky two-week ride from Charleston, the Louisianan reached Tupelo on January 15 to find his worst fears confirmed by his first sight of the Army of Tennessee in the two months since he parted from it at Tuscumbia, about to set out in balmy weather on a march designed to carry the war to the Ohio. Now only about 15,000 infantry were on hand, huddled miserably in their camps, and of these fewer than half had shoes or blankets to help them withstand the coldest winter the Deep South had known for years. In shock from the sudden fall of the scales from his eyes, Beauregard saw in their faces the horror of Franklin and in their bearing the ravage of the long retreat that followed their rout on the near bank of the Cumberland. He looked at the tattered, shattered ranks, the shot-torn flags and gunless batteries, and could scarcely recognize what he himself had once commanded. "If not, in the strictest sense of the word, a disorganized mob," he later wrote, "it was no longer an army." Rage at Hood for having misled him so grievously these past three weeks, in slanted and delayed reports, gave way in part to sadness when he realized that the distortion had proceeded, not so much from deception, as from embarrassment; not so much from confusion, even, as from shame. Still, it was clear enough that the Kentucky-born Texan had to go, and the sooner the better for all concerned. Hood in fact had already spared him the unpleasant ritual of demanding his resignation. "I respectfully request to be relieved from the command of this army," he had wired Seddon two days ago, and by now the Secretary's answer was on the way: "Your request is complied with. . . . Report to the War Department in Richmond."

Beauregard now had seen for himself the all-too-wretched condition of the main western force, and this seemed on the face of it to preclude action on the second purpose of his trip — the reinforcement of Bragg and Hardee for the defense of the Carolinas against Sherman. "An attempt to move Hood's army at this time would complete its destruction," Dick Taylor wired Davis from Meridian as he prepared to set out for Tupelo to assume command of what one of its members described as "the shattered debris of an army." Old Bory was inclined to agree: the more so because he found it necessary to grant immediate furloughs to some 3500 of the worse broken-down troops, while another 4000 had to be sent to Mobile to help meet what the local commander said was an all-out threat from Canby in New Orleans. Taylor replaced Hood on January 23, and Forrest next day was put in charge of the Department of Mississippi, East Louisiana, and West Tennessee, which he would defend with his three cavalry divisions, now detached. Returning stragglers by then had brought the army's total strength to 18,742 of all arms, including the furloughed men and those on their way to Mobile, whose deduction left only about 11,000 so-called effectives. Not only was this fewer, in all, than the number Beauregard had hoped to send East, but the bedraggled state of this remnant was such that both he and Taylor doubted whether the troops could survive the move from Tupelo to the Carolinas, even if the crippled railroads could manage to get them there before Sherman took up, or indeed completed, his northward drive on Richmond.

Both generals were mistaken, at least in regard to the first of these assessments. Like so many others down the years, they underestimated the toughness of this most resilient of Confederate armies, whose ability to survive mistreatment and defeat was rivaled only by the Army of the Potomac. Even as Taylor assumed command, Stephen Lee's corps — now under Stevenson, pending Lee's recovery from the wound he had suffered on the retreat — was loading aboard the cars, 3078 strong, for its eastern journey over the bucking strap-iron and rotted crossties of a dozen railroads. Despite the Creole's telegraphed protest that "to divide this small army at this juncture to reinforce General Hardee would expose to capture Mobile, Demopolis, Selma, Montgomery, and all the rich valley of the Alabama River," the War Department would neither cancel nor delay the transfer. Cheatham's corps left two days later, and part of Stewart's followed before the month was out. Taylor thus lost practically his whole army within a week of taking over from Hood. Including Forrest's troopers, the furloughed men, the strengthened Mobile garrison, and detachments scattered at random from the Mississippi River to the Georgia line, he retained in all perhaps as many as 30,000 troops for use against greatly superior possible combinations by Thomas, Canby, Washburn, and others. Few as that was, it still was better than five times the number headed east with Beauregard, who was recalled simultaneously to organize and take charge of the defense of the Carolinas.

He reached Augusta on February 1, the day Sherman set out in earnest from Savannah. That was well in advance of the first relay of reinforcements from the Army of Tennessee, who had a more circuitous route to follow. Cheatham's men, for example, after leaving Tupelo on foot, trudged to West Point, where they boarded the cars for Meridian, then changed for Selma and a steamboat ride from there to Montgomery, after which they went by rail again to Columbus, Georgia. From Columbus they marched through Macon and Milledgeville to Mayfield, where they took the cars for Augusta — ten days after Beauregard passed that way — then marched again to Newberry, South Carolina, for a reunion with Stevenson's corps, which had preceded them by a no less roundabout route. Presently, sixty miles across the state, Mrs Chesnut watched them pass through the streets of Camden. In proof of their unquenchable spirit they were singing as they swung along, and the sound of it nearly broke her heart, combined as it was with the thought of all they had been through in the grim three years since Donelson. "So sad and so stirring," she wrote in her diary at nearby Mulberry that night. "I sat down as women have done before and wept. Oh, the bitterness of such weeping! There they go, the gay and gallant few, the last flower of Southern manhood. They march with as airy a tread as if they still believed the world was all on their side, and that there were no Yankee bullets for the unwary."

She had seen their former commander some weeks before, at the end of January, when Hood stopped off in Columbia on his way to Richmond. He no more considered his war career at an end now than he had done after losing a leg at Chickamauga. "I wish to cross the Mississippi River to bring to your aid 25,000 troops," he wired his friend the President on leaving Tupelo. "I know this can be accomplished, and earnestly desire this chance to do you so much good service. Will explain my plan on arrival." Breaking his journey at the South Carolina capital — which no one yet suspected lay in Sherman's path — he visited the family of Brigadier General John S. Preston, whose daughter Sally he was engaged to marry and whose son Willie had been killed fighting under him at Atlanta. "He can stand well enough without his crutch," Mrs Chesnut observed, "but he does very slow walking. How plainly he spoke out those dreadful words, 'My defeat and discomfiture. My army destroyed. My losses.' He said he had nobody to blame but himself."

She found him changed, remote, profoundly grieved, and so did Sally's younger brother Jack, who took her aside to ask: "Did you notice how he stared in the fire, and the livid spots which came out on his face, and the huge drops of perspiration that stood out on his forehead?"

"Yes, he is going over some bitter hours," Mrs Chesnut said. "He sees Willie Preston with his heart shot out. He feels the panic at Nashville, and its shame."

"And the dead on the battlefield at Franklin," Jack agreed. "That agony in his face comes again and again. I can't keep him out of those absent fits. . . . When he looks in the fire and forgets me, and seems going through in his own mind the torture of the damned, I get up and come out as I did just now."

In and around Richmond — where Hood was headed with a scheme no more farfetched, and considerably less expensive, than the one that put him in motion for the Ohio, ten weeks back — R. E. Lee and his troops had just endured their worst hunger crisis of the war to date. Heavy January rains washed out trestles on the Piedmont Railroad, completed last year as a link between Danville and the western Carolinas, and floods at the same time cut off supplies from the upper valley of the James, obliging the army to fall back on its meager food reserve. Within two days Commissary General Lucius Northrop's storehouses were as empty as the men's bellies. Lee's anger flared. "If some change is not made and the commissary department reorganized," he protested to Seddon, "I apprehend dire results. The physical strength of the men, if their courage survives, must fail under this treatment." Davis saw the letter and added his endorsement: "This is too sad to be patiently considered, and cannot have occurred without criminal neglect or gross incapacity." In early February he followed through by replacing the detested Northrop with Colonel Isaac St John, who had performed near miracles in charge of the Nitre and Mining Corps. Promoted to brigadier, St John reorganized the system for delivering supplies from outlying regions and instigated a plan whereby a local farmer undertook to ration an individual soldier for six months: all of which helped to some degree, though not enough. Hunger, even starvation, was a specter that stalked the camps of the Army of Northern Virginia.

Lee fretted and sometimes fumed. "Unless the men and animals can be subsisted," he informed the government, "the army cannot be kept together, and our present lines must be abandoned. Nor can it be moved to any other position where it can operate to advantage without provisions to enable it to move in a body." The implications were clear. There could be but one end for an army that could neither remain where it was nor shift its ground. "Everything, in my opinion, has depended and still depends upon the disposition and feelings of the people. Their representatives can best decide how they will respond to the demands which the public safety requires." Invited to Richmond for a meeting with Virginia congressmen, he told them of his army's plight and repeated what he had said in his report. They replied with professions of loyalty and devotion, expressing a willingness to make any sacrifice required; but that was as far as it went. They had nothing to propose, either to Lee or anyone else, as to what the sacrifice might be. That night after supper, which he took in town with his eldest son Custis, a major general serving under Ewell in the capital defenses, Lee paced up and down the room, gravely troubled. Suddenly he stopped and faced his son, who was seated reading a newspaper by the fire. "Well, Mr Custis," he said angrily, "I have been up to see the Congress and they do not seem able to do anything except eat peanuts and chew tobacco, while my army is starving. I told them the condition my men were in, and that something must be done at once, but I can't get them to do anything." He fell silent, resumed his pacing, then came back. "Mr Custis, when this war began I was opposed to it, bitterly opposed to it, and I told these people that unless every man should do his whole duty, they would repent it. And now" — he paused — "they will repent."

Hunger distressed him, but so did the dwindling number of the hungry. His strength was below 50,000 mainly because of recent detachments which left him with barely more than a man per yard of his long line, including Ewell's reserve militia and the three divisions of troopers, most of whom were posted a hard day's ride or more away, where forage was available for their mounts. Following Hoke's departure for Wilmington, Lee declined a request from the War Department that he send Bushrod Johnson's division as well. "It will necessitate the abandonment of Richmond," he told Davis, who deferred as usual to his judgment in such matters. In early January, however, with Sherman in occupation of Savannah and Governor Andrew G. Magrath calling urgently for troops to reinforce Hardee, Lee sent him a veteran South Carolina brigade from Kershaw's division of Longstreet's corps. That was little enough, considering the risk, not only to Charleston but also to his own rear, if Sherman marched northward unchecked for a link-up with Grant at Petersburg. Still, it was all he felt he could afford, at any rate until Wade Hampton approached him soon afterward with a proposal that Calbraith Butler's troopers be sent to South Carolina for what remained of the winter, leaving their horses behind and procuring new ones for the harassment of the invader once they reached their native state. Lee scarcely enjoyed the notion of losing a solid third of his cavalry, even temporarily, but he saw in this at least a partial solution to the growing remount problem. Accordingly, on January 19 — his fifty-eighth birthday — after a conference with the President, he authorized the horseless departure of Butler's division by rail for the Palmetto State, "with the understanding that it is to return to me in the spring in time for the opening of the campaign." Moreover, having thought the matter through ("If Charleston falls, Richmond follows," Magrath had written; "Richmond may fall and Charleston be saved, but Richmond cannot be saved if Charleston falls") he ordered Hampton himself to go along, explaining to Davis that the South Carolina grandee, badly needed as he was at his Virginia post, would "be of service in mounting his men and arousing the spirit and strength of the State and otherwise do good."

With his chief of cavalry gone far south, along with a third of his veteran troopers — gone for good, events would show, though he did not know that yet — Lee could find small solace elsewhere, least of all in any hope of distracting the host that hemmed him in at Petersburg and Richmond. Off in the opposite direction, conditions were tactically even worse for Jubal Early out on the fringes of the Shenandoah Valley. Discredited and unhappy, down in strength to a scratch collection of infantry under Wharton, called by courtesy a division though it numbered barely a thousand men, and two slim brigades of cavalry under Rosser, he could only observe from a distance Sheridan's continued depredations, which consisted by now of little more than a stirring of dead coals. In mid-January, however, Rosser struck with 300 horsemen across the Alleghenies at Beverly, West Virginia, a supply depot guarded by two Ohio regiments, one of infantry, one of cavalry. At scant cost to himself, he killed or wounded 30 of the enemy and captured 580, along with a considerable haul of rations. Welcome as these last were to his hungry troopers, the raid was no more than a reminder of the days when Jeb Stuart had done such things, not so much to obtain a square meal as to justify his plume. George Crook, the outraged commander of the blue department, secured the dismissal of a pair of lieutenant colonels, heads of the two regiments, "in order that worthy officers may fill their places, which they have proved themselves incompetent to hold," but otherwise the Federals suffered nothing they could not easily abide: certainly not Sheridan, who was chafing beyond the mountains for a return to the main theater. He soon would receive and execute the summons, despite Old Jube, who was charged with trying to hold him where he was.

Meantime Grant did not relax for a moment his close-up hug on Lee's thirty-odd miles of line from the Williamsburg Road to Hatcher's Run. Though he had attempted no movement that might bring him to grips with his opponent since the early-December strike down the Weldon Railroad, no day passed without its long-range casualties and the guns were never silent; not even at night, when the spark-trickling fuzes of mortar bombs described their gaudy parabolas above the rebel earthworks. Boredom provoked strange responses, as when some outdone soldier on either side would leap atop the parapet and defy the marksmen on the other. But a more common phenomenon was the "good run of Johnnies" who came over — "rejoining the Union," they called it — while, across the way, one grayback complained that "the enemy drank coffee, ate fat, fresh beef and good bread, and drank quantities of whiskey, as their roarings at night testified." Reactions varied, up and down the trenches. "There are a good many of us who believe this shooting match had been carried on long enough," one Maryland Confederate declared. "A government that has run out of rations can't expect to do much more fighting and to keep on in a reckless and wanton expenditure of human life. Our rations are all the way from a pint to a quart of cornmeal a day, and occasionally a piece of bacon large enough to grease your palate." On the other hand, a North Carolinian regretted to hear that people back home were in despair over the loss of Fort Fisher. "If some of them could come up here and catch the good spirits of the soldiers," he wrote his family, "I think they would feel better."

Lee himself was a military realist, and as such he had said nine months ago, a month before Grant maneuvered him into immobility south of the James, that a seige could only end in defeat for his penned-up army. He had also shown, however, that as a fighter he was perhaps most dangerous when cornered. Long odds encouraged his fondness for long chances, and not even the present gloom was deep enough to suppress an occasional flash of his old aggressive outlook. "Cheer up, General," a Virginia representative told him on the Richmond visit; "we have done a good work for you today. The legislature has passed a bill to raise an additional 15,000 men for you." Lee did not seem heartened by the news. "Passing resolutions is kindly meant," he replied with a bow, "but getting the men is another matter." He paused, and in that moment his eye brightened. "Yet if I had 15,000 fresh troops, things would look very different," he said. Hope died hard in Lee, whose resolution was shared by those around him. "My faith in this old Army is unshaken," a young staff colonel wrote his sweetheart at the time, adding: "Like a brave old lion brought to bay at last, it is determined to resist to the death and, if die it must, to die game. But we have not quite made up our minds to die, and if God will help us we shall yet prove equal to the emergency."

In essence, that was the view Jefferson Davis applied to the whole Confederacy. He had never embraced the notion that, without allies, the South could win an offensive war against the North; but this was not to say that her people could not confirm her independence for all time, provided they stood firm in the conviction that sustained their forebears in the original Revolution. What had worked for that other infant nation would work for this one. Moreover, once its enemy came to understand that defeat did not necessarily mean submission, that nothing much short of annihilation could translate conquest into victory, a nation willing to "die game" was unlikely to have to die at all. That had been at the root of his November claim that "not the fall of Richmond, nor Wilmington, nor Charleston, nor Savannah, nor Mobile, nor of all combined, can save the enemy from the constant and exhaustive drain of blood and treasure which must continue until he shall discover that no peace is attainable unless based on the recognition of our indefeasible rights." Since then, Savannah had fallen, and Wilmington and Charleston were directly threatened, as Mobile had been for the past six months and Richmond had been from the outset. Yet even here there was comfort for those who saw as Davis and Lee's young colonel did. As the odds lengthened, the margin for choice narrowed; the grimmer the prospect, the readier the people would be to accept their leader's view that resolution meant survival; or so he believed at any rate. After all, the only alternative was surrender, and he considered them no more ready for that than he was, now or ever.

Throughout January, while Sherman reposed in Savannah, letters and telegrams with the familiar signature *Jeffn Davis* went out to Beauregard, Taylor, Bragg, and Hardee, as well as to the governors of North and South Carolina, Georgia, Alabama, and Mississippi, urging mutual support in the present crisis and vigorous preparation for the day when the tiger unsheathed his claws and started north. Not even Kirby Smith, remote and all but inaccessible, was overlooked as a possible source of borrowed strength. "Under these circumstances," Davis wrote him, stressing the massive Federal shift of troops from west to east, "I think it advisable that you should be charged with military operations on both banks of the Mississippi, and that you should endeavor as promptly as possible to cross that river with as large a force as may be prudently withdrawn." Nothing was likely to come of this; nor did it; yet when Hood showed up the following month, big with his plan for recruiting volunteers in his adoptive Texas, Davis gladly approved the mission and sent him on his Quixotic way, reduced to his previous rank of lieutenant general. Another defeated hero who returned at the same time, Raphael Semmes, was also welcomed and employed. Crossing the Atlantic in late October, four months after he fought and lost the famous channel duel off Cherbourg, he landed at Matamoros, Mexico, then worked his way on a wide swing east from Brownsville to his home in Mobile, where he rested before pushing on to Richmond, saddened by the devastation he saw had been visited on the land since his departure in the summer of '61. Promoted to rear admiral, he was given command of the James River squadron, though Davis in turn was saddened by his inability to award the former captain of the *Alabama* with anything more substantial than three small ironclads and five wooden gunboats, which collectively were no match for a single enemy monitor and in fact could do little more than support the forts and batteries charged with guarding the water approach to the capital in their rear.

Intent as he was on gathering and bracing his scattered and diminished armies for the shock of an eastern Armageddon, Davis had the still harder concomitant task of preparing the nation at large for survival after the defeat made probable by the odds. He too was a military realist, in his way, and as such he knew that, far more important than the loss of any battle — even one on such a promised cataclysmic scale as this — was the possible loss of the will to fight by those behind the lines. There was where wars were ultimately won or lost, and already there were signs that this will, though yet unbroken, was about to crumble. "It is not unwillingness to oppose the enemy," Governor Magrath informed him from threatened South Carolina, "but a chilling apprehension of the futility of doing so which affects the people." Just so: and Davis took as his chief responsibility, as the people's leader, the task of replacing this chill with the warmth of resolution. Whatever the odds, whatever the losses, he believed that so long as they had that, to anything like the degree that he possessed it, their desperate bid for membership in the family of nations could never be annulled.

His need to rally the public behind him had never been more

acute, but neither had it ever been more stringently opposed by his political adversaries, who saw in the current dilemma a fulfillment of all the woes they had predicted from the outset if Congress continued to let him have his way on such issues as conscription and the periodic suspension of the writ of habeas corpus, in violation of the rights not only of the states but also of individuals. Under the press of circumstance, Davis by now had gone beyond such preconceptions. "If the Confederacy falls," he told one congressman in a fruitless effort to bring him over, "there should be written on its tombstone, *Died of a Theory.*"

That might be; still, the hard-line States Righters could not see it. Desist from such wicked practices, they were saying, and volunteers would flock again to the colors in numbers sufficient to fling the invader back across the Mason-Dixon line. Yet here was the Chief Executive, clearly seeking to move toward the arming of the slaves, with emancipation to follow as the worst of all possible violations of the rights they held dearest. "What did we go to war for, if not to protect our property?" R. M. T. Hunter wanted to know. A Virginian, he was president pro tempore of the Senate and one of its largest slave-holders, known privately to favor a return to the Union on terms likely to be gentler now than after the South's defeat, which the present crisis had convinced him was inevitable. Some colleagues agreed, while others believed the war could still be won if the Commander in Chief only had men around him who knew how to go about it. In mid-January, accordingly, Speaker of the House Thomas Bocock, after conferring with other Virginia members of that body, informed the President that his state desired a complete change in the Cabinet, all but Treasury Secretary George A. Trenholm, who had succeeded his fellow South Carolinian Christopher Memminger in July; otherwise they would put through a vote of censure that might bring the Government down. Davis had no intention of yielding to this unconstitutional threat, but the maneuver was partly successful anyhow, paradoxically costing him — and them — the only remaining member of his official family from the Old Dominion. Affronted by this slur from representatives of his native state, and wearied by two years and two months of almost constant tribulation, James Seddon promptly submitted his resignation and declined to withdraw it, only consenting to remain through the end of the month and thus give his successor, Kentuckian John C. Breckinridge, time to clear up matters in his Department of Southwest Virginia before coming to Richmond to take over as the Confederacy's fifth Secretary of War.

Under pressure, men responded in accordance with their lights. Some were convinced the time had come for one-man rule, not by Davis but by Lee, the one leader they believed could "guide the country through its present crisis." This went up in smoke, however, when Representative William C. Rives, a fellow Virginian and chairman of the

Committee on Foreign Affairs, went to the general with the proposal carefully worded to lessen the shock. Lee reacted as he might have done if presented with a gift-wrapped rattlesnake. Not only did he consider this man-on-horseback scheme a reflection on his loyalty as a soldier and a citizen, he also sent back word by Rives "that if the President could not save the country, no one could." Others were busy on their own. One-time U.S. Supreme Court Justice John A. Campbell of Alabama, for example, having failed to stave off war by his negotiations with Seward over Sumter, four years back, was in correspondence with a former associate, Supreme Court Justice Samuel Nelson of New York, "proposing to visit him [in Washington] and confer," a confidant noted, "with a view to ascertaining whether there is any way of putting an end to the war and suggesting conference, if Judge Nelson thinks it may lead to any good result, to be held by Judge Campbell with Mr Stanton or one or two other leading men." Supporters of Joe Johnston also stepped up their clamor for his reinstatement at this time, partly as a way of striking at the Administration, while some among them favored more drastic methods. "One solution which I have heard suggested," a War Department official confided in his diary, "is an entire change of the Executive by the resignation of the President and Vice President. This would make Hunter, as president of the Senate, the President, would really make Lee commander-in-chief, and would go far to restore lost confidence."

Davis was spared at least one measure of exacerbation through this period by the absence of his long-time stump opponent Henry Stuart Foote, who had defeated him in a Mississippi race for governor ten years before the war, but now represented a Tennessee district in Congress, where he fulminated alternately against the Yankees and the government. Arrested in early January while trying to cross the Potomac, he announced that he had been on his way to Washington to sue for peace and deliver his people from despotism. On his release, a vote to expel him from the House having failed for lack of a two-thirds majority, he struck out again. This time he made it all the way to Canada, only to find that no Federal authority would treat with him: whereupon he sailed for London, and there issued a manifesto calling on his constituents to secede from the Confederacy and again find freedom in the Union.

Good riddance, friends of the President said. But such relief as his departure brought was more than offset by the simultaneous reappearance of Alexander Stephens, who reacted in just the opposite way to a gloom as deep as Foote's. Instead of entering, he emerged from exile to lead a headlong attack on the Administration, not only for its failure to check Sherman's march through his beloved Georgia, but also for all its previous sins of omission and commission. Resuming his vice-presidential chore of presiding over the Senate, he arrived in time to cast the deciding vote restoring habeas corpus, then moved on to deliver a ringing speech in which he arraigned the government for incompetence, slack judgment, and despotic arrogance at all levels. The war having failed, he called for the removal of Davis or, short of impeachment, the opening of direct negotiations for peace with Washington, ignoring the Executive entirely, since there could be no end to the fighting so long as the present leader remained in control of the nation's destiny. Thus Stephens, whom Davis in friendlier days had referred to as "the little pale star from Georgia," and the Richmond *Examiner* took up the cry in its January 17 issue, urging the assembly of a convention to abolish the Constitution and remove the Chief Executive from office, both in preparation for a return to principles long since betrayed by those in whom the people, to their current dismay, had placed their trust.

On that same day Virginia's General Assembly passed and sent to the President a resolution calling for the appointment of R. E. Lee as commander of all the Confederate armies, on grounds that this would promote their efficiency, reanimate their spirit, and "inspire increased confidence in the final success of our arms." Though Davis saw the request as an attempt to infringe on his constitutional designation as Commander in Chief, he handled the matter tactfully in a letter to Lee, asking whether he wished to undertake this larger duty "while retaining command of the Army of Northern Virginia." Lee promptly replied that he did not. "If I had the ability I would not have the time.... I am willing to undertake any service to which you think proper to assign me, but I do not wish you to be misled as to the extent of my capacity." This was written on January 19, but Davis had known so well what Lee would say that he had not waited for an answer. His letter of response to the Assembly had gone out the day before. Thanking the members for their suggestion, as well as for "the uncalculating, unhesitating spirit with which Virginia has, from the moment when she first drew the sword, consecrated the blood of her children and all her natural resources to the achievement of the object of our struggle," he assured them "that whenever it shall be found practicable by General Lee to assume command of all the Armies of the Confederate States, without withdrawing from the direct command of the Army of Northern Virginia, I will deem it promotive of the public interest to place him in such command, and will be happy to know that by so doing I am responding to [your] expressed desire."

That more or less took care of that; or should have, except that the issue would not die. While the Virginians were framing their request, the Confederate Senate — by a 14–2 vote, January 16 — passed a resolution not only favoring Lee's elevation to general-in-chief, but also proposing that Beauregard take charge in South Carolina and that Johnston be restored to command of the Army of Tennessee. Varina Davis was indignant at this attempt to clip her husband's presidential wings. "If I were he," she told one cornered senator, "I would die or be hung before I would submit to the humiliation that Congress intended him." Davis himself had no intention of complying with the resolution, which landed on his desk a few days later. For one thing, he had just disposed of the Lee question, at least to his and the general's satisfaction, and Beauregard was already slated to assume the recommended post on his return from Mississippi, where he was busy turning Hood's army over to Richard Taylor. As for Johnston, Davis was presently engaged in composing a 5000-word survey of that other Virginian's war career from First Manassas to Peachtree Creek, a thorny indictment rounded off with a brief summation: "My opinion of General Johnston's unfitness for command has ripened slowly and against my inclination into a conviction so settled that it would be impossible for me again to feel confidence in him as the commander of an army in the field." Moreover, the lengthy document would close with a final cutting answer to those critics who sought to curtail the Chief Executive's military prerogatives. "The power to assign generals to appropriate duties is a function of the trust confided in me by my countrymen. That trust I have ever been ready to resign at my country's call; but, while I hold it, nothing shall induce me to shrink from its responsibilities or to violate the obligations it imposes."

He would not bow to the three-count resolution. However, now that Lee's deferential reply to the recent feeler had been received, he saw a chance for a compromise that would cost him nothing, either in principle or in practical application, yet would serve to placate his congressional foes, at least in part, and would also, as the Virginia members put it, "inspire increased confidence in the final success of our arms." Accordingly, on January 26 he gladly signed, apparently with no thought of the predicted veto, an act that had passed both houses three days ago, providing for the appointment of a Confederate general-in-chief. Congress of course had Lee in mind, and on the last day of the month Davis recommended his appointment, which the Senate quickly approved. Lee's response, addressed to Adjutant General Samuel Cooper, was something of a snub to the politicians who had worked for his elevation. "I am indebted alone to the kindness of His Excellency the President for my nomination to this high and arduous office," he declared, and a final sentence indicated how little he was likely to assert his independence at the post: "As I have received no instructions as to my duties, I do not know what he desires for me to undertake." To Davis himself, soon afterward, Lee expressed his thanks for "your indulgence and kind consideration.... I must beg you to continue these same feelings to me in the future and allow me to refer to you at all times for counsel and advice. I cannot otherwise hope to be of service to you or the country. If I can relieve you from a portion of the constant labor and anxiety which now presses upon you, and maintain a harmonious action between the great armies, I shall be more than compensated for the addition to my present burdens." This was no more and no less than Davis had expected. Not to be outdone in graciousness, he replied: "The honor designed to be bestowed has been so fully won, that the fact of conferring it can add nothing to your fame."

Greeted with enthusiasm, Lee's appointment encouraged many waverers to hope that his genius, which had transformed near-certain defeat into triumph in Virginia two and one half years ago, would now work a like miracle on a larger scale; the man who had saved beleaguered Richmond from McClellan, flinging him back in confusion, first on his gunboats and then on his own capital, would save the beleaguered Confederacy from Grant. But Davis knew only too well that the confirmed defeatists — men like Hunter, Campbell, and Stephens — were not converted by this stroke, which after all was of the pen and not the sword. They were for peace, peace *now*, and would not believe that anyone, even Robert E. Lee, could do anything more than stave off defeat and thus make the terms for surrender that much stiffer when it came. Above all, they and the Impossiblists, who wanted him removed for other reasons, mainly having to do with his overriding of States Rights, believed that Davis would never consent to the mildest compromise the Union authorities might offer, not only because of his known conviction that the loss of the war meant the loss of honor, but also because of his personal situation as the leader of a failed rebellion. "We'll hang Jeff Davis on a sour apple tree!" blue-clad troops were singing now, to the tune of *John Brown's Body*, and Republican politicians were saying much the same thing, in words as harsh and even more specific, from stumps all over the North, to wild applause.

Davis knew this, and knew as well that he had to find some way to answer and, if possible, discredit his domestic critics before he could unite the nation to meet the impending crisis. But how? He watched and waited. Then it came: from Lincoln, of all people — or, more specifically, Old Man Blair.

Blair, that long-time adviser to all the Presidents back through Jackson, wanted to add one more to his list in the person of Jefferson Davis, who had been his friend for more than twenty years, but was now beyond his reach. Or perhaps not. Approaching seventy-four, the distinguished Marylander hoped to crown a life of public service with a trip to Richmond for the purpose of persuading Davis to treat for peace and thereby end the war. In mid-December, shortly after Sherman reached the coast, Blair went to Lincoln and asked permission to make the trip. "Come to me after Savannah falls," the President told him; which he did, and on December 28 was handed a card inscribed, "Allow the bearer, F. P. Blair, Senr. to pass our lines, go South and return. A. Lincoln."

He left at once, and on December 30 sent Davis two letters from Grant's headquarters at City Point. One was brief, requesting admission to the Confederacy to search for some title papers missing since Jubal Early's July visit to his home in Silver Spring. The other, considerably longer, remarked that the first would serve as a cover for his true purpose, which was to "unbosom my heart frankly and without reserve" on matters regarding the "state of affairs of our country." He was "wholly unaccredited," he said, but he hoped to offer certain "suggestions" he believed would be of interest.

There were delays. Davis recognized another peace feeler, and though he did not expect to find anything advantageous in the exchange under present circumstances, he knew that a refusal to see the Washington emissary was apt to bring still heavier charges of intransigence on his head. Besides, his wife encouraged the visit for old times' sake. In the end he wrote the elder statesman to come on, and Blair did. Lodged unregistered at the Spotswood on January 12, he came that evening to the White House, where Mrs Davis met him with a hug.

Alone with Davis in the presidential study, he elaborated on what he had meant by "suggestions." In brief, his plan was for the North and South to observe a cessation of hostilities for such time as it might take to drive the French and their puppet Maximilian out of Mexico, possibly with none other than Jefferson Davis in command of the joint expeditionary force; after which the two former combatants, flushed with victory from their common vindication of the Monroe Doctrine, could sit down and discuss their various differences in calm and dignity. Davis did not think highly of the plan, mainly because it sounded to him like one of Seward's brainstorms, concocted for some devious purpose. Blair replied that the crafty New Yorker had had and would have no part in the matter. "The transaction is a military transaction, and depends entirely on the Commander in Chief." Whatever Seward's shortcomings, which admittedly were many, Lincoln was altogether trustworthy, Blair declared. Davis said he was glad to hear it. In point of fact, he added, he was willing now, and always had been, to enter into negotiations for ending the war by this or any other honorable method, and in demonstration of his sincerity he drafted a letter for Blair to take back and show Lincoln. "Notwithstanding the rejection of our former offers," the letter read in closing, "I would, if you could promise that a commission, minister, or other agent would be received, appoint one immediately, and renew the effort to enter into a conference with a view to secure peace to the two countries."

Back in Washington, Blair had a second interview with Lincoln on January 18. After giving him Davis's letter to read he reported that he had seen a number of prominent Confederates in the southern capital, many of them friends of long standing, and had found them for the most part despondent about the outcome of the war. Lincoln appeared more interested in this last than in the letter, which seemed to him to promise little in the way of progress, but in the end gave Blair a letter of his own, in indirect answer to the one from Davis. "You may say to him that I have constantly been, am now, and shall continue, ready to receive any agent whom he, or any other influential person now resisting the national authority, may informally send to me with the view of securing peace to the people of our one common country."

There in the final words of the paired notes — "the two countries": "our one common country" — the impasse was defined and, paradoxically, the maneuvering began in earnest: not so much between the two leaders, though there was of course that element in what followed, as between them and their respective home-front adversaries. Blair went back to Richmond four days later, then returned, his part complete, and newspapers North and South began to speculate frantically on what might come of the old man's go-between travels back and forth. Southern journalists accused Davis of near treason for having entertained a "foreign enemy" in the White House, while those who were for peace at almost any price expressed fears that he had rejected an offer to end the war on generous terms. Conversely, up in Washington, the Jacobins set up a hue and cry that Lincoln was about to stop the fighting just short of the point where they could begin to exact the vengeance they saw as their due from the rebellion. Each of the two Presidents thus had much to fret him while playing their game of high-stakes international poker, and they functioned in different styles: different not only from each other, but also different each from what he had been before. During this diplomatic interlude, Lincoln and Davis — fox and hedgehog — swapped roles. Lincoln remained prickly and unyielding, almost stolid, though always willing to engage on his own terms as he defined them. It was Davis who was foxy, secretive and shifty, quick to snap.

He began by inviting the Vice President to a consultation — their first since the government moved to Richmond, nearly four years ago — at which he showed him Lincoln's letter, reviewed its background, and requested an opinion. Stephens replied that he thought the matter should be pursued, "at least so far as to obtain if possible a conference upon the subject." Asked for recommendations on the makeup of the proposed commission, he suggested the Chief Executive as the most effective member, then added the names of several men who were known to be as strong for peace as he was, including John A. Campbell, the former Supreme Court Justice, now Assistant Secretary of War. Davis thanked him for his time and trouble, and next day, January 25, summoned the chosen three to his office. They were Campbell, Robert Hunter — who presided over the Senate, as president pro tem, in the Vice President's frequent absences — and Stephens himself. The frail Georgian protested but was overruled, and all three were handed their instructions: "In conformity with the letter of Mr Lincoln, of which the foregoing is a copy, you are requested to proceed to Washington City for an informal conference with him upon the issues involved in the existing war, and for the purpose of securing peace to the two countries."

There again were the critical words, "two countries." Judah Benjamin in the original draft had written, "for conference with him upon the subject to which it relates," but Davis had made the revision, not wanting to leave the trio of known "submissionists" any leeway when they reached the conference table. He knew well enough how little was likely to come of the effort with this stipulation attached, though he did not go into that at present. He merely informed the commissioners that they would set out four days from now, on Sunday the 29th, passing beyond the farthest Petersburg outworks under a flag of truce, presumably bound for Washington and a talk with Lincoln about the chances of ending the war without more bloodshed.

✗ 3 ✗

And so it was. Due east of Petersburg on that designated Sunday, near the frost-rimed scar of the Crater, a white flag appeared on the rebel parapet and a messenger came over with a letter addressed to Lieutenant General U. S. Grant. Word spread up and down the opposing lines that something was up; something important, from the look of things — something that maybe had to do with peace.

As it turned out, there was plenty of time for speculation. Grant was down the coast, looking over the Wilmington defenses with Schofield, who was to move against them as soon as his transports could descend the ice-jammed Potomac. By the time a fast packet got the flag-of-truce message to Fort Fisher, and word came back that the applicants were to be admitted and lodged at headquarters pending Grant's return, two days had passed. Then at last, on the final afternoon in January, a carriage bearing the three would-be commissioners came rolling out the Jerusalem Plank Road, which was lined with gray-clad soldiers and civilians, and on to an opening in the works, which were crowded left and right, as far as the eye could follow — northward to the Appomattox and south toward Fort Hell and Fort Damnation — with spectators who jammed the parapets for a look at what some were saying meant an end to all the killing. Across the way, the Union works were crowded too, and when the carriage turned and began to jolt eastward over the shell-pocked ground between the trenches, a roar of approval went up from opposite sides of the line of battle. "Our men cheered loudly," Meade would write his wife that night, "and the soldiers on both sides cried out lustily, 'Peace! Peace!'" Blue and gray alike, west and east of that no-man's land the carriage rocked across, spokes twinkling in the sunlight, men swung their hats and hollered for all they were worth. "Cheer upon cheer was given," a Federal artillerist would recall, "extending for some distance to the right and left of the lines, each side trying to cheer the loudest. 'Peace on the brain' appeared now to have spread like a contagion. Officers of all grades, from lieutenants to major generals, were to be seen flying in all directions to catch a glimpse of the gentlemen who were apparently to bring peace so unexpectedly."

Grant had returned by then, and though he saw to it that the three Confederates were made comfortable on a headquarters steamer tied up at the City Point wharf, he was careful not to discuss their mission with them. Which was just as well, since he received next morning a wire from the Commander in Chief, warning against any slackening of vigilance or effort on his part. "Let nothing which is transpiring change, hinder, or delay your military movements or plans," Lincoln told him, and Grant replied: "There will be no armistice in consequence of the presence of Mr Stephens and others within our lines. The troops are kept in readiness to move at the shortest notice if occasion should justify it." That afternoon Major Thomas Eckert, who normally had charge of the War Department telegraph office in Washington, arrived with instructions from the President to interview the proposed commissioners. Seward was on his way to Fort Monroe, and Eckert was to send them there to talk with him, provided they would state in writing that they had come for the purpose Lincoln had specified; that is, "with a view of securing peace to the people of our one common country."

Eckert saw them that evening. One look at their instructions quickly convinced him the main condition was unmet. At 9.30 he wired Washington, "I notified them that they could not proceed."

That seemed to be that; another peace effort no sooner launched than sunk. Lincoln inclined to that view next morning, February 2, when he received a somewhat puzzled telegram Seward had sent last night from Fort Monroe: "Richmond party not here." Eckert's followed, explaining the holdup. Lincoln was about to recall them both, ending the mission, when Stanton came in with a message just off the wire from Grant, a long and earnest plea that negotiations go forward despite Eckert's disapproval. In it, the general seemed to have come under the influence of the contagion that infected his soldiers, two days ago, while they watched the rebel carriage approach their lines. He had had a letter from and a brief talk with two of the Confederates, following Eckert's refusal to let them proceed, and he had been favorably impressed. "I will state confidentially, but not officially to become a matter of record," he wired Stanton, "that I am convinced, upon conversation with Messrs Stephens and Hunter, that their intentions are good and their desire sincere to restore peace and union. . . . I fear now their going back without any expression from anyone in authority will have a bad influence." He himself did not feel free to treat with them, of course; "I am sorry however that Mr Lincoln cannot have an interview with the two named in this dispatch, if not all three now within our lines. Their letter to me was all the President's instructions contemplated to secure their safe conduct if they had used the same language to Major Eckert."

For Lincoln, this put a different face on the matter. He got off two wires at once. One was to Seward, instructing him to remain where he was. The other was to Grant. "Say to the gentlemen I will meet them personally at Fortress Monroe as soon as I can get there."

He left within the hour, not even taking time to notify his secretary or any remaining member of his cabinet, and by nightfall was with Seward aboard the steamer *River Queen*, riding at anchor under the guns of Fort Monroe. The rebel commissioners were on a nearby vessel, also anchored in Hampton Roads; Seward had not seen them yet, and Lincoln sent word that he would receive them next morning in the *Queen*'s saloon. His instructions to the Secretary of State had been brief and to the point, listing three "indispensable" conditions for peace. One was "restoration of the national authority throughout all the states"; another was that there be no "receding" on the slavery question; while the third provided for "no cessation of hostilities short of the end of the war, and the disbanding of all forces hostile to the government." Lincoln considered himself bound by these terms as well, and had no intention of yielding on any of them, whatever else he might agree to.

The Confederates were punctual, coming aboard shortly after breakfast Friday morning, February 3. Handshakes and an exchange of amenities, as between old friends, preceded any serious discussion. "Governor, how is the Capitol? Is it finished?" Hunter asked. Seward described the new dome and the big brass door, much to the interest of the visitors, all three of whom had spent a good part of their lives in Washington, Campbell as a High Court justice, Hunter as a senator, and Stephens as a nine-term congressman. Lincoln was particularly drawn to the last of these, having admired him when they served together in the House at the time of the Mexican War, which they both opposed. "A little, slim, pale-faced, consumptive man," he called him then, writing home that his fellow Whig had "just concluded the very best speech of an hour's length I ever heard." Stephens, though still pale-faced, seemed to have put on a great deal of weight in the past few years; that is until he took off a voluminous floor-length overcoat fashioned from blanket-thick cloth, a long wool muffler, and several shawls wound round and round his waist and chest against the cold. Then it was clear that he had not added an ounce of flesh to his ninety-four pounds of skin and bones. "Never have I seen so small a nubbin come out of so much husk," Lincoln said with a smile as they shook hands.

That too helped to break the ice, and when the five took seats in the saloon, conversing still of minor things, the Union President and Confederate Vice President spoke of their days as colleagues, sixteen years ago. There had been a welcome harmony between the states and sections then, Stephens remarked, and followed with a question that went to the heart of the matter up for discussion: "Mr President, is there no way of putting an end to the present trouble?" Lincoln responded in kind, echoing the closing words of his recent message to Congress. "There is but one way," he said, "and that is for those who are resisting the laws of the Union to cease that resistance." Although this was plain enough, so far as it went, Stephens wanted to take it further. "But is there no other question," he persisted, "that might divert the attention of both parties for a time?" Lincoln saw that the Georgian was referring to the Mexico scheme, about which he himself had known nothing until Blair's return from Richmond, and declared that it had been proposed without the least authority from him. "The restoration of the Union is a *sine qua non* with me," he said; anything that was to follow had to follow that. Stephens took this to mean that a Confederate pledge for reunion must precede such action, and maintained that it was unneeded. "A settlement of the Mexican question in this way would necessarily lead to a peaceful settlement of our own." But that was not what Lincoln had meant — as he now made clear. He would make no agreement of any kind, he said, until the question of reunion was disposed of once and for all. That had to come first, if only because he could never agree to bargain with men in arms against the government in his care. Hunter, who had preceded Benjamin as Secretary of State and prided himself on a wide knowledge of international precedents, remarked at this point that Charles I of England had dealt with his domestic foes in just that way. Lincoln looked askance at the Virginian, then replied: "Upon questions of history I must refer you to Mr Seward, for he is posted in such things. My only distinct recollection of the matter is that Charles lost his head."

Hunter subsided, at least for a time, and the talk moved on to other concerns. Campbell, ever the jurist, wanted to know what the northern authorities had in mind to do, when and if the Union was restored, about southern representation in Congress, the two Virginias, and wartime confiscation of property, including slaves. Lincoln and Seward, between them, dealt with the problems one by one. Congress of course would rule on its own as to who would be admitted to a seat in either house. West Virginia was and would remain a separate state. As for compensation, both considered it likely that Congress would be

lenient in its handling of property claims once the war fever cooled
down, and Lincoln added that he would employ Executive clemency
where he could, though he had no intention of revoking the Emancipation Proclamation, which was still to be tested in the courts. At this
point Seward broke the news of the Thirteenth Amendment, approved
while the commissioners were entering Grant's lines three days ago, and
Lincoln remarked that he still favored some form of compensation by
the government for the resultant loss in slaves — provided, of course,
that Congress would go along, upon ratification, and vote the money for
payment to former owners; which seemed unlikely, considering the
present reported mood and makeup of that body.

All this came as a considerable shock to the three rebel listeners,
but the shock was mild compared to what followed when Hunter,
having recovered a measure of his aplomb, expressed their reaction in a
question designed to demonstrate just how brutally intransigent such
terms were. "Mr President, if we understand you correctly, you think
that we of the Confederacy have committed treason; that we are
traitors to your government; that we have forfeited our rights, and are
proper subjects for the hangman. Is that not about what your words
imply?" There was a pause while they waited for Lincoln's answer,
and presently he gave it. "Yes," he said. "You have stated the proposition
better than I did. That is about the size of it."

That remained about the size of it throughout the four-hour exchange in the *River Queen* saloon. He was unyielding, and though he
told a couple of tension-easing stories — causing Hunter to observe
with a wry smile, "Well, Mr Lincoln, we have about concluded that we
shall not be hanged as long as you are President: if we behave ourselves"
— the most he offered was a promise to use Executive clemency when
the time came, so far at least as Congress would allow it. The Confederates, bound as they were by their own leader's "two countries"
stipulation, could offer quite literally nothing at all, and so the conference wound down to a close.

Amid the flurry of parting handshakes, Lincoln said earnestly:
"Well, Stephens, there has been nothing we could do for our country.
Is there anything I can do for you personally?" Little Aleck, once more
immured within his bulky overcoat and wrappers, shook his head. "Nothing," he said. But then he had a thought. "Unless you can send me my
nephew who has been for twenty months a prisoner on Johnson's Island."
Lincoln brightened at the chance. "I'll be glad to do it. Let me have his
name." He wrote the name in a notebook, and that was how it came
about that Lieutenant John A. Stephens, captured at Vicksburg in
mid-'63, was removed from his Lake Erie island prison camp and brought
to Washington the following week for a meeting with the President
at the White House. Lincoln gave him a pass through the Union lines

and a photograph of himself as well, saying of the latter: "You had better take that along. It is considered quite a curiosity down your way, I believe."

Young Stephens and the photograph were about all the South got out of the shipboard conference in Hampton Roads, except for an appended gift from the Secretary of State. Reaching their own steamer the commissioners looked back and saw a rowboat coming after them, its only occupant a Negro oarsman. He brought them a basket of champagne and a note with Seward's compliments. As they waved their handkerchiefs in acknowledgment and thanks, they saw the genial New Yorker standing on the deck of the *Queen*, a bosun's trumpet held to his mouth. "Keep the champagne," they heard him call to them across the water, "but return the Negro."

Stephens, Hunter, and Campbell spent another night tied up to the wharf at City Point, and then next day recrossed the Petersburg lines, their mission ended. "Today they returned to Richmond," Meade wrote his wife that evening, "but what was the result of their visit no one knows. At the present moment, 8 p.m., the artillery on our lines is in full blast, clearly proving that at this moment there is no peace."

★　★　★

A basket of wine, supplemented in time by a homesick Georgia lieutenant bearing a photograph of Lincoln, seemed a small return for the four-day effort by the three commissioners, who came back in something resembling a state of shock from having learned that negotiations were to follow, not precede, capitulation. Davis, however, was far from disappointed at the outcome. His double-barreled purpose — to discredit the submissionists and unite the country behind him by having them elicit the northern leader's terms for peace — had been fulfilled even beyond a prediction made in the local *Enquirer* while the conference was in progress down the James. "We think it likely to do much good," the editor wrote, "for our people to understand in an authoritative manner from men like Vice President Stephens, Senator Hunter, and Judge Campbell the exact degree of degradation to which the enemy would reduce us by reconstruction. We believe that the so-called mission of these gentlemen will teach our people that the terms of the enemy are nothing less than unconditional surrender." Now that this had been borne out, Davis used much the same words in a note attached to a formal report of the proceedings, submitted to Congress on the Monday after the Saturday the three envoys reappeared in Richmond: "The enemy refused to enter into negotiations with the Confederate States, or with any of them separately, or to give to our people any other terms or guaranties than those which the conqueror may grant, or to permit us to have [peace] on any other basis than our unconditional submission to their rule."

Wasting no time, he struck while the propaganda iron was hot. Amid the rush of indignation at the news from Hampton Roads, Virginia's redoubtable Extra Billy called a meeting at Metropolitan Hall that same evening, February 6, to afford the public a chance to adopt resolutions condemning the treatment its representatives had received three days ago, on board the *River Queen*, at the hands of the northern leader and his chief lieutenant. Robert Hunter was one of the speakers. "If anything was wanted to stir the blood," he informed the close-packed gathering, "it was furnished when we were told that the United States could not consent to entertain any proposition coming from us as a people. Lincoln might have offered *some*thing. . . . No treaty, no stipulation, no agreement, either with the Confederate States jointly or with them separately: what was this but unconditional submission to the mercy of the conquerors?"

The crowd rumbled its resentment, subsiding only to be aroused by other exhortations, then presently stirred with a different kind of excitement as a slim figure in worn gray homespun entered from Franklin Street, paused in the doorway, and started down the aisle. It was Davis. Governor Smith greeted the unexpected visitor warmly and escorted him to the platform, where he stood beside the lectern and looked out over the cheering throng. "A smile of strange sweetness came to his lips," one witness later wrote, "as if the welcome assured him that, decried as he was by the newspapers and pursued by the clamor of politicians, he had still a place in the hearts of his countrymen."

When the applause died down at last he launched into an hour-long oration which all who heard it agreed was the finest he ever delivered. Even Pollard of the *Examiner*, his bitterest critic south of the Potomac, noting "the shifting lights on the feeble, stricken face," declared afterwards that he had never "been so much moved by the power of words spoken for the same space of time." Others had a similar reaction, but no one outside the hall would ever know; Davis spoke from no text, not even notes, and the absence of a shorthand reporter caused this "appeal of surpassing eloquence" to be lost to all beyond range of his voice that night. Hearing and watching him, Pollard experienced "a strange pity, a strange doubt, that this 'old man eloquent' was the weak and unfit President" he had spent the past three years attacking. "Mr Davis frequently paused in his delivery; his broken health admonished him that he was attempting too much; but frequent cries of 'Go on' impelled him to speak at a length which he had not at first proposed. . . . He spoke with an even, tuneful flow of words, spare of gestures; his dilated form and a voice the lowest notes of which were distinctly audible, and which anon rose as a sound of a trumpet, were yet sufficient to convey the strongest emotions and to lift the hearts of his hearers to the level of his grand discourse."

Apparently the speech was in part a repetition of those he had made last fall, en route through Georgia and the Carolinas, in an attempt to whip up the flagging spirits of a people distressed by the loss of Atlanta. Now, as then, he praised the common soldier, decried the profiteer, and expressed the conviction that if half the absent troops would return to the ranks no force on earth could defeat the armies of the South. In any case, with or without these shirkers, he predicted that if the people would stand firm, the Confederacy would "compel the Yankees, in less than twelve months, to petition us for peace on our own terms." The darker the hour, the greater the honor for having survived it — and, above all, the deeper the discouragement of the enemy for his failure to bring a disadvantaged nation to its knees. As it was, he had nothing but scorn for those who spoke of surrender: especially now that Lincoln had unmasked himself at Hampton Roads, revealing the true nature of his plans for the postwar subjugation of all who had opposed him and his Jacobin cohorts in the North. The alternative to continued resistance was unthinkable. Not only did he prefer death "sooner than we should ever be united again" with such a foe; "What shall we say of the disgrace beneath which we should be buried if we surrender with an army in the field more numerous than that with which Napoleon achieved the glory of France — an army standing among its homesteads?" All this he said, and more, in response to enthusiastic urgings from the crowd, before he reached the ringing peroration. "Let us then unite our hands and hearts; lock our shields together, and we may well believe that before another summer solstice falls upon us, it will be the enemy who will be asking us for conferences and occasions in which to make known *our* demands."

There followed a series of patriotic rallies featuring speakers who took their cue from this lead-off address by the President in Metropolitan Hall. Three days later, at the African Church — requisitioned for the occasion because of its vast capacity — Hunter once more described how Lincoln had "turned from propositions of peace with cold insolence," and told his indignant listeners: "I will not attempt to draw a picture of subjugation. It would require a pencil dipped in blood." Benjamin, the next man up, came forward with his accustomed smile. "Hope beams in every countenance," he said. "We know in our hearts that this people must conquer its freedom or die." He brought up the touchy subject of arming the slaves, calling on Virginia to set the example by furnishing 20,000 black recruits within the next twenty days, and was pleased to find that the subject was not so touchy after all. The outsized crowd approved with scarcely a murmur of dissent. Davis spoke too, though briefly, again predicting a Confederate victory by the end of summer, then left the rostrum to other dignitaries who continued the daylong oratory into the evening. Judge Campbell, unstrung by his recent visit beyond the enemy lines, was not among them; nor was Stephens, who — though he was present, as Campbell was not —

was too disheartened to join the chorus of affirmation. Like all the rest, he was swept along by the President's address, which he praised for its "loftiness of sentiment and rare form of expression," as well as for the "magnetic influence in its delivery."

Even so, looking back on it later, he pronounced it "little short of demention." Asked by Davis after the meeting what his plans were, he replied that he intended "to go home and remain there." He would "neither make any speech, nor even make known to the public in any way of the general condition of affairs, but quietly abide the issue of fortune." Discredited, outmaneuvered, he threw in the sponge at last. He left Richmond next day, returning to Liberty Hall, his home near Crawfordville — a deserter, like some hundred thousand others — and there remained, in what he termed "perfect retirement," for the balance of the war.

Such defection was rather the exception through this time, even among the Vice President's fellow Georgians who lately had been exposed to the wrath or whim of Sherman's bummers. Howell Cobb, whose plantation had been gutted on specific orders from the red-haired destroyer himself, spoke fervently in Macon that same week, calling on the people to unite behind their government, which he said could never be conquered if they held firm. "Put me in my grave," he cried, "but never put on me the garments of a Submissionist!" Benjamin Hill followed Stephens back to their native state, but for a different purpose. Addressing crowds in Columbus, Forsyth, and La Grange, he declared that the Confederacy still had half a million men of military age, together with plenty of food and munitions; all it lacked was the will to win. "If we are conquered, subjugated, disgraced, ruined," the senator asserted with a figurative sidelong glance at Joe Brown in Milledgeville and Little Aleck in nearby Liberty Hall, "it will be the work of those enemies among us [who] will accomplish that work by destroying the faith of our people in their government." Robert Toombs, the fieriest Georgian of them all, emerged from his Achilles sulk to assume the guise of Nestor in reaction to the news from Hampton Roads. All that was needed was resolution, a recovery of the verve that had prevailed in the days when he himself was in the field, he told a wrought-up audience in Augusta. "We have resources enough to whip *forty* Yankee nations," he thundered, "if we could call back the spirit of our departed heroes." Similarly, in North Carolina, even so confirmed an obstructionist as Zeb Vance came over when he learned of Lincoln's "terms" for acceptance of the South's surrender. In response, the governor issued a mid-February proclamation calling for all Tarheels to "assemble in primary meetings in every county in the State, and let the whole world, and especially our enemies, see how a free people can meet a proposition for their absolute submission.... Great God! Is there a man in all this honorable, high spirited, and noble Commonwealth so steeped in every conceivable meanness, so blackened with all the guilt of treason, or so damned with all the leprosy of cowardice as to say: 'Yes, we will submit to this' . . . whilst there yet remains half a million men amongst us able to resist? . . . Should we willfully throw down an organized government, disband our still powerful armies, and invite all these fearful consequences upon our country, we would live to have our children curse our gray hairs for fastening our dishonor upon them."

Editors formerly critical of practically everything Davis did or stood for, especially during the twenty months since Gettysburg and the fall of Vicksburg, now swung abruptly to full support of his administration, as if in admission of their share in reducing public morale to so low a point that Lincoln felt he could afford to spurn all overtures for peace except on terms amounting to unconditional surrender. Formerly gloomy, they turned hopeful, claiming to find much that was encouraging in the current military situation. "Nil Desperandum," writing in the *Enquirer*, pointed out that less of the Confederacy was actually occupied by the enemy now than there had been two years ago; Sherman had marched through it, true enough, but had not garrisoned or held what he traversed, except for Savannah, where he had been obliged to stop and catch his breath. What was more, he had not really whipped anyone en route, according to the Georgia humorist Charles H. Smith, who signed himself Bill Arp: "Didn't the rebellyun klose rite up behind him, like shettin a pair of waful irons?" Pollard of the *Examiner* agreed. "His campaign comes to nought if he cannot reach Grant; nothing left of it but the brilliant zig-zag of a raid, vanishing as heat lightning in the skies."

Clergymen throughout the South, of varied denominations, prepared to undertake a new crusade designed to reunite their congregations, along with any number of strayed sheep, in resistance to the unholy fate it now was clear the enemy had in mind to impose in the wake of their defeat. Army units began sending home letters signed in mass, expressing confidence in victory if only those behind the lines would emulate the soldiers at the front. In response, a hundred Mobile citizens established the League of Loyal Confederates, dedicated to the promotion of such support, ánd vowed to expand the society to cover every section of the nation, whether occupied or still free of blue contamination. Congress too was caught up in the fervor of the occasion. Indignant over Lincoln's reported terms at Hampton Roads, both houses voted overwhelmingly for a set of resolutions asserting that "no alternative is left to the people of the Confederate States, but a continuance of the war or submission to terms of peace alike ruinous and dishonorable." The choice was plain, and Congress made it with no opposing vote in the Senate and only one in the House. Fighting would continue, the joint resolution declared, until "the independence of the Confederate States shall have been established."

Davis thus gained more than he had planned for when, at the urging of Old Man Blair, he first decided to send the trio of sub-missionists to confer with Lincoln on the prospect of "securing peace to the two countries." Not only had they returned discredited, as he had expected and assured in their instructions, but the nature of their failure — made evident by Hunter when he repeated at rallies the harsh terms laid out for them aboard the *River Queen* — united the clashing factions within the Confederacy more effectively than any single event had done since far-off Chancellorsville. Elation had been the causative reaction then. Now it was indignation, quite as heady an emotion and even more cohesive in effect, since not to feel it was to confess a lack of honor sensible to insult. And yet there was a measure of elation, too, this cold first week in February, based on the simul-taneous elevation of Lee as general-in-chief, the replacement of Nor-throp with Isaac St John as commissary general, and the appointment of Breckinridge — even more popular as the hero of New Market than he had been as the South's favorite candidate in the presidential election that brought on the current struggle for independence — to the post vacated by Seddon, who was associated with all the military disasters that had occurred since he took office, two long years ago. Men noted these administrative changes and found in them a cause for hope that the war, which Lincoln had just made clear would have to be fought to the finish, had taken a sharp turn for the better, at least in the way it would be run.

How deep the emotion went was another matter. It might be what Pollard, reverting to type, would call "a spasmodic revival, or short fever of the popular mind"; in which case not even the indignation, let alone the tentative elation, would outlast the march begun that week by Sherman, north through the Carolinas from Savannah. "The South's condition is pitiable," Seward had told his wife after talking with Blair on the eve of the Hampton Roads conference, "but it is not yet fully realized there." That too might be true; in which case, deep or shallow, the unifying reaction came too late. Davis had silenced his most vocifer-ous critics, driving them headlong from the public view; but he knew well enough, from hard experience, that they were only waiting in the wings. One bad turn of fortune, left or right, would bring them back, stage center and full-voiced.

✗ 4 ✗

Lee received formal notice of his appointment to command of all the armies on February 6, midway through a heavy three-day attack on his right flank at Hatcher's Run, word of which had reached him the day before, a Sunday, while he was at church in Petersburg. Contrary to his usual custom, though he waited out the service, he went with the first group to the chancel for Communion before he left to ride down the Boydton Plank Road, where guns were growling and infantry was engaged on the far side of the frozen stream. Some green recruits, exposed to their first large-scale action, were in a state of panic along one critical part of the line, and when the good gray general rode out to rally them — a heroic figure, accustomed to exciting worshipful fervor in veterans who then would set up a shout of "Lee to the rear! Lee to the rear!" — one badly rattled soldier flung both hands above his head in terror and exclaimed: "Great God, old man, get out of the way! You don't know nothing!"

Grant had made no serious effort to attack or flank the Petersburg defenses since his late-October drive to cut the Southside Railroad was turned back at Burgess Mill, where the Boydton Plank Road straddled Hatcher's Run. Mindful however of Lincoln's admonition on the eve of Hampton Roads — "Let nothing which is transpiring change, hinder, or delay your military movements or plans" — he considered it time, despite the bitterness of the weather, to give the thing another try, less ambitious both in size and scope, but profitable enough if it worked out. This time he would not attempt to seize the railroad; he would be content to reach and hold the Boydton pike, which ran northeast from Stony Creek and Dinwiddie Courthouse, believing that this was the route Lee's supply wagons took from the new Petersburg & Weldon railhead at Hicksford, just beyond the Meherrin River. Accordingly, on February 4 — the Saturday the three rebel envoys returned to their

own lines from City Point — Warren and Humphreys were instructed to move out next morning, each with two of his three divisions, preceded by Gregg's troopers, who were to strike and patrol the objective from Dinwiddie to Burgess Mill, capturing whatever enemy trains were on it, until the infantry arrived to establish permanent occupation. So ordered: Gregg set out before dawn Sunday, and Warren followed from his position on the Union left, two miles west of Globe Tavern. Humphreys brought up the rear, his marchers breathing steam in the frosty air while their boots crunched ice in puddles along the way.

Hard as the weather was on men in the open, mounted or afoot, it had much to do with their success, first in reaching the Boydton Road unchallenged and then in holding their own through most of the three-day action which presently went into the books as the Battle of Hatcher's Run. Thinly clad and poorly fed, shivering in their trenches north of the stream, the Confederates apparently had not believed that any general, even Grant, would purposely expose his troops to the cutting wind, whistling over a bleak landscape frozen iron hard, for a prize of so little worth. As it turned out, Lee was scarcely using the Dinwiddie artery as a supply route at all, considering it too vulnerable to just such a strike as now was being made. Early on the scene, the blue troopers captured only a few wagons out on a foraging expedition, and when the infantry came up — Warren on the left, confronting Burgess Mill, and Humphreys opposite Armstrong's Mill, two miles below — there was little for them to do but dig in under long-range fire from guns in the rebel works beyond the run. Late that afternoon the graybacks tried a sortie against Humphreys, who rather easily turned it back. Reinforced that night by two divisions sent by Meade from the lines on the far side of Petersburg — one from Wright, the other from Parke — he was joined before daylight by Warren and Gregg, who gave up holding and patrolling the unused Boydton Plank Road in favor of a concentration of all available forces. Next morning (February 6; Lee was notified of his confirmation as general-in-chief, and Davis would speak that night in Metropolitan Hall) scouts reported the defenders hugging their works, but a probe by Warren that afternoon provoked a counterattack that drove him back in some disorder until he stiffened alongside Humphreys. Together they broke up the butternut effort, which turned out to have involved all three of Gordon's divisions, as well as one of Hill's. Despite this evidence of compacted danger and a total of 1474 casualties — most of them Warren's; Humphreys lost 155, all told — the Federals remained on the south bank of the creek well into the following day, then recrossed to take up a new position extending Grant's left to the Vaughan Road crossing of Hatcher's Run, three miles downstream from Burgess Mill and about the same distance southwest of where his flank had rested prior to this latest attempt to turn his adversary's right.

Militarily, the results of this latest flanking try were negligible except on two counts. One was that it required a corresponding three-mile extension of Lee's own line, now stretched to a length of more than 37 miles, exclusive of recurrent jogs and doublings, while the army that held it was reduced by casualties and desertion to a strength of 46,398, the number listed as "present for duty" although many among them were too weak for anything more rigorous than answering roll call from their widespread posts along the fire step. The other negative outcome was the loss of John Pegram, the only professional among Gordon's three division commanders. Shot through the heart, he fell leading the counterattack on the second day of battle, two weeks past his thirty-third birthday, and was buried two days later from St Paul's Church in Richmond, just three weeks after he was married there. Such a loss came hard. But hardest of all, perhaps, was the feeling of what the three-day fight portended, coming as it did at a time when the food reserve was quite exhausted. Throughout the action, the troops received no issue of meat, only a scant handful of meal per man. Lee protested to the War Department about this and the absence of his cavalry, dispersed for lack of forage. "Taking these facts in connection with the paucity of our numbers," he informed his superiors in the capital at his back, "you must not be surprised if calamity befalls us."

At the same time, he spoke to those below him not of calamity but of fortitude and courage. On February 11, four days after the fighting subsided along Hatcher's Run, he issued with the concurrence of the President a final offer of pardon for all deserters who would return to the colors within twenty days. Included in this general order, the first since he took over as general-in-chief, was an address to all the nation's soldiers, present and absent. The choice, he said, had been narrowed "between war and abject submission," and "to such a proposal brave men with arms in their hands can have but one answer. They cannot barter manhood for peace, nor the right of self-government for life or property. . . . Taking new resolution from the fate which our enemies intend for us," Lee's appeal concluded, "let every man devote all his energies to the common defense. Our resources, wisely and vigorously employed, are ample, and with a brave army, sustained by a determined and united people, success with God's assistance cannot be doubtful. The advantages of the enemy will have but little value if we do not permit them to impair our resolution. Let us then oppose constancy to adversity, fortitude to suffering, and courage to danger, with the firm assurance that He who gave freedom to our fathers will bless the efforts of their children to preserve it."

Sherman by then was eleven days out of Savannah, and though all was confusion in his path and ruin in his rear, his purpose was becoming clearer with every northward mile he covered toward a link-up with Schofield, moving inland from Fort Fisher against Wilmington and Bragg. So too was Grant's purpose, which Lee believed was to act on his own before the intended conjunction. Petersburg now had been under seige for eight relentless months — five times the length of Vicksburg's previous forty-eight-day record — but the chances were that the blue commander wanted to avoid having it said that he could never have taken the place without the help of the forces coming up through the Carolinas. "I think Genl Grant will move against us soon," Lee wrote his wife some ten days later, "within a week if nothing prevents, and no man can tell what may be the result."

★ ★ ★

"I want to see the long deferred chastisement begin. If we don't purify South Carolina it will be because we *can't get a light*," an Illinois major wrote home while awaiting orders to cross the Savannah River. Six weeks later, when he got his next chance to post a letter, he could look back on a job well done and satisfaction achieved. "The army burned everything it came near in the State of South Carolina," he informed his wife, "not under orders, but in spite of orders. The men 'had it in' for the state, and they took it out in their own way. Our track through the state is a desert waste."

In some commands — Judson Kilpatrick's, for one — there were at least informal orders for such destruction. "In after years," the cavalry leader told his staff at a dinner he gave on the eve of setting out, "when travelers passing through South Carolina shall see chimney stacks without houses, and the country desolate, and shall ask, 'Who did this?' some Yankee will answer, 'Kilpatrick's Cavalry.'" Moreover, he did what he could to fulfill this prophecy en route. Descending on Barnwell four days later, just beyond the Salkehatchie, his troopers left little behind them but ashes and the suggestion that the town be renamed Burnwell.

"It seems to be decreed that South Carolina, having sown the wind, shall reap the whirlwind," a veteran infantryman asserted, and was echoed by a comrade: "South Carolina has commenced to pay an installment, long overdue, on her debt to justice and humanity. With the help of God, we will have principal and interest before we leave her borders. There is a terrible gladness in the realization of so many hopes and wishes."

Sherman, having cast himself in the role of avenging angel, saw his long-striding western veterans as crusaders, outriders for the Union, charged with imparting to the heathen Carolinians a wisdom that began with fear, and they in turn were proud to view their service in that light; "Do Boys," they called themselves, happy to be at the bidding of a commander who did not intend to restrain his army unduly, "lest its vigor and energy should be impaired." Anticipating a two-way profit from such license — high spirits within the column, panic in its path — he was hard put to say which of these benefits he valued most. "It is impossible to conceive of a march involving more labor and exposure," he would say, "yet I cannot recall an instance of bad temper." Throughout what was known from the outset as the Smoky March, a free-swinging jocularity obtained, as if to demonstrate that the damage, however severe, was being inflicted in high good humor, not out of meanness or any such low motivation. "There goes your damned old gospel shop!" the soldiers crowed, by way of a warmup for the march, as they pulled down the steeple and walls of a church in Hardeeville. "Vandalism, though not encouraged, was seldom punished," according to an artillery captain who also served as an undercover reporter for the New York *Herald*. He noted that, while "in Georgia few houses were burned, here few escaped," with the result that "the middle of the finest day looked black and gloomy" because of the dense smoke rising on all sides. Here again the cavalry did its share, Kilpatrick being under instructions to signal his whereabouts out on the flank by setting fire to things along the way. "Make a smoke like Indians do on the plains," Sherman had told him.

By way of further protection against the pangs of conscience, in case any tried to creep in, the marchers developed a biding dislike for the natives, especially those who had anything to lose. "In Georgia we had to respect the high-toned feelings of the planters," the *Herald*'s artillerist explained, "for they yielded with a dignity that won our admiration. In Carolina, the inhabitants, with a fawning, cringing subserviency, hung around our camps, craving a bite to eat." Enlarging on this, a Massachusetts colonel declared that he felt no sympathy for these victims of the army's wrath or high jinks. "I might pity individual cases brought before me," he wrote home, "but I believe that this terrible example is needed in this country as a warning to those men in all time to come who may cherish rebellious thoughts; I believe it is necessary in order to show the strength of this Government and thoroughly to subdue these people."

For the most part, though, no matter how amusing all this was for the soldiers trudging northward, or painful for the victims in their path, such depredations had little more to do with the success or failure of the operation, at least at this stage, than did the marksmanship or battle skill of the invaders, who went unchallenged except by skittish bands of butternut horsemen on the flanks. What mattered now was endurance, the ability of the marchers to cover a dozen miles of icy calf-deep bog a day, and the dexterity of the road-laying pioneers, charged with getting the 3000-odd wagons and ambulances through, as well as the 68 guns. On the right, where Howard had taken a steam-propelled head start up Port Royal Sound, then overland to Pocotaligo, this was not so much of a problem; he had only the Salkehatchie to cross before he reached the railroad linking Charleston and Augusta, Sherman's initial tactical objective; whereas Slocum, on the left, had first the Savannah River and then the Coosawhatchie Swamp to get across before he even approached the Salkehatchie. Howard made it in seven days. The wonder was that Slocum took only two days longer, considering the obstacles he encountered — especially the Coosawhatchie, which was three rain-swollen miles across and belt-buckle-deep, or sometimes worse, for nearly a mile on either side of the main channel. "Uncle Billy seems to have struck this river end-ways," one floundering veteran complained, submerged to his armpits in liquid muck and crackling skim-ice.

In addition to a 300-foot bridge that spanned the deeper-bottomed channel, the pioneers had to corduroy both approaches, in and out of the morass, and pin down the split-sapling mats, laid crosswise two and three feet underwater, to keep them from floating away. All this was managed handily, using materials on the scene; the six divisions crossed with a minimum of delay, if not of discomfort. By February 9 Slocum had all his men and vehicles over the Salkehatchie and in camp along the railroad west of Blackville, alongside Howard, who had reached and begun wrecking it two days ago, east to Bamberg, within fifteen miles of Branchville. For two more days they stayed there, converting thirty miles of track into twisted scrap iron, and then both wings were off again, slogging northward for the Congaree and the capital on its opposite bank, some fifty miles away. In addition to the "terrible gladness" the marchers felt because of the destruction they had wrought, official and unofficial, along and on both sides of their line of march, they also felt considerable hindsight amazement at the speed they had made through the midwinter swamps.

Nor were they by any means the only ones to feel this. Up in western North Carolina, where he was awaiting the outcome of efforts by friends in Richmond to achieve his reinstatement to the command from which he had been removed just over half a year before, Joe Johnston was even more amazed than were the soldiers who had accomplished this near miracle of stamina and logistics. He had been told by experts that the South Carolina hinterland was impenetrable at this season of the year, all the roads being under water, and he had believed it. "But when I learned that Sherman's army was marching through the Salk swamps, making its own corduroy roads at the rate of a dozen miles a day and more," he said later, "I made up my mind that there had been no such army in existence since the days of Julius Caesar."

Sherman rather agreed with this assessment. He had ridden with Howard on the less-obstructed right, northwest from Pocotaligo across the Salkehatchie, and when Slocum came up on the left along the railroad, having also encountered little formal opposition, the red-haired general's enthusiasm flared. For one thing, it was evident that his strategy of striking at a central objective while feinting simultaneously at others beyond his flanks was still effective, and for another it was equally clear that his policy of giving his troops a freer hand, not only to forage but also to visit their frisky wrath on the property of aboriginal secessionists along both routes of march, was bearing fruit; soldiers and civilians alike, the Confederates seemed unstrung by indecision and alarm. So far, the only resistance had come from cavalry snapping ineffectively at his wingtips, and already he could see that Magrath's appeal for South Carolinians to ambuscade the bluecoats in their midst was even less productive than Joe Brown's had been, two months ago in Georgia — with the result that, in his attitude toward the enemy ahead, Sherman become more confident and high-handed than ever. "I had a species of contempt for these scattered and inconsiderable forces," he afterwards declared, and the record sustained his claim. Midway of the two-day pause for railroad twisting, for example, when he received a flag-of-truce note from Wheeler, offering to quit burning cotton in the path of the invaders if they in turn would "discontinue burning houses," he kept his answer brief and to the point. He was unwilling to waste time now in an argument over the propriety of gratuitous destruction, nor did he intend to fall into the fibrous trap that had snared Banks last spring up the Red River. In short, he declined to enter into any discussion of the matter, except to tell the rebel cavalryman: "I hope you will burn all cotton and save us the trouble. All you don't burn I will."

Next day — February 9 — he was off again, across the Edisto, hard on the go for the Congaree and Columbia, just beyond. The two wings marched in near conjunction now, and once more it was as if the friction match had replaced the rifle as the basic infantry weapon. Barns exploded in flame as soon as the foragers emptied them of stock and corn; deserted houses loosed heavy plumes of smoke on the horizon; even the split-rail fences crackled along roadsides, and Kilpatrick was complaining of how "the infernal bummers," outstripping his troopers in the race for booty, "managed to plunder every hamlet and town before the cavalry came up." Aware that their next prize was the state capital, the very cradle of secession, the veterans chanted as they swung along the roads converging northward on their goal:

> "*Hail Columbia, happy land!*
> *If I don't burn you, I'll be damned.*"

Riding among them, his spirits as high as their own — "sandy-haired, sharp-featured," an associate described him; "his nose prominent, his lips thin, his gray eyes flashing fire as fast as lightning on a summer's day; his whole face mobile as an actor's, and revealing every shade of thought or emotion that flitters across his active mind" — Sherman would have been in even higher feather if he had known that Schofield's troops, long ice-bound up the Potomac, began unloading that same day at Fort Fisher, preparatory to moving against Wilmington and points inland, as agreed upon beforehand. Not only would this provide the northward marchers with supplies and reinforcements when the time came; it would create still more confusion for Beauregard, who was confused enough already by his instructions from Richmond to intercept the invaders with a force that was even more "scattered and inconsiderable" than his adversary knew.

The Creole had returned from Mississippi the week before, called back to conduct the defense of the Carolinas, where his name retained a measure of the magic it once evoked, first as the Hero of Sumter and then as the deliverer who turned back Du Pont's iron fleet. On February 2, the day after his arrival in Augusta, he assembled a council of war for discussion of how to go about intercepting Sherman's double-pronged advance, which had begun in earnest just the day before. Hardee was there, summoned by rail from Charleston, as were G. W. Smith, in command of the Georgia militia, and D. H. Hill, who had volunteered, as at Petersburg nine months before, for service under Beauregard in a time of national trial. Taking count, the council came up with a figure of 33,450 men available for the task. But this was a considerable over-estimate, since it included some 7500 veterans from the Army of Tennessee, only 3000 of whom were yet on hand, as well as Hoke's 6000, pinned down at Wilmington by the fall of Fort Fisher, and Smith's 1500 Georgians, forbidden by law to move outside their home state. The actual number available was just over 20,000, barely more than a third as many as Sherman had moving against them from Sister's Ferry and Pocotaligo. Moreover, they were grievously divided. Hardee had 12,500 in and around Charleston — 8000 in two divisions under Major Generals Lafayette McLaws and Ambrose Wright, 3000 South Carolina militia under Brigadier General William Taliaferro, and M. C. Butler's 1500 troopers, recently detached from the Army of Northern Virginia — while Harvey Hill had 9500 near Augusta, including Stevenson's 3000, just off the cars from Tupelo, and Wheeler's 6500 cavalry, already in motion to challenge the invaders in case they tried to cross the "impassable" Salkehatchie. Beauregard's decision, made in the absence of any information as to which blue wing was making the main effort, was to defend both cities, 120 miles apart, until such time as evidence of a feint allowed the troops in that direction to be shifted elsewhere. He himself would set up headquarters at Columbia, he said. If worse came to worse, both Hardee and Hill could fall back and join him there, evacuating Charleston and Augusta rather than suffer the loss of their commands to overwhelming numbers, and thus combine for an attack on one or another of the two blue columns toiling northward.

Poor as the plan was in the first place, mainly because of its necessary surrender of the initiative to the enemy, it was rendered even poorer — in fact inoperative — by the speed with which Sherman moved through the supposedly impenetrable swamps. By the time Beauregard set up headquarters in the capital on February 10, the invaders, having reached and wrecked the railroad between Charleston and Augusta, were over the Edisto and hard on the march for the Congaree, no longer by two routes but in a single unassailable column; Sherman, like a diving hawk, had closed his wings for a rapid descent on Columbia before either Hill or Hardee, outflanked on the left and right, had time to react as planned for the combined attack on some lesser segment of the Union host. Despondent, Beauregard wired Hill to leave Augusta and join him at once with Stevenson's men at Chester, fifty miles north of the South Carolina capital. Similar orders to Hardee struck a snag, however. Though he promptly detached Butler's remounted troopers to assist Wheeler in delaying the blue advance, Richmond had urged him not to abandon Charleston until it was absolutely necessary, and he wanted his chief to make that judgment in person, on the scene. Unable to end the Georgian's indecision by telegraph, Beauregard went to Charleston on February 14, convinced him there was no longer any choice in the matter, prepared written instructions for the evacuation, and returned that night to Columbia: only to learn next day that Hardee had suffered another change of heart, prompted by still another Richmond dispatch urging him to postpone the evacuation until it was certain that Beauregard could not stop the Federals on his own. Exasperated, the Creole wired peremptory orders for Hardee to get the endangered garrison aboard the cars for Chester while there still was time. Sherman by then was maneuvering for a crossing of the Congaree, upstream and down, and Columbia itself was being evacuated in hope of sparing the capital the destruction that would attend any attempt to defend it against the 60,000 bluecoats on its doorstep.

That was February 15. Beauregard stayed through the following day and set out north by rail for Chester after nightfall, leaving Wade Hampton, whose splendid peacetime mansion rivaled the new brick State House as the showplace of the capital, to conduct the final stage of the withdrawal before the Federals arrived. Placed in command of all the cavalry, the post he had filled in Virginia until Lee detached him for his present task, the South Carolina grandee was promoted to lieutenant general over Wheeler, who, though nearly two decades his junior in age — Hampton would be forty-seven next month; Wheeler was twenty-eight — had half a year's seniority on him as a major general. Like most evacuations under pressure, this one was attended with considerable disorder and a confusion enlarged by particular circumstances. Columbia, a neat, well-laid-out little city with a charm befitting its uplands heritage as a center for culture and commerce, had grown in the course of the past two years from a population of about 8000 to better than 20,000, largely as a result of the influx of people from threatened areas on the seacoast and, more recently and in even larger numbers, from regions along or near the Georgia border thought to lie in the path of Sherman's burners. Convinced that the capital was strategically unimportant, especially in comparison with directly menaced Charleston and Augusta, prominent landowners and businessmen sought refuge here for their families, as well as for their valuables and house slaves. Before the war, there had been three banks in Columbia; now there were fourteen, including all of bombarded Charleston's, shifted beyond reach of the heaviest naval guns. Moreover, this notion of inland security persisted well beyond the time that Sherman left Savannah. Just last week, on February 9, the editor of the local *South Carolinian* had assured his readers that there was "no real tangible cause" for supposing that the Yankees had Columbia in mind.

Then suddenly they knew better; Sherman was two days off, then one, then none, guns booming from the Congaree bottoms, just across the way; there was neither time nor means for removing their sequestered goods beyond his reach. Offers as large as $500 hired no wagons, and men and women competed testily for seats or standing room on every northbound train. Earlier, the authorities had ordered all cotton transported from intown warehouses for burning in open fields beyond the city limits, and the bales were trundled into the streets for rapid loading when the time came. They sat there still, spilling their fluffy, highly combustible fiber through rents in the jute bagging. Columbia thus was a tinderbox, ready to burst into flame at the touch of a match or a random spark, by the time the rear-guard handful of gray troopers pulled out Friday morning, February 17, and Mayor T. J. Goodwyn set out with three aldermen in a carriage flying a white flag, charged by Hampton with surrendering the capital to the bluecoats already entering its outskirts.

Sherman rode in about midday, close on the heels of Howard's lead brigade. Part of Logan's XV Corps, whose mere proximity he had said would obviate the need for sowing any hated place with salt, its members were given the customary privilege, as the first troops in, of policing the captured town and enjoying all it had to offer in the way of food and fun. A blustery wind had risen and was blowing the spilled cotton about the streets in wisps and skeins. Asked later why, under these explosive circumstances, he had not kept his veterans in formation and under control while they were in occupation of the surrendered capital, the red-haired Ohioan replied indignantly: "I would not have done such a harshness to save the whole town. They were men, and I was not going to treat them like slaves."

Liquor shops were among the first establishments to be looted when the troops broke ranks and scattered. But this was more from habit than from need, since friendly house slaves stood in front of many residences, offering the soldiers drinks from bottles they had brought up from abandoned cellers. "Lord bless you, Massa. Try some dis," a genial white-haired butler said, extending a gourd dipper he kept filled with fine old brandy from a bucket in his other hand. Breakfastless and exuberant, a good part of the command was roaring drunk in short order. Slocum, whose left wing crossed upstream and went into camp beyond the city, saw in this the main cause for what would follow after sundown. "A drunken soldier with a musket in one hand and a match in the other is not a pleasant visitor to have about the house on a dark, windy night," he afterwards remarked, "particularly when for a series of years you have urged him to come so that you might have an opportunity of performing a surgical operation on him." Sherman apparently thought so, too. "Look out," he told Howard, observing the effect of all this proffered whiskey, "or you'll have hell to pay. You'd better go and see about it in person."

Howard did go and see about it. Alarmed, he stopped the informal distribution of spirits and, after nightfall, ordered the drunken brigade

relieved by another from the same division, which had marched through
the city earlier to camp on the far side. But it was altogether too late by
then. The men of the first having scattered beyond recall, the practical
outcome was that a second XV Corps brigade was added to the milling
throng of celebrants and looters. By then, moreover, the frightened
citizens had learned what the soldiers meant when, passing through the
windy streets that afternoon, they told them: "You'll catch hell tonight."
Sherman could have interpreted for them, though as it happened he only
found out about the prophecy after it had been fulfilled. Weary, he
took an early supper and lay down to rest in a bedroom of the house
his staff had commandeered for headquarters. "Soon after dark," he
would remember, "I became conscious that a bright light was shining
on the walls."

Columbia was burning, and burning fiercely, in more than a dozen
places simultaneously. Hampton's mansion was one of the first to go,
along with Treasury Secretary Trenholm's, and lest it be thought that
these had been singled out because of their owners' wealth or politics,
the Gervais Street red-light district was put to the torch at the same
time, as well as Cotton Town, a section of poorer homes to the northwest, and stores and houses along the river front. One object of special
wrath was the Baptist church where the South Carolina secession convention had first assembled, but the burners were foiled by a Negro
they asked for directions. As it happened, he was the sexton of the
church they sought and he pointed out a rival Methodist establishment
just up the block, which soon was gushing flames from all its windows.
So presently was the nearby Ursuline convent, whose Mother Superior
was known to be the sister of Bishop Patrick N. Lynch, an outspoken
secessionist who had celebrated the breakup of the Union, back in '61,
with thanksgiving rites in his Charleston cathedral. Hardest hit of all
was the business district. Terrified pigeons flapped and wheeled in the
drifting smoke, unable to find a place to light, and the hysterical screams
of women combined strangely with the lowing of cattle trapped in their
stalls. "All around us were falling thickly showers of burning flakes," a
seventeen-year-old girl wrote in her diary next day. "Everywhere the
palpitating blaze walled the streets as far as the eye could reach, filling
the air with its terrible roar. On every side [was] the crackling and
devouring fire, while every instant came the crashing of timbers and the
thunder of falling buildings. A quivering molten ocean seemed to fill the
air and sky."

Mindful perhaps of a statement he had made to Mayor Goodwyn,
who served as his guide on an afternoon tour of inspection: "Go home
and rest assured that your city will be as safe in my hands as if you had
controlled it," Sherman himself turned out to fight the flames, along with
his staff, a number of unit commanders, and as many of their troops as
could be rounded up and persuaded to serve as firemen. Of the rest,

unwilling to end their fun or too drunk to follow orders, 370 were placed in arrest, two were shot and killed, and thirty wounded. That still left enough at large to defeat the efforts being made to confine the conflagration. Some among them hurried from block to block, carrying wads of turpentine-soaked cotton for setting fire to houses so far spared, while others used their rifles to bayonet hoses and cripple pumpers brought into play by the civilian fire department. Before the night was over, another whole division was summoned into the city to help sub-due the arsonists and the flames, but even that did not suffice until about 4 o'clock in the morning, when the wind relented enough to let the flames die down and save the capital from annihilation. As it was, when the sun rose two hours later, blood red through the murk of heavy smoke, two thirds of Columbia lay in ashes. Fire had raged through 84 of its 124 blocks, with such effect that the girl diarist could see nothing from her position near the center "but heaps of rubbish, tall dreary chimneys, and shattered brick walls." Burned-out families gathered in the parks and on the common, huddled among such possessions as they had managed to save. Some of the women were weeping uncontrollably. Others were dry-eyed, either from shock or from a sharpened hatred of the Yankees. An Illinois surgeon moved among them for a time, then withdrew sadly. "I talked with some," he wrote in his diary that night, "but it made me feel too bad to be endured."

Sherman had a different reaction. "Though I never ordered it, and never wished it," he was to say of the burning, "I have never shed any tears over it, because I believe that it hastened what we all fought for — the end of the war." As for blame, he fixed that on Hampton for starting the fire and on God for enlarging it. He charged the rebel general with "ripping open bales of cotton, piling it in the streets, burning it, and then going away"; at which point "God Almighty started wind sufficient to carry that cotton wherever He would." Originally, while the fire was in progress, he had seen whiskey as the overriding cause of the catastrophe, available in quantity because the departed graybacks had foolishly made "an evacuated city a depot of liquor for an army to occupy." Under its influence, he admitted, his soldiers "may have as-sisted in spreading the fire after it once began, and may have indulged in unconcealed joy to see the ruin of the capital of South Carolina," but he did not dwell long on this aspect of the case, saying instead: "I dis-claim on the part of my army any agency in this fire, but, on the con-trary, claim that we saved what of Columbia remains unconsumed. And without hesitation I charge General Wade Hampton with having burned his own city of Columbia, not with malicious intent, or as the manifesta-tion of a silly 'Roman stoicism,' but from folly and want of sense in filling it with lint, cotton, and tinder." So he declared in his formal report of the campaign, although he conceded in his memoirs, ten years later, that there had been method in his arraignment of his adversary for the burning. "I distinctly charged it to General Wade Hampton," he wrote then, "and confess I did so pointedly, to shake the faith of his people in him, for he was in my opinion a braggart, and professed to be the special champion of South Carolina."

For two more days the army remained in and around Columbia, probing the rubble for overlooked spoils and expanding the destruction by burning down the Confederate arsenal and a Treasury printing office, legitimate targets which somehow had survived the conflagration. The Preston mansion, where Hood had visited his fiancée on his way to Richmond two weeks back, escaped entirely: first, because John Logan occupied it during the three-day stay, and finally because Sherman gave permission for the homeless wards of the Ursuline convent to take up residence there on February 20, the day his troops moved out. Logan was supervising the placement of barrels of pitch in the cellar, intending to set them ablaze on his departure, when the white-clad pupils were herded in by the Mother Superior, armed with Sherman's order. Black Jack loosed a string of oaths at this sparing of a rebel general's ornate property, but had no choice except to let the house go unburned when he took up the march.

It was northward, as before. The feint now was at Chester, fifty miles away, and at Charlotte, about the same distance farther on, across the North Carolina line. Beyond Winnsboro, however — which the outriding bummers set afire next day, though not soon enough to keep the main body from coming up in time to save most of it from the flames — both infantry wings turned hard right for a crossing of the Wateree River, a dozen miles to the east, and a fast march on Cheraw, en route to Fayetteville and Goldsboro, where Sherman had arranged for Schofield to meet him with supplies brought inland from Wilmington and New Bern.

Alas, it was just at this critical stage, with by far the worst stretch of the march supposedly behind him, that the pace slowed to a crawl. Coming down to the Wateree on February 23, Howard's wing made it over the river in a driving rain, but only half of Slocum's crossed before the bridge collapsed under pressure from logs and driftwood swept downstream by the rush of rising water; Davis's XIV Corps was left stranded on the western bank, and the other three, having made it over, soon had cause to wish they hadn't. The mud, though thinner, was slick as grease on the high red ground beyond the river, and grew slicker and deeper throughout the record three-day rainfall, until at last — "slipping, stumbling, swearing, singing, and yelling" — the head of the column reached Hanging Rock Post Office on February 26, having covered barely twenty miles in the past four days; while the XIV Corps, still on the far side of the Wateree, had made no miles at all. Furious, Sherman called a halt and ordered Slocum to ride back and expedite a crossing. If necessary, he was to have Davis burn his wagons, spike his guns, shoot the mules, and ferry or swim his troops across; he was in fact to do anything, within reason or beyond, that would avoid prolonging the delay now that a solid half of the long trek to Goldsboro was behind the main body, slathered with mud and resting close to exhaustion at Hanging Rock, within twenty air-line miles of the North Carolina line.

No such drastic steps were needed. That afternoon the sun came out, beaming down on "bedraggled mules, toiling soldiers, and seas of mud," and by the next the river had fallen enough for Davis to improvise a bridge; his laggard corps got over that night with its guns and train, followed by the cavalry, which had kept up the feint against Chester after the infantry swung east. Sherman meanwhile improved the interim by sending a reinforced brigade to nearby Camden, with instructions to destroy all "government property, stores, and cotton." Reinspired despite their bone-deep weariness, the detached troops accomplished this and more, burning a large flour mill and both depots of the South Carolina Railroad, along with the Masonic Hall, and looting almost every private residence in town, then returned to Hanging Rock in time to take their place in column when the reunited army resumed its march on Cheraw, just under fifty miles away. They had recovered their high spirits, and so too, by now, had their commander. He had learned from newspapers gathered roundabout that Charleston, evacuated by Hardee on the night Columbia burned, had been occupied next morning by units from Foster's garrison at Savannah: a splendid example of what Sherman had meant when he told him to be ready to "pick up the apples." Symbolically, at any rate — for it was here, not quite two months under four long years ago, that the war began — this was the biggest apple of them all. Four days later, moreover, while the inland marchers were turning east to cross the Wateree, Schofield had captured Wilmington, freeing his and Terry's men for the appointed meeting in the interior next month.

One other piece of news there was, but Sherman was not sure, just yet, whether he was glad or sorry to receive it. Joe Johnston, he learned, had replaced Beauregard as commander of the "scattered and inconsiderable forces" assembling in his front.

★   ★   ★

Often, down the years, it would be said that Lee's first exercise of authority, following his confirmation as general-in-chief, had been to recall Johnston to active duty; whereas, in fact, one of his first acts at his new post was the denial of a petition, signed by the Vice President and seventeen prominent Senators, urging him to do just that by restoring his fellow Virginian to command of the Army of Tennessee. "The three corps of that army have been ordered to South Carolina and are now under the command of Genl Beauregard," he replied on February 13, one week after his elevation. "I entertain a high opinion of Genl

Johnston's capacity, but think a continual change of commanders is very injurious to any troops and tends greatly to their disorganization. At this time, as far as I understand the condition of affairs, an engagement with the enemy may be expected any day, and a change now would be particularly hazardous. Genl Beauregard is well known to the citizens of South Carolina, as well as to the troops of the Army of Tennessee, and I would recommend that it be certainly ascertained that a change was necessary before it was made." Besides, he told Stephens and the others, "I do not consider that my appointment . . . confers the right which you assume belongs to it, nor is it proper that it should. I can only employ such troops and officers as may be placed at my disposal by the War Department."

Old Joe it seemed would have to bide his time in the Carolina piedmont, awaiting the outcome of further efforts by his supporters. But developments over the course of the next week provoked a reassessment of the situation. For one thing, Beauregard's health was rumored to be "feeble and precarious," which might account for his apparent shakiness under pressure. Shifting his headquarters, formerly at Augusta, from Columbia to Chester, then to Charlotte, the Creole seemed confused and indecisive in the face of Sherman's "semi-amphibious" march through the boggy lowlands. "General Beauregard makes no mention of what he proposes or what he can do, or where his troops are," Lee complained to Davis. "He does not appear from his dispatches to be able to do much." Columbia by then had been abandoned, along with outflanked Charleston, and Wilmington was under heavy pressure from Schofield; at which point, on February 21, Davis received and passed on to Lee a wire just in from Beauregard, once more proposing a "grand strategy" designed to bring the Yankees to their knees. In the Louisianian's opinion, Sherman (who would not turn east, away from Chester, until the following day) was advancing upon Charlotte and Salisbury, North Carolina, on his way to a conjunction with Grant in rear of Richmond, and Old Bory saw in this — as he so often had done before, under drastic circumstances — the opportunity of a lifetime. "I earnestly urge a concentration of at least 35,000 infantry and artillery at [Salisbury], if possible, to give him battle there, and crush him, then to concentrate all forces against Grant, and then to march on Washington and dictate a peace. Hardee and myself can collect about 15,000 exclusive of Cheatham and Stewart, not likely to reach in time. If Lee and Bragg can furnish 20,000 more, the fate of the Confederacy would be secure."

Unknowingly, Beauregard had proposed his last air-castle strategy of the war. "The idea is good, but the means are lacking," Lee told Davis two days later. He had by then made up his mind that the Creole had to go, and by way of providing a successor he had already sounded out Breckinridge on the matter. "[Sherman] seems to have everything his own way," he informed the War Secretary on February 19, the day after Charleston fell, adding that he could get little useful information from the general charged with contesting the blue advance through the Carolinas. "I do not know where his troops are, or on what lines they are moving. His dispatches only give movements of the enemy. He has a difficult task to perform under present circumstances, and one of his best officers, Genl Hardee, is incapacitated by sickness. I have also heard that his own health is indifferent, though he has never so stated. Should his strength give way, there is no one on duty in the department that could replace him, nor have I anyone to send there. Genl J. E. Johnston is the only officer whom I know who has the confidence of the army and people, and if he was ordered to report to me I would place him there on duty. It is necessary to bring out all our strength. . . ."

Puzzled by Lee's indirectness, the Kentuckian asked just what it was he wanted, and when. Lee replied that he had intended "to apply for Genl J. E. Johnston, that I might assign him to duty, should circumstances permit." Understanding now that by "circumstances" Lee meant the President's objections, Breckinridge passed the request along, and Davis — despite his recent expression of "a conviction so settled that it would be impossible for me again to feel confidence in [Johnston] as the commander of an army in the field" — agreed, however reluctantly, to the recall and appointment, though he was careful to point out that he did so only "in the hope that General Johnston's soldierly qualities may be made serviceable to his country when acting under General Lee's orders, and that in his new position those defects which I found manifested by him when serving as an independent commander will be remedied by the control of the general-in-chief."

That was how it came about that Johnston received on February 23, the day after they were issued, simultaneous orders from the War Department and from Lee, recalling him to active duty and assigning him to command of the troops now under Beauregard, including the Army of Tennessee. He was then at Lincolnton, North Carolina — "I am in the regular line of strategic retreat," Mrs Chesnut, who preceded him there in her flight from threatened Mulberry, had remarked sarcastically when she learned that he was expected any day — thirty miles northwest of Charlotte, where Beauregard had established headquarters after falling back from Chester. Instructed to "concentrate all available forces and drive back Sherman," Johnston replied much as he had done on his arrival in Mississippi just under two years ago, preceding the fall of Vicksburg: "It is too late. . . . The remnant of the Army of Tennessee is much divided. So are the other troops. . . . Is any discretion allowed me? I have no staff."

Before taking over he went by rail to Charlotte to confer with his predecessor, now designated his second in command. Beauregard assured him of his support, having just wired Lee that he would "at all

times be happy to serve with or under so gallant and patriotic a soldier."
Privately, though, the Louisianian was bitterly disappointed at having
once more been relegated to a subordinate position, as at Manassas, Shiloh, and Petersburg. "My greatest desire has always been to
command a good army in the field," he had recently declared. "Will I
ever be gratified?" Now in the Carolinas — as in Mississippi nearly three
years before, following his canny withdrawal from Halleck's intended
trap at Corinth — another chance had come and gone, and he knew this
was the last; Fate and Davis had undone him, now as then.

Johnston was by no means correspondingly elated. Though he was
grateful for Beauregard's loyalty, he believed the post afforded little
opportunity for success or even survival. He had, as he informed one of
his Richmond supporters, "not exactly no hope, but only a faint hope,"
and even this was presently seen to have been an overstatement of the
case. He said later that he took over in Charlotte, February 25, "with a
full consciousness . . . that we could have no other object, in continuing
the war, than to obtain fair terms of peace; for the Southern cause must
have appeared hopeless then, to all intelligent and dispassionate Southern
men."

Sherman by now was astride Lynch's Creek, midway between the
Wateree and the Pee Dee, closing fast on Cheraw, his final intermediary
objective before he entered North Carolina. Moreover, the invaders by
then had still another powerful column in contention; Wilmington's fall,
on the day of Johnston's restoration by the War Department, freed
Schofield to join Sherman for a northward march across the Roanoke,
the last strong defensive line south of the Appomattox. Lee pointed out
that the only way to avoid the consequences of such a penetration
would be for him to combine with Johnston for a strike at Sherman before that final barrier was crossed, even though this would require him
not only to give up his present lines covering Petersburg and the national
capital, but also to manage the evacuation so stealthily that Grant would
not know he was gone until it was too late to overtake and crush him
on the march. How long the odds were against his achieving such a
deliverance Lee did not say, yet he did what he could to warn his superiors of the sacrifice involved in the attempt. On the day after Foster
occupied Charleston — February 18: the fourth anniversary of Davis's
provisional inauguration in Montgomery — he notified Breckinridge:
"I fear it may be necessary to abandon all our cities, and preparation
should be made for this contingency." Similarly, on the day after
Wilmington fell — February 22: the third anniversary of Davis's permanent inauguration in Richmond — he made it clear to Davis himself that
any attempt to "unite with [Johnston] in a blow against Sherman" would
"necessitate the abandonment of our position on James River, for which
contingency every preparation should be made." One other alternative
there was, and he mentioned it one week later in a different connection.

This was the acceptance of Lincoln's terms, as set forth aboard the *River Queen* four weeks ago in Hampton Roads. "Whether this will be acceptable to our people yet awhile," he told Davis, "I cannot say."

"Yet awhile" was as close as Lee had come, so far, to foreseeing surrender as the outcome of the present situation. As for himself, this detracted not a whit from the resolution he had expressed in a letter to his wife the week before: "Sherman and Schofield are both advancing and seem to have everything their own way. But trusting in a merciful God, who does not always give the battle to the strong, I pray we may not be overwhelmed. I shall however endeavor to do my duty and fight to the last."

Victory, and Defeat

★ ✗ ☆

"EVERYTHING LOOKS LIKE DISSOLUTION in the South. A few more days of success with Sherman will put us where we can crow loud," Grant wrote his congressional guardian angel Elihu Washburne on the day after Schofield captured Wilmington, hard in the wake of Foster's occupation of Charleston and Sherman's burning of Columbia. By coincidence, this February 23 was also the day Lee warned Davis of the need for abandoning Richmond when the time came for him to combine with Johnston in a last-ditch effort to stop Sherman and Schofield before they crossed the Roanoke River, sixty miles in what had been his rear until he was cooped up in Petersburg. Far from being one of the things Grant looked forward to crowing about, however, such a move by his adversary, even though it would mean possession of the capital he had had under siege for eight long months, was now the Union commander's greatest fear. Looking back on still another of those "most anxious periods," he afterwards explained: "I was afraid, every morning, that I would awake from my sleep to hear that Lee had gone, and that nothing was left but a picket line. He had his railroad by the way of Danville south, and I was afraid that he was running off his men and all stores and ordnance except such as it would be necessary to carry with him for his immediate defense. I knew he could move much more lightly and more rapidly than I, and that, if he got the start, he would leave me behind so that we would have the same army to fight again farther south." In other words, he feared that Lee might do to him what he had done to Lee after Cold Harbor; that is, slip away some moonless night while the bluecoats, snug in their trenches across the way, engaged in lackadaisical speculation on "a good run of Johnnies." The result would be recovery by the old fox of his freedom to maneuver, a resumption of the kind of warfare at which he and his lean gray veterans had shown themselves to be past masters, back in May and early June; in which case, Grant summed it up, still shuddering at the prospect, "the war might be prolonged another year."

Three factors prevented or delayed effective Federal interference with either the preparation or execution of such a breakout plan. One was the weather, which had turned the roads into troughs of mud and the fields into quagmires, unfit for pursuit or maneuver if Lee, who had the use of the Danville and Southside lines for the removal of all he chose to put aboard them, was to be overtaken and overwhelmed before he achieved a link-up with Johnston in the Carolinas. Another was the strength of the Richmond-Petersburg defenses, which, combined with his skill in tactical anticipation, had withstood all efforts to penetrate or outflank them. The third was the prevailing cavalry imbalance, occasioned by Sheridan's protracted absence with two of his three ·divisions in the Shenandoah Valley, which made it highly inadvisable to attempt a strike at the tenuous rail supply lines deep in Lee's rear, vital though they were, not only to the subsistence of his army, but also to its breakout when the time came. There was little or nothing Grant could do about the first two of these three discouraging factors, except wait out a change in the weather and the continuous sapping effect of rebel desertions, neither of which was likely to prove decisive before Lee found a chance to slip away. However, the third factor was quite another matter, and Grant had already begun to do something about it three days ago, on February 20, in a letter assigning Sheridan the task of slamming shut Lee's escape route, west or southwest, through Lynchburg or Danville.

He had decided, as a result of his fear of the growing risk of a getaway by Lee, on an alteration in the bandy-legged cavalryman's role in the close-out plan devised to bring the Confederacy to its knees. Instead of awaiting a fair-weather summons, Sheridan was to leave the Valley "as soon as it is possible to travel," and instead of rejoining Meade by the shortest route, down the Virginia Central, he was to move with his two mounted divisions against Lynchburg, where the Southside Railroad and the Orange & Alexandria came together to continue west as the Virginia & Tennessee. A thorough wrecking of that important junction, together with an adjacent stretch of the James River Canal, would cut Lee off from supplies coming in from Southwest Virginia and would also end any hope he had for a flight beyond that point. "I think you will have no difficulty about reaching Lynchburg with a cavalry force alone," Grant wrote. "From there you could destroy the railroads and canal in every direction, so as to be of no further use to the rebellion." Then came the real surprise. "From Lynchburg, if information you might get there would justify it, you could strike south, heading the streams in Virginia to get to the westward of Danville, and push on and join Sherman."

Explaining this change — not only of route, in order to deny Lee both the Southside and the Richmond & Danville lines for use as all-weather avenues for escape, but also of destination — Grant tied what he called "this additional raid" in with those about to be launched by Canby and Wilson through Alabama and by Stoneman into North Carolina. Seen in that light, with these three on the rampage and Sherman "eating out the vitals of South Carolina," the proposed operation was "all that will be wanted to leave nothing for the rebellion to stand upon." There followed a final touch of the spur, applied as insurance against discouragement or delay. "I would advise you to overcome great obstacles to accomplish this. Charleston was evacuated on Tuesday last."

Sheridan seldom needed much urging on either count, and he did so less than ever now, having engaged in no large-scale fighting in the four months since his celebrated mid-October "ride" from Winchester to Cedar Creek, where he turned apparent defeat into a smashing victory and drove the shattered remnant of Early's army headlong out of the Valley. This was not to say that he had been idle all this time; far from it; but his activity was rather in the nature of common labor, directed more against enemy resources than against enemy soldiers, of which by now there were none on the scene; or almost none, if guerillas (or "rangers," as they preferred to call themselves) were taken into account. Such times as his troops were engaged in the devastation Grant had ordered, burning mills and barns, rounding up or butchering livestock, and removing or destroying all food and forage, they were in danger of being bushwhacked, and wagon trains also had to be heavily escorted, going and coming, to keep them from being captured. Not only did this interfere with the speedy conversion of the once-lush region into a wasteland, it was also hard on morale, requiring the blue troopers to turn out in freezing weather, at night and on days better spent in bed or round the campfire. Sometimes, indeed, the damage was far worse. For example, at 3 o'clock in the morning of the day Grant's letter arrived — February 21 — a small party of guerillas stole into Cumberland, Maryland, on the Potomac and the Baltimore & Ohio, fifty-odd miles above Harpers Ferry, and into the hotel room of George Crook himself, recently promoted to major general and put in charge of the Department of West Virginia as a reward for his performance as Sheridan's star corps commander at Winchester and Fisher's Hill. Undetected, they grabbed Crook and his ranking subordinate, Brigadier General B. F. Kelley, and got them onto waiting horses for a fast ride south, once more through the unsuspecting pickets, all the way to Libby Prison. Both generals were presently released by the terms of a special exchange worked out between Richmond and Washington, but the incident rankled badly as an example of what such brigands could accomplish without fear of personal reprisal.

That had not always been the case. At the outset, with the approval of Grant, Sheridan adopted a policy of reprisal that was personal indeed, especially against members of Colonel John S. Mosby's Partisan Rangers, two battalions with just under a hundred men in each, who claimed as their own a twenty-mile-square district containing most of Loudon and Fauquier counties; "Mosby's Confederacy," they dubbed it, cradled between the Bull Run Mountains and the Blue Ridge, through whose passes they raided westward across the Shenandoah River. Farmers by day, they rode mostly by night, and their commander, a former Virginia lawyer, thirty-three years old and sandy-haired, weighing less than 130 pounds in his thigh-high boots, red-lined cape, and ostrich plume, was utterly fearless, quite uncatchable, and altogether skillful in the conduct of operations which Lee himself, though he had small use for partisans in general, had praised as "highly creditable." In the past six months, in addition to keeping his superiors accurately informed of enemy activities in the Valley, he had killed, wounded, or captured more than a thousand Federals of all ranks, at a cost of barely twenty casualties of his own, and had taken nearly twice that many beeves and horses, along with a considerable haul of rations and equipment. Most of this came from Sheridan, who arrived on the scene in August. Appealing to Grant for permission to deal harshly with such guerillas as he was able to lay hands on, by way of deterring the rest, he was told: "When any of Mosby's men are caught, hang them without trial."

Promptly Sheridan passed the word to his subordinates, and in late September, having captured six of the rangers in a sudden descent on Front Royal, Custer shot four and hanged the other two, leaving their bodies dangling with a crudely lettered placard around the neck of one. "This will be the fate of Mosby and all his men," it read.

Mosby bided his time, even though another ranger was similarly captured, hanged, and placarded the following month in Rappahannock County. All this time, however, he was taking captives of his own, some 700 within a six-week span, and forwarding them to Richmond: unless, that is, they were from Custer's division, in which case they were set apart and kept under guard in an abandoned schoolhouse near Rectortown, just across the Blue Ridge from Front Royal. By early November he had 27 of Custer's men in custody, and he lined them up to draw folded slips of paper from a hat, informing them beforehand of his purpose. Twenty of the slips were blank; the rest, numbered 1 to 7, signified that those who drew them would be executed in retaliation for the postcapture death of his seven rangers. Harrowing as the lottery was for the participants, the game took an even crueler turn when it developed that one of the hard-luck seven was a beardless drummer, barely into his teens; Mosby had the delivered twenty draw again to determine who would take the boy's place. This done, a detail escorted the seven losers out into the night, under orders to hang them in proximity to Custer's headquarters at Winchester. One scampered off in the rainy darkness as they approached the scene of execution near Berryville, where three of the remaining six were hanged and the other three were lined up to be shot. One of these also managed to get away in the confusion, but Mosby later said that he was glad the two troopers escaped to "relate in Sheridan's camps the experience they had with Mosby's men." Meantime, under a flag of truce, a ranger scout — his safe conduct ensured by the remaining hostages — was on his way to deliver in person a note to Sheridan, informing him of what had been done, and why. "Hereafter," it concluded, "any prisoners falling into my hands will be treated with the kindness due to their condition, unless some new act of barbarity shall compel me reluctantly to adopt a line of policy repugnant to humanity. Very respectfully, your obedient servant, John S. Mosby."

Deterred himself, Sheridan called off the hanging match and agreed to deal henceforward with Mosby's men as he did with other prisoners of war. It came hard for him just now, though, for the rangers lately had wrecked and robbed a B. & O. express, dividing among themselves a $73,000 Federal payroll, and followed up this "Greenback Raid," as they called it, by capturing Brigadier General Alfred Duffié, out for a buggy ride near Bunker Hill, within ten miles of army headquarters. Besides, the Valley commander had more or less carried out by then his instructions to "peel this land"; little remained to protect or patrol except the trains bringing in rations for his troops, whose number had dwindled steadily as the infantry — first Wright's whole corps, then most of Crook's, and finally part of Emory's — was detached, all but a couple of rest-surfeited divisions, for transfer to more active theaters. Grant's letter, outlining plans for an all-out cavalry strike at Lynchburg and a subsequent link-up with Sherman, was greeted by Sheridan as a reprieve from boredom, a deliverance from uncongenial idleness in what had become a backwash of the war. He did not much like the notion of a detour into Carolina, preferring to be in on the smashing of Lee from the outset, but he was pleased to note that Grant had left him room for discretion in the matter, just as he had done about the date for setting out, saying merely that Sheridan could take off southward "as soon as it is possible to travel."

Unleashed, he wasted no time in getting started, even though, as he later reported, "the weather was very bad. . . . The spring thaw, with heavy rains, had already come on, [and] the valley and surrounding mountains were covered with snow which was fast disappearing, putting all the streams nearly past fording." A more cautious man would have waited; but not this one. Soon after sunrise, February 27 — one week from the date on Grant's letter — he had 10,000 veteran troopers pounding south up the turnpike out of Winchester, leaving Mosby and boredom and other such problems to Hancock, who returned to active duty to replace him in command of all he left behind in the lower Valley. Thirty miles the two divisions made that day, and thirty the next, to make camp at the end of the third day out — March 1 — within seven miles of Staunton, where Early had established headquarters after his rout at Cedar Creek. Next morning Sheridan rode into town to find Old Jube had departed eastward the day before, apparently headed for Charlottesville by way of Rockfish Gap. The question was whether to take out after him, in hope of completing his destruction, or press on south without delay to Lynchburg, leaving Early's remnant stranded in his wake; perhaps to bedevil Hancock. Sheridan chose the former course, and scored next day, as a result, a near Cannae that abolished what little remained of Stonewall Jackson's fabled Army of the Valley.

Twelve miles east out the Virginia Central almost to Waynesboro, a hamlet perched on the slope leading up to the snowy pass through the Blue Ridge in its rear, he came upon the thrice-whipped rebels posted in what he termed "a well chosen position" on the near side of a branch of the South Fork of the Shenandoah. They numbered about 1200 of all arms, all but a handful of Rosser's troopers being still en route from their rest camp forty miles west of Staunton. Early had stopped here in hope of delaying the bluecoats long enough to get his eleven guns across the mountain in double-teamed relays; otherwise, lacking horses enough to haul them up the slippery grade, he would have had to abandon five of them. "I did not intend making my final stand on this ground," he afterwards explained, "yet I was satisfied that if my men would fight, which I had no reason to doubt, I could hold the enemy in check until night, and then cross the river to take position in Rockfish Gap; for I had done more difficult things than that during the war."

He had indeed done more difficult things, but not with the disjointed skeleton of a command that had been trounced, three times running, by the general now closing fast upon his rear. As it turned out, holding his ground was not only difficult; it was impossible, mainly because Sheridan would not be denied even an outside chance at the total smash-up he had been seeking from the start. One division, under Brigadier General Thomas Devin — successor to Wesley Merritt, who had replaced Torbert as chief of cavalry — was delayed by orders to clean out a depot of supplies on the far side of Staunton, and though this left only Custer's division for the work at hand, Sheridan judged it would be enough, not only because he still enjoyed a better than four-to-one numerical advantage, but also because of Custer's nature, which he knew to be as aggressive as his own. He knew right. Told to move against the position, the yellow-haired Michigander — lately brevetted a major general on the eve of his twenty-fifth birthday — sent one brigade to strike the rebel left, which was somewhat advanced, and led the other two in a saber-swinging charge on the hastily thrown-up breastworks dead ahead. He had his favorite mount shot from under him in the assault, but that did not disrupt the breakthrough in either direction or slow down the lunge for the one bridge over the river in the Confederate rear. The result, according to the cartographer Jed Hotchkiss, posted by Early as a lookout, was "one of the most terrible panics and stampedes I have ever seen." Early himself agreed, though he caught no more than a tail-end glimpse of the rout. "I went to the top of a hill to reconnoiter," he later wrote, "and had the mortification of seeing the greater part of my command being carried off as prisoners, and a force of the enemy moving rapidly toward Rockfish Gap."

What was worse, "the greater part" was a considerable understatement. Merritt claimed "over 1000 prisoners" — a figure enlarged by Sheridan to 1600 and by Custer to 1800 in their reports, although the latter came to half again more than Early had on hand — along with 11 guns, close to 200 wagons, and 17 flags. Best of all, according to Sheridan, was the seizure of Rockfish Gap, "as the crossing of the Blue Ridge, covered with snow as it was, at any other point would have been difficult." The other division coming up next morning, March 3, he sent his captives and spoils back to Winchester under escort — all but the rebel battle flags, which he kept to flaunt in the faces of future opponents, if any — then moved on to make camp that night at Charlottesville, twenty miles away. For two days he rested his men and horses there, what time he did not have them ripping up track on the Virginia Central, before he set out southwest down the Orange & Alexandria on March 6, wrecking it too in his wake, bound for Lynchburg in accordance with the instructions in Grant's letter, written two weeks ago that day.

Old Jubilee had a harder road to travel. Escaping over the mountains with a few members of his staff — all that managed a getaway when Wharton's two brigades collapsed — he turned up at Lee's headquarters two weeks later. He had left with a corps, nine months ago; now he returned with nothing. Lee comforted him as best he could, but instead of restoring him to the post occupied by Gordon, ordered him back to the Valley. Although there was little to command there, Rosser's 1200 troopers having been summoned to Petersburg in partial replacement for the division still with Hampton in the Carolinas, Lee's hope was that he would be able to collect and attract such fugitives and under- or over-aged volunteers as remained in that burned-out region. Early departed on this mission, but before the month ended Lee rescinded the order, explaining to Breckinridge that he did so, despite his fellow Virginian's "great intelligence, good judgment, and undoubted bravery," because it was clear that his defeats in the lower Valley, capped by the recent final debacle at Waynesboro, had cost him the confidence of those he would be attempting to reassemble or recruit. To Early himself, at the same time, went a letter expressing Lee's "confidence in your ability, zeal, and devotion to the cause" and thanking him "for the fidelity and energy with which you have always supported my efforts, and for the courage and devotion you have ever manifested in the service."

This letter remained Old Jube's most treasured possession down the years, and did much to relieve the bitterness of the next few weeks — no doubt for him the hardest of the war — while he waited at home in Franklin County for orders to return to duty; orders that never came.

★ ★ ★

On March 3, about the time Sheridan's troopers were approaching Charlottesville, still jubilant over yesterday's lopsided victory at Waynesboro, Lincoln was up at the Capitol signing last-minute bills passed by Congress in preparation for adjournment tomorrow on Inauguration Day. He was interrupted by Stanton, who had just received a wire from Grant requesting instructions on how to reply to a formal query from Lee "as to the possibility of arriving at a satisfactory adjustment of the present unhappy difficulties, by means of a military convention."

There was more behind this than many people knew; Grant gave some of the details in his wire. Longstreet and Ord, it seemed, had met between the lines ten days ago, ostensibly to arrange a prisoner exchange, and Ord had advanced the notion that, the politicians having failed to agree on terms for peace at Hampton Roads, it might be well for the contestants themselves — the men, that is, who had been doing the actual bleeding all along — to "come together as former comrades and friends and talk a little." Grant and Lee could meet for an exchange of views, as could others, not excluding a number of their wives; Mrs Grant and Mrs Longstreet, for example, intimates before the war, could visit back and forth across the lines, along with their husbands, so that "while General Lee and General Grant were arranging for better feeling between the armies, they could be aided by intercourse between the ladies and officers until terms honorable to both sides could be found." Thus Ord spoke to his old army friend James Longstreet, who went to Lee with the proposal. Lee in turn conferred with Davis and Breckinridge. Both agreed the thing was worth a try: particularly the Kentuckian, who, as Old Peter later remarked, "expressed especial approval of the part assigned for the ladies." So Lee returned to Petersburg and sent his letter across the lines to Grant, suggesting "a military convention" as a means of ending the bloodshed, and Grant wired the War Department for instructions, saying: "I have not returned any reply, but promised to do so at noon tomorrow."

Noon tomorrow would be the hour at which Lincoln was scheduled to take the inaugural oath to "preserve, protect, and defend the Constitution of the United States" against what he conceived to be its domestic foes, and he did not intend to break — or, what might be worse, stand by while a clubby group of West Point professionals, North and South, broke for him — either that or another public oath he had taken just under nine months ago in Philadelphia: "We accepted this war for an object, a worthy object, and the war will end when that object is attained. Under God, I hope it never will until that time." The thing to do, as he saw it, was to nip this infringement in the bud. Accordingly, he wrote out in his own hand, for Stanton's signature, a carefully worded reply to Grant's request for instructions. "The President directs me to say to you that he wishes you to have no conference with General Lee unless it be for the capitulation of Gen. Lee's army, or on some minor and purely military matter. He instructs me to say that you are not to decide, discuss, or confer upon any political question. Such questions the President holds in his own hands; and will submit them to no military conferences or conventions. Meantime you are to press to the utmost your military advantages."

That ended that; Grant informed Lee next day that he had "no authority to accede to your proposition. . . . Such authority is vested in the President of the United States alone." Lincoln meantime had wound up his bill-signing chores and returned to the White House for the last night of his first term in office, having received on February 12 — his fifty-sixth birthday — formal notice from the Electoral College of his victory over McClellan, back in November, by a vote of 212 to 21.

Inauguration Day broke cold and rainy. High on the dome of the Capitol, unfinished on this occasion four years ago, Thomas Crawford's posthumous bronze Freedom, a sword in one hand, a victory wreath in the other, peered out through the mist on a scene of much confusion, caused in part by deepening mud that hampered the movement of the throng of visitors jammed into town for the show, and in part by Mrs Lincoln, who, growing impatient at a long wait under the White House portico, ordered her carriage to proceed up Pennsylvania Avenue at a gallop, disrupting the schedule worked out by the marshals. Her husband had already gone ahead to a room in the Senate wing, and was occupied with signing another sheaf of bills rammed through to beat the deadline now at hand. The rain let up before midmorning, though the sun did not break through the scud of clouds, and around 11 o'clock a small, sharp-pointed, blue-white diamond of a star — later identified as the planet Venus — appeared at the zenith, directly over the Capitol dome, bright in the murky daylight sky.

First the Senate would witness the swearing in of Andrew Johnson; for which purpose, shortly before noon, all the members of both houses and their distinguished guests fairly packed the Senate chamber. Diplomats in gold lace and feathers rivaled the crinolined finery of the ladies in the gallery. Joe Hooker, hale and rosy in dress blues, represented the army, Farragut the navy; "The dear old Admiral," women cooed as the latter entered, wearing all of his sixty-three years on his balding head. Governors of most loyal states were there, together with the nine Supreme Court justices, clad, as one observer noted, in "long black silk nightgowns (so to speak) though it's all according to law." These last — five of them of Lincoln's making, including the new Chief

Justice — were seated in the front row, to the right of the chair, while the Cabinet occupied the front row on the left. Lincoln sat between the two groups, looker trimmer than usual because of a shorter clip to his beard and hair.

As the clock struck 12, Vice President Hamlin entered, arm in arm with the man who would replace him. They had no sooner taken their seats than Hamlin rose and opened the ceremony by expressing his "heartfelt and undissembled thanks" to his colleagues for their kindness over the past four years. He paused, then asked: "Is the Vice President elect now ready to take and subscribe the oath of office?" Johnson got up. "I am," he said firmly, and launched without further preamble into an unscheduled oration. "Senators, I am here today as the chosen Vice President of the United States, and as such, by constitutional provision, I am made the presiding officer of this body." He wore his habitual scowl, as if to refute some expected challenge to his claim. "I therefore present myself here, in obedience to the high behests of the American people, to discharge a constitutional duty, and not presumptuously to thrust myself in a position so exalted." He spoke impromptu, without notes, and his words boomed loud against a hush more puzzled than shocked; just yet. "May I at this moment — it may not be irrelevant to the occasion — advert to the workings of our institutions under the Constitution which our fathers framed and George Washington approved, as exhibited by the position in which I stand before the American Senate, in the sight of the American people? Deem me not vain or arrogant; yet I should be less than man if under the circumstances I were not proud of being an American citizen, for today one who claims no high descent, one who comes from the ranks of the people, stands, by the choice of a free constituency, in the second place in this Government."

By now a buzz had begun in the chamber, spreading from point to point as his listeners gradually perceived that his near incoherence was not the result of faulty hearing or a lapse of comprehension on their part. "All this is in wretched bad taste," Speed whispered to Welles on his right. Welles agreed, saying to Stanton on his other side: "Johnson is either drunk or crazy." Stanton wagged his head. "There is evidently *some*thing wrong," he admitted. Then Welles had another thought. "I hope it is sickness," he said.

It was, in part. Six weeks ago, emerging shaky from a bout with typhoid and the strain of the campaign, the Tennessean had sought permission to stay in Nashville for the taking of the oath, but when Lincoln urged him to come to Washington he did so, though he still was far from well. "I am not fit to be here, and ought not to have left my home," he said that morning after he reached Hamlin's office in the Capitol. Someone brought him a tumbler of whiskey, which he drank to settle his nerves and get his strength up, then followed it with another just before he entered the overheated Senate chamber, saying: "I need all the strength for the occasion I can have." The result was the present diatribe, which continued despite tugs on his coattail from Hamlin, seated behind him, and unseen signals from his friends in front. He had stumped his way through a long campaign and he was stumping still. "Humble as I am, plebeian as I may be deemed," he went on, red-faced and unsteady, "permit me in the presence of this brilliant assemblage to enunciate the truth that courts and cabinets, the President and his advisers, derive their power and their greatness from the people." He wore on, croaking hoarsely toward the end, and when at last the oath had been administered he turned to the crowd with the Bible in both hands and kissed it fervently, saying as he did so: "I kiss this Book in the face of my nation of the United States."

Reactions varied. A reporter noted that, while Seward remained "bland and serene as a summer's day" and Charles Sumner "wore a saturnine and sarcastic smile," few others among those present managed to abide the harangue with such aplomb or enjoyment. Lincoln, for example, kept his head down throughout the blusterous display, apparently engaged in profound study of his shoe tips. Later he would discount the fears and rumors going round about the man who might replace him at any tragic moment. "I have known Andy for many years," he would say. "He made a bad slip the other day, but you need not be scared. Andy aint a drunkard." Just now, though, he had had enough embarrassment on so solemn an occasion. As he rose to join the procession filing out onto the inaugural platform set up along the east face of the building, he said pointedly to a marshal: "Do not let Johnson speak outside."

Emerging, he saw beneath the overcast of clouds what a journalist described as "a sea of heads in the great plaza in front of the Capitol, as far as the eye could reach, and breaking in waves along its outer edges." When he came out to take his seat a roar of applause went up from the crowd, which subsided only to rise again when the sergeant-at-arms, performing in dumb show, "arose and bowed, with his shining black hat in hand . . . and Abraham Lincoln, rising tall and gaunt among the groups about him, stepped forward." Just as he did so, the sun broke through and flooded the platform with its golden light. "Every heart beat quicker at the unexpected omen," the reporter declared. Certainly Lincoln's own did. "Did you notice that sunburst?" he later asked. "It made my heart jump." He moved to the lectern, unfolding a single large sheet of paper on which his speech was printed in two broad columns. "Fellow countrymen," he said.

There was, as he maintained, "less occasion for an extended address" than had been the case four years ago, when his concern had been to avoid the war that began soon afterward. Nor would he much con-

cern himself just now with purely military matters or venture a prediction as to the outcome, though his hope was high in that regard.
"Both parties deprecated war; but one of them would make war rather
than let the nation survive, and the other would accept war rather than
let it perish. And the war came.... Neither party expected for the
war the magnitude or the duration which it has already attained. Neither
anticipated that the cause of the conflict might cease with, or even before, the conflict itself should cease. Each looked for an easier triumph,
and a result less fundamental and astounding. Both read the same Bible
and pray to the same God, and each invokes His aid against the other.
It may seem strange that any men should dare to ask a just God's assistance in wringing their bread from the sweat of other men's faces;
but let us judge not, that we be not judged. The prayers of both could
not be answered; that of neither has been answered fully. The Almighty
has His own purposes. 'Woe unto the world because of offenses! for it
must needs be that offenses come; but woe to that man by whom the
offense cometh!'"

"Bless the Lord!" some down front cried up: Negroes mostly,
who took their tone from his, and responded as they would have done in
church. Lincoln kept on reading from the printed text in a voice one
hearer described as "ringing and somewhat shrill."

"If we shall suppose that American slavery is one of those offenses
which, in the providence of God, must needs come, but which, having
continued through His appointed time, He now wills to remove, and
that He gives to both North and South this terrible war, as the woe due
to those by whom the offense came, shall we discern therein any departure from those divine attributes which the believers in a living God
always ascribe to Him? Fondly do we hope — fervently do we pray —
that this mighty scourge of war may speedily pass away. Yet, if God
wills that it continue until all the wealth piled by the bondman's two
hundred and fifty years of unrequited toil shall be sunk, and until every
drop of blood drawn with the lash shall be paid by another drawn with
the sword, as was said three thousand years ago, so still it must be said:
'The judgments of the Lord are true and righteous altogether.'"

"Bless the Lord!" came up again through the thunder of applause,
but Lincoln passed at once to the peroration. He was beyond the war
now, into the peace which he himself would never see.

"With malice toward none; with charity for all; with firmness in
the right, as God gives us to see the right, let us strive on to finish the work
we are in; to bind up the nation's wounds; to care for him who shall have
borne the battle, and for his widow, and his orphan — to do all which
may achieve and cherish a just and a lasting peace, among ourselves and
with all nations."

Thus ended, as if on a long-held organ note, the shortest inaugural any President had delivered since George Washington was sworn in the second time. When the applause subsided, Chase signaled the clerk of the Supreme Court to come forward with the Bible held open-faced before him; Lincoln rested one hand on it while repeating the oath of office. "So help me God," he said, then bent and kissed the Book. Cheers went up as he rose once more to his full height and guns began thudding their shotless, flat-toned salutes in celebration. He turned to the crowd and bowed in several directions before he reëntered the Capitol and emerged again from a basement entrance, where a two-horse barouche waited to take him and Tad back to the White House in time for him to rest up for the reception scheduled there that evening. Between 8 and 11 o'clock, newsmen reckoned, he shook hands with no less than six thousand people, though these were by no means all who tried to get close enough to touch him. Walt Whitman, caught in the press of callers, was one of those who had to be content with watching from a distance. "I saw Mr Lincoln," the poet wrote in his notebook that night, "dressed all in black, with white kid gloves and a clawhammer coat, receiving, as in duty bound, shaking hands, looking very disconsolate . . . as if he would give anything to be somewhere else."

He was concerned about the reception of his speech that afternoon. "What did you think of it?" he asked friends as they passed down the line. He had heard and seen the cheers and tears of people near the platform, but tonight he was like a neglected author in wistful search of a discerning critic. Later, writing to Thurlow Weed, he said that he expected the address "to wear as well — perhaps better than — anything I have produced; but I believe it is not immediately popular. Men are not flattered by being shown that there has been a difference of purpose between the Almighty and them." Actually, the difficulty lay elsewhere. Some among his hearers and readers found his style as turgid, his syntax as knotty to unravel, as that of the new Vice President in the tirade staged indoors. "While the sentiments are noble," a disgruntled Pennsylvanian would complain this week in a private letter, "[Lincoln's inaugural] is one of the most awkwardly expressed documents I ever read — if it be correctly printed. When he knew it would be read by millions all over the world, why under the heavens did he not make it a little more creditable to American scholarship? Jackson was not too proud to get Van Buren to slick up his state papers. Why could not Mr Seward have prepared the Inaugural so as to save it from the ridicule of a sophomore in a British university?"

In point of fact, the British reaction was quite different from the one this Keystone critic apprehended. "It was a noble speech," the Duke of Argyll wrote his friend Sumner, "just and true, and solemn. I think it has produced a great effect in England." The London *Spectator* thought so, too, saying: "No statesman ever uttered words stamped at once with the seal of so deep a wisdom and so true a simplicity." Even the *Times*, pro-Confederate as it mostly was, had praise for the address. Nor was approval lacking on this side of the Atlantic, even among those with valid claims to membership in the New World aristocracy. "What think you of the inaugural?" C. F. Adams Junior wrote his ambassador father. "That rail-splitting lawyer is one of the wonders of the day. Once at Gettysburg and now again on a greater occasion he has shown a capacity for rising to the demands of the hour which we should not expect from orators or men of the schools. This inaugural strikes me in its grand simplicity and directness as being for all time the keynote of this war; in it a people seemed to speak in the sublimely simple utterance of ruder times. What will Europe think of this utterance of the rude ruler, of whom they have nourished so lofty a contempt? Not a prince or minister in all Europe could have risen to such an equality with the occasion."

Others besides Adams drew the Gettysburg comparison, being similarly affected, and presently there was still another likeness in what followed. Lincoln fell ill, much as he had done after the earlier address, except then it had been varioloid, a mild form of smallpox, and this was a different kind of ailment — noninfectious, nonspecific, yet if anything rather more debilitating. In fact, that was at the root of his present indisposition. He was exhausted. "Nothing touches the tired spot," he had begun to say within a year of taking office, and lately he had been referring again to "the tired spot, which can't be got at," somewhere deep inside him, trunk and limbs and brain. "I'm a tired man," he told one caller. "Sometimes I think I'm the tiredest man on earth."

If so, he had cause. In the past five weeks — hard on the heels of a bitter campaign for reëlection, which only added to the cumulative strain of leadership through four bloody years of fratricidal conflict — he had cajoled and logrolled Congress into passing the Thirteenth Amendment, dealt with the Confederate commissioners aboard the *River Queen* in Hampton Roads, and kept a watchful eye on Grant while raising the troops and money required to fuel the war machine. All this, plus the drafting and delivery of the second inaugural, was in addition to his usual daily tasks as Chief Executive, not the least of which consisted of enduring the diurnal claims of office-seekers and their sponsors, often men of political heft and high position. Two cabinet changes followed within a week, both the result of his acceding to Fessenden's plea that the time had come for him to leave the Treasury and return to his seat in the Senate. Lincoln replaced him on March 7 with Hugh McCulloch, a Maine-born Hoosier banker, only to have Interior Secretary John P. Usher resign on grounds that he too was from Indiana. Iowa Senator James Harlan was named to take his place, a felicitous choice, since he was a close family friend and the President's son Robert was courting the senator's daughter with the intention of marrying her as soon as he completed his military service.

This too was a problem for Lincoln — or, more specifically, for his wife; which came to the same thing. Just out of college, the young man wanted to enter the army despite strenuous objections by his mother, who grew sick with fear of what might happen to him there. As a result, Lincoln had worked out a compromise, back in January, that might satisfy them both, depending on Grant's response to a proposal made him at the time: "Please read and answer this letter as though I was not President, but only a friend. My son, now in his twenty-second year, having graduated from Harvard, wishes to see something of the war before it ends. I do not wish to put him in the ranks, nor yet to give him a commission to which those who have already served long are better entitled, and better qualified to hold. Could he, without embarrassment to you or detriment to the service, go into your military family with some nominal rank, I, and not the public, furnishing his necessary means? If no, say so without the least hesitation, because I am as anxious, and as deeply interested that you shall not be encumbered, as you can be yourself." Grant replied that he would be glad to have the young man on his staff as an assistant adjutant, his rank to be that of captain and his pay to come from the government, not his father. In mid-February the appointment came through. Soon after attending the inaugural ceremonies in the hard-galloping carriage with his mother and his prospective father-in-law, Robert set out down the coast for City Point. Lincoln was glad to have the difficult matter settled, but it came hard for him that he had had to settle it this way, knowing as he did that he had drafted into the shot-torn ranks of the nation's armies hundreds of thousands of other sons whose mothers loved and feared for them as much as Mary Lincoln did for hers.

As a result of all these pressures and concerns, or rather of his delayed reaction to them, what should have been for him a time of relieved tension — Congress, having adjourned, was not scheduled to reconvene until December, so that he had hope of ending the war in much the same way he had begun it; that is, without a host of frock-coated politicians breathing down his neck — turned out instead to be the one in which he looked and felt his worst. It was as if, like a spent swimmer who collapses only after he has reached the shore, he had had no chance till now, having been occupied with the struggle to keep afloat in a sea of administrative and domestic frets, to realize how close he was to absolute exhaustion. "His face was haggard with care and seamed with thought and trouble," Horace Greeley noted after a mid-March interview. "It looked care-ploughed, tempest-tossed and weather-beaten." One reporter diagnosed the ailment as "a severe attack of influenza," but another remarked more perceptively that the President was "suffering from the exhausting attentions of office hunters." In any case, on March 14 — ten days after the inauguration — Lincoln was obliged to hold the scheduled Tuesday cabinet meeting in his bedroom, prone beneath the covers but with his head and shoulders propped on pillows stacked against the headboard of his bed.

That day's rest did some good, and even more came from a new rule setting 3 o'clock as the close of office hours, so far at least as scheduled callers went. By the end of the week he felt well enough to go with his wife and guests to a performance of Mozart's *Magic Flute* at Grover's Theatre, enjoying it so much indeed that when Mrs Lincoln suggested leaving before the final curtain reunited the fire-tested lovers, he protested: "Oh, no. I want to see it out. It's best, when you undertake a job, to finish it." Much of his fascination was with one of the sopranos, whose feet were not only large but flat. "The beetles wouldn't have much of a chance there," he whispered, nodding toward the stage.

Here was at least one sign that he was better, though it was true he often joked in just this way to offset the melancholia that dogged him all his life. He still felt weary — "flabby," as he called it — and no amount of rest, by night or day, got through to the tired spot down somewhere deep inside him. He considered a trip, perhaps a visit to the army in Virginia, "immediately after the next rain." Then on March 20 a wire from Grant seemed to indicate that the general either had read his mind or else had spies in the White House. "Can you not visit City Point for a day or two? I would like very much to see you, and I think the rest would do you good."

Lincoln at once made plans to go. He would leave in the next day or two, aboard the fast, well-armed dispatch steamer *Bat*. "Will notify you of exact time, once it shall be fixed upon," he replied to Grant. But when he told his wife, she announced that she too would be going; it had been two weeks since Robert left for City Point, and she would see him there. So the expanded party shifted to the more commodious *River Queen*, retaining the *Bat* for escort. Tad would go, along with Mrs Lincoln's maid, a civilian bodyguard, and a military aide. Lincoln had heard from Grant on Monday, and on Thursday he was off down the Potomac, sailing from the Sixth Street wharf in the early afternoon.

2 ✕

That same Thursday — March 23 — Sherman reached Goldsboro, the goal of his 425-mile slog up the Carolinas, to find Schofield waiting for him with reinforcements enough to lift his over-all strength to just under 90,000 of all arms. Both had run into their first hard fighting of the double-pronged campaign, and both had come through it more or less intact, despite losses they would rather have avoided until they combined to inflict the utter destruction of whatever gray fragments presumed to stand in the path of their northward conjunction with Grant at the gates of Richmond.

What was more, for all the wretched weather and sporadic opposition, the two blue columns — themselves divided and out of touch, each with the other, until they arrived at their common objective — had made good time. Two weeks after Columbia went up in smoke, Sherman got both wings of his army up to the Pee Dee River and called a halt at Cheraw, March 3–5, to give his bedraggled troops a chance to dry their clothes and scrape away the mud they had floundered through while crossing the rain-bulged Wateree and soft-banked Lynch's Creek. Then he was off again, out of the Palmetto State at last. Reactions differed, up and down the long line of marchers; some looked back with cackling glee on the destruction, while others felt a softening effect. "South Carolina may have been the cause of the whole thing," a Michigan lieutenant wrote in a running letter home, "but she has had an awful punishment."

She had indeed, and now ahead lay the Old North State; a quite different prospect, Sherman believed, one that entailed a much higher degree of Union sentiment, which he intended to woo and play upon en route. "Deal as moderately and fairly by North Carolinians as possible," he told subordinates, "and fan the flame of discord already subsisting between them and their proud cousins of South Carolina. There never was much love lost between them. Touch upon the chivalry of running away, always leaving their families for us to feed and protect, and then on purpose accusing us of all sorts of rudeness."

Accordingly, guards were posted at the gates or on the steps of roadside houses, barring entrance to the marchers filing past, and the women, emboldened by this protection, came out on their porches to watch the invaders go by, shoulders hunched against the rain, feet made heavy with balled-up mud, and spirits considerably dampened. The women looked at the men, and the men looked back. "We glanced ruefully at them out of the shadow of our lowering, drenched hat rims," one soldier was to say, recalling freer times a week ago, when their red-haired commander had scorned to practice such restraint. Denied access to residences, they exercised their arsonist proclivities on the forests of pine through which they passed between the Pee Dee and Cape Fear rivers — and found the result even more spectacular than those produced when they set fire to barns and gins, back in Georgia and South Carolina. Notched for the drawing of sap, the trees burned like enormous torches, often hundreds at a time, when a match was put to them. Overhead, "the smoke could hardly escape through the green canopy, and hung like a pall," an Ohio colonel noted. "It looked like a fire in a cathedral." A New York private, highly conscious of being part of what he saw, found himself awed by the tableau, "all to be heard and seen only by glimpses under the smoke and muffled by the Niagara-like roar of the flames as they licked up turpentine and pitch. Now came rolling back from the depths of the pine forest the chorus of thousands singing 'John Brown's body lies a-moldering.'" He considered it "at once a prophecy and a fulfillment."

This final leg of the march, just over a fourth of the whole, would be covered in two sixty-mile jumps, with a rest halt in between: Cheraw to Fayetteville, a major Confederate supply base, and Fayetteville to Goldsboro, where Sherman had arranged to meet Schofield, barring serious complications. Driving rains and deepening mud, together with the washout of all bridges over the Wateree, had thrown him a bit off schedule by now, but he hoped to get back on it by making better time through the piny highlands. And so he did, despite the unrelenting downpour. "It was the damndest marching I ever saw," he said of an Illinois regiment's covering fifteen soggy miles in five hours. Delighted, he detached three enlisted volunteers — two of them disguised as rebel officers, the third as a civilian — to pick their way through enemy country, ninety-odd miles east to Wilmington, with a note for whoever Schofield had left in charge there: "If possible, send a boat up Cape Fear River. . . . We are well and have done finely. The rains make our roads difficult, and may delay us about Fayetteville, in which case I would like to have some bread, sugar, and coffee. We have abundance of all else. I expect to reach Goldsboro by the 20th instant." He kept going, crossing the Lumber River by the light of flaming pine knots, and made it into Fayetteville before midday, March 11, five days out of Cheraw; Hardee, he learned, had left the night before, and Hampton had come close to being captured by the first blue troopers riding in that morning. After running the national flag up over the market place and establishing headquarters in the handsome former U.S. arsenal — now U.S. again — his first concern was to find out whether anything had been heard from downriver in response to the note, written three days ago, which the three-man detail had been charged with getting through to Wilmington.

Nothing had. But at noon next day the Sabbath quiet was shattered by the scream of a steamboat whistle; Alfred Terry, in command at Wilmington, had sent the army tug *Davidson* upriver in response to Sherman's note, all three copies of which had reached him the day before. Armored with cotton bales to shield her crew from snipers, the boat's main cargo was not sugar, coffee, or hardtack, but news of the outside world, as set forth in dispatches and a bundle of the latest papers, North and South. "The effect was electric," Sherman was to say, "and no one can realize the feeling unless, like us, he has been for months cut off from all communication with friends and compelled to listen to the croakings and prognostications of open enemies." He ordered the tug to return downriver at sunset, passing the word that she would take with her all the letters anyone cared to write, and gave instructions for a larger vessel to be sent back up as soon as possible, this time with the hardtack, coffee, and sugar he had requested in the first place, plus all the shoes, stockings, and drawers that could be spared. Which done, he put his men back to work destroying rebel installations, including the Fayetteville arsenal itself, and spent much of the night and the following day studying the dispatches and perusing newspapers crammed with speculations as to his whereabouts and fate.

The best of the news was that Schofield, his strength increased above 30,000 by the addition of two new divisions, one made up of convalescents sent from Washington, the other of troops from coastal garrisons such as Beaufort, was hard on the go for Goldsboro and seemed likely to get there well within the time allotted. Leaving Terry to hold Wilmington with his X Corps, in case improbable rebel combinations obliged Sherman to veer in that direction at the last minute, he had sent Jacob Cox by sea to New Bern with his beefed-up XXIII Corps, under instructions to move west along the Atlantic & N.C. Railroad — which was not only shorter and more repairable than the Wilmington & Weldon, but was also provided with locomotives and cars, as the other was not — thus establishing a rapid-transit link between Goldsboro and the coast, not at the mouth of the Cape Fear River, as originally intended, but instead at the mouth of the Neuse in Pamlico Sound, which afforded the navy far better all-weather harbor facilities for unloading the mountain of supplies Sherman's 60,000 footsore, tattered veterans would need at the end of their long swing through the Carolinas. Cox had set out from New Bern on March 1, repairing the railroad as he went, and Schofield had left Wilmington to join him, wanting to be on hand in case he ran into serious opposition from Hoke, whose division, flung out of Wilmington two weeks before, was reported to have fallen back on Kinston, where the Atlantic & N.C. crossed the Neuse, about midway between Goldsboro and New Bern.

Sherman was pleased with this news of Schofield's progress across the way, promising as it did an early combination for the follow-up march into Virginia. He had grown more cautious since learning that Johnston, his wily Georgia adversary, was back in command of the forces in his front. So far, here inland, nothing had come of the shift, however, and Terry's report assured him that all was well in the other direction, too. "Jos. Johnston may try to interpose between me here and Schofield about New Bern," he had written Grant in a letter the *Davidson* carried downriver at sunset, March 12, "but I think he will not try that." His notion was that the Virginian would "concentrate his scattered armies at Raleigh": in which case, he told his friend the general-in-chief, "I will go straight at him as soon as I get our men reclothed and our wagons reloaded." Meantime, before he moved on, there was the arsenal to be disposed of, a handsome cluster of cream-colored brick structures whose well-kept grounds served Fayetteville as a municipal park. "The arsenal is in fine order, and has been much enlarged," he informed Stanton in a letter that went along with Grant's. "I cannot leave a detachment to hold it, therefore shall burn it, blow it up with gunpowder, and then with rams knock down its walls. I take it for granted the United States will never again trust North Carolina with an arsenal to appropriate at her leisure."

In point of fact, he had been right to suspect that Johnston was up to something, and wrong to think that all he was up to was a concentration at Raleigh. Terry's latest information about Schofield's other column, toiling westward out the Atlantic & N.C., was three days old; within which span, as a result of Johnston's caginess, Cox had had to fight a battle on disadvantageous ground. Schofield had reached New Bern by sea from Wilmington on March 7, and when he went forward next morning, beyond the spike-hammer din of rail repair crews, he found the head of the infantry column under fire from graybacks who had lain in wait along the high ground just this side of Southwest Creek, the western limit of Dover Swamp, a thirty-mile-wide marsh through which the railroad threaded its way to within three miles of Kinston and the Neuse. A sudden, unexpected attack had struck and scattered two blue regiments in advance, capturing three fourths of the men, and the attackers seemed determined to expand this opening setback into a full-scale defeat. What was more, they might be able to do just that, by the sheer weight of their numbers. Prisoners taken were found to be not only from Hoke's division, already suspected of lurking up ahead, but also from Stewart's and S. D. Lee's corps of the Army of Tennessee, a good five hundred miles from home.

It was Johnston, urged by R. E. Lee to strike before the Federals united in his front, who had made this possible by reinforcing the troops opposing Cox. Moreover, he had other such moves in mind, and was even now in the process of effecting them: not so much with the intention of actually defeating his red-haired antagonist — each of whose two wings, like Schofield's two-corps army over toward the coast, was nearly half again larger than his total force — but rather in the hope of delaying the blue combination until Lee could give Grant the slip and join him, here in Carolina, for an offensive combination of their own. Although by ordinary he was far from being the cut-and-slash sort of general who seized upon long chances as a means of redressing odds that were even longer, desperation had made him bold. Indeed, there was no better indication of the extent of Confederate desperation, at this stage, than Joseph E. Johnston's overnight conversion into the kind of commander he became, at least for a time, hard on the heels of having told Lee, while en route to take over from Beauregard at Charlotte: "It is too late," and following this with a letter in which, having studied the strength reports on hand, he said flatly: "In my opinion these troops form an army too weak to cope with Sherman."

He had at the time fewer than 20,000 men, considerably scattered. Hardee's 10,000 at Cheraw, the rail terminus he fell back on after evacuating Charleston, were joined by Hampton's 4000 cavalry, three fourths of them under Wheeler and the rest under Butler, while another 4000 infantry, on hand or still on the way from the Army of Tennessee, brought the total to 18,000 of all arms. Presently, on March 4, this figure was enlarged by Lee's extension of Johnston's authority to include Hoke's 5500, withdrawn by Bragg to Goldsboro after the fall of Wilmington. By then, however, Hardee had been obliged to evacuate Cheraw, under pressure from Howard and Slocum, and had fallen back on Fayetteville, reduced to about 8000 by desertions and the detachment of his South Carolina militia, who were forbidden by law to follow him out of the state. Sherman continued his march, obviously toward Fayetteville now, but Johnston was hard put to determine whether his adversary would be headed next for Goldsboro or for Raleigh. Splitting the difference, he decided to concentrate at Smithfield, on the railroad midway between the two, for a strike at one or another of Sherman's wings before they came together at whichever city was their goal. There was hope in this, but only by contrast with the surrounding gloom of the piecemeal and seemingly endless retreat. Desertions were heavy and getting heavier, particularly by Carolinians, South and North, whose homes lay in the path or wake of the blue despoilers tramping northward. Ambrose Wright, commanding one of Hardee's two divisions, took the occasion to return to his native Georgia, where he had been elected *in absentia* to the senate; Taliaferro took over his undersized division, adding the Sumter garrison to its roll — a disgruntled body in which tempers ran short among men unaccustomed to marching or going hungry. A sergeant, for example, on being reproved for advising comrades to desert, drew his pistol and attempted to use it on the lieutenant who had reproached him. Arrested, he was tried before a drumhead court and sentenced to be shot. He died without the consolation of religion. "Preacher, I never listened to you at Fort Sumter," he said bitterly to the chaplain who came to pray with him on the night before his execution, "and I won't listen to you now."

These were brave men; Wright had been one of the Army of Northern Virginia's hardest-hitting brigadiers, all the way from the Seven Days to the Siege of Petersburg, and the sergeant had stood up to everything the U.S. Navy had to throw at him in the rubble and brick dust of Sumter. What they mainly suffered from was despair, a discouragement verging into disgust as they were shuttled about, invariably rearward, to avoid being crushed by the compact masses of bluecoats in their front. Johnston knew well enough that the best correction for flagging morale lay in delivery of the blow he planned to throw as soon as he completed the concentration now in progress around Smithfield, although this was a necessarily slow procedure, scattered as his 21,500 soldiers were in their attempt to confront the 90,000 invaders moving against them from the south and east, unchecked so far, and scarcely even delayed. Then Bragg suggested an interim maneuver that might not only lift morale but also disrupt the Federal convergence. Schofield had divided his army, holding one corps at Wilmington while the other went to New Bern; Bragg's notion was for Johnston to reinforce him at Goldsboro for an attack, just east of Kinston, on the corps slogging westward along the Atlantic and N.C. Railroad; after which he would hurry back east by rail in time for a share in the strike at one of Sherman's wings before they closed on Raleigh or Goldsboro, whichever they headed for after reaching Fayetteville. "A few hours would suffice to unite the forces at Smithfield with mine and assure a victory," he telegraphed headquarters on March 6. Johnston thought it over, and then next day — uncharacteristically; for the shift involved a division of force in the presence of a greatly superior foe — decided to give the thing a try. All he had on hand just now were some 3000 men from the Army of Tennessee, forwarded by Beauregard, who had remained in Charlotte to expedite such movements; but he alerted them for the shift, and notified Bragg that they were at his disposal. "Send trains when fight is impending," he wired, "and send back troops as soon as it is over."

That was how it came about that Bragg was able to surprise and crumple the head of Cox's column next morning, March 8, just before it reached the western rim of Dover Swamp. Encouraged by this initial rout, which netted him close to a thousand prisoners, he pressed his assault on the main body. Schofield had arrived by then, however, and had ordered light intrenchments thrown up during the lull that followed the opening attack: with the result that Bragg rebounded to search elsewhere along Southwest Creek for a breakthrough point. He never found it, though he tried for the rest of that day and the next, when Cox brought up the remainder of his 15,000-man corps, including the railroad workers, to stand fast against the graybacks, whom he estimated at better than twice their actual number of 8500. On the third day, March 10, Bragg withdrew across the Neuse, burning the wagon and railway bridges in his rear, and got his troops aboard the cars for a fast ride west to Smithfield, as he had said he would do, in time for a share in the sequential attack on Sherman. The Battle of Kinston — or Wise's Forks, as the Federals sometimes called it — was a long way short of the triumph he had predicted, but the respective casualty lists went far toward sustaining his claim that he had scored a tactical success. He lost 134 men in all, while Cox lost 1257, most of them captured at the outset. What was more, the engagement had served its larger purpose

as a check to Schofield's progress toward Goldsboro. It was March
14 before he got the bridges rebuilt across the Neuse, and still another
week, after summoning Terry up from Wilmington, before he reached
his appointed goal. Even so, he reached it well before Sherman, whom
Johnston had struck not once but twice in the course of Schofield's
final week of marching west along the railroad toward their common
objective.

Old Joe was of course disappointed that Bragg had not been able
to do Schofield all the damage promised in his plea for reinforcements,
but he was grateful for the resultant easing of pressure from the east
while he continued his efforts to pull his scattered units together for the
projected strike at Sherman, about to move out of Fayetteville by now.
Still uncertain whether this main blue force was headed for Raleigh or
Goldsboro, he held Bragg and the Tennessee contingent near Smithfield, midway between them, and divided his cavalry to patrol the roads
in both directions, Butler's troopers on the left and Wheeler's on the
right, the latter covering Hardee's northward withdrawal from Fayetteville under instructions to slow down, if he could, the march of the
Federals in his rear. For all his grave numerical disadvantage, Johnston
at least had no shortage of brass in the corps-sized army he planned to
unite and throw at one or another of Sherman's wings; Bragg was a
full general, Hardee, Stewart, and Hampton lieutenant generals, and in
addition he had fourteen major generals and innumerable brigadiers, not

to mention another full general, Beauregard, expediting the movement of troops through Charlotte, and still a fourth lieutenant general, S. D. Lee, present but not yet recovered enough from his post-Nashville wound to take the field. For all their various prickly characteristics — including, in several paired cases, a stronger dislike for each other than for anything in blue — they made a distinguished roster, one that augured well for the conduct of the impending battle. Johnston took much comfort from that, and also from something else he learned about this time. Texas Senator Louis Wigfall, one of his most ardent supporters in the capital, wrote that both the President and Mrs Davis appeared to be in deep distress over the current situation. The Virginian replied on March 14: "I have a most unchristian satisfaction in what you say of the state of mind of the leading occupants of the Presidential Mansion. For me, it is very sufficient revenge."

Sherman began his march out of Fayetteville that same day, and by the next — having completed his demolition of the arsenal by alternately blowing it up and battering it down — had both wings over the Cape Fear River, trudging north for a feint at Raleigh before he turned east to keep his March 20 appointment with Schofield at Goldsboro, five days off. Terry had not been able to send shoes or clothing on the *Davidson*'s return upriver, but he had sent coffee and sugar, to the delight of the tattered, half-barefoot veterans, and he had relieved the column of "twenty to thirty thousand useless mouths," started downriver by Sherman under escort, white and black, to be herded into refugee camps at Wilmington; "They are a dead weight to me and consume our supplies," the red-haired commander explained. He was in higher spirits than ever, having learned that Sheridan would likely be joining him in a week or two. Far from resenting the prospect of sharing laurels with the man who next to himself was the chief hero of the day, he looked forward to his fellow Ohioan's arrival as "a disturbing element in the grand and beautiful game of war.... If he reaches me, I'll make all North Carolina howl," he told Terry, adding the further inducement: "I will make him a deed of gift of every horse in the state, to be settled for at the day of judgment."

For all his lightness of heart as he set out on the final leg of his march, he was thoroughly aware of possible last-minute dangers in his path. Indeed, he was overaware of them, not only because of his great respect for Johnston, who had shown in the past a capacity for reading his mind as accurately as if he were reading his mail, but also because he more than doubled his adversary's true numerical strength with an estimate of 45,000 of all arms; a not unreasonable error after all, since the Virginian had been in command for better than two weeks, presumably with every Confederate resource at his disposal for fending off this ultimate strike through the Carolinas. Properly cautious now that he was within a few days of his goal, Sherman ordered four divisions in each wing to travel light, ready for action, while the others — two in Slocum's case, three in Howard's — accompanied the train and guns to help them along through the mud, thereby assuring speed in case of breakdowns and alertness in case of attack. "I can whip Joe Johnston if he don't catch one of my corps in flank," he had written Terry from Fayetteville, "and I will see that my army marches hence to Goldsboro in compact form."

So he said. But compactness was no easy thing to achieve on roads that varied greatly in condition, especially under the pelting of rain, which now began to come down harder than ever. Besides, in the opening stage of this final leg of the march, while Howard's wing traveled a fairly direct route (a little north of east) toward Cox's Bridge, a dozen miles above Goldsboro on the Neuse, Slocum's followed a more circuitous route (a little east of north) up the Fayetteville-Raleigh road along the left bank of the Cape Fear River — a move designed to mislead Johnston into assembling all his troops for the defense of the state capital, in the belief that it was the Federal objective. If successful, this would remove the graybacks from contention; for Slocum meantime would have swung due east at Averasboro, twenty miles upriver from Fayetteville, to get back in touch with Howard near Bentonville, twelve miles short of Cox's Bridge, where both would cross for an on-schedule meeting with Schofield at Goldsboro and a brief pause for rest and refitment before turning to deal with Johnston, once and for all, preparatory to setting out for Virginia to join Grant. In any case, that was Sherman's plan, and he rode with Slocum to see that all went well.

All did, despite frequent clashes between Kilpatrick's horsemen, screening the outer flank, and Wheeler's. On the first night out, March 15, Slocum made camp about eight miles south of Averasboro, where he would swing east tomorrow to reunite the two blue columns before they reached the Neuse, ninth of the nine major rivers between Savannah and their goal. Or so Sherman thought until Slocum took up the march next morning, shortly after sunrise, only to run into heavy infantry fire from dead ahead.

It was Hardee. Instructed by Johnston to keep between Sherman and Raleigh for the double purpose of slowing the bluecoats down and determining their objective (if it was the capital, as seemed likely, he would be joined by Bragg and the Tennesseans for a strike before the Federals got there. If not, if instead they were marching somewhat roundabout on Goldsboro, he would move toward Smithfield, where Bragg and the Tennesseans were posted, for a combined attack somewhere short of the Neuse) he had decided the night before to make a stand, as he later explained, "to ascertain whether I was followed by Sherman's whole army, or part of it, and what was its destination." Half a dozen miles south of Averasboro, where the Cape Fear and

Black rivers were only four miles apart, he came upon suitable ground for such a delaying action. Adopting the tactics used by Daniel Morgan eighty-four years ago at Cowpens, just under two hundred miles away in northwest South Carolina, he placed Taliaferro's less experienced troops in a double line out front, astride the Fayetteville-Raleigh road and facing south between the rivers, with orders to fall back on Mc-Laws' veterans, dug in along another double line 600 yards to the north, as soon as the attackers pressed up close enough to overrun them. These six infantry brigades — Taliaferro's two were mostly converted artillerists from the Sumter garrison — together with Wheeler's two mounted brigades, gave Hardee an overall strength of about 11,000. How many the Federals had, except that they had a lot, the Georgian did not know. He expected to find out soon, however, since that was one of his three main reasons for stopping to fight them in the first place, the other two being to slow them down and find out for certain whether their march was a feint or a true drive on the North Carolina capital, thirty-odd miles in his rear.

They had about twice his number, as it turned out, immediately available under Kilpatrick and in the four divisions Sherman had ordered to travel light for ready use, plus half again as many more who could be called up from the train if they were needed; which they were not. Slocum advanced two divisions in support of the skirmishing troopers, and when at last around 10 o'clock, their progress badly hampered by muddy ravines and a driving rain, they encountered Taliaferro's makeshift force in position astride the road, they halted, pinned down by spattering fire, and sent back word that they had struck Hardee's main line of resistance, intrenched across the swampy neck of land between the rivers. Anxious to waste no more time, Sherman had Slocum commit a third division for an immediate assault. That burned still more daylight, however. It was 3 o'clock before the concerted push could be made, and though it was altogether successful in flinging the graybacks rearward with the loss of three guns and more than two hundred prisoners, the attackers pursued them less than a quarter of a mile before they were pinned down again by fire from a stronger line of works, some 600 yards in rear of the first. "It would have been worse than folly to have attempted a farther advance," one division commander would report, and Sherman and Slocum agreed. Long-range fire continued past sundown into dusk, then stopped. Hardee, who had suffered about 500 casualties, pulled back after nightfall, leaving Wheeler's horsemen to cover his rear, and issued next day a congratulatory order commending his troops, green and seasoned alike, for "giving the enemy the first check he has received since leaving Atlanta."

There was truth in that, and it was also true that Sherman wanted no more of it just now. Unlike Johnston, he was not seeking to fight his enemy piecemeal; he wanted him whole, for total destruction when the time came — after his and Schofield's forces were combined beyond the Neuse. Averasboro had gained him nothing more than control of the field next morning, and had cost him 682 casualties, 149 of them dead or missing, which left 533 wounded to fill the left-wing ambulances and hinder still further the train's hard-grinding progress through the mire. It had also cost him a day of critical time, both for Slocum and for Howard, who had to be told to slow his pace across the way, lest the space between them grow so great that mutual support would no longer be possible in a crisis. There seemed little likelihood of this last, however; Wheeler's troopers faded back up the Raleigh pike which Hardee's men had traveled the night before, apparently in delayed obedience to Johnston's orders for a concentration in front of the threatened capital. Satisfied that his feint had worked, Sherman turned the head of Slocum's column east for Bentonville and Cox's Bridge, as originally planned, when he came in sight of Averasboro at midday, March 17. The rain was pouring down harder than ever, and one officer later testified that St Patrick's Day and the two or three that followed were "among the most wearisome of the campaign. Incessant rain, deep mud, roads always wretched but now nearly impassable, seemed to cap the climax of tedious, laborious marching. . . . In spite of every exertion," he added, "the columns were a good deal drawn out, and long intervals separated the divisions."

In short, aside from the irreducible disparity in numbers, blue and gray, Johnston could scarcely have asked for a situation more favorable to his purpose than the one reported to him before daybreak, March 18. As a result — for the first time since Seven Pines, nearly three years ago, with his back to Richmond's eastern gates — he went over to the offensive. Informed by Hardee, who had fallen back not on Raleigh but to a point where the road forked east to Smithfield, and by Hampton, who was in touch with Butler and Wheeler, that both of Sherman's wings were across Black River, bound for Goldsboro in separate columns, a day's march apart and badly strung out on sodden, secondary roads, Old Joe called for a concentration at Bentonville that night and an all-out strike just south of there next morning, first at one and then the other of Slocum's corps toiling eastward through the mud. By the time Bragg and the Tennesseans left Smithfield, shortly after sunrise, he had matured his plan so far that he could direct Hardee, a day in advance, to take position "immediately on their right" when he arrived. Hampton, already with Butler on the chosen field, two miles beyond the town, would skirmish with Slocum's leading elements in an attempt to fix him in position for the execution Johnston had designed.

Sherman, having remained with the left wing so long as he supposed it was in graver danger than the other, set out crosscountry next morning — Sunday, March 19 — to join Howard for the crossing of the Neuse and the meeting with Schofield the following day, as scheduled. Soon after he started he heard what he called "some cannonading over about Slocum's head of column," but he kept going, on the assumption that it amounted to nothing more than another try by Hampton to divert and slow him down. Nine air-line miles to the south and east, after a wearing day spent doubling the right-wing column — as badly strung out, tail to head, as was Slocum's across the way — he came upon Howard at Falling Creek, where the roads from Fayetteville and Averasboro came together, four miles from Cox's Bridge; Howard had made camp there, less than twenty miles from Goldsboro, to give his two corps a chance to close up before crossing the river next day. All seemed well in this direction, and any worries Sherman might have had about the cannonade that erupted in his rear when he set out that morning, just short of Bentonville, had been allayed by a staff officer Slocum sent to overtake him with word that the clash was with butternut cavalry, which he was "driving nicely." Still, the rumble and thump of guns had continued from the northwest all day and even past sundown, when a courier reached Falling Creek with another left-wing message, altogether different from the first. Headed 1.30 p.m. and written under fire, it read: "I am convinced the enemy are in strong force to my front. Prisoners report Johnston, Hardee, Hoke and others present. They say their troops are just coming up. I shall strengthen my position and feel of their lines, but I hope you will come up on their left rear in strong force. Yours, truly, H. W. Slocum, Major General."

After reading the message in Howard's tent, where he had removed his boots and uniform to get some rest, Sherman rushed out to stand ankle-deep in the ashes of a campfire, hands clasped behind him — a lanky figure dressed informally, to say the least, in a red flannel undershirt and a pair of drawers. He seemed bemused, but not for long. Presently he was barking orders, and there was much of what one startled witness called "hurrying to and fro and mounting in hot haste." Once a courier was on the way with a note advising Slocum to fight a purely defensive action until the rest of the army joined him, Sherman told Logan, whose corps was in the lead today, to march for Bentonville on the road from Cox's Bridge, and sent word for Blair to follow by the same route; which hopefully would put them in the rebel rear, provided Slocum could hold his position until they got there. Whether this last was possible, however, in the light of subsequent dispatches from the field, was highly doubtful. "I deem it of the greatest importance that the Right Wing come up during the night," Slocum urged in a message written an hour after dark.

That could scarcely be; Bentonville was a good ten miles by road from Falling Creek. Moreover, by way of indicating the fury of the conflict up to now, he requested "all the ammunition and empty ambulances and wagons that can be spared," and added that he had positive information that "the corps and commands of Hardee, Stewart, Lee, Cheatham, Hill, and Hoke are here."

Which Lee? Which Hill? Sherman might have wondered as he stood amid the ashes, convinced as he had been till now that Old Joe would not risk fighting with the Neuse at his back. Still, as a roster — a Confederate order of battle — the list was not only accurate but complete: although it had not been the latter until past midday, when Hardee at last came up. Otherwise Slocum might not have survived the ambush Johnston had devised for his piecemeal destruction.

Bragg and the Tennesseans had reached Bentonville the night before, as ordered, and were deployed for combat by midmorning, two miles south of town. Hoke's 5500 were posted athwart the road on which Slocum was advancing, slowed by Hampton's skirmishing troopers, while the 4000 western veterans were disposed behind a dense screen of scrub oaks, north of the road and parallel to it, facing south. Johnston's plan was for Hoke to bring the bluecoats to a jumbled halt with a sudden blast of fire from dead ahead, at which point they would be struck in flank by the Tennesseans and Hardee, charging unexpectedly out of the brush. The trouble was that Old Reliable's 7500 — more than a third of the gray total, mounted and afoot — were not yet there to extend and give weight to the strike force stretching westward along the north side of the road. Misled by Johnston, who had himself been misled by a faulty map, Hardee had found yesterday's march twice its reckoned length; with the result that he had had to go into camp, long after dark, some six miles short of Bentonville. He notified his chief of this, but said that he hoped to make up for it by setting out again at 3 a.m. Even so, he did not reach the town until around 9 o'clock, and then found the single road leading south through the blackjack thickets badly clogged by rearward elements of the units already in position. It was well past noon before he approached the field, and by that time the trap had been sprung by pressure on Hampton, whose vedettes were driven back through the line of works Hoke's men had thrown across the road to block the Federal advance.

The trap snapped, but lacking Hardee it lacked power in the jaw that was intended to bite deeply into the flank of the startled Union column. Brigadier General William Carlin's division of Davis's corps had the lead today, and when the woods exploded in his front — a crash of rifles, with the roar of guns mixed in — he recoiled, then rallied and came on again, having called for help from Brigadier General James D. Morgan, whose other XIV Corps division was close behind. While Carlin pressed forward, as if to storm Hoke's light intrenchments, Morgan came up in time to help resist the rebel effort against the flank. They made a good team: Carlin, a thirty-five-year-old Illinois West

Pointer, and Morgan, twenty years his senior, an Illinoisian too, but born and raised in Massachusetts, a workhorse type who had risen by hard fighting. Holding in front, the Federals fell back south of the road and took up a new position facing north, where the graybacks were regrouping in the thickets for a follow-up assault. These were the three corps, so called, of the Army of Tennessee, though all three combined amounted to little more, numerically, than a single full division in the old days, and not one of the three was led today by its regular commander; Harvey Hill had replaced S. D. Lee, still out with his wound, while Bate had charge of his own and the remnant of Cleburne's division, Cheatham not having arrived with the third, and Loring had taken over from Stewart, whose rank gave him command of the whole. They lacked the strength for an overwhelming strike at the bluecoats intrenching rapidly in the woods, and not even Hardee's arrival from Bentonville at this critical juncture was of much help, as it turned out. From the left, dug in athwart the road, Bragg sent word that Hoke was on the verge of being overrun; whereupon Johnston — "most injudiciously," he later said — responded by ordering Hardee to send McLaws to his assistance. That left only Taliaferro's division to reinforce the effort on the right, and it was not enough.

It was especially not enough in light of the fact that Williams by now had his two available XX Corps divisions hurrying forward to close the gap between him and Davis, and the other two divisions, one from each corps, were presently summoned to move up from escort duty with the train. Methodical as always, Hardee extended Stewart's line with Taliaferro's Carolinians, hoping to overlap the enemy left, and then at last, soon after 3 o'clock, resumed the attack on the Federals intrenched by then in the woods to the south of the road. He suffered heavy losses in coming to grips with Morgan's men, and though he was successful in driving a good part of them from their hastily improvised works, taking three guns in the process — "We however showed to the Rebs as well as to our side some of the best running ever did," a Wolverine lieutenant would write home — it was only for a few hundred yards before they stiffened, and he had to call a halt again to realign his strike force in the tangled underbrush. While he did so, Williams' lead division came up and the Union right held firm against a belated attempt by Bragg to add to the confusion. Both commanders then had about 15,000 infantry on the field, and now that surprise was no longer a factor there was scant hope of an advantage for either side in any fighting that might ensue: barring, of course, the arrival of substantial reinforcements. In regard to this last, Slocum already had the other half of his two-corps wing moving up, and what was more he had hopes that Sherman, in response to repeated crosscountry pleas, would land Howard's wing in the Confederate rear tonight, or early tomorrow morning at the latest. But for Johnston there was no such hope and no such reassurance. He could expect no additional troops even in his own rear, let alone the enemy's; he could only try to make better use of those he had — including the solid fourth of his infantry under Mc-Laws, whose division, after groping blind around unmapped ponds and impenetrable thickets, finally reached the left to find that it was not only unneeded for the defense of Hoke's position, but was also too late for a share in the follow-up demonstration against Carlin. As a result of Hardee's miscalculated approach march and McLaws' futile detachment, Seven Pines now had a rival for the distinction of being at once the best-planned and worst-conducted battle of the war.

Still Hardee pressed on, as thorough as he was methodical. Cheered by the western veterans he had last commanded back in Georgia, he was also saddened by the thinness of their ranks. For example, the 1st, 13th, and 19th Tennessee, each of which had contained an average of 1250 effectives at the outset of the war, now had 65, 50, and 64 respectively present for duty; nor were these by any means the worst-off units in this gaunted aggregation, the ghost of the one-time Army of Tennessee, fighting southward now and farther from home than it had been even at Perryville, the northernmost of its lost victories. "It was a painful sight," one of Hoke's men wrote after watching these transplanted remnants of a departed host surge forward in their first charge since Franklin, "to see how close their battle flags were together, regiments being scarcely larger than companies and a division not much larger than a regiment should be." Blown as they were, their third attack — launched shortly after 5 o'clock, within an hour of sunset — was less successful than their second, two hours before; Morgan's men, stoutly dug in and reinforced by Williams' lead division, yielded nothing. The graybacks rebounded, then came on again, and the wierd halloo of the rebel yell rang out in the dusky Carolina woods, given with a fervor that seemed to signify a knowledge by the tattered Deep South veterans that this would be their last. "The assaults were repeated over and over again until a late hour," Slocum reported, "each assault finding us better prepared for resistance."

Convinced by now, if not sooner, that all had been done that could be done once his plan for exploiting the initial shock had gone awry, Johnston instructed Hardee to pull Stewart's and Taliaferro's men back in the darkness to their original position north of the road, confronting with Bragg the reunited half of Sherman's army under Slocum, while Wheeler's troopers, just arrived from their decoy work in front of Raleigh, proceeded east toward Cox's Bridge to delay the advance of the other half under Howard, who was no doubt hard on the way from that direction in response to the eight-hour boom and growl of guns near Bentonville today. (In point of fact, Old Joe would have had to do this, or something like it, in any case — preferably an outright skedaddle — since, even if he had succeeded in abolishing Slocum's wing entirely, despite its three-to-two preponderance in numbers, Sherman could then have brought Schofield across the Neuse to combine with Howard for a counterattack with the odds extended to three-to-one or worse.) Hardee managed the withdrawal before dawn, and when Wheeler sent word that he was in contact with Howard's advance, some half-dozen miles in rear of Hoke's division, Johnston had Bragg pull Hoke back, too, and place him in a newly intrenched position from which he would confront the blue right wing when it came up. Formerly concave, the gray line was now convex, a spraddled V, one arm opposing Slocum, the other Howard, whose first corps arrived by noon, followed shortly by the second. Before the day was over — March 20: the vernal equinox — Sherman thus had close to 60,000 soldiers on or near the field, while Johnston, bled down by his losses in yesterday's failed assault, had fewer than 20,000.

Here then for the red-haired Ohioan was a rare chance, not only to score the Cannae every general prayed for, but also to refute the charge leveled by scorners that he lacked the moral courage to commit his whole army in a single all-out effort. It was true he had never done so, yet it was also true he had never before had such an opportunity as this. Discouraged by their failure to snap shut the trap Old Joe had laid for Slocum, frazzled by hard fighting well into the previous night, confronted left and right today by three times their number, the Confederates clung to the spraddled V whose apex was three miles from the lone bridge over Mill Creek in their rear, and though their purpose was to afford the medical details time to evacuate the wounded, they knew well enough that in remaining within this snare of their own making they were also giving Sherman time to accomplish their destruction — provided, of course, he was willing to attempt it; which he was not. "I would rather avoid a general battle," he cautioned Slocum when the New Yorker concluded his report, "but if [Johnston] insists, we must accommodate him."

He stayed his hand, not so much from lack of moral courage as from mistrust of his own impulsive nature, which he only gave free rein in times of relaxation, while writing letters, say, or dealing with civilians, and almost never when men's lives were at stake. There was that deterrent, plus the fact that he knew little of Johnston's position, except that it was skillfully intrenched, or of his strength, except that it seemed great indeed, to judge by the number of units yielding prisoners from the Army of Tennessee; Sherman, unaware that most of its regiments had dwindled to company size, could assume that the whole army was in his front, as formidable in North Carolina as it had been in Georgia. Besides, his Bentonville casualties, though unreported yet, were clearly heavy; in fact, they would come to 1646 in all, and of these 1168 were wounded. Combined with the 533 from Averasboro, that gave him 1700 sufferers to find room for in his train. Any more such — and who knew how many more there would be if he pressed the issue here? — would overflow the ambulances and crowd the aid stations far beyond the capacity of his surgeons to give them even minimal attention. At Goldsboro, on the other hand, he would be in touch by rail with mountains of supplies, medical and otherwise, unloaded from ships at New Bern and Wilmington, and that was where he wanted to go, as soon as possible, for a combination with Schofield in the open country beyond the Neuse, where he could deal with Johnston at his leisure, fully rested and with half again more men than he had now. Ten days ago, he had promised Schofield to meet him there today, and though Averasboro and Bentonville had thrown him a couple of days off schedule, he hoped to arrive without further delay. If Johnston would only pull back, he himself would be free to go his way, and he was somewhat puzzled by his opponent's apparent reluctance to cooperate by retiring — as he plainly ought to do. "I cannot see why he remains," Sherman complained, but added: "[I] still think he will avail himself of night to get back to Smithfield."

In this he was mistaken, or at any rate premature. Night fell, ending the first day of spring, and the following dawn, March 21, showed Old Joe still in occupation of the works across the way. His reason for staying — concern for his wounded — was similar to Sherman's for wanting to leave, except that in Johnston's case the problem was evacuation, with heavier losses and even slimmer means of transportation. He suffered 2606 casualties in the battle, almost a thousand more than his adversary, and of these 1694 were wounded, who, for lack of enough wagons, had to be taken rearward across Mill Creek Bridge in relays; all of which took time, and time was why he stayed, gambling that the greatly superior enemy force would not overrun him while the work was in progress.

As it turned out, that was nearly what happened: not by Sherman's orders, but rather by a flaunting of them by one of Blair's division commanders, Major General Joseph Mower. Vermont-born, a Massachusetts carpenter in his youth, Mower had served as a private in the Mexican War, and staying on in the army had been commissioned a second lieutenant by the time of Sumter. Since then, he had risen steadily, always as an officer of the line; "the boldest young soldier we have," Sherman had said of him the year before, when he was a thirty-six-year-old brigadier, and here today, posted on the far right, he demonstrated that such praise was deserved. Slipping the leash, he committed his division in a headlong charge that broke through on the rebel left, then drove hard for the single bridge in Johnston's rear. Struck front and flank by a sudden counterattack, he paused and called on Blair and Howard for reinforcements, certain that if he got them nothing could prevent him from closing the only Confederate escape hatch. What he got instead was a peremptory order from Sherman to return to his original position.

Hardee had stopped him with reinforcements brought over from the right, including the 8th Texas Cavalry, which sixteen-year-old Willie Hardee, the general's only son, had joined that morning after finally overcoming his father's objections that he was too young for army duty. "Swear him into service in your company, as nothing else will suffice," Old Reliable told the captain who reported to head-quarters with him. Then he kissed the boy and sent him on his way for what turned out to be a share in the critical job of checking Mower's penetration. Elated by the retirement of the bluecoats — which he did not know had been ordered by Sherman — Hardee grinned and said to Hampton, as they rode back from directing the counteraction: "General, that was nip and tuck, and for a while I thought Tuck had it." Laughing, they continued across the field, only to encounter a pair of litter bearers bringing Willie from the front, badly wounded in his first charge. It was also his last; he would die three days later, with his father at his side, and be buried in a Hillsborough churchyard after the military funeral he would have wanted. For the present, Hardee could only dismount and spend a moment with him before rejoining Hampton for deployment of their troops in case the Yankees tried for another breakthrough, somewhere else along the line.

There was no such attempt, and Johnston, having completed the evacuation of his wounded, pulled back that night across Mill Creek and took the road for Smithfield the next morning, unpursued. He had failed to carry out his plan for wrecking Slocum, but he had at least achieved the lesser purpose of delaying Sherman's march to the back door of Richmond, thereby gaining time for Lee to give Grant the slip and combine with him for another, more substantial lunge at the blue host slogging north. As for himself, now that all six Union corps were about to consolidate at Goldsboro, close to 90,000 strong — "I wonder if Minerva has stamped on the earth for our foes?" Beauregard marveled, contemplating their numbers in intelligence reports — Johnston was convinced that he could accomplish nothing further on his own, and he said as much in a wire to Lee when he crossed the Neuse the follow-ing day, March 23.

"Sherman's course cannot be hindered by the small force I have. I can do no more than annoy him," he told the general-in-chief. His only hope, slight as it was, lay in the proposed combination of the two gray armies for a sudden strike, here in the Old North State, and he con-tinued to urge the prompt adoption of such a course. "I respectfully suggest that it is no longer a question whether you leave present position; you have only to decide where to meet Sherman. I will be near him."

In point of fact he was near him now; Sherman by then was in

Goldsboro, barely twenty miles from Smithfield, a morning's boatride down the Neuse. Schofield had been there for two days, awaiting the arrival of his other corps under Terry, which Sherman had diverted from its direct route up the Wilmington & Weldon, with instructions to prepare a pontoon crossing for Slocum and Howard at the site of Cox's Bridge, burned by the rebels while the fighting raged a dozen miles to the west. As a result, there was no delay when the lead wing reached the river on March 22; Sherman rode into Goldsboro next morning, only three days off the time appointed. Fifty days out of Savannah, ten of which he had had his troops devote to halts for rest or intensive destruction, he had covered well over four hundred miles of rough terrain in wretched weather, crossing rivers and plunging full-tilt through "impenetrable" swamps, and now, after three battles of mounting intensity — Kinston, Averasboro, Bentonville — he combined his four corps with Schofield's two for a total of 88,948 effectives, half again more than he had had when he set out on what he called "one of the longest and most important marches ever made by an organized army in a civilized country." Best of all, from the tactical point of view, Goldsboro was within eighty miles of Weldon, and Weldon was more than halfway to Richmond, already under pressure from 128,046 Federal besiegers. Combined, as they soon could be, the two forces would give Grant 217,000 veterans for use in closing out R. E. Lee, whose own force had been ground down by combat and depleted by desertion to less than one fourth that number of all arms. Impatient for the outcome, which seemed to him foregone, Sherman said later, "I directed my special attention to replenishing the army for the next and last stage of the campaign."

First off, by way of preparation for the prospective meeting with the paper-collar Easterners, the outriding "bummers" were unhorsed and told to rejoin their units for reconversion into soldiers of the line. That came hard for them, accustomed as they had become to hard-handed, light-fingered living and the special pleasure of frightening civilians on their own, independent of the usual military restrictions. What might have been worse, their red-haired commander took it into his head to stage an impromptu review as they came striding into town, mud-spattered and ragged as they were. Oddly enough, the notion appealed to them about as much as it did to him; they saw that he was eager to show them off, and they were glad to please him. "They don't march very well, but they will fight," he told Schofield, who had ridden out to meet him. Half were shoeless, and their trousers were in tatters; "a sorry sight," one brigadier admitted, while a staff colonel noted that "nearly every soldier had some token of the march on his bayonet, from a pig to a potato." Uncle Billy was altogether delighted by their appearance, even their rags, which lent a rollicking touch to the column, and was amused by their unavailing efforts, as they swung past him, to close files that had not been closed in months. When Frank Blair remarked, "Look at those poor fellows with bare legs," Sherman scoffed at such misplaced sympathy.

"Splendid legs! Splendid legs!" he sputtered between puffs on his cigar. "I'd give both of mine for any one of them."

He had never cared for parades and such, and even in this case, for all his pride in the weathered marchers and his amusement at the show they made, he seemed to a reporter "to be wishing it was over. While the troops are going by he must be carrying on a conversation or smoking or fidgeting in some way or other." Self-distracted as he was, the approach of the colors nearly caught him unaware; "he looks up just in time to snatch off his hat. And the way he puts that hat on again! With a jerk and drag and jam, as if it were the most objectionable hat in the world and he was specially entitled to entertain an implacable grudge against it." So great was his impatience, indeed, that he can-cancelled the rest of the review as soon as the second regiment passed. However, there was more to this than the reporter knew. Sherman had just found out that neither railroad was in working order to the coast, and in his anger he fired off a wire to Schofield's chief quartermaster — now his own — demanding to know the whereabouts of "the vast store of supplies I hoped to meet here. . . . If you can expedite the movement of stores from the sea to the army, do so, and don't stand on expenses. There should always be three details of workers, of eight hours each, making twenty-four hours per day of work on every job, whether building a bridge, unloading vessels, loading cars, or what not. Draw everything you need from Savannah, Port Royal, Charleston, &c. for this emergency. . . . I must be off again in twenty days, with wagons full, men reclad, &c."

As a result of this round-the-clock prodding, the road to New Bern was in operation within two days, and Sherman himself was one of its first eastbound passengers, March 25. He was off on a trip: first to, then up, the coast. "If I get the troops all well placed, and the supplies working," he had written Grant when he entered Goldsboro, "I might run up to see you for a day or two before diving again into the bowels of the country." A year ago this week, he and the new general-in-chief had huddled over their maps in a Cincinnati hotel room, planning the vast campaign that was about to enter its final stage. He had not seen him since, and it occurred to him, now that his soldiers were at last in camp, idly awaiting delivery of their new clothes and other luxuries, that this would be a good time for him and his chief to get back in touch, to put their heads together again over plans for the close-out maneuver. Privately, in a jesting mood, he remarked to friends that he was going to see Grant in order to "stir him up," fearing that so long a time behind breastworks might have "fossilized" him. Actually, though, he saw the prospective conference as a means of saving

time and lives by hastening the showdown operation and avoiding mis-
understandings once it began. By way of preamble, he suggested in a
follow-up letter, March 24, his notion of what could be done. "I think
I see pretty clearly how, in one more move, we can checkmate Lee,
forcing him to unite Johnston with him in the defense of Richmond, or,
by leaving Richmond, to abandon the cause. I feel certain if he leaves
Richmond, Virginia leaves the Confederacy."

Next day he was off. Leaving Schofield in command at Goldsboro, he took the cars for New Bern, where he spent the night before
getting aboard the steamer *Russia* Sunday morning, March 26, for the
trip to City Point. "I'm going up to see Grant for five minutes and have
it all chalked out for me," he said, "and then come back and pitch in."

★ ★ ★

"How d'you do, Sherman."

"How are you, Grant."

Smiles broadened into laughter for them both as they shook hands
on the wharf at City Point late Monday afternoon, then proceeded
at once to headquarters for the reunion that ended their year-long
separation. En route, the red-head launched into a description of his
two marches, first across Georgia to the sea, then up through the Carolinas to within 150 miles of where they presently were sitting, Grant
smoking quietly and Sherman talking, talking. He spoke for the better
part of an hour, scarcely pausing — "Columbia; pretty much all burned,
and burned *good*," a staffer heard him say — until his companion,
jogged by a sudden recollection, interrupted to remark that the President too was there on a visit. Arriving late Friday he had spent the past
three nights tied up to the City Point dock, aboard the *River Queen*. "I
know he will be anxious to see you. Suppose we go and pay him a
visit before supper?"

Lincoln was indeed on hand, and what was more, in leaving
Washington four days ago for the double purpose of escaping the press
of executive duties and seeing something of the war first-hand, he had
arrived in time to have his first night's sleep disrupted before dawn,
March 25, by what seemed to him a tremendous uproar over toward
Petersburg, as if all the guns in this part of Virginia were being fired
at once, barely half a dozen miles from his stateroom on the presidential
yacht. They boomed and they kept booming; he thought surely a
full-scale battle must be raging; that is until his son Robert, still proud
of his untarnished captain's bars, came aboard for breakfast and informed him that there had been "a little rumpus up the line this morning, ending about where it began." There must have been more to it
than that, however, because when Lincoln expressed a desire to visit the
scene of the fight — or "rumpus," as Robert had it, affecting the jargon
of the veterans whose life he had shared these past two weeks — Grant

sent word that he couldn't permit the Commander in Chief to expose himself to the danger of being shot.

Presently, though, the general relented. Lincoln not only could view the scene of this morning's disturbance; he would also — along with Tad and Mrs Lincoln, as well as a number of visiting army wives — attend a review by a V Corps division, previously scheduled for noon, but postponed now till 3 o'clock, to be staged in rear of a sector adjoining the one where the predawn uproar had erupted.... Here, for those who could spot it in passing, was another of those unobtrusive but highly significant milestones on the long road to and through the war. This prompt rescheduling of the review, combined with young Robert's offhand reference to "a little rumpus up the line," was indicative of the extent to which the strength of the pent-up rebels had declined in the past few months. For what had awakened Lincoln before daylight was the last of the Army of Northern Virginia's all-out offensive strikes, so awesome in effect these past three years, but now more pitiful than savage. Despite casualties totaling close to 7000 on both sides — more, in fact, than had been suffered in all three battles down in North Carolina during the past two weeks — the only tangible result, once the smoke cleared, was a three-hour postponement of a formal review by part of a corps that had stood idle, within easy supporting distance, while another contained and repelled, unassisted, the heaviest assault the Confederates could manage at this late stage of the drawn-out siege of Petersburg and their national capital. Here indeed was a milestone worth remarking by those on the lookout, blue or gray, aboard the juggernaut fast approaching the end of its four-year grind across the landscape of the South.

No one knew better than Lee himself the odds against survival, by his army or his country — the two were all but synonymous by now, in most men's eyes — of the showdown that drew nearer as the lengthening days wore past. Early's defeat at Waynesboro not only had abolished his last conceivable infantry reserve, it had also cleared the way for a rapid descent on his westward supply lines by Sheridan's win-prone troopers; "against whom," Lee told a colleague, "I can oppose scarcely a vedette." At the same time he learned of this reverse, March 4, he received from Grant a reply to his proposal that ranking officers of their two armies meet to discuss a possible armistice. Declining, Grant informed him that all such matters were up to Lincoln, whose reinauguration day this was and who had said flatly, a month ago in Hampton Roads, that negotiations must follow, not precede, surrender. Lee perceived that his only remaining course, if he was to stave off disaster, was to set out southward for a combination with Johnston before Sherman overwhelmed or moved around him to combine with Grant and serve Petersburg's defenders in much the same fashion. Such a march, he had warned Davis nine days back, would "necessitate the abandonment of our position on James River, for which contingency every preparation should be made." Now he went in person to the capital, that same day, to notify the President that the time for such a shift — and such an abandonment — was closer at hand than he had presumed before Early's defeat and Grant's concomitant refusal to enter into negotiations that might have led to peace without more bloodshed.

In confirmation of what Lee called "his unconquerable will power," Davis did not flinch at the news that Richmond might have to be given up sooner than had been supposed till now. In fact, he countered by asking whether it wouldn't "be better to anticipate the necessity by withdrawing at once." Lee replied that his horses were too weak to haul his guns and wagons through the still-deep mud; he would set out when the roads had dried and hardened. What he had in mind for the interim, he went on, was a strike at Grant that might disrupt whatever plans he was making, either for a mass assault on the Confederate defenses or another westward extension of his line. The Mississippian approved that too, hoping, as he said later, that such a blow would "delay the impending disaster for the more convenient season for retreat." Nothing in his manner indicated that he viewed the loss of Richmond as anything worse than yet another shock to be absorbed in the course of resistance to forces that would deny him and his people the right to govern themselves as they saw fit, and Lee returned to Petersburg impressed and sustained by his chief's "remarkable faith in the possibility of still winning our independence."

That he termed such faith "remarkable" was a measure of his discouragement at this stage, as well as of his military realism in assessing the likely outcome of the problems he and his hungry soldiers faced. Yet in planning the strike just mentioned to Davis he demonstrated anew that none of his old aggressive fire was lacking. "His name might be Audacity. He will take more desperate chances, and take them quicker, than any other general in the country, North or South," a subordinate had said of him when he first assumed command of the army now clinging precariously to its 37 miles of works from White Oak Swamp to Hatcher's Run, and that this was as true now as the Seven Days had proved it to be then, nearly three years back, was shown by his reaction to a report from John Gordon, whom he instructed to study the works confronting his part of the line — due east of Petersburg and closer to the enemy defenses than either Hill's, winding off to the west, or Longstreet's, north of the James — with a view to recommending the point most likely to crumple under attack.

The Georgian chose Fort Stedman, a somewhat run-down Federal installation, midway between the Appomattox and the Crater, only 150 yards from the nose of a bulge in his own line known as Colquitt's Salient. His plan was to use all three of his divisions in a predawn assault, preceded by fifty axmen, whose job it would be to chop a path through the sharp-pointed abatis in front of the objective, and three groups of a hundred men each, who would make their way into the Union rear to seize three open-ended forts Gordon had spotted there, turning their captured guns on the works to the right and left of Stedman, so that the main body could widen the breach in both directions. One beauty in the choice of this location was that it lay in close proximity to the City Point Railroad, a vital supply route leading rearward to Grant's headquarters and main base; Grant would have little choice, if the opera-tion went as planned, except to withdraw troops from his far left to meet the danger, thus shortening his line in just the direction Lee would be moving when the time came for him to set out on his march to join Joe Johnston.

Lee not only approved, he expanded the operation. Leaving the tactical details to Gordon, much as he had done in the old days with Jackson, he reinforced him with four brigades from Hill and two from Anderson — which lifted the total to about half of his southside in-fantry — as well as with Rooney Lee's cavalry division, summoned up from Stony Creek to be used in spreading havoc in the Union rear once the breakthrough had succeeded.

Although he thus would be stripping the Petersburg front prac-tically bare of men except at the point of concentration, he was more than willing to accept the risk for the sake of the possible gain. For one thing, having told his wife some weeks ago that he intended to "fight to the last," he was going about it in his familiar style: all out. For another, in the nearly three weeks since his talk with Davis in Rich-mond, the over-all situation had worsened considerably. Sheridan, after disposing of Early, was reported to be moving toward a junction with Grant that would give the besiegers the rapid-fire mobility they had been needing for a raid-in-force around the Confederate right, which would not only menace the tenuous gray supply lines but would also block the intended escape route for the link-up down in Carolina. Moreover, things had gone from bad to worse in that direction too. On March 11 Johnston warned that if Sherman and Schofield combined, "their march into Virginia cannot be prevented by me." Twelve days and three lost battles later, on March 23, he sent word that the two blue armies had met at Goldsboro. "I can do no more than annoy him," he said of Sherman, whose 90,000 troops were closer to Grant at Globe Tavern, say — a ten-day march at worst — than Johnston, with scarcely one fifth that number around Smithfield, was to Lee at Petersburg.

Time had all but run out. Lee called Gordon in that night and told him to assemble his force next day for the strike at Fort Stedman before dawn, March 25. Gordon requested that Pickett's division be detached from Longstreet to strengthen the effort, and Lee agreed, though he doubted that it would arrive in time from beyond the Ap-pomattox. "Still we will try," he said, adding by way of encouragement to the young corps commander, who at thirty-three was twenty-five years his junior: "I pray that a merciful God may grant us success and deliver us from our enemies."

Gordon cached his reinforced corps in Colquitt's Salient the following day, as ordered, and after nightfall had the obstructions quietly removed to clear the way for the attack. Exclusive of Pickett, who was not up, and the division of cavalry en route from Stony Creek, he had 12,000 infantry poised for the 4 o'clock jump-off, an hour before dawn and two hours before sunrise. Lee arrived on Traveller after moonset and took position on a hill just in rear of the trenches; he would share in the waiting, though he would of course be able to see nothing until daylight filtered through to reveal Fort Stedman, out ahead on Hare's Hill; by which time it should be in Gordon's possession, along with a considerable stretch of line in both directions. On schedule, the signal — a single rifle shot, loud against the bated silence — rang out, and the skirmishers overwhelmed the drowsy enemy pickets, followed by the fifty axmen and the 300-man assault force, all wearing strips of white cloth across their breasts and backs for ready identification in the darkness.

There was no alarm until the first wave started up the rising ground directly under the four guns in the fort. Then suddenly there was. All four guns began to roar, and the force of their muzzle blasts and the wind from passing shells tore at the hats of the attackers. "We went the balance of the way with hats and guns in hand," one would recall. At the moat, the axmen came forward to hack at the chevaux-de-frise, and the charging graybacks went up and over the parapet so quickly that the defenders, some 300 members of a New York heavy artillery outfit, had no time to brace themselves for hand-to-hand resistance. Stedman fell in that first rush, along with its guns, which were seized intact and turned on the adjacent works. Battery 10, on the immediate left, was promptly taken, as was Battery 11 on the right. Gordon was elated. A lean-faced man with a ramrod bearing, long dark hair, and glowing eyes — "as fierce and nearly cruel blue eyes as I ever looked into," a reporter was to note — he was much admired by his men, one of whom said of him: "He's most the prettiest thing you ever did see on a field of fight. It would put heart in a whipped chicken just to look at him." Happy and proud, he sent back word of his success and his intention to enlarge it, left and right and straight ahead.

Dawn had glimmered through by then, and the three 100-man assault teams pressed on beyond the captured works, toward the rim of sky tinted rose by the approaching sun. Trained artillerists were among them, assigned to serve the guns in the three backup forts, once they were taken, and thus bring them to bear on the rear of front-line redoubts north and south of fallen Stedman and its two companion batteries. This unexpected shelling from the rear, combined with pressure from the front and flanks, would assure enlargement of the gap through which the waves of graybacks could push eastward, perhaps within reach of City Point itself, where the wide-ranging cavalry would take over the task of rounding up high-rank prisoners — conceivably including U. S. Grant himself, whose headquarters was known to be in the yard of the Eppes mansion — while setting fire to the main enemy supply base and disrupting the very nerve center of the encircling Union host. Gordon saw that the pressure from the rear had better come soon, though, for the bluecoats in Batteries 9 and 12 were standing firm, resisting all efforts to widen the breach. Then at sunup he got the worst possible news from runners sent back by officers in charge of the assault teams. They could not locate the three open-ended forts on the rearward ridge: for the simple reason, discovered later, that they did not exist, being nothing more than the ruins of old Confederate works along the Dimmock line, abandoned back in June by Beauregard. Meantime the counterbattery fire was getting heavier and more accurate from adjoining redoubts and Fort Haskell, within easy range to the south, as well as from massed batteries of field artillery, brought forward to help contain the penetration. Fort Stedman and its two flank installations were subjected to converging fire from every Yankee gun along this portion of the line; a fire so intense that the air seemed filled with shells whose burning fuzes, one observer said, made them resemble "a flock of black-birds with blazing tails beating about in a gale." Pinned down, the stalled attackers huddled under what shelter they could find, waiting for the metallic storm to lift.

Instead of lifting it grew heavier as the red ball of the sun bounced clear of the landline. Gordon saw plainly that without help from the nonexistent forts he not only could not deepen or widen the dent he had made, he would not even be able to hold what he had won by the predawn rush. Accordingly, he notified Lee of his predicament, and word came back, shortly before 8 o'clock, for him to call off the attack and withdraw. The Georgian was altogether willing to return to his own lines, but the same could not be said for hundreds of his soldiers, who preferred surrender to running the gauntlet of fire that boxed them in. As a result, Confederate losses for this stage of the operation came to about 3500 men, half of them captives, as compared to a Federal total of 1044. Nor was that all. Convinced that Lee must have stripped the rest of his southside line to provide troops for the strike at Stedman, Grant ordered a follow-up assault to be launched against the rebel right, where Hill's intrenched picket line was overrun near Hatcher's Run, inflicting heavy casualties and taking close to a thousand additional prisoners, not to mention securing a close-up hug on Hill's main line of resistance. By the time a truce was called that afternoon for collecting the dead and wounded on both sides, the casualty lists had grown to 4800 for Lee and 2080 for Grant. The bungled affair of the Crater — which today's effort so much resembled, both in purpose and in outcome — had been redressed, although with considerably heavier losses all around.

Another difference was that the southern commander could ill afford what his opponent had shrugged off, eight months ago and less than a mile down the line, with no more than a brief loss of temper. Riding rearward, Lee met Rooney coming forward in advance of his division. With him was his younger brother Robert, now a captain on his staff. Both greeted their father, who gave them the news that there would be no cavalry phase of the operation. The assault had failed, and badly, at great cost. "Since then," Robert declared long afterwards, "I have often recalled the sadness of his face, its careworn expression."

Lee's depression was well founded. On no single day since the Bloody Angle was overrun at Spotsylvania had he lost so many prisoners, and these combined with the killed and wounded had cost him a solid tenth of his command, as compared to Grant's loss of less than a sixtieth. "The greatest calamity that can befall us is the destruction of our armies," he had warned Davis eleven days ago, while Gordon was planning the Stedman operation. "If they can be maintained, we may recover from our reverses, but if lost we have no resource." Today marked a sizeable step toward the destruction of the first army of them all. Moreover, it had gained him nothing, while costing him Hill's outer defenses, now occupied by Grant, who could be expected to launch a swamping assault from this new close-up position — a sort of Stedman in reverse — in just the direction Lee would be obliged to move when he tried for a breakout west and south: no longer for the purpose of combining with Johnston for a lunge at Sherman before the red-head crossed the Roanoke, but simply as the only remaining long-shot chance of postponing the disaster he foresaw. Notifying Breckinridge of the failed attack, he made no complaint of Gordon's miscalculations; he merely remarked that the troops had "behaved most handsomely." But next day, in following this with a report to the President, he confessed himself at a loss as to his next move, except that he knew he had to get away, and soon. "I fear now it will be impossible to prevent a junction between Grant and Sherman," he frankly admitted, "nor do I deem it prudent that this army should maintain its position until the latter shall approach too near."

He was warning again that Richmond would have to be given up any day now, but what would follow that abandonment he did not say; perhaps because he did not know. All he seemed to have in mind was a combination with Johnston for the confrontation that was bound to ensue. "I have thought it proper to make the above statement to Your Excellency of the condition of affairs," he concluded, "knowing that you will do whatever may be in your power to give relief."

But the power was Grant's, and Grant knew it. When Lincoln

came to headquarters, shortly after the Confederates began their withdrawal from Fort Stedman — those of them, that is, who did not choose
surrender over running the gauntlet of fire — the general observed that
the assault had been less a threat to the integrity of the Union position
than it was an indication of Lee's desperation in regard to the integrity
of his own. Accordingly, he rescheduled the V Corps review, which
would be staged in rear of a sector just south of the one where Gordon's
attack had exploded before dawn, and decided as well that the President
would be safe enough in taking a look at the ground where the struggle
had raged between 4 and 8 o'clock that morning.

So it was that Lincoln, going forward on the railroad to the margin
of that field, saw on a considerably larger scale what he had seen at Fort
Stevens eight months earlier, just outside Washington. Mangled corpses
were being carted rearward for burial in the army cemetery near City
Point — which incidentally, like everything else in that vicinity, had
been much expanded since his brief visit in June of the year before —
and men were being jounced on stretchers, writhing in pain as they
were lugged back for surgeons to probe their wounds or remove their
shattered arms and legs. There was pride and exhilaration in statements
that Parke, cut off from communication with Meade and Grant while
the fighting was in progress, had used only his three IX Corps divisions
to contain and repulse the rebels without outside help. But for Lincoln, interested though he always was in military matters, the pleasure he would
ordinarily have taken in such reports was greatly diminished by the sight
of what they had cost. He looked "worn and haggard," an officer who
accompanied him declared; "He remarked that he had seen enough
of the horrors of war, that he hoped this was the beginning of the end,
and that there would be no more bloodshed."

Still another shock was in store for him before the day was over,
this one involving his wife. For some time now, particularly since the
death of her middle and favorite son, eleven-year-old Willie, Mary
Lincoln had been displaying symptoms of the mental disturbance that
would result, a decade later, in a medical judgment of her case as one of
insanity. Her distress, though great, was scarcely greater than her family
misfortunes — exclusive of the greatest, still to come. Four of her five
Kentucky brothers had gone with the South, and three of them died at
Shiloh, Baton Rouge, and Vicksburg. Similarly, three of her four sisters
were married to Confederates, one of whom fell at Chickamauga. Such
losses not only brought her grief, they also brought on a good deal
of backhand whispering about "treason in the White House." All this,
together with Lincoln's lack of time to soothe her hurts and calm her
fears, combined to produce a state in which she was quick to imagine
slights to her lofty station and threats to all she valued most, including
her two surviving sons and her husband.

It was the latter who was in danger today, or so she conceived from something she heard as she rode with Mrs Grant and Lieutenant Colonel Adam Badeau, Grant's military secretary, in an ambulance on the way to the review that had been rescheduled for 3 o'clock. Badeau happened to remark that active operations could not be far off, since all army wives had recently been ordered to the rear: all, that is, but the wife of Warren's ranking division commander, Mrs Charles Griffin, who had been given special permission by the President to attend today's review. The First Lady flared up at this. "What do you mean by that, sir? Do you mean to say that she saw the President alone? Do you know that I never allow the President to see any woman alone?" Speechless with amazement at finding her "absolutely jealous of poor, ugly Abraham Lincoln," the colonel tried to assume a pleasant expression in order to show he meant no malice; but the effect was otherwise. "That's a very equivocal smile, sir," Mrs Lincoln exclaimed. "Let me out of this carriage at once! I will ask the President if he saw that woman alone."

Badeau and Mrs Grant managed to persuade her not to alight in the mud, but it was Meade who saved the day. Coming up to pay his respects on their arrival, he was taken aside by Mrs Lincoln for a hurried exchange from which she returned to fix the flustered staffer with a significant look. "General Meade is a gentleman, sir," she told him. "He says it was not the President who gave Mrs Griffin the permit, but the Secretary of War." Badeau afterwards remarked that Meade, the son of a diplomat, "had evidently inherited some of his father's skill."

Unfortunately, the Pennsylvanian was not on hand for a similar outburst the following day, when the troops reviewed were Ord's, beyond the James. Arriving late, again in an ambulance with the staff colonel and Mrs Grant, Mrs Lincoln found the review already in progress, and there on horseback beside her husband, who was mounted too — he wore his usual frock coat and top hat, though his shirt front was rumpled and his strapless trouser legs had worked up to display "some inches of white socks" — was Mrs Ord. She was neither as young nor as handsome as Mrs Griffin, but that was no mitigation in Mary Lincoln's eyes. "What does the woman mean by riding by the side of the President? And ahead of me! Does she suppose that *he* wants *her* by the side of *him*?" She was fairly launched, and when Mrs Grant ventured a few words of reassurance she turned on her as well, saying: "I suppose you think you'll get to the White House yourself, don't you?" Julia Grant's disclaimer, to the effect that her present position was higher than any she had hoped for, drew the reply: "Oh, you had better take it if you can get it. 'Tis very nice."

Mrs Ord, seeing the vehicle pull up, excused herself to the dignitaries around her. "There come Mrs Lincoln and Mrs Grant; I think I had better join them," she said, unaware of the tirade in progress across the way, and set out at a canter. It was not until she drew rein beside the ambulance that she perceived that she might have done better to ride in the opposite direction. "Our reception was not cordial," an aide who accompanied her later testified discreetly. Badeau, a former newsman, gave a fuller account of Mrs Ord's ordeal. "Mrs Lincoln positively insulted her, called her vile names in the presence of a crowd of officers, and asked what she meant by following up the President. The poor woman burst into tears and inquired what she had done, but Mrs Lincoln refused to be appeased, and stormed till she was tired. Mrs Grant tried to stand by her friend, and everybody was shocked and horrified. But all things come to an end, and after a while we returned to City Point."

Things were no better there, however: certainly not for Lincoln, who was host that night at a dinner given aboard the *Queen* for the Grants and Grant's staff. Mrs Lincoln, with the general seated on her right, spent a good part of the evening running down Ord, who she said was unfit for his post, "not to mention his wife." Making no headway here, she shifted her scorn toward her husband, up at the far end of the table, and reproached him for his attentions to Mrs Griffin and Mrs Ord. Lincoln "bore it," Badeau noted, "with an expression of pain and sadness that cut one to the heart, but with supreme calmness and dignity. He called her Mother, with old-time plainness; he pleaded with eyes and tones, and endeavored to explain or palliate the offenses." Nothing worked, either at table or in the saloon afterwards; "she turned on him like a tigress," until at last "he walked away, hiding that noble, ugly face that we might not catch the full expression of its misery." Yet that did not work either; she kept at him. After the guests had retired, she summoned the skipper of the *Bat*, Lieutenant Commander John S. Barnes, who had been present at today's review, and demanded that he corroborate her charge that the President had been overattentive to Mrs Ord. Barnes declined the role of "umpire," as he put it, and earned thereby her enmity forever. He left, and when he reported aboard next morning to inquire after the First Lady, Lincoln replied that "she was not at all well, and expressed the fear that the excitement of the surroundings was too great for her, or for any woman."

By then it was Monday, March 27. Sherman's courtesy call that evening, within an hour of his arrival from down the coast, was all the more welcome as a diversion: for Lincoln at any rate, if not for the red-haired Ohioan, who had accepted Grant's suggestion — "Suppose we pay him a visit before supper?" — with something less than delight at the prospect. "All right," he said. He had small use for politicians, including this one, whom he had met only once, four years ago this week, at the time when the Sumter crisis was heading up. Introduced at the White House by his senator brother as a first-hand witness of recent activities in the South, he testified that the people there were preparing for all-out conflict. "Oh, well," he heard the lanky Kentuckian say, "I guess we'll manage to keep house." Disgusted, he declined to resume his military career, and though he relented when the issue swung to war, he retained down the years that first impression of a lightweight President.

Now aboard the *Queen*, however — perhaps in part because he could later write, "He remembered me perfectly" — he found himself in the presence of a different man entirely, one who was "full of curiosity about the many incidents of our great march" and was flatteringly concerned "lest some accident might happen to the army in North Carolina in my absence." Sherman's interest, quickened no doubt by Lincoln's own, deepened into sympathy as the exchange continued through what he called "a good, long, social visit." He saw lights and shadows unsuspected till now in a figure that had been vague at best, off at the far end of the telegraph wire running back to Washington. "When at rest or listening," he would say of his host, now three weeks into a second term, "his arms and legs seemed to hang almost lifeless, and his face was careworn and haggard; but, the moment he began to talk, his face lighted up, his tall form, as it were, unfolded, and he was the very impersonation of good-humor and fellowship."

Taking their leave, the two generals returned to Grant's quarters, where Mrs Grant, laying out tea things, asked if they had seen the First Lady. They had not; nor had they thought to tender their respects. "Well, you are a pretty pair!" she scolded.

After some badinage about the risk of having Julia within earshot ("Know all men by these presents," he observed, might just as well read "Know one woman," if what you wanted was to spread the word) Grant brought his companion up to date on the progress of other forces involved in his plan for closing out the rebellion. Mainly it had been a vexing business, especially in regard to the strikes by Canby, Stoneman, and Wilson, from which so much had been expected, both on their own and by way of diversion, if they had been launched in conjunction with Sherman's march through the Carolinas; which they had not. Canby was the worst offender, delaying his movement against Mobile while he gathered materials and built up a construction corps for laying seventy miles of railroad supply line. Moreover, he had put Gordon Granger in charge of one wing of his army, despite Grant's known dislike of the New Yorker, and had wanted to give Baldy Smith the other, until Grant vetoed the notion and flatly told him to get moving with what he had. Finally he did. Two columns of two divisions each, one under Granger, the other under A. J. Smith, together with a division of cavalry and a siege train, were put in motion around the east side of Mobile Bay, while a third column, also of two divisions, set out from Pensacola under Frederick Steele, resurrected from Arkansas, where he had spent the past ten months recuperating from his share in the Red River expedition. This brought a total of 45,000 men converging on an estimated 10,000 defenders in the works that rimmed Mobile; surely enough to assure reduction in short order. But it was March 17 by the time Canby got started, more than a month behind schedule, and March 26 — just yesterday — by the time Spanish Fort, an outwork up at the head of the bay, nine miles east of the city, was taken under fire. How long it might be at this rate before the Mobile garrison surrendered or skedaddled, Grant did not try to guess, but he saw clearly enough that it would not be in time to free any portion of Canby's army for the projected march on Selma in coöperation with the mounted column Thomas had been ordered to send against that vital munitions center, the loss of which would go far toward ending Confederate resistance in the western theater.

There was however another rub, no less vexing because it had been more or less expected with Old Slow Trot in command. Late as Canby was in setting out, Thomas was even later: not only in getting Wilson headed south for Selma, but also in launching Stoneman eastward into the Carolinas, where he had been told to operate against the railroad between Charlotte and Columbia and thus disrupt the rebel effort to assemble troops in the path of Sherman's army slogging north. As it turned out, Sherman had fought at Averasboro and was midway through the Bentonville eruption, within a day's march of his Goldsboro objective, by the time Stoneman left Knoxville on March 20, and it took him and his 4000 horsemen a week, riding through Morristown, Bull's Gap, and Jonesboro, before he crossed the Smokies to approach the western North Carolina border. By then — today, March 27; Sherman would reach City Point at sundown — there was little raiders could do in that direction; so Grant wired Thomas to have Stoneman turn north into Southwest Virginia instead, and there "repeat the raid of last fall, destroying the [Virginia & Tennessee] railroad as far toward Lynchburg as he can." That way, at least he might be able to cripple Lee's supply line and be on hand in case the old fox tried a getaway westward. Perhaps it would even work out better, Grant reasoned, now that Sherman had managed to come through on his own. But it was vexing, in much the same way Sigel's and Butler's ineptitudes had been vexing at the outset of the previous campaign, back in May of the year before.

Wilson posed a somewhat different problem, in part because Grant had a fondness for him dating back to their Vicksburg days, when the young West Pointer had been a lieutenant colonel on his staff, and also because real danger was involved. Danger was always an element in military ventures, but in Wilson's case the danger was Bedford Forrest, who could be depended on to try his hand at interfering with this as he had done with other Deep South raids, all too often disastrously — as Abel Streight, Sooy Smith, and Samuel Sturgis could testify, along with Stephen Hurlbut, A. J. Smith, Cadwallader Washburn, and several others who had encountered him at various removes, including Grant and Sherman. However, his recent promotion to lieutenant general was no measure of the number of soldiers he now had at his disposal; Wilson, with 12,500 troopers armed to a man with Spencer carbines, three batteries of horse artillery, and a supply train of 250 wagons (a command he described, on setting out, as being "in magnificent condition, splendidly mounted, perfectly clad and equipped") would outnumber his adversary two-to-one in any likely confrontation. Even without the distraction Canby would fail to supply, and even though the long delay had given Forrest and Richard Taylor an extra month to prepare for its reception, Grant believed the blue column would be able to ride right over anything they were able to throw in its path.

Still, this delay was as vexing as the others — and even longer, as it turned out. It was March 18 before Wilson, who had been having remount troubles, was able to start crossing the Tennessee, swollen by the worst floods the region had ever known. The steamboat landing at Eastport, his crossing point into Mississippi's northeast corner, was so far under water that he needed three whole days to get his horsemen over the river and reassembled on the southern bank. Finally, on March 22, he set out across the hilly barrens of Northwest Alabama, hard on the go for Selma, two hundred miles to the southeast. Five days later — March 27; Sherman was steaming up the James for a handshake with Grant, a visit with Lincoln, and later that night the present informal briefing by the general-in-chief — Wilson began to cross the upper forks of the Black Warrior River near Jasper, almost halfway to his goal. So far, he had encountered nothing he could not brush aside with a casual motion of one hand; but up ahead, somewhere between there and Selma, Forrest no doubt was gathering his gray riders for whatever deviltry he had in mind to visit on the invading column's front or flank or rear. Grant, conferring with Sherman that evening in his quarters, could only hope it was nothing his twenty-seven-year-old former staff engineer couldn't handle on his own.

By way of contrast with Canby, Stoneman, and Wilson — whose efforts, as Grant declared in his vexation, might turn out to be "eminently successful, but without any good results" because they were launched too near the end they had been designed to hasten — Phil Sheridan had demonstrated, here in the eastern theater, the virtue of promptness when striking deep into enemy territory. Leaving Winchester a month ago today, within a week of receiving orders to set out "as soon as it is possible to travel," he had caught Early unprepared at Waynesboro, his back to the Blue Ridge, and after wrecking him there moved on through Rockfish Gap to Charlottesville, where he tore up track on two vital rail supply lines, first the Virginia Central and then the Orange & Alexandria, the latter while proceeding south in accordance with his instructions to cross the James for a link-up with Sherman beyond the Carolina line. As he approached Lynchburg, however — the main objective of his raid, as defined by Grant, because it was there that the Orange & Alexandria and Lee's all-important Southside Railroad came together to continue west as the Virginia & Tennessee — he received reports from scouts that the place had been reinforced too heavily for him to move against it. What was more, the rebels had burned all the nearby bridges over the James, which was swollen to a depth past fording and a width beyond the span of his eight pontoons. Accordingly, he drew rein, thought the matter over briefly, and turned east, intending to move down the north bank of the river to the vicinity of Richmond, where he would rejoin Grant. This was not a difficult decision, since it led to what he had wanted in the first place. Regardless of orders, which required him either to cross the James or turn back to the Valley, he wanted to be where the action was. And in his eyes, the action — the real action: so much of it as remained, at any rate — was not with Sherman in North Carolina, opposing Johnston, but here in Virginia with Grant, opposing Lee. "Feeling that the war was approaching its end," he afterwards explained in fox-hunt terms, "I desired my cavalry to be in at the death."

At Columbia on March 10, fifty-odd miles upstream from the rebel capital, he gave his troopers a day's rest from their exertions, which included the smashing of locks on the James River Canal, and got off a crosscountry message to Grant, "notifying him of our success, position, and condition, and requesting supplies to be sent to White House." That was his goal now, McClellan's old supply base on the Pamunkey River, well within the Union lines on the far side of Richmond. To reach it, he turned away from the James next day at Goochland and rode north across the South Anna to Beaver Dam Station, which he had visited back in May on the raid that killed Jeb Stuart. From there he turned east and south again, down the Virginia Central to Hanover Courthouse, then crossed the North Anna to proceed down the opposite bank of the Pamunkey to White House, arriving on March 20 after three full weeks on the go. Though his loss in horses had been "considerable — almost entirely from hoof-rot," he noted — his loss in men "did not exceed 100," including some "left by the wayside, unable to bear the fatigues of the march." The rest, he said, "appeared buoyed up by the thought that we had completed our work in the Valley of the Shenandoah, and that we were on our way to help our brothers-in-arms in front of Petersburg in the final struggle."

Assurance that he and they would have a share in the close-out operation against Lee was contained in a dispatch the general-in-chief had waiting for him at White House, along with the supplies he had requested. Dated yesterday, the message instructed him to cull out his broken-down horses and men, give the others such rest and refitment as they needed to put them back in shape, and prepare to cross the James for a strike around Lee's right flank at Petersburg, in conjunction with some 40,000 infantry who would be shifted in that direction. "Start for this place as soon as you conveniently can," Grant told him. His assignment would be to wreck the Southside and Danville railroads, "and then either return to this army or go on to Sherman, as you may deem most practicable." Which of the two he chose, Grant said, "I care but little about, the principal thing being the destruction of the only two roads left to the enemy at Richmond."

Sheridan was delighted, knowing already which course he would "deem most practicable" when the time came. Next day, March 21, a follow-up message arrived. "I do not wish to hurry you," it began, and then proceeded to do just that, explaining: "There is now such a possibility, if not probability, of Lee and Johnston attempting to unite that I feel extremely desirous not only of cutting the lines of communication between them, but of having a large and properly commanded cavalry force ready to act with in case such an attempt is made." Elsewhere, Grant added, things were moving at last. "Stoneman started yesterday from Knoxville"; "Wilson started at the same time from Eastport"; "Canby is in motion, and I have reason to believe that Sherman and Schofield have formed a junction at Goldsboro." As for Sheridan, "I think that by Saturday next you had better start, even if you have to stop here to finish shoeing up."

Saturday next would be March 25. On Friday, still busy getting his horses and troopers reshod and equipped, the bandy-legged cavalryman received from Grant a letter — copies of which also went to Meade and Ord, as heads of armies: proof, in itself, of his rise in the military hierarchy since his departure for the Valley, back in August — giving details of the maneuver designed to accomplish Lee's undoing. "On the 29th instant the armies operating against Richmond will be moved by our left, for the double purpose of turning the enemy out of his present position around Petersburg and to insure the success of the cavalry under General Sheridan, which will start at the same time, in its efforts to reach and destroy the South Side and Danville railroads." That was the opening sentence; specific instructions followed. Ord was to cross the James with four of his seven divisions, including one of cavalry, and take over the works now occupied by Humphreys and Warren on the Federal left, thus freeing their two corps to move west beyond Hatcher's Run, where Sheridan's three mounted divisions — 13,500 strong — would plunge north, around Lee's right, to get astride the vital rail supply routes in his rear. Meantime, Ord's other three divisions under Weitzel, north of the James and across Bermuda Hundred, together with the two corps under Parke and Wright and Ord's four divisions south of the river, were to keep a sharp lookout and attack at once if they saw signs that Lee was drawing troops from the works in their front to meet the threat to his flank and rear.

In short, what Grant had devised was another leftward sidle, the maneuver he had employed all the way from the Rapidan to the James, with invariable success in obliging his adversary to give ground. Since then, in the nine months spent on this side of the James, the maneuver had been a good deal less successful, achieving little more in fact than a slow extension of the rebel earthworks, along with his own, more or less in ratio to his lengthening casualty lists. Much of that time, however, Sheridan had been on detached service up the country; whereas, this time, Little Phil and his hard-hitting troopers would not only be on hand — "the left-hand man of Grant the left-handed," someone dubbed him — but would also lead the strike intended to dispossess Lee, first of his tenuous rail supply lines and then of Petersburg itself, whose abandonment would mean the loss of his capital as well.

Presently it developed that Grant intended to dispossess him of even more than that, right here and now. Sheridan began crossing his horsemen on March 26, riding ahead for a talk with his chief at City Point. Pleased though he was at having been told he could do as he chose, "return to this army or go on to Sherman" once he and his troops had completed their share in the upcoming sidle, he still worried that Grant might change his mind and send him south against his will. And, indeed, further written instructions he found waiting for him at headquarters reinforced this fear by stressing the possibility of having him "cut loose from the Army of the Potomac" and continue his ride "by way of the Danville Railroad" into North Carolina. Watching him scowl as he read that part of the order, Grant took him aside, out of earshot of the staff, and quietly told him: "General, this portion of your instructions I have put in merely as a blind." He explained that if the sidle failed, as others had done in the course of the past nine months, he would be able to head off criticism by pointing to these orders as proof that it had been designed as nothing more than a sidelong slap at Lee by Sheridan, en route to a junction with Sherman. Actually, Grant assured him, he had no intention of sending him away. He wanted him with him, in the forefront of the strike about to be launched and the chase that would ensue. Little Phil began to see the light; a light that grew swiftly into a sunburst when he heard what his chief said next. "I mean to end the business here," Grant told him. The cavalryman's raid-weathered face brightened at the words; Lee was to be dispossessed, not only of Petersburg and Richmond, but also of his army — here and now. Sheridan grinned. "I am glad to hear it," he said. He slapped his thigh. "And we can do it!" he exclaimed.

Elated by this private assurance from the general-in-chief (and flattered by Lincoln, who told him later that morning, in the course of a boatride down the James: "General Sheridan, when this peculiar war began I thought a cavalryman should be at least six feet four inches high, but I have changed my mind. Five feet four will do in a pinch") he was alarmed the following afternoon by news that Sherman was expected at City Point that evening. His concern proceeded from awareness that his fellow Ohioan was not only badly in need of mounted reinforcements, still having only Kilpatrick's frazzled division on hand at Goldsboro, but was also an accomplished talker, possessed of considerable "zeal and powers of emphasis," which might well enable him to persuade his friend Grant to revise his plan for keeping Sheridan and all three of his divisions in Virginia. Disturbed by the threat, he got the last of his troopers over the James by nightfall — one month, to the day, since they left Winchester — then boarded a train and set out for headquarters. Breakdowns delayed his arrival till nearly midnight, just as Grant and Sherman were ending the conference that followed their meeting with Lincoln aboard the *River Queen.* So far as he could tell, the interloper had not changed their chief's mind about the use of cavalry in the pending operation against Lee, if indeed the subject had come up. Still the danger remained, and Sheridan continued to fret about it, even after all three of them had turned in for the night. His alarm increased next morning, March 28, when the red-head came to his room and woke him up, talking earnestly of "how he would come up through the Carolinas and hinting that I could join him." Sheridan responded so angrily, however, that Sherman dropped the subject and retired.

There was by now little time for argument, even if Sherman had thought it would do any good. He and Grant were scheduled to see Lincoln again this morning, and the President's concern for the safety of his army in his absence had led him to promise that he would start back for Goldsboro as soon as this second meeting aboard the *Queen* was over; in which connection David Porter, who was there to give advice on naval matters, had volunteered to substitute the converted blockade-runner *Bat* for the sluggish *Russia,* thus assuring the western general a faster voyage down the coast. This time, coming aboard the presidential yacht, Grant remembered to tender his and Sherman's respects to the First Lady, but when her husband went to her stateroom she sent word that she hoped they would excuse her; she was unwell. Whereupon the four men — Grant and Sherman, Porter and Lincoln — took their seats in the saloon, and the high-level conference began.

It was not, properly speaking, a council of war; "Grant never held one in his life," a staffer was to note; but it did begin with a discussion of the military situation here and in North Carolina. In regard to the former, Grant explained that Sheridan's horsemen had crossed the James in preparation for a strike at Lee's rail supply lines, which, if successful, would leave the old fox no choice except to surrender or (as he had done on a lesser scale three days ago at Fort Stedman, no doubt to his regret) come out and fight: unless, that is, he managed to slip away beforehand, in which case Meade and Ord would be close on his heels in pursuit. As for the danger to Sherman, in the event that Lee made it south to combine with Johnston, the red-head assured Lincoln that his army at Goldsboro was strong enough to hold its own against both rebel forces, "provided Grant could come up within a day or so." As for a matching attempt by Johnston to give him the slip, either on foot or by rail, he saw little chance of that; "I have him where he cannot move without breaking up his army, which, once disbanded, can never be got together."

Tactically, the Commander in Chief was satisfied that victory was at last within reach. But it seemed to him, from what had just been pointed out, that all this squeezing and maneuvering was leading to a high-loss confrontation, an Armageddon that would serve no purpose on either side except to set the seal on a foregone conclusion. "Must more blood be shed?" he asked. "Cannot this last bloody battle be avoided?" Both generals thought not. In any case, that was up to the enemy; Lee being Lee, there was likely to be "one more desperate and bloody battle." Lincoln groaned. "My God, my God," he said. "Can't you spare more effusions of blood? We have had so much of it."

In the pause that followed — for they had no answer, except to repeat that the choice was not with them — Sherman observed again, as he had done the night before, the effect four years of war had had on the leader charged with its conduct all that time. "When in lively conversation, his face brightened wonderfully, but if the conversation flagged his face assumed a sad and sorrowful expression." Presuming somewhat on his feeling of sympathy, and wanting to be prepared for what was coming, he then "inquired of the President if he was all ready for the end of the war" and, more specifically, "What was to be done with the rebel armies when defeated?" That was the question, as he recalled it a decade later, when he also set down Lincoln's answer. "He said he was all ready; all he wanted of us was to defeat the opposing armies, and to get the men composing the Confederate armies back to their homes, at work on their farms and in their shops." Warming to the subject, Lincoln went on to expand it. He was also ready, he declared, "for the civil reorganization of affairs in the South as soon as the war was over." In this connection, the general would remember, "he distinctly authorized me to assure Governor Vance and the people of North Carolina that, as soon as the rebel armies laid down their arms, and resumed their civil pursuits, they would at once be guaranteed all their rights as citizens of a common country," and he added that in order to avoid anarchy in the region, "the state governments then in existence, with their civil functionaries, would be recognized by him as the government *de facto* till Congress could provide others."

Sherman, "more than ever impressed by his kindly nature, his deep and earnest sympathy with the afflictions of the whole people, resulting from the war and the march of hostile armies through the South," perceived (or gathered) from these remarks, uttered offhand and in private, that Lincoln's "earnest desire seemed to be to end the war speedily, without more bloodshed or devastation, and to restore all the men of both sections to their homes." *All*, he said; but did he mean it? Did that apply to the fire-eaters who had engineered secession; to the stalwarts, in and out of uniform, who sustained the rebellion after the fire-eaters fell by the wayside? Coming down to the most extreme example, Sherman wanted to know: Did the hope for such restoration apply to Jefferson Davis?

Now it was Lincoln's turn to pause, though not for long. As Chief Executive, the possible reviewing authority for any future legal action taken in the matter, he was "hardly at liberty to speak his mind fully," he declared, yet he was willing to reply, as he had done so often down the years, with a story. "A man once had taken the total-abstinence pledge. When visiting a friend he was invited to take a drink, but declined, on the score of his pledge; when his friend suggested lemonade, which was accepted. In preparing the lemonade, the friend pointed to the brandy bottle, and said the lemonade would be more palatable if he were to pour in a little brandy; when his guest said, if he could do so 'unbeknown' to him, he would not object." Thus Sherman retold the story, no doubt tightening it up a bit in the transcription, from which he inferred that the northern President hoped his southern counterpart would "escape, 'unbeknown' to him" — clear out, leave the country — "only it would not do for him to say so openly."

By then it was close to leaving time; Barnes had steam up on the *Bat*, waiting for Sherman to come aboard, and Lincoln was no less anxious for him to get started down the coast, where he could look to the security of his army and prepare for the movement scheduled to begin on April 10, first on Raleigh to dispose of Johnston, then north across the Virginia line to Burkeville, chosen as his objective because it was there that the Southside and Danville railroads crossed, fifty miles west of Petersburg; which meant that, once he reached that point, he would not only have cut Lee's two remaining all-weather supply lines — if, indeed, they survived till then — but would also be in position to intercept him if he retreated in that direction. Before he left, however, he and Grant and the President took a walk along the river bank, glad of a chance to stretch their legs after confinement in cramped quarters on the *Queen* for the past three hours. A reporter saw and described them as they strolled. "Lincoln, tall, round-shouldered, loose-jointed, large-featured, deep-eyed, with a smile upon his face, is dressed in black and wears a fashionable silk hat. Grant is at Lincoln's right, shorter, stouter, more compact; wears a military hat with a stiff, broad brim, has his hands in his pantaloon pockets, and is puffing away at a cigar. Sherman, tall, with a high, commanding forehead, is almost as loosely built as Lincoln; has sandy whiskers, closely cropped, and sharp, twinkling eyes, long arms and legs, shabby coat, slouched hat, his pantaloons tucked into his boots." As usual, the red-head did most of the talking —

"gesticulating now to Lincoln, now to Grant," the newsman noted, "his eyes wandering everywhere" — but at one point the President broke in to ask: "Sherman, do you know why I took a shine to Grant and you?"

"I don't know, Mr Lincoln," he replied. "You have been extremely kind to me, far more than my deserts."

"Well, you never found fault with me," Lincoln said.

This was not true. Sherman had found a good deal of fault with the President over the past four years, beginning with the day he heard him say, almost blithely, "Oh, well, I guess we'll manage to keep house." But it was true from this day forward. For one thing, Lincoln had in fact managed to "keep house," though sometimes only by the hardest, and for another, now that Sherman knew him he admired him, perhaps beyond all the men he had ever known. Again at the wharf, he boarded the *Bat* and set out down the James. Afterwards, looking back, he said of Lincoln, who had walked him to the gangplank: "I never saw him again. Of all the men I ever met, he seemed to possess more of the elements of greatness, combined with goodness, than any other."

✗ 3 ✗

Grant began his close-out sidle in earnest the following day. Ord's four divisions, after crossing the James in the wake of Sheridan's troopers, had replaced the six under Humphreys and Warren at the far end of the line the night before, freeing them to move in support of the cavalry strike around Lee's right, and Grant was leapfrogging his headquarters twenty miles southwest down the Vaughan Road, beyond the western limit of his intrenchments at Hatcher's Run, so he could watch the progress of events and make, first hand, such last-minute adjustments as might be needed in that direction. After breakfast, around 8.30, while he and his staff waited beside the tracks at City Point for their horses and gear to be loaded onto boxcars, Lincoln joined them and stood talking with the general for a time. Finally, after handshakes with the President all round — including one for Robert, about to take the field in his first campaign — Grant and his military family got aboard the cars. As the engine began to strain they raised their hats in salute to Lincoln, who lifted his in turn to them, and the train chuffed off, south then west, behind the long slow curve of trenches the army had dug in the course of the past nine months of stalemate here in front of Petersburg, a type of warfare the present shift had been designed to end.

In Richmond, that same March 29, Brigadier General Josiah Gorgas received at his office in the Ordnance Department, which he headed, a hastily written note signed Jefferson Davis. "Will you do me the favor to have some cartridges prepared for a small Colt pistol, of which

I send the moulds?" Gorgas, a Pennsylvania-born West Pointer who had married south — and who, starting with next to nothing in the way of machinery, skilled labor, raw materials, or the means of producing them, in the past four years had turned out seventy million rounds of small-arms ammunition, along with so much else, including weapons, that no Confederate army, whatever it suffered from being deprived of food and clothing, ever lost a battle for lack of ordnance equipment or supplies — filled the requisition overnight. The cartridges were not for Davis himself, but for his wife. He gave her the pistol and showed her how to load, aim, and fire it, saying: "You can at least, if reduced to the last extremity, force your assailants to kill you."

Four days ago, at the time of Lee's latest warning that Richmond was to be given up, he had told her she must prepare to leave without him. "My headquarters for the future may be in the field, and your presence would embarrass and grieve me instead of giving comfort." Though she begged to stay and help relieve the tension, he was firm in refusal. "You can do this in but one way: by going yourself and taking the children to a place of safety. If I live, you can come to me when the struggle is ended," he said: adding, however, that he did not "expect to survive the destruction of constitutional liberty." Regretfully she began her preparations for departure, hampered by his insistence that she not ask friends to look after the family silver, lest they be "exposed to inconvenience or outrage" when the Yankees took the city. So she sent the silver, together with some of the furniture, to an auctioneer for sale under the hammer. Then she "made the mistake," as she later said, of telling her husband that she intended to take along several barrels of flour she had bought — at the going price of $1500 a barrel — to help withstand the expected siege. He forbad this, saying flatly: "You can't take anything in the shape of food from here. The people need it." Saddened, she turned to packing what little was left, mainly clothes for herself and the four children, who ranged in age from ten years to nine months.

Others had done what Varina Davis was doing now, though with less conscientious interference by their husbands with regard to such household items as flour and silver. Since early February, foreseeing that the end of winter meant the end of Richmond, men of substance had been sending their wives and children to outlying estates, north and west of the threatened capital, or to North Carolina towns and cities so far spared a visit from Sherman. All through March the railway stations were crowded with well-off "refugees" boarding trains to avoid the holocaust at hand. Having no choice, those with nowhere to go (and no money either to pay the fare or live on when they got there) remained, as did the heads of families whose government duties or business interests required their presence; with the result that by the time the First Lady started packing, alerted for a sudden removal to

Charlotte, where Davis had rented a house for her and the children, Richmond's population was predominantly black and poor and male. A sizeable group among these last had been composed of the 105 congressmen and 26 senators, most of them eager for adjournment so they too could get aboard the cars rattling westward, away from the seven-hilled capital and the blue flood lapping the earthworks east and south — muddy dikes buttressed only by the scarecrow infantry under Lee, who was rumored to have given the government notice that they would not be there long.

In any case, these 131 elected representatives of the people felt that they had done all they could by March 18, when they adjourned and scattered for their homes, those who still had them. And, indeed, they had done much this term: including the unthinkable. After long and sometimes acrimonious debate, the House on February 20 and the Senate on March 8 authorized the enlistment of Negroes for service in the armies of the Confederacy. On March 13 a joint bill to that effect was forwarded for approval by the Chief Executive, who promptly signed it despite objections that it fell considerably short of what he — and Pat Cleburne, fifteen months ago — had wanted. For one thing, the recruits must all be volunteers, and at second hand at that; only "such able-bodied slaves as might be patriotically rendered by their masters" were to be accepted, although the President was authorized to call on the states to fill their respective quotas, limited in each case to no more than one fourth of its male slaves between the ages of eighteen and forty-five. Moreover, while it was stipulated that Negro soldiers were to receive the same pay, rations, and clothing as other troops, no mention was made of emancipation as a reward for military service, and it was even stressed in a final rider that nothing in the act was "to be construed to authorize a change in the relation which the said slaves shall bear toward their owners, except by the consent of their owners and of the states in which they may reside." Mainly, though, Davis regretted the extended debate that had kept the bill so long from his desk. "Much benefit is anticipated from this measure," he remarked, "though far less than would have resulted from its adoption at an earlier date, so as to afford time for organization and instruction during the winter months."

Grim as the warnings leading up to passage of the act had been, the fulminations that followed were even grimmer. "If we are right in passing this measure," Robert Hunter told his fellow senators, "we were wrong in denying the old government the right to interfere with the institution of slavery and to emancipate slaves." Howell Cobb agreed, writing from Georgia: "Use all the Negroes you can get, for the purposes for which you need them" — cooking, digging, chopping, and such — "but don't arm them. The day you make soldiers of them is the beginning of the end of the revolution. If slaves will make good soldiers our whole theory of slavery is wrong." Even Robert Kean, head of the Bureau of War, who knew better than most the urgent need for men in the ranks of the nation's armies, saw nothing but evil proceeding from a measure which, he noted in his diary, "was passed by a panic in the Congress and the Virginia Legislature, under all the pressure the President indirectly, and General Lee directly, could bring to bear. My own judgment of the whole thing is that it is a colossal blunder, a dislocation of the foundations of society from which no practical results will be reaped by us." Robert Toombs, after his brief return to the service during Sherman's march through Georgia, was strongest of all in condemnation of this attempt to convert the Negro into a soldier; a Confederate soldier, anyhow. "In my opinion," he wrote from his plantation in Wilkes County, where he had put down a full crop of cotton last year in response to a Davis proclamation calling on planters to shift to food crops, "the worst calamity that could befall us would be to gain our independence by the valor of our slaves. . . . The day that the army of Virginia allows a negro regiment to enter their lines as soldiers they will be degraded, ruined, and disgraced."

Toombs need not have fretted about the prospect of disgrace to his former comrades, either in Virginia or elsewhere. For though the army, by and large, had favored adoption of the measure (144 out of 200 men in an Alabama regiment, for example, signed a petition addressed to Congress in its favor, and the proportion was about the same in a Mississippi outfit) the legislation failed in application: not so much because of the shortness of "time for organization and instruction," of which Davis had complained, as because of a lack of support by the owners of prospective black recruits — and possibly by the slaves themselves, though of the latter there was little chance to judge. Some few came or were sent forward to Richmond before the end of March; new gray uniforms were somehow found for them, and there was even a drill ceremony in Capitol Square, performed to the shrill of fifes and throb of drums; but that was all. Small boys jeered and threw rocks at the paraders, not one of whom reached the firing line while there was still a firing line to reach.

Nor was it only on this side of the Atlantic that the proposal to invoke the assistance of the Negro in the struggle which so intimately concerned him failed to achieve its purpose. Judah Benjamin, ever willing to play any last card in his hand, had written to Mason and Slidell in late December, instructing them to sound out the British prime minister and the French emperor, respectively, as to what effect a Confederate program for emancipation — "not suddenly and all at once, but so far as to insure abolition in a fair and reasonable time" — might have on their views with regard to recognition of the Confederacy and possible intervention in the war. Napoleon rather blandly replied that slavery had never been an issue so far as France was concerned, and Lord Palmerston said much the same of England in an interview on March 14 with Mason, who wrote Benjamin that he was "satisfied that the most ample concessions on our part in the matter referred to would have produced no change in the course determined by the British government." Twelve days later, in conversation with the Earl of Donoughmore, a Tory leader friendly to the South, the Virginian's view was confirmed by a franker response to the same question. If the proposal had been made in midsummer of 1863, while Lee was on the march in Pennsylvania, the earl did not doubt that recognition would have followed promptly. But that was then. What about now? Mason asked, and afterwards informed the Secretary: "He replied that the time had gone by."

It would have been at best a deathbed conversion, and as such would have lacked the validity of conviction and free will. Meantime, opponents of the earlier and more limited proposal — to induct blacks into the army, even without the promise of freedom as a reward for any suffering short of death — were no doubt pleased that, in practical application, the Lost Cause was spared this ultimate "stain" on its record. In any case the Confederacy's chief opponent, Abraham Lincoln, professed not to care one way or another about the success or failure of the experiment. "There is one thing about the Negro's fighting for the rebels which we can know as well as they can," he remarked, "and that is that they cannot at the same time fight in their armies and stay home and make bread for them. And this being known and remembered, we can have but little concern whether they become soldiers or not." Something else he saw as well, and when news of the action by the Richmond lawmakers reached Washington he expressed it in an address to an Indiana regiment passing through the capital on March 17, six days before he set out down the coast for City Point. "I am rather in favor of the measure," he told the Hoosiers, "and would at any time, if I could, have loaned them a vote to carry it. We have to reach the bottom of the insurgent resources, and that they employ or seriously think of employing the slaves as soldiers gives us glimpses of the bottom. Therefore I am glad of what we learn on this subject."

Davis by now had caught more than "glimpses" of the scraped bottom. Yet for all his West Point training and his regular army background, both of which contributed to the military realism that had characterized his outlook as Commander in Chief — and paradoxically, because of his unblinking recognition of the odds, had made him a believer in long chances and a supporter of those generals who would take them — it was also in his nature, as the leader of his people, to deny, even to himself, the political consequences of whatever of this kind he saw, even with his own eyes. "I'd rather die than be whipped," Jeb Stuart had said at Yellow Tavern, ten months back. So would Davis, but he took this a step further in his conviction that no man was ever whipped until he admitted it; which he himself would never do. Earlier this month, writing to thank a Virginia congressman for support "in an hour when so many believed brave have faltered and so many esteemed true have fallen away," he declared his faith in survival as an act of national will. "In spite of the timidity and faithlessness of many who should give tone to the popular feeling and hope to the popular heart, I am satisfied that it is in the power of the good man and true patriots of the country to reanimate the wearied spirit of our people. The incredible sacrifices made by them in the cause will be surpassed by what they are still willing to endure in preference to abject sub-mission, if they are not deserted by their leaders. Relying upon the sublime fortitude and devotion of my countrymen, I expect the hour of deliverance."

His resolution was to be tested to the full before the month was out. Gordon's failure at Fort Stedman prompted Lee to state unequiv-ocally next day that he would have to give up Richmond before Sherman and Grant effected a junction he could do nothing to prevent, and two days later, March 28, in response to a query from Breckinridge as to how much notice the capital authorities could expect — "I have given the necessary orders in regard to commencing the removal of stores, &c.," the Secretary wrote, "but, if possible, would like to know whether we may probably count on a period of ten or twelve days" — Lee replied: "I know of no reason to prevent your counting upon the time suggested." So he said. But next morning he learned that Grant had begun another crablike sidle around his thin-stretched right. Both infantry and cavalry were involved, and the movement was across Monk's Neck Bridge, over Rowanty Creek just below the confluence of Hatcher's and Gravelly runs; their initial objective seemed to be Dinwiddie Courthouse, a scant half-dozen miles beyond, which would give them a clear shot north at Five Forks, a critical intersection out the White Oak Road, about the same distance west of Burgess Mill, the right-flank anchor of Lee's line. Five Forks, defended now by no more than a handful of gray vedettes, was within three miles of the Southside Railroad, whose loss would interfere grievously — perhaps disastrously — with the army's projected withdrawal, not only from its lines below the James but also from those above, since the Richmond & Danville would also be exposed beyond the Appomattox.

Informed of this, Davis requisitioned from Gorgas ammunition for the pistol he gave his wife next day, along with instructions on how to use it. By that time Lee had troops in motion westward to meet the threat, which further reports had identified as substantial; Sheridan was at Dinwiddie with his cavalry, and two blue corps had also crossed the Rowanty, apparently to lend heft to the roundhouse left Lee believed was about to be thrown at Five Forks. Unable to stretch his line that far, lest it snap, the gray commander detached Pickett from Longstreet, reinforcing his division to a strength of 6400, and posted him there, four miles beyond the farthest reach of the intrenchments on that side of Hatcher's Run. Fitzhugh and Rooney Lee's divisions, as well as Rosser's, lately arrived from the Valley — a total of 5400 troopers; all but a handful of all the army had — were called in from roundabout and sent to bolster Pickett. Nor was that all Lee did. Aggressive as always, he visited the outpost position the following morning, March 30, and ordered an advance toward Dinwiddie the following day, hoping thus to seize the initiative and throw the flankers into confusion, despite odds he knew were long. This done, he rode back to Petersburg. "Don't think he was in good humor," a young lieutenant entered in his diary.

Heavy rain had been falling with scarcely a let-up since the night before, and it continued through the final day of March, hampering last-minute preparations for the departure that evening of Mrs Davis, made urgent by the threat to the Danville line. Guns boomed daylong east of Richmond, mixed with peals of thunder; Grant no doubt was feeling the works in that direction, as well as elsewhere along the nearly forty random miles of their extent, for evidence that Lee had weakened them to confront the movement around his right. Soon after dark an over-loaded carriage set out from the White House for the railroad station, bearing Mrs Davis and her sister Margaret Howell, the four children and their nurse, a young midshipman assigned as escort, and Burton Harrison, the President's secretary, who was to help them get settled in Charlotte, then rejoin his chief — wherever he might be by then. They arrived well before leaving time, 8 o'clock, and boarded a passenger coach which, though dilapidated and "long a stranger to paint," was the best the Confederacy could provide for its First Lady at this late stage of its existence. She looked with dismay at the lumpy seats, with threadbare plush the color of dried blood, and made the children as comfortable as she could; Billy, three, and the baby Pie were stretched out asleep by the time their father arrived to see them off. He sat talking earnestly with his wife, ten-year-old Maggie clinging to him all the while and eight-year-old Jeff trying hard to keep from crying. When the whistle blew, an hour and a half past schedule, he rose, kissed the children, embraced Varina, and turned to go, still with an appearance of great calm, though he came close to giving way to his emotion when Maggie persisted in clinging to him, sobbing, and Little Jeff begged tearfully to remain with him in Richmond. "He thought he was looking his last upon us," Mrs Davis later wrote.

There was a further wait on the station platform; he walked up and down it, talking with Harrison until 10 o'clock, when the train gave a sudden lurch that left the secretary barely time to leap aboard. Davis stood and watched the tail light fade and vanish, then rode back to the big empty-seeming house at Clay and 12th streets, there to await word from Lee that he too must leave the city.

All the evidence was that it would not be long, and next morning — All Fools Day — a message from the general-in-chief served notice that the time was shorter than he or anyone else had known. Pickett's advance the day before, supported by Fitz Lee's troopers, had driven the startled Federals back on Dinwiddie by sunset, but there they rallied, pumping lead from their rapid-fire carbines, and Pickett felt obliged to pull back in the rainy predawn darkness, leaving the situation much as it had been when he set out from Five Forks yesterday morning. Sheridan still held Dinwiddie, cutting the Stony Creek supply line, and had followed up Pickett's withdrawal so closely as to deny him use of the critical White Oak Road leading east to Hatcher's Run. Supported as it was by at least two corps of infantry, Lee told Davis, this movement of Grant's "seriously threatens our position and diminishes our ability to maintain our present lines in front of Richmond and Petersburg. . . . I fear he can cut both the South Side and the Danville railroads, being far superior to us in cavalry. This in my opinion obliges us to prepare for the necessity of evacuating our position on James River at once, and also to consider the best means of accomplishing it, and our future course."

★   ★   ★

"Grant has the bear by the hind leg while Sherman takes off the hide," Lincoln had told a White House caller some weeks back, explaining the situation as it then obtained. But now the holder-skinner roles were to be reversed, and Sheridan — much to his delight — was the catalytic agent injected by Grant to bring the change about. At Dinwiddie on the 29th, just as the rain began to patter on the roof of the tavern where he had set up for the night, he received a dispatch that sent his spirits fairly soaring. "I feel now like ending the matter, if it is possible to do so, before going back," his chief informed him. "In the morning, push around the enemy, if you can, and get onto his right rear. The movements of the enemy's cavalry may, of course, modify your action, [but] we will all act together as one army until it is seen what can be done."

"Onto," Grant said, not *into* Lee's rear: meaning that the strike at the two railroads had become incidental to his main purpose, which was to crush the rebel army where it stood. "My hope was that Sheridan would be able to carry Five Forks, get on the enemy's right flank and rear, and force them to weaken their center to protect their right so that an assault in the center might be successfully made." That was how he put it later; Warren and Humphreys would support the cavalry effort west of Hatcher's Run, and Wright was to lunge at Petersburg on signal, supported on the left and right by Ord and Parke, while Weitzel maintained pressure on Richmond's defenses beyond the James, partly to hold Longstreet in position, but also to be ready to move in when

the breakthrough came, beyond the Appomattox. Glad to find his
superior following through on what he had told him in private, three
days back — "I mean to end the business here" — Sheridan briefed
his subordinates on their share in the operation. All during the conference, however, rain drummed hard and harder on the tavern roof;

daylight showed a world in flood, with no sign of a let-up; roads were
practically bottomless, preventing the movement of supplies, and the
rain continued to fall in sheets, converting meadows into ponds. To
make things worse, a bogged observer noted, "the soil was a mixture
of clay and sand, partaking in some places of the nature of quicksand."
Grant could testify to this, his headquarters beside the Vaughan Road
being one such place. Formerly a cornfield, it now resembled a slough,
with effects at once comic and grim on men and mounts, coming and
going or even trying to stand still. "Sometimes a horse or mule would
be standing apparently on firm ground," he later wrote, "when all at
once one foot would sink, and as he commenced scrambling to catch
himself, all his feet would sink and he would have to be drawn by
hand out of the quicksands so common in that part of Virginia."
    Veterans wagged their heads, remembering Burnside's Mud March,
and some declared the situation was no worse than might have been
expected, what with all the glib predictions that Bobby Lee was about
to be outfoxed. They had heard that kind of talk before, with results
that varied only in the extent of their discomfort when the smoke
cleared. "Four years of war, while it made the men brave and valorous,"
a Pennsylvania private would point out, "had entirely cured them

of imagining that each campaign would be the last." Still they were not dispirited; soggy crackers and soaked blankets often went with soldiering, especially on occasions like the present; "When are the gunboats coming up?" they called to one another as they slogged along the spongy roads or stood about in fields too wet for sitting.

Sheridan, on the other hand, fumed and fretted. He had scouting parties working northward out of Dinwiddie in accordance with his orders, but he feared the arrival of a dispatch changing those orders because of the weather. Sure enough, just such a message came from Grant around midmorning. "The heavy rain of today will make it impossible for you to do much until it dries up a little, or we get roads around our rear repaired." His suggestion was that Sheridan "leave what cavalry you deem necessary to protect the left" and return with the rest to a station on the military railroad, where he could draw rations and grain for his troopers and their mounts. Or, better yet: "Could not your cavalry go back by the way of Stony Creek Depot and destroy or capture the store of supplies there?"

Go back! Sheridan frowned as he read the words, then set out instead for Grant's command post, seven miles northeast, to argue for all he was worth against postponement of the forward movement. Hoping to save time — "a stumpy, quadrangular little man," a subsequent acquaintance was to say, "with a forehead of no promise and hair so short that it looks like a coat of black paint" — he rode a long-legged Kentucky pacer, much admired for its mile-eating gait. But the going was slow on the mud-slick roads, pelted by unrelenting rain, and slower still around midday when he turned off the Vaughan Road, a mile beyond Gravelly Run, and urged his mount across the drowned headquarters cornfield. "Instead of striking a pacing gait now," a staffer noted, "[the horse] was at every step driving its legs knee-deep into the quicksand with the regularity of a pile driver." Grant was in conference just then, but Little Phil, "water dripping from every angle of his face and clothes," launched forthwith into his protest to such listeners as were handy. Give him his head, he said, and Lee would be whipped in short order. How about forage? someone asked; to his disdain. "Forage?" he snorted. "I'll get all the forage I want. I'll haul it out if I have to set every man in the command to corduroying roads, and corduroy every mile of them from the railroad to Dinwiddie. I tell you I'm ready to strike out tomorrow and go to smashing things!"

Such enthusiasm was contagious. Twenty minutes alone with the general-in-chief, once he was free, resulted in agreement that the cavalry would "press the movement against the enemy with all vigor." Ord, Wright, and Parke were to remain on the alert for the signal to assault the rebel works in their front, and Sheridan would not only have the diversionary support of Humphreys and Warren, he would also be given direct command of the latter's corps at any time he requested it, thereby assuring full coöperation despite any difference of opinion that might arise. "Let me know, as early in the morning as you can, your judgment of the matter," Grant told him in parting, "and I will make the necessary orders." Elated, the bandy-legged Ohioan remounted and set out to rejoin his troopers around Dinwiddie, waving goodbye to the admiring group of staffers who came out into the still-driving rain to see him off, most of them as happy as he was over his success in getting their chief to cancel the postponement.

Still, a day had been lost to mud and indecision. And so, as it developed, was another — the last in March — not so much because of the weather, though rain continued to pelt the roads and sodden fields, as because of a double-pronged attack by Lee, who went over to the offensive in an attempt to disconcert the combinations moving against him west of Hatcher's Run. True to his word, Sheridan put Custer's whole division to work that morning, corduroying the Dinwiddie supply routes, while Devin probed northwest up the road to Five Forks, reinforced by a brigade from the third division, formerly Gregg's but now under George Crook; Gregg had resigned in February, exhausted or disheartened by a winter spent on the Petersburg front, and Crook was exchanged, one month after his capture up in Maryland, in time to take Gregg's place on the eve of the present maneuver, covering Dinwiddie today with his two remaining brigades while the other moved out with Devin for a share in what turned out to be a retreat in the face of heavy odds.

Approaching Five Forks around noon Devin encountered Pickett, who had been instructed by Lee to move out with his nearly 12,000 infantry and cavalry in order to beat the advancing Federals to the punch; which he did, emptying more than 400 U.S. saddles in the process. Outnumbered almost three to one, Devin had all he could do to make it back to Dinwiddie by sunset, still under heavy pressure. Crook's and Custer's troopers, called up and thrown dismounted into line alongside Devin's, managed to stop the graybacks in plain view of Sheridan's headquarters. Night came down, and with it came word of a similar repulse suffered by Warren across the way. Advancing in the direction of Lee's right, which he had been told to "feel," the New Yorker's corps was badly strung out on the muddy byroads, various units marking time while others ran heavy-footed to catch up; Brigadier General Romeyn Ayres' division, struck a sudden blow by a butternut host that came screaming out of the dripping woods ahead, took off rearward in such haste that Crawford's, next in line and with no chance to brace for the shock, was also overrun. The attack was delivered by veterans from Bushrod Johnson's division — all that remained of Anderson's improvised corps — reinforced by others brought over from A. P. Hill beyond the run, and was directed by Lee himself, who had no way of knowing that this would be his and the Army of Northern Virginia's last. In any case, the drive did not falter until it reached Griffin's division, posted in reserve, and even then was only contained with help from Humphreys, whose corps was advancing in better order on the right. After sundown, the attackers — some 5000 in all, of whom about 800 had fallen or been captured — withdrew to their works apparently satisfied with the infliction of just over 1400 casualties on Warren and just under 400 on Humphreys, both of whom testified that the call had been a close one, indicative of the need for caution while groping for contact with the rebel flank.

Sheridan did not agree. Nettled, but no more daunted by Devin's repulse than he was by Warren's, he was convinced that what had been learned from these two encounters far outweighed the loss of 2700 men on the Union left, today and yesterday. After all there still were some 50,000 blue-clad veterans west of Hatcher's Run, mounted and afoot, and he believed in using them all-out, with emphasis on getting the job done, rather than on caution. Lee had scarcely that many troops in his whole command, from White Oak Swamp to Five Forks, and if Little Phil had his way tonight the old fox would have a good many less before the sun went down tomorrow. What he had in mind was Pickett's detachment. Its movement against him today, while tactically successful, had increased its isolation and thereby exposed it to destruction, if only the right kind of pressure could be brought to bear. Even before sundown, with the issue still apparently in doubt, he said as much to a staff colonel sent over by Grant, who expressed alarm at finding Devin's troopers thrown back on the outskirts of Dinwiddie, skirmishing hotly within carbine range of the headquarters tavern. "This force is in more danger than I am," Sheridan told him. "If I am cut off from the Army of the Potomac, it is cut off from Lee's army, and not a man in it should ever be allowed to get back to Lee. We at last have drawn the enemy's infantry out of its fortifications, and this is our chance to attack it."

One doubt he had, which he also expressed. He would need a corps of infantry to help inflict Pickett's destruction, and today's encounter across the way had increased his mistrust of Warren as a fit partner, or even subordinate, in such an undertaking. Consequently, recalling how well he and Wright had worked together in the Valley, he urged the staffer to pass on to Grant his fervent request that the VI Corps be sent to him instead. Departing after nightfall, the colonel promised to support the plea, despite doubts that the change would be made this late, and presently these doubts were confirmed. Near midnight, word came from Grant — whose headquarters had been shifted that afternoon to Dabney's Sawmill, a mile northwest of the boggy Vaughan Road cornfield — that Wright could not be sent: first, because he was too far away to make the march tonight, and second because he would be needed where he was, to score the breakthrough scheduled to follow upon the smashing of Lee's right. In any case, Warren had been detached from Meade and ordered to proceed down the Boydton Plank Road to Dinwiddie, where he would report for such duty as Sheridan had in mind for him. He and his three divisions should arrive by midnight, Grant wrote, followed next morning by Brigadier General Ranald Mackenzie's troopers, one of the four divisions brought over from beyond the James two days ago. This would raise Sheridan's total to around 30,000 effectives, half cavalry, half infantry; quite enough, presumably, for the resumption of his stalled offensive. "You will assume command of the whole force sent to operate with you," the message ended, "and use it to the best of your ability to destroy the force which your command has fought so gallantly today."

More or less reconciled, Little Phil turned in for a few hours' sleep, only to have his wrath flare up again when he rose at dawn to find none of Warren's troops on hand. The rain had stopped at last, but even so their march had been a snarl of mud and confusion, including a four-hour jumbled wait for the washed-out bridge over Gravelly Run to be rebuilt. It was broad open daylight by the time the head of the 16,000-man column reached Dinwiddie, and crowding noon before Warren himself came up with his third division, eleven hours behind the schedule sent by Grant, but apparently satisfied that he and his men had done their best under difficult conditions. Sheridan took a less tolerant view. "Where's Warren?" he growled at a brigadier who arrived with the first of the mud-slathered infantry. Back toward the rear, attending to some tangle, the other replied. "That's where I expected to find him," the cavalryman snapped.

His impatience mounted with the fast-climbing sun, right up to midday, when he rode over to give the New Yorker instructions for his share in the attack. Pickett had withdrawn to Five Forks this morning and reoccupied breastworks along the White Oak Road, on both sides of the Ford Road crossing; Sheridan's plan was for his troopers, advancing northwest up the road from Dinwiddie — which bisected the southeast quadrant of the intersection and gave it the name Five Forks — to apply and maintain pressure in front, thus pinning the defenders in position while the infantry attacked their eastern flank in a turning movement whose main effort would be against the angle where their line bent north to confront a possible blue approach out the White Oak Road from Hatcher's Run, where Lee's intrenchments ended. By hitting this knuckle with one division and rounding the brief northward extension with the other two, Warren could throw two thirds of his corps — a force equal to everything Pickett had, mounted and dismounted — into their rear, and perhaps bag the lot when they gave way under double pressure, front and flank, in full flight for their lives. The important thing just now, the cavalryman stressed, was to get going before the rebs escaped or used still more of the time allowed them to improve their position. Warren nodded agreement, but it did not seem to Sheridan that much of his western enthusiasm had been communicated to the paper-collar Easterner, who left to rejoin his tired and sleepy men, muttering something about "Bobby Lee getting people into difficulties."

Actually, for all his chafing, Sheridan was to find that the delay had worked to his advantage by lulling the defenders into believing there would be no serious confrontation at Five Forks today: so much so, indeed, that when the attack did come — as it finally did, around 4 o'clock — neither the infantry nor the cavalry commander was even present to oppose him.

Reporting this morning on his two-day movement to Dinwiddie and back, Pickett was somewhat miffed by the tone of Lee's reply. "Hold Five Forks at all hazards," he was told. "Protect road to Ford's Depot and prevent Union forces from striking the Southside Railroad. Regret exceedingly your forced withdrawal, and your inability to hold the advantage you had gained." Not only did this seem tinged with unaccustomed panic, it also seemed to the long-haired hero of Gettysburg inappreciative of his efforts yesterday, which he was convinced had shocked the Federals into deferring whatever maneuver they had intended before he struck and drove them back. At any rate, on his return he put his five brigades of infantry in line along the White Oak Road, astride the Ford Road intersection, and covered their flanks and rear with cavalry, Rooney Lee's division on the right, Fitz Lee's on the left, and Tom Rosser's on guard with the train beyond Hatcher's Run, two miles to the north. All seemed well; he had no doubt that he could maintain his position against Sheridan's horsemen, even if they ventured to attack, and there had been no word of a farther advance by the blue infantry whose reported presence west of Gravelly Run had provoked his withdrawal this morning. Consequently, when an invitation came from Rosser to join in an alfresco meal of shad caught in the Nottoway River on his way from Stony Creek, Pickett gladly accepted, as did Fitzhugh Lee, who turned his division over to Colonel T. T. Munford around 1 o'clock, then set out for the rear with his ringleted superior for a share in their fellow Virginian's feast. Neither told any subordinate where he was going or why, perhaps to keep from dividing the succulent fish too many ways; with the result that when the attack exploded — damped from their hearing, as it was, by a heavy stand of pines along Hatcher's Run — no one knew where to find them. Pickett only made it back to his division after half its members had been shot or captured, a sad last act for a man who gave his name to the most famous charge in a war whose end was hastened by his three-hour absence at a shad bake.

Nor was he the only Gettysburg hero whose reputation suffered from his participation — or, strictly speaking, nonparticipation — in the fight that raged at Five Forks during the final daylight hours of April 1. Sheridan's wrath had continued to mount as the sun declined past midday and the V Corps plodded wearily up the road past Gravelly Run Church to execute its share of the fix-and-shatter maneuver already begun by the dismounted troopers banging away with their rapid-fire weapons in front of the enemy right and center. "This battle must be fought and won before the sun goes down," he grumbled on being told that it would be 4 o'clock by the time the three infantry divisions were deployed. "All the conditions may be changed in the morning; we have but a few hours of daylight left us. My cavalry are rapidly exhausting their ammunition, and if the attack is delayed much longer they may have none left." Warren, however, "seemed gloomy and despondent," Little Phil said later, and "gave me the impression that he wished the sun to go down before dispositions for the attack could be completed." If so, the New Yorker was in graver danger than he knew. Another staff colonel had arrived from Grant with a message for Sheridan, authorizing Warren's removal "if in your judgment the V Corps would do better under one of its division commanders." Sheridan saw this not only as an authorization but also as a suggestion, knowing that his chief was as displeased as he was by Warren's performance these past two days, despite his aura as the savior of Little Round Top, twenty-one months ago in Pennsylvania. All the same, he stayed his hand, controlling his temper by the hardest, and finally, not long after 4 o'clock, all three divisions started forward on a thousand-yard front, Ayres on the left, Crawford on the right, and Griffin in support, intending to strike and turn the rebel left, preliminary to the combined assault that would sweep the graybacks from the field and net them as they fled northward.

Alas, it was just at this critical moment that the bill for the worst of the day's inadvertencies came due. Informed by Sheridan that the road past Gravelly Run Church entered the White Oak Road at the point where the enemy works bent north, Warren had aligned his left division on it as a guide for the attack. Emerging from the woods, however, Ayres saw that the rebel angle — his objective — was in fact about half a mile west of the junction he was approaching. Accordingly, he swung left as he crossed the White Oak Road, then lunged westward: only to find that he was charging on his own. Crawford, on the right, kept going north, followed by Griffin close in his rear, while Mackenzie, who had arrived that morning to support the turning movement, led his troopers eastward, as instructed, to block the path of any reinforcements Lee might send across the three-mile gap between him and Pickett. Alarmed at the widening breach in the ranks of his supposed attackers, Warren spurred after the two divisions trudging north. He overtook Griffin and ordered him to turn west, where Ayres was taking concentrated punishment from guns that bucked and fumed along that end of the gray line. Then he rode on after Crawford, who continued to drift into the northward vacuum, unaware of the battle raging ever farther in his rear.

Sheridan reacted fast. Over on the left and center, Custer and Devin surged forward on schedule, their clip-fed weapons raising a clatter that sounded to one observer "as if a couple of army corps had opened fire," while Crook stood by for the mounted pursuit that was to follow. Just now, however, their chief gave his attention to the infantry in trouble on the right. "Where's my battle flag?" he cried. Snatching the swallow-tailed guidon from its bearer, he spurred Rienzi into the confusion Ayres had encountered on his lonely approach to the fuming rebel flank. "Come on, men!" he shouted, brandishing his twin-starred banner along their cowered ranks, a prominent if diminutive target, high on his huge black horse amid twittering bullets. "Go at 'em with a will. Move on at a clean jump or you'll not catch one of them! They're all getting ready to run now, and if you don't get on to them in five minutes they'll every one get away from you." Converted by such assertiveness, the wavering troops responded by resuming their advance. It was as if he addressed them individually: as, indeed, he sometimes did. Just then a nearby skirmisher was struck in the throat, blood gushing from the severed jugular. "I'm killed," he moaned as his legs gave way. But Sheridan would not have it. "You're not hurt a bit," he told the fallen soldier. "Pick up your gun, man, and move right on to the front." Dazed but convinced, the skirmisher rose, clutching his rifle, and managed to take a dozen forward steps before he toppled over, dead beyond all doubt.

For all the certainty in his voice and manner while hoicking the laggards into line, Little Phil's assurance that the rebs were "ready to run" was based not on what he could discern beyond the flame-stabbed bank of smoke that boiled up from their breastworks (he could in fact see very little, even at close range) but rather on his conviction of what would happen once the blue machine got rolling in accordance with his orders. With close to three times as many troops, and well over half of them deployed as flankers, he had no doubt about the outcome — if only they could be brought to bear as he intended. Then suddenly they were. No sooner had Ayres resumed his stalled advance than the lead elements of Griffin's division, redirected west just now by Warren, began to come up on his right, overlapping the northward extension of the enemy works. "By God, that's what I want to see: general officers at the front!" Sheridan greeted a commander who rode at the head of his brigade. He put these late arrivers in line alongside Ayres, adding others as they came up in rapidly growing numbers, then ordered the attack pressed home, all out.

Still brandishing his red and white guidon, he was in the thick of the charge that shattered the rebel left, where more than a thousand prisoners were trapped within the confines of the angle. He leaped Rienzi over the works and landed amid a group of startled graybacks. Hands shot skyward in surrender all around him. "Whar do you want us-all to go to?" one asked, and he replied, suddenly conversational if not quite genial, grinning down at them: "Go right over there. Go right along now. Drop your guns; you'll never need them any more. You'll all be safe over there. Are there any more of you? We want every one of you fellows."

There were in fact a great many more such fellows to be gathered up. Devin — known as "Sheridan's hard hitter" — broke through in front, just west of the shattered angle, and Mackenzie, finding no reinforcements on the way from Lee, returned to assist in the round-up; Griffin was into the rebel rear, and so by now was Crawford, overtaken at last by Warren and hustled westward to arrive in time for a share in the butternut gleaning. All told, at a cost of 634 casualties, the V Corps took 3422 prisoners; while the dead, plus fugitives who slipped through the infantry dragnet only to be snagged by the wider-ranging Federal troopers, raised the Confederate total above 5000; more, even, than had been lost at Fort Stedman, a week ago today. Sheridan, though exhilarated, was far from satisfied. When a jubilant brigadier reported the capture of five rebel guns, he roared back at him: "I don't care a damn for their guns — or you either, sir! What I want is the Southside Railway." He said as much to the troops themselves as they crowded round him, cheering and waving their caps. "I want you men to understand we have a record to make before that sun goes down that will make hell tremble." He stood in his stirrups, pointing north toward the railroad three miles off. "I want you there!" he cried. Encountering Griffin beyond Five Forks, shortly after sunset at 6.20, he told him: "Get together all the men you can, and drive on while you can see your hand before you."

Griffin — crusty Griffin, whom Grant had advised Meade to place in arrest for insubordination on his second day over the Rapidan — now headed the V Corps. Warren, deep in the rebel rear with Crawford, corralling prisoners as they came streaming north across the fields and up Ford Road, had sent a staff colonel to inform headquarters of his whereabouts and his success in carrying out the flanking operation, only to have Sheridan scoff at the report. "By God, sir," he interrupted hotly, "tell General Warren he wasn't in that fight." Astonished, the colonel replied that he would dislike to deliver any such message verbally. Might he take it down in writing? "Take it down, sir!" Sheridan barked. "Tell him by God he was not at the front." Nor was that all. At their sundown meeting he formally notified Griffin that he was to take over in place of Warren, to whom a hastily scrawled field order soon was on its way: "Major General Warren, commanding the Fifth Army Corps, is relieved from duty, and will at once report for orders to Lieutenant General Grant, commanding Armies of the United States. By command of Major General Sheridan."

All the same, though he now felt he had an infantry chief he could depend on, he called off the pursuit he had been urging. In part this was because of the encumbrance of so many grayback prisoners that he used their discarded rifles to corduroy the worst stretches of road; but mainly it was because, on second thought — detached as he was from the rest of the army — he concentrated instead on bracing his victory-scattered troops for the counterattack Lee's opponents had long since learned to expect in such a crisis. Nightfall cooled his blood, and with it his temper, even to the point where he came close to a downright apology for some of the rough talk he had unloaded on subordinates today. "You know how it is," he told a group of V Corps officers gathered around a Five Forks campfire. "We had to carry this place, and I was fretted all day until it was done." None of this applied to their former chief, however, and he had said as much to Warren himself when the New Yorker rode up to headquarters in the gathering dusk and asked him to reconsider the order issued for his removal in the heat of battle. "Reconsider, hell," Sheridan snorted; "I don't reconsider my decisions. Obey the order."

Sedgwick, Burnside, Hancock, Warren: now all four of the men commanding infantry corps at the time of the Rapidan crossing had departed, the last under conditions not unlike those attending the removal of his predecessor Fitz-John Porter, with whom he had shared an admiration for George McClellan, rejected like them by the powers that were. Reporting as ordered to headquarters at Dabney's Mill about 10 o'clock that night, he found a celebration of Sheridan's victory in progress. Grant, he said later, "spoke very kindly of my past services and efforts," though the best he could do for him now, apparently, was put him in charge of the inactive City Point area, where he sat in the backwash while the guns boomed westward. . . . Warren began at once to press for a court of inquiry to right the hot-tempered wrong he believed had been done him today. He finally got it, fourteen years later, and after nearly three more years of hearings and deliberation he also received a measure of vindication by the court, which not only cleared him of Sheridan's charges that he had been negligent at Five Forks, but also criticized the manner of his relief. However, that came three months after Warren himself was in his grave. Buried, as he directed in his will, in civilian clothes and without military ceremony, he would in time stand fully accoutered in bronze on the crest of Little Round Top, where he had saved Meade and, some would say, the Union.

Back at Dabney's, before Warren's appearance put something of a damper on the scene, the victory celebration had been set off by Horace Porter's arrival from Five Forks about an hour after dark; he had sent couriers, but overtook the last and most joyously burdened of these in his haste to share the good news with his friends and fellow members of the staff. They were sitting around a blazing campfire — Grant among them, wrapped in a long blue overcoat and smoking his usual cigar — when the young colonel rode into the firelight, shouting from horseback of Sheridan's success. "For some minutes," he would recall, "there was a bewildering state of excitement, grasping of hands, tossing up of hats, and slapping of each other on the back. It meant the beginning of the end, the reaching of the 'last ditch.' It pointed to peace and home."

Only the general-in-chief remained seated, puffing stolidly at his cigar while Porter burbled of six guns captured along with thirteen rebel flags. "How many prisoners have been taken?" Grant asked. More than 5000, he was told. He rose, went into his tent, and began to write telegraphic dispatches by the flickering light of a candle. When these were done he gave them to an orderly for transmission, then came back out to resume his seat beside the fire. "I have ordered an immediate assault along the lines," he said.

★   ★   ★

Hearing before sunset of the reverse at Five Forks (though not of its extent, which would leave Pickett gunless by nightfall and unable to muster 2000 infantry in his shattered ranks next morning) Lee ordered Anderson to have Bushrod Johnson march his three remaining brigades at once to Sutherland Station, three miles north on the Southside Railroad, to combine with Pickett and Fitz Lee for the defense of that vital supply line and the even more vital Richmond & Danville, farther west. In partial compensation for this stripping of his right, and though the shift reduced by about 400 the number of defenders in A. P. Hill's two divisions east of Burgess Mill — already so thin-spread, one of them declared, that the pickets were "as far apart as telegraph poles" — he brought two of Heth's regiments across Hatcher's Run to patrol the empty works along the south bank of that stream. Still robbing Peter to pay Paul, when he returned to his headquarters near the Appomattox, two miles west of Petersburg, he wired Longstreet to bring Field's division south by rail tonight from beyond the James. That would leave only Kershaw's reduced division and Ewell's reservists to cover Richmond: a grave risk, but no graver than the one Lee ran in gambling that Grant would not launch an all-out southside attack before Old Peter arrived to help prevent the breaking of Hill's line. Situated as he was, his right flank turned and a deep river at his back, if he had known that Pickett's losses today, combined with those a week ago at Stedman, had cost him a solid fourth of his army, he probably would have evacuated Petersburg that night. Instead, he held on where he was, shifting and sidling his few troops to meet a crisis whose true dimensions were unknown to him, in hope of deferring his departure until such time — quite possibly tomorrow night — as would allow him to alert his subordinate commanders, not to mention the Richmond authorities, at least a few hours in advance.

In any case, having done what he could within his means to meet the problem caused by the loss of Five Forks, he turned in early, so weary that he only removed his boots and outer garments before lying down to sleep. It was as well; for he had no sooner rested his head on the pillow, shortly after 9 o'clock, than guns began to growl all up and down the long curve of Union works, possibly signifying that he would have to turn out in a hurry to meet what Grant had in mind to do when the bombardment lifted. Whatever it was, he hoped it would not come before Field arrived to chink the undermanned stretches of his line. At 1.45 (April 2 now, a Sunday, though dawn was three hours off) a sudden ripple of picket fire intensified the duller rumble of artillery. Awake or asleep, Lee may or may not have heard it, intermittent at first and then a rising clatter. Certainly A. P. Hill did, for he appeared at the Turnbull house, Lee's command post, about an hour before dawn. Disturbed by the weakness of his six-mile front along the Boydton Plank Road leading down to Burgess Mill — especially those portions of it whose outworks had been overrun by the Federals in reaction to Gordon's storming of Fort Stedman, eight days back — Little Powell had returned from sick leave yesterday, though he still was far from well. Unable to sleep tonight, what with the roar of cannons and the stutter of small-arms fire, he had ridden from his own headquarters, back on the outskirts of Petersburg, a mile and a half out Cox Road to the Turnbull house to inquire whether anyone there knew what the Yankees were up to in the rackety, flame-stabbed darkness out beyond his front.

Lee was awake, though still in bed, when Hill arrived, hazel eyes glittering feverishly above his auburn beard, high-set cheekbones hectic with the illness that had kept him from duty so much of the past year. Nearly two decades apart in age — one fifty-eight and looking it, prone beneath the bedclothes, the other eight months short of forty, slim and immaculately uniformed as always — the two generals began a discussion of what could be done if, as seemed likely from the step-up in the firing with the swift approach of dawn, a blue assault preceded Field's arrival from beyond the James. Then Longstreet entered, burly and imperturbable despite the persistent lameness of his sword arm from the bullet that had cut him down at the height of his Wilderness flank attack, just one month less than a year ago this week. His arrival, as commander of the reinforcements ordered southward in all haste, was encouraging until he explained that he and his staff had ridden ahead on horseback to save space on the crowded cars for Field's 4600 infantry. They were still on the way, so far as he knew, though he could not say how long it would be before the first of them reached Petersburg, let alone the front. Daylight was glimmering through by now, and Lee was indicating on a map the route he wanted these troops to take as soon as they detrained, when a staff colonel rushed into the room exclaiming that panicked teamsters were dashing their wagons "rather wildly" up the Cox Road past the Turnbull gate, apparently in flight from a Federal breakthrough somewhere down near Hatcher's Run. A wounded officer, hobbling back on crutches, had even told of being driven from his quarters more than a mile behind the center of Hill's line.

Alarmed — as well he might be, since this first word of a penetration also indicated the likelihood of a rout — Lee drew a wrapper around him and went to the front door. Sure enough, though swirls of ground fog obscured the color of their uniforms in the growing light, long lines of men resembling skirmishers were moving toward him from the southwest, the nearest of them not over half a mile away. Uncertain whether they were retreating Confederates or advancing Federals, he sent an aide to take a closer look. Just then, however, they halted as if in doubt, and as they did the quickening daylight showed their clothes were blue. Lee turned to Longstreet and told him to go at once to the Petersburg station and hurry Field's men westward, relay by relay, as fast as they unloaded from the cars. Then he turned to speak to Hill; but Hill was already running toward his horse, intent on reaching and rallying the troops in rear of his broken line. He mounted and rode south, accompanied by Sergeant G. W. Tucker, his favorite courier. Disturbed by something desperate in his fellow Virginian's manner — or perhaps because he had heard that during the recently interrupted sick leave, spent with kinsmen in a Richmond rife with rumors of impending evacuation, Little Powell had said he had no wish to survive the fall of the capital — Lee sent a staffer to caution Hill not to expose himself unduly.

Out front, across the open fields to the southwest, the line of bluecoats remained halted in a swale. Apparently made cautious by the activity in the Turnbull yard, they seemed to be waiting for reinforcements to come up before they continued their advance. Lee studied them briefly, then went into the house to finish dressing. When he reappeared, he wore his best gray uniform and had buckled on his sword. This last was so unusual that it occurred to at least one member of his staff that the general had decided to be in "full harness" in case he was obliged to surrender before the rising sun went down. In any event, he mounted Traveller and rode out for a closer examination of whatever calamity was at hand.

Piecemeal, in the absence of reports from subordinates who were too busy just then to do anything but fight to hang on where they were or hurry rearward to avoid capture, he managed to gather at least a notion of what had happened as a result of the massive three-corps blue assault launched at daybreak, 60,000 strong, against nearly the whole twelve miles of works, defended by less than one fourth that number, from the Appomattox down to Burgess Mill. On the left, east and directly south of Petersburg, Gordon's front-line troops were driven back on their inner fortifications by the force of Parke's attack. There they rallied, supported by Pendleton's reserve artillery, which Lee had massed in their rear the day before, and not only resisted all further efforts to dislodge them, but were counterattacking even now to recover the outworks they had lost. Southwest along the thinly manned stretch of Hill's line, whose forward positions had been overrun the week before, events took a different turn. Attacking from close up, one of Wright's three divisions broke through a single line of works defended by two of Wilcox's brigades. Swept from their trenches, these veterans fell back north through the soggy woods, firing as they went. Beyond the Boydton Plank Road — within two miles of the Turnbull house, where Lee was conferring with A. P. Hill and Longstreet — their pursuers fanned out to the left, southwest down the plank road toward Hatcher's Run, in rear of that part of the gray line under assault by Ord. Heth's division and the other half of Wilcox's, pressed in front and threatened from the rear, gave way in turn, withdrawing northwest up the left bank of the run, and Ord's and Wright's men followed for a time, then veered northeast into the angle between the Boydton Plank Road and Cox Road. These were the bluecoats Lee discerned through wisps of fog when he came to the Turnbull front door in his wrapper, and this was the breakthrough — the two breakthroughs, really — that had more or less abolished Hill's half dozen miles of line between Gordon's right and Hatcher's Run.

Fortunately for him, at this stage the attackers were about as disorganized by their sudden gains as his own troops were by their retreat. Straggling was heavy among the pursuers, and various units were intermingled, shaken loose from their regular order of battle and strung out in long lines like skirmishers. Their pause for realignment and the ensuing wait for reinforcements, at a time when absolutely nothing stood between them and his headquarters, gave Lee the chance to dress and mount Traveller for a first-hand study of the situation. Westward there was scattered firing, and a heavier clatter rolled in from the east, where the sun by now was rising over Petersburg, obscured by smoke from Pendleton's guns supporting Gordon in his fight to hold back Parke. Southward, however, there was an ominous silence along the lines where Ord and Wright had undone Heth and Wilcox. Riding toward the Turnbull gate for a look across the fields in that direction, Lee saw a group of horsemen turn in from the road: members of Hill's staff, he observed as they drew nearer, and then noted with a pang of apprehension that the man astride the corps commander's handsome dapple-gray was Sergeant Tucker. This could only mean that Hill was dead or wounded.

He was dead; Tucker, who had been with him when he fell, told how it happened. Proceeding south from the Turnbull house before sunrise, just short of the Boydton Plank Road they found Union soldiers cavorting among the huts the men of Mahone's division had occupied, as the army's one reserve, until they were detached and shifted north of the Appomattox to take over Pickett's position on Bermuda Hundred. This in itself showed the depth of the breakthrough, but Hill, skirting the celebration being staged a mile behind his lines, was determined to continue the search for his missing troops, even though all that could be seen in any direction were random groups of blue-clad stragglers from the attack that had swept this way and then moved on. Beyond the plank road he turned right, explaining that he hoped to reach Heth on the far side of the break that seemed to have made a clean sweep of Wilcox and all four of his brigades. The two rode west about a mile along a screening fringe of woods, through which from time to time they sighted still more clots of Federals on the prowl, but no Confederates at all. "Sergeant," Hill said at last, for the sense of danger grew as they proceeded, "should anything happen to me, you must go back to General Lee and report it." Tucker responded by taking the lead, and removed his navy Colt from its holster to be prepared for whatever loomed. Presently he drew rein, having spotted a squad-sized cluster of bluecoats in the woods directly ahead, the two closest of whom scuttled for shelter behind a large tree and extended their rifle barrels around its trunk, one above the other. "We must take them," Hill said, coming forward. But Tucker would not have it. "Stay there: I'll take them," he said, and shouted to the hidden pair, some twenty yards away: "If you fire you'll be swept to hell! Our men are here. Surrender." Beside him now, Hill too had drawn his pistol and held it at the ready. "Surrender!" he cried, his gauntleted left hand extended palm-out toward the two blue soldiers crouched behind their tree. "I can't see it," Tucker heard one of them say, and then: "Let's shoot them." One rifle had been lowered. Now it rose and both went off. A bullet whistled past the courier's head: but not past Little Powell's. Unhorsed, he lay sprawled and motionless on the ground, arms spread. Later, when his body was recovered, friends discovered that the bullet had passed through the gauntlet, cutting off his thumb, before it entered his heart and dropped him, dead perhaps before he struck the earth. Tucker dodged and grabbed the bridle of the riderless gray horse, spurring his own mount back the way they had come. Beyond range of the two soldiers — Corporal John W. Mauk and Private Daniel Wolford, stragglers from a Pennsylvania regiment in one of Wright's divisions — he changed to the faster horse and made good time, first to Hill's headquarters, then to Lee's, where he told and retold what had happened to his chief, back there amid the wreckage of what had been his rear until this morning.

Lee's eyes brimmed with tears. "He is at rest now, and we who are left are the ones to suffer," he said on learning thus of his loss of fiery, high-strung Little Powell, the hard-hitting embodiment of his army's offensive spirit and the one troop commander Stonewall Jackson had called on in his last delirium, back in the days when that spirit burned its brightest. "Go at once, Colonel, and get Mrs Hill and her children across the Appomattox," he told the Third Corps chief of staff, adding: "Break the news to her as gently as possible."

As it turned out, there was no gentle way to break such news. Hesitating at the front door of the cottage she and Hill and their two small daughters had shared on an estate near Petersburg, the staffer could hear the unsuspecting widow singing as she went about her housework. He entered without knocking, hoping to spare her so abrupt a summons. But when Mrs Hill — John Morgan's younger sister Kitty, auburn-haired like the husband she did not yet know had fallen, though she had learned to live with apprehension of such loss throughout the nearly four years of her marriage — heard his slow footsteps in the hall, then turned and saw him, the singing stopped. "The general is dead," she said in a strained voice, numbed by shock. "You would not be here unless he was dead."

Back at the Turnbull house by then, Lee had begun planning to do for his southside units what he had told the colonel to do for Hill's widow and children; that is, get them over the Appomattox before the victory-flustered Union host completed its mission of cutting them off from a crossing. Tucker's account of all that he and his chief had seen, en route to their encounter with the two blue stragglers in rear of the crumpled right, was enough to convince him that the time had come — if, indeed, it was not already past — for him to order the evacuation not only of Petersburg but also of Richmond. Beyond Burgess Mill, Humphreys by now had added a fourth corps to the general assault, and Sheridan was reported driving north and east with his and Griffin's men, lifting the total to six full corps, any one of which had more troops on its roster than Lee had in all on this side of Hatcher's Run, including those in flight. Moreover, this would continue to be the case until Field arrived: if, in fact, he did arrive in time to stop or hinder Wright and Ord, whose buildup southwest of headquarters had continued to the point where they seemed ready to resume their stalled advance, unopposed by anything more than Lee and his staff and a single battery of guns just unlimbered in the Turnbull yard.

Around 10 o'clock, firing over the heads of infantry massing for attack, Federal gunners ended the providential four-hour lull by opening on the battery and the house itself. Before disconnecting the telegraph for departure, Lee dictated a series of dispatches to the Secretary of

War, the President, and Ewell, who had taken over from Longstreet north of the James. "I see no prospect of doing more than holding our position here till night. I am not certain that I can do that. If I can I shall withdraw tonight north of the Appomattox, and if possible it will be better to withdraw the whole line tonight from James River." This was the message to Breckinridge, ending summarily: "I advise that all preparation be made for leaving Richmond tonight." The one to Davis added that he was sending "an officer to Your Excellency to explain the routes by which the troops will be moved," as well as "a guide and any assistance that you may require." Ewell in turn was cautioned to "make all preparations quietly and rapidly to abandon your position.... Have your field transportation ready and your troops prepared for battle or marching orders, as circumstances may require."

But the time was short. When Lee came out again into the yard, where the gray cannoneers were getting badly knocked about in the process of limbering their pieces for withdrawal, a shell tore over his head and into the house, starting fires that soon would leave only four tall chimneys standing where his headquarters had been. "This is a bad business," he remarked as he mounted for the ride to find shelter in the inner fortifications, which Field's troops were to man when they arrived. Still, he waited for the guns to complete their displacement before he set out eastward, trailed by his staff. He rode at a walk, not looking back until a shell exploded close behind him, disemboweling a horse. Others followed rapidly, now that the enemy gunners had the range, and an officer riding beside him watched as Lee reacted to what he evidently considered a highly personal affront. "He turned his head over his right shoulder, his cheeks became flushed, and a sudden flash of the eye showed with what reluctance he retired before the fire directed upon him." Rearward he saw blue infantry moving out ahead of the bucking guns, their rifle barrels gleaming in the sunlight. Suppressing his defiance, if not his anger, he gave Traveller the spur and rode on nearly a mile to the thinly-held works about the same distance west of Petersburg. "Well, Colonel," he said to one of his staff as he drew rein, "it has happened as I told them it would at Richmond. The line has been stretched until it has broken."

These inner fortifications, where he and his staff took refuge from the shells that pursued them on their ride, were the so-far unused western portion of the old Dimmock Line, other parts of whose original half-oval had been put to such good use in June. Beauregard then had been grievously outnumbered, but Lee's predicament now was even worse. East and south, on the far side of town, Gordon had all he could do to hold off Parke, and Field's veterans had not yet appeared. The few garrison troops available to man this empty stretch of works extending from Gordon's hard-pressed right, northward a mile and a half to the Appomattox, were scarcely enough to delay, let alone prevent, a breakthrough by Ord and Wright, whose renewed advance, if undeterred, would end the war in the streets of Petersburg before the midday sun went down. Lee's hope, pending Field's arrival, was in two small earthworks under construction out the Boydton Plank Road, half a mile in front of the main line; Fort Gregg and Battery Whitworth, they were called. Less than a quarter-mile apart and mutually supporting, they were occupied by four slim regiments from Nathaniel Harris's Mississippi brigade — some 400 men in all, left on line when the rest of Mahone's division was shifted north — together with about a hundred North Carolinians, fugitives cut off from Wilcox by the collapse of his left center. Harris put just under half his troops into Gregg, along with two of his five guns, and took the rest with him to Whitworth, 300 yards north of the plank road. A Natchez-born former Vicksburg lawyer, thirty years old, he passed Lee's orders to Gregg's defenders when he left. "Men," he told them, shouting above the uproar of the opening cannonade, "the salvation of the army is in your keep. Don't surrender this fort. If you can hold out for two hours, Longstreet will be up." Behind him, as he turned to go, he heard someone call out after him: "Tell them we'll not give up."

It was noon by now, and presently they showed that they meant what their spokesman said, and more. Given the reduction assignment, Ord passed it along to John Gibbon and the two 6000-man divisions he had brought southside from his XXIV Corps, one against each of the outworks, intending to overrun them in short order. The attack on Whitworth was delayed by a wait for some huts set afire by the rebels to burn out in its front, but the one on Gregg was launched promptly at 1 o'clock, as soon as the bombardment lifted. A brigade in each, the advance was in three columns, which converged as they drew near the objective. Hit by massed volleys, they fell back in some disorder to reform, and then came on again; only to have the same thing happen. "In these charges," a defender would recall, "there was no shooting but by us, and we did cruel and savage work with them." Between attempts, observers back on the Confederate main line, where Field's leading elements were at last beginning to file into the trenches, heard faint cheering from the fort, as well as from Battery Whitworth, still not under immediate pressure. Lee watched from a high vantage point: as did Longstreet, who thought he recognized his old friend Gibbon when he studied the close-packed attackers through his glasses. "[I] raised my hat," he later wrote, "but he was busy and did not see me."

Gibbon was indeed busy, having learned by now that the only way he was going to reduce the two-gun earthwork was by swamping it. Fortunately he had the men, and the men themselves were willing. He brought down a brigade from the division standing idle in front of Whitworth, thus increasing the assault force to 8000, and sent them forward, no longer in successive waves but in a single flood. Inside the place, wounded graybacks loaded rifles taken from the dead and dying, and passed them up to rapid-firing marksmen perched atop the walls. Still the attackers came on, taking their losses to sweep past the flanks and into the rear of the uncompleted installation. Near the end, a butternut captain noted, "The battle flags of the enemy made almost a solid line of bunting around the fort. The noise was fearful, frightful, indescribable. The curses and groaning of frenzied men could be heard over the din of our musketry. Savage men, ravenous beasts — we felt there was no hope for us unless we could keep them at bay. We were prepared for the worst, and expected no quarter." Tumbling over the parapets, sometimes onto the lifted bayonets of the defenders, the Federals gained the interior, and there the struggle continued, hand to hand. One gun was out by then, but the other, trained on the still-advancing bluecoats on the far side of the ditch, was double shotted with canister, its lanyard held taut by a single cannoneer. "Don't fire that gun! Drop the lanyard or we'll shoot!" the attackers yelled, their rifles leveled at him. "Shoot and be damned!" he shouted back, leaning on the lanyard. Canister plowed the ranks out front, and the cannoneer, riddled with bullets, sprawled dead across the trail of the smoking gun.

For another twenty minutes the fight continued at close quarters with clubbed muskets, rammer staffs, and any weapons that were handy, including brickbats from a toppled chimney. By the time it ended, Gibbon's loss of 122 killed and 592 wounded more than tripled the rebel garrison of 214 men, of whom 55 were dead, 129 wounded — 86 percent — and only 30 surrendered uninjured. Northward, their flank exposed by Gregg's collapse and the huts at last burned out in front, Whitworth's defenders scuttled rearward, losing about 60 captives in the final rush by Gibbon's other division's other two brigades. By then it was just after 3 o'clock. Harris's Mississippians and the Tarheel fugitives had given Lee the two hours he asked of them, plus still another for good measure.

Something else they gave as well: an example for Field's veterans, now on line, to follow when and if the Federals tried to continue their advance: which they did not. "The enemy, not finding us inclined to give way for him," Field afterwards reported, "contented himself with forming line in front of us, but out of range. We stood thus in plain view of each other till night, when the army began its retreat."

While the contest for Gregg was in progress Lee and his staff worked on plans for the removal that night of the divided army, northward over the Appomattox and southward over the James, and its subsequent concentration at Amelia Courthouse on the Richmond & Danville, forty miles west-northwest and west-southwest, respectively, of Petersburg and the capital. From there, reunited for the first time since Cold Harbor, ten months back, the command was to follow the line of the railroad, via Burkeville, for a combination with Joe Johnston some-where beyond Danville, which was just over a hundred miles from Amelia. What Grant would do with his greatly superior force, by way of interfering with this proposed march of a hundred and fifty miles or more, depended in part on how much of a head start Lee managed to gain between nightfall and daylight — at the latest — when the Union lookouts woke to find him gone. Accordingly: "The movement of all troops will commence at 8 o'clock," the evacuation order read, "the artillery moving out quietly first, infantry following, except the pickets, who will be withdrawn at 3 a.m." Copies went to Longstreet and Gordon, close at hand, to Ewell in Richmond and Mahone on the Bermuda Hundred line, and to Anderson, who was instructed to collect the shattered remnants of Pickett's, Johnson's, Heth's, and Wilcox's divisions beyond Hatcher's Run, cut off from Petersburg by the enemy now astride the Southside Railroad east of Sutherland Station.

Except for his anger at the Federals for their shelling of the Turn-bull house that morning, the southern commander kept his temper all through this long and trying day; save once. This once was when he received a wire from Davis in the capital, protesting that "to move tonight will involve the loss of many valuables, both for the want of time to pack and of transportation. Arrangements are progressing," the President added, however, "and unless you otherwise advise, the start will be made." Lee bristled at the implied rebuke — perhaps forgetting that five days ago he had promised Breckinridge a ten- or twelve-day warning — and ripped the telegram to pieces. "I am sure I gave him sufficient notice," he said testily, and dictated a reply that left no doubt whatever about his intentions: "I think it is absolutely necessary that we should abandon our position tonight. I have given all necessary orders on the subject to the troops, and the operation, though difficult, I hope will be performed successfully."

It was, and on schedule. Less than an hour after dark, Pendleton, close in rear of the Second Corps, began withdrawing the reserve artil-lery through the cobbled streets of Petersburg and then across the Ap-pomattox bridges, followed by other batteries from all parts of the line. Field's First Corps division led the infantry displacement under Longstreet, who had also been put in charge of those Third Corps units cut off east of this morning's breakthrough. Assigned the rear-guard duty, Gordon pulled his three divisions back in good order, with little need for stealth and none at all for silence, since any noise his departing soldiers made was drowned by the nightlong roar of Union guns, firing all-out in apparent preparation for another dawn assault; an assault which, if made at all, would be made upon a vacuum. Beyond the river, approaching a road junction whose left fork Longstreet had taken to ease the crowding when his own corps took the right, Gordon came upon Lee, dismounted and holding Traveller's rein in one gauntleted hand. All the troops left in Petersburg at sundown — fewer than 15,000 of all arms — would pass this way, and the gray-bearded commander had chosen this as his post for supervising the final stage of the evacuation. About the same number of graybacks were in motion elsewhere, miles away in the chilly early-April darkness. Kershaw was with Ewell up in Richmond, withdrawing too by then, along with reservists from the capital fortifications, guncrews from the heavy batteries on James River, and even a battalion of sailors, homeless landsmen now that they had burned their ships to keep them out of enemy hands. Mahone was on the march from Bermuda Hundred, just to the north, and Anderson presumably was working his way west along the opposite bank of the Appomattox with the remnants of Johnson's and Pickett's divisions, as well as parts of Hill's two, driven in that direction by the collapse of his line at daybreak, and Fitz Lee's troopers. South of the river, from point to scattered point along the otherwise empty eight-mile curve of intrenchments, the pickets kept their shell-jarred vigil. Soon now they too would be summoned rearward and engineer details would carry out their work of demolition, first on the abandoned powder magazines and then on the bridges, which were to be fired when the last man crossed, leaving Petersburg to the bluecoats who, at a cost of well over 40,000 casualties, had been doing all they could to take it for the past two hundred and ninety-three days.

Lee did not wait for that. About an hour before midnight, having observed that both gray columns were well closed up as they slogged past him there in the fork of the two roads, he mounted and set out westward for Amelia Courthouse, just under forty miles away.

By that time, up in the capital, Davis and his cabinet were departing from the railway station where, two nights ago, he had seen his wife and children off for Charlotte, three hundred miles to the southwest. His own destination was Danville, half as far away, just short of the North Carolina line. That was to be the new seat of government at least until Lee and his army got there, en route to a combination with Johnston; at which time another shift would no doubt be required, though how far and in what direction — still within or else beyond the borders of the Old Dominion, every vestige of whose "sacred soil" would in the latter case be given over to the invader — no one could say at this stage of a crisis that had become acute some twelve hours earlier, when a War Department messenger brought to the presidential pew in St Paul's Church, midway through the morning service, Lee's telegram advising that "all preparation be made for leaving Richmond tonight."

Nearby worshipers saw "a sort of gray pallor creep over his face" as he read the dispatch, then watched him rise and stride back down the aisle "with stern set lips and his usual quick military tread." Some few rose to follow, knowing the summons must be urgent for him to leave before taking Communion this first-Sunday; but for the most part, he said later, "the congregation of St Paul's was too refined to make a scene at anticipated danger." He went directly to the War Office to confer with Breckinridge and other cabinet members available at short notice on the Sabbath. One such was Judah Benjamin, who strolled over from his quarters on North Main, apparently unperturbed, "his pleasant smile, his mild Havana, and the very twirl of his slender gold-headed cane contributing to give casual observers an expression of casual confidence."

Davis's manner was almost as calm, though by no means as debonair, as he told the assembled ministers of the breaking of Lee's line and the impending evacuation, then directed them to have their most valuable records packed for delivery to the Richmond & Danville Depot, where they would meet that evening for departure as a group. Special instructions for the Treasury Department covered the boxing of Confederate funds on hand — some $528,000 in double-eagle gold pieces, Mexican silver coins, gold and silver bricks and ingots — for shipment aboard a special train, with a guard of sixty midshipmen from their academy training vessel *Patrick Henry*. These last would of course be furnished by Mallory, who was also told to pass the word for Raphael Semmes to see to the destruction of this and all other ships of the James River Squadron, iron and wood; after which their crews would proceed to Danville for service under Lee.

Later that afternoon, his desk cleared and his office put in order for tomorrow's faceless blue-clad occupant — Grant himself, for all he knew, or whoever else would command the occupation force — Davis set out through Capitol Square for the last of his familiar homeward walks to the White House, where he still had to pack for the journey south. More people were abroad today than usual, but they were strangely quiet, shocked by rumors that they and their city were about to be abandoned to the foe. Asked if it was true, he replied that it was, adding however that he hoped to return under better auspices. Some wept at the news, while others replaced false hope with resolution. "If the success of the cause requires you to give up Richmond, we are content," one matron came out of her house to tell him as he walked by, and he afterwards declared that "the affection and confidence of this noble people in the hour of disaster were more distressing to me than complaint and unjust censure would have been."

At the mansion there was much to do, including the disposition of certain effects he could not take with him yet did not want to have fall into enemy hands: the family cow, for instance, lent by a neighbor and now returned: a favorite easy chair, which he had carted to Mrs R. E. Lee's home on Franklin Street with a message expressing hope that it would comfort her arthritis: an oil painting, "Heroes of the Valley," and a marble bust of Davis himself, both turned over to a friend who offered to put them where "they will never be found by a Yankee." While a servant packed his valise he gave final instructions to the housekeeper, emphasizing that everything must be in decent order, swept and dusted, when the Federals arrived to take possession tomorrow morning. This done, he dressed carefully — trousers and waistcoat of Confederate gray, a dark Prince Albert frock coat, polished Wellingtons, a full-brimmed planter's hat — brushed his hair and tuft of beard, and waited in his pale-rugged private office — long the terror of muddy-booted officers reporting from the field — for word that the special train was ready for boarding. Shortly after 8 o'clock it came. He went out the front door and down the steps, mounted his saddle horse Kentucky, and set out for the railway station beside the James on the far side of town.

The ride was just over half a mile through crowded streets, and his impressions now were very different from those he had received four hours ago, in the course of his walk home from Capitol Square. Numbed decorum had given way to panic, a hysteria that grew more evident as he drew near the river and the depot. Government warehouses stocked with rations for the anticipated siege were there, and word had spread that the food was to be distributed to the public, on a first-come first-served basis, before the buildings were destroyed along with whatever remained in them by the time the army left. Some among those gathered were marauders out for spoils in the business district, their number swollen by convicts who, deserted by their guards, had broken out of jail and were rifling shops for clothing to replace their prison garb; "a crowd of leaping, shouting demons," one observer called these last, "in parti-colored clothes and with heads half-shaven. . . . Many a heart which had kept its courage to this point quailed at the sight." All in all, another witness would declare, this was "the saddest of many of the sad sights of war — a city undergoing pillage at the hands of its own mob, while the standards of an empire were being taken from its capitol and the tramp of a victorious enemy could be heard at its gates." Davis rode on, forcing his way through the throng, and finally reached the station. There the cabinet awaited his arrival; all but Breckinridge, who would remain behind to supervise the final stages of the evacuation, then follow Lee to observe and report on the military situation before rejoining his colleagues at Danville, or wherever they might be by then.

All got aboard the waiting coach, but there was another long delay while the treasure train, preceding them with its cargo of precious metals and its sixty nattily-uniformed midshipmen, cleared the southbound track and the bridge across the James. Glum but resigned, the ministers took their seats on the dusty plush. Trenholm, down with neuralgia and attended by his wife, the only woman in the party, had brought along a demijohn of peach brandy, presumably for medicinal purposes though it helped to ease the tension all around: especially for Benjamin, who smiled in his curly beard as he spoke from his fund of historical examples of other national causes that had survived reverses even more dismal than the one at hand. Mallory however remained somber, aware that the flotilla he had improvised for the capital's defense — three small ironclads and half a dozen wooden vessels — would be abolished, by his own orders, before dawn. By contrast, Attorney General George Davis was limited to theoretical regrets, his department having existed only on paper from the outset: and paper, unlike ships, could be replaced. Finally, at 11 o'clock — as Lee headed Traveller west from the road-fork on the near side of the Appomattox, twenty miles to the south — the train creaked out of the station. While the gaslit flare of Richmond faded rearward beyond the river, the fleeing President could reflect on the contrast between his departure tonight and his arrival, four bright springs ago, when the city had been festooned with flowers to bid him welcome. Whatever he was thinking, though, he kept his thoughts to himself. So did John Reagan, the selfmade Texan who had kept the mail in motion, if not on time, throughout the shrinking Confederacy all those years. He chewed morosely at his habitual quid, a colleague would recall, "whittling a stick down to the little end of nothing without ever reaching a satisfactory point."

Behind them as the train crept southward, worn wheels clacking on worn track, Richmond trembled for the last time from the tramp of gray-clad soldiers through her streets; Ewell was leaving, and only a cavalry rear guard, a small brigade of South Carolina troopers, stood between the city and some 20,000 bluecoats confronting the unmanned fortifications north of the James. On their way through town, demolition squads set fire to tobacco warehouses near the river, while others stood by to put the torch to buildings stocked with munitions of all kinds. City officials protested, but to no avail; the army had its orders, and no ranking member of the government was available to appeal to, all having left by midnight except John A. Campbell, who was not available either; he had last been seen at sundown, talking rapidly to himself as he walked along 9th Street with two books under his arm. A south wind sprang up, spreading flames from the burning tobacco, and soon the great waterside flour mills were on fire. Around 2 o'clock, a huge explosion jolted the city with the blowing of a downstream magazine, followed presently by another, closer at hand, that shattered plate glass windows all over Shockoe Hill. This last was a sustained eruption, volcano-like in its violence, for its source was the national arsenal, reported to contain 750,000 loaded projectiles, which continued to go off for hours. "The earth seemed fairly to writhe as if in agony," a diarist recorded; "the house rocked like a ship at sea, while stupendous thunders roared around." When the three ironclads went, near Rocketts Landing shortly afterward, Semmes pronounced the spectacle "grand beyond description," especially the one produced by his flagship, C.S.S. *Virginia Number 2*. "The explosion of her magazine threw all the shells, with their fuses lighted, into the air. The fuses were of different lengths, and as the shells exploded by twos and threes, and by the dozen, the pyrotechnic effect was very fine." By then both railway bridges were long lines of fire, reflected in the water that ran beneath them. Only Mayo's Bridge remained, kept open for the rear guard, though barrels of tar were stacked at intervals along it, surrounded by pine knots for quick combustion when the time came. At last it did. Shortly after dawn, having seen the last of his troopers across, the South Carolina brigadier rode out onto the span and touched his hat to the engineer in charge. "All over. Goodbye. Blow her to hell," he said, and trotted on.

From where he stood, looking back across the river at the holocaust in progress along Richmond's waterfront, a butternut horseman afterwards observed, "The old war-scarred city seemed to prefer annihilation to conquest." What was more, she appeared well on the way toward achieving it. Both the Haxall and Gallego mills, reportedly the largest in the world, were burning fiercely, gushing smoke and darting tongues of flame from their hundreds of windows, while beyond them, after spreading laterally the better part of a mile from 8th to 18th streets, the fire licked northward from Canal to Cary, then on to Main, dispossessing residents and driving looters from the shops. Within this "vista of desolation," known henceforward as "the burnt district," practically everything was consumed, including two of the capital's three newspaper offices and plants. Only the *Richmond Whig* survived to continue the long-term verbal offensive against the departed government. "If there lingered in the hearts of our people one spark of affection for the Davis dynasty," its editor would presently declare, "this ruthless, useless, wanton handing over to the flames [of] their fair city, their homes and altars, has extinguished it forever." But that was written later, under the once-dread Union occupation. Just now, with the Confederate army gone and the fire department unequal to even a fraction of the task at hand, the only hope of stopping or containing the spread of destruction lay with the besiegers out on the city's rim, who perhaps would restore order when they arrived: if, indeed, they arrived in time for there to be anything left to save.

They barely did, thanks to the lack of opposition and an urgent plea by the mayor himself that they not delay taking over. From near the crest of Chimborazo, easternmost of Richmond's seven hills, a hospital matron watched the first of the enemy infantry approach. "A single bluejacket rose over the hill, standing transfixed with astonishment at what he saw. Another and another sprang up, as if out of the earth, but still all remained quiet. About 7 o'clock there fell upon the ear the steady clatter of horses' hoofs, and winding around Rocketts came a small and compact body of Federal cavalry in splendid condition, riding closely and steadily along." At that distance she did not perceive that the enemy troopers were black, but she did see, moving out the road at the base of the hill to meet them, a rickety carriage flying a white flag. In it was eighty-year-old Mayor Joseph Mayo. Dressed meticulously, as another witness remarked, "in his white cravat and irrepressible ruffles, his spotless waistcoat and his blue, brass-buttoned coat," he had set out from Capitol Square with two companions to urge the invaders to hasten their march, which he hoped would end with their bringing the mob and the fire under control, and he took with him, by way of authentication, a small leather-bound box containing the seal of the city he intended to surrender.

About that time — already some eight hours behind schedule, with other delays to follow — the presidential special crossed the Roanoke River and rolled creakily into Clover Station, two thirds of the way to Danville. A young lieutenant posted there had watched the treasure train go through at daybreak, loaded with bullion and cadets, and now came the one with the Chief Executive and his ministers aboard, all obviously feeling the strain of a jerky, sleepless night. "Mr Davis sat at a car window. The crowd at the station cheered. He smiled and acknowledged their compliment, but his expression showed physical and mental exhaustion." Finally the engine chuffed on down the track and over Difficult Creek, drawing its brief string of coaches and boxcars. Others followed at various intervals. Increasingly as they went by, jammed to overflowing with the archives and employees of the Treasury Department, Post Office, and Bureau of War, the conviction grew in the young officer that all, or nearly all, was lost; "I saw a government on wheels." Moreover, as he watched the passage of car after car, burdened with "the marvelous and incongruous débris of the wreck of the Confederate capital," it seemed to him that each grew more bizarre in its contents than the one before — as if whoever was loading them was getting closer and closer to the bottom of some monstrous grab bag. "There were very few women on these trains, but among the last in the long procession were trains bearing indiscriminate cargoes of men and things. In one car was a cage with an African parrot, and a box of tame squirrels, and a hunchback! Everybody, not excepting the parrot, was wrought up to a pitch of intense excitement." Then at last, near midday, the final train passed through. "Richmond's burning. Gone; all gone!" a man called from the rear platform, and it occurred to the lieutenant that Clover Station, within forty miles of the Carolina line, "was now the northern outpost of the Confederacy."

This was to discount or overlook Lee, whose army was even then making its way west from Richmond and Petersburg to converge on Amelia Courthouse, sixty miles back up the track. Davis, when he reached Danville in the midafternoon, did not make that mistake. Weary though he was — the normal four-hour run had taken just four times that long, and sleep had been impossible, what with the cinders and vibration, not to mention the crowds at all the many stops along the way — he had no sooner established headquarters in a proffered residence on Main Street than he set out on an inspection tour of the nearly four-year-old intrenchments rimming the town. Finding them "as faulty in location as in construction," he said later, "I promptly proceeded to correct the one and improve the other." So far, despite anxious inquiries, he had heard nothing of or from the general-in-chief, yet he was determined to do all he could to prepare for his arrival, not only by strengthening the fortifications Lee's men were expected to occupy around Danville, but also by collecting food and supplies with which to feed and refit them when they got there. "The design, as previously arranged with General Lee," he afterwards explained, "was that, if he should be compelled to evacuate Petersburg, he would proceed to Danville, make a new defensive line of the Dan and Roanoke rivers, unite his army with the troops in North Carolina, and make a combined attack upon Sherman. If successful," Davis went on, "it was expected that reviving hope would bring reinforcements to the army, and Grant being then far removed from his base of supplies, and in the midst of a hostile population, it was thought we might return, drive him from the soil of Virginia, and restore to the people a government deriving its authority from their consent."

Although this was unquestionably a great deal to hope or even wish for, it was by no means out of proportion to his needs; that is, if he and the nation he represented were to survive the present crisis. He went to bed that night, still with no word from Lee or any segment of his army, and woke Tuesday morning, April 4, to find that none had come in, either by wire or by courier, while he slept. Around midday Raphael Semmes arrived with 400 crewmen from the scuttled James flotilla; Davis made him a brigadier, reorganized his sailors into an artillery brigade, and put him in charge of the Danville fortifications, with orders to defend and improve them pending Lee's arrival from Amelia, one hundred miles to the northeast. This done, he retired to his office to compose a proclamation addressed "To the People of the Confederate States of America," calling on them to rally for the last-ditch struggle now so obviously at hand.

"It would be unwise, even if it were possible, to conceal the great moral as well as material injury to our cause that must result from the occupation of Richmond by the enemy." He admitted as much from the outset, but promptly added: "It is equally unwise and unworthy of us, as patriots engaged in a most sacred cause, to allow our energies to falter, our spirits to grow faint, or our efforts to become relaxed under reverses, however calamitous. . . . It is for us, my countrymen, to show by our bearing under reverses how wretched has been the self-deception

of those who have believed us less able to endure misfortune with fortitude than to encounter danger with courage." Squaring his shoulders
for the test to come, he urged his compatriots to do likewise. "We have
now entered upon a new phase of the struggle, the memory of which is
to endure for all ages and to shed an increasing luster upon our country.
Relieved from the necessity of guarding cities and particular points, important but not vital to our defense; with an army free to move from point
to point and strike in detail the garrisons and detachments of the enemy;
operating in the interior of our own country, where supplies are more
accessible and where the foe will be far removed from his own base and
cut off from all succor in case of reverse, nothing is now needed to
render our triumph certain but the exhibition of our own unquenchable
resolve. Let us but will it, and we are free — and who, in the light of
the past, dare doubt your purpose in the future?" He asked that, then
continued. "Animated by that confidence in your spirit and fortitude
which never yet has failed me, I announce to you, fellow countrymen,
that it is my purpose to maintain your cause with my whole heart and
soul; that I will never consent to abandon to the enemy one foot of the
soil of any one of the States of the Confederacy. . . . If by stress of numbers we should ever be compelled to a temporary withdrawal from
[Virginia's] limits, or those of any other border State, again and again
will we return, until the baffled and exhausted enemy shall abandon in
despair his endless and impossible task of making slaves of a people
resolved to be free. Let us not then despond, my countrymen, but,
relying on the never-failing mercies and protecting care of our God, let
us meet the foe with fresh defiance, with unconquered and unconquerable hearts."

Davis himself said later that the appeal had been "over-sanguine"
in its expression of what he called his "hopes and wishes" for deliverance;
but to most who read it, South as well as North, the term was all too
mild. To speak of the present calamitous situation as "a new phase of the
struggle," which ultimately would result in the withdrawal of Grant's
"baffled and exhausted" armies, seemed now — far more than two
months ago, when Aleck Stephens applied the words to Davis's speech
in Metropolitan Hall — "little short of demention," if indeed it was
short at all. However, this was to ignore the alternative which to Davis
was unthinkable. He was no readier to submit, or even consider submission, than he had been when fortune's scowl was a broad smile. Now
as in the days when he played Hezekiah to Lincoln's Sennacherib, he
went about his duties as he saw them, his lips no less firmly set, his
backbone no less rigid.

Mainly, once the proclamation had been composed and issued,
those duties consisted of overseeing the pick-and-shovel work Brigadier
Admiral Semmes's landlocked sailors were doing on the fortifications
Lee and his men were to occupy when they arrived from Amelia. In the

two days since his and their abandonment of Petersburg and Richmond, there had been no news of them whatever. Davis could only wait, as he had done so often before, for some word of their progress or fate, which was also his.

★ ★ ★

Lincoln spent the better part of that Tuesday in the capital Davis had left two nights ago, and slept that night aboard a warship just off Rocketts Landing, where he had stepped ashore within thirty hours of the arrival of the first blue-clad troops to enter the city in four years. The two-mile walk that followed, from the landing to the abandoned presidential mansion — Weitzel had set up headquarters there, as chief of occupation, less than twelve hours after Davis's departure — was a fitting climax to three days of mounting excitement that began soon after sundown, April 1, when he learned of Sheridan's coup at Five Forks. "He has carried everything before him," Grant wired, exulting over the taking of "several batteries" and "several thousand" prisoners. Other trophies included a bundle of captured flags, which he sent to City Point that evening by a special messenger. Lincoln was delighted. "Here is something material," he said as he unfurled the shot-torn rebel colors; "something I can see, feel, and understand. This means victory. This *is* victory."

Mrs Lincoln had left for Washington that morning, frightened by a dream of her husband's that the White House was on fire, and Lincoln, perhaps feeling lonesome, had decided to sleep on board Porter's flagship *Malvern*, a converted blockade runner. As a result, having declined the admiral's offer of his own commodious quarters, he spent an uncomfortable night in a six- by four-foot cubicle whose built-in bunk was four inches shorter than he was. Asked next morning how he had slept, he replied somewhat ruefully: "You can't put a long blade into a short scabbard. I was too long for that berth." In the course of the day — Sunday, April 2 — Porter had the ship's carpenter take down the miniature stateroom and rebuild it, together with the bed and mattress, twice as wide and half a foot longer. Lincoln however knew nothing of this; he was up at the telegraph office, reading and passing along to Stanton in Washington a series of high-spirited messages from the general-in-chief. Lee's line had been shattered in several places; Grant was closing in on what remained; "All looks remarkably well," the general wired at 2 o'clock, and followed this with a 4.30 dispatch — Fort Gregg and Battery Whitworth had just been overrun — announcing that "captures since the army started out will not amount to less than 12,000 men and probably 50 pieces of artillery." He had no doubt he would take Petersburg next morning, and he urged the President to "come out and pay us a visit." Lincoln replied: "Allow me to tender to you, and all with you, the nation's grateful thanks for this additional and magnificent success. At your kind suggestion, I think I will visit you tomorrow."

Back aboard the *Malvern* after dark, he and Porter watched from her deck the flash of guns against the sky to the southwest, where Grant had ordered a dawn assault if Lee was still in Petersburg by then. "Can't the navy do something now to make history?" Lincoln asked, unsated by the daylong flow of good news from the front. The admiral pointed out that the fleet had quite enough to do in standing by to counter a downriver sally by the Richmond flotilla, but he did send instructions for all the ships above Dutch Gap to open on the rebel forts along both banks of the James. Presently the northwest sky was aglow with flashes too, and Lincoln, his impatience relieved to some degree, turned in for another presumably fitful sleep in the cramped quarters he did not yet know had been enlarged. Next morning, rising early and well rested, he announced that a miracle had happened in the night. "I shrunk six inches in length, and about a foot sideways," he told Porter, straight-faced.

Their laughter was interrupted by a dispatch Lincoln passed along to Stanton at 8 o'clock: "Grant reports Petersburg evacuated, and he is confident Richmond also is. He is pushing forward to cut off, if possible, the retreating army. I start to join him in a few minutes." Accompanied by Tad and a civilian White House guard, he also took Porter with him on the train ride to the outskirts of Petersburg, where Robert was waiting with an escort and horses for them to ride the rest of the way. Tightly shuttered, the town seemed deserted except for a few Negroes on the roam amid the wreckage; Robert explained that Meade had been told to leave only a single division in occupation while he pressed on after Lee with all the rest. Proceeding up Market Street, the riders came to a house where Grant was waiting on the porch. A staffer watched as the President "dismounted and came in through the gate with long and rapid strides, his face beaming." Grant rose and met him on the steps. When they had shaken hands and exchanged congratulations, Lincoln said with a smile: "Do you know, General, I have had a sort of a sneaking idea for some days that you intended to do something like this." Grant replied that, rather than wait for Sherman and his Westerners to come up from Goldsboro, he had thought it better to let the Armies of the Potomac and the James wind up, unassisted, their long-term struggle against Lee's Army of Northern Virginia. That way, he believed a good deal of sectional jealousy and discord, East and West, would be avoided. Lincoln nodded. He could see that now, he said, but his anxiety had been so great that he had not cared what help was given, or by whom, so long as the job got done.

They talked for more than an hour, not only of the pursuit in progress but also of the peace to come, and it seemed to the staffer, listening while the President spoke, that "thoughts of mercy and mag-

nanimity were uppermost in his mind." Before long the yard was
crowded with former slaves, drawn by reports that Lincoln was there
in the flesh: proof, if proof was needed, of their sudden deliverance from
bondage. Round-eyed, they looked at him, and he at them, intently,
neither saying a word to the other. Grant was eager to be off, yet he
lingered in hope of hearing that Richmond had been taken before he
set out to join the long blue columns toiling westward on this side of
the Appomattox, intent on intercepting Lee when he turned south, as
Grant felt sure he would try to do, for a link-up with Johnston in
North Carolina. Finally he could wait no longer. He and Lincoln
shook hands and parted; Lincoln stood on the porch and watched him
ride off down the street.

Near Sutherland Station, eight miles out the Southside Railroad,
a courier overtook the general and handed him a message. He read it
with no change of expression, then said quietly: "Weitzel entered
Richmond this morning at half past eight." Word spread rapidly down
the line of marchers, accompanied by cheers. "Stack muskets and go
home!" some cried, although there was no slackening of the pace. At
Sutherland, Grant stopped long enough to wire Sherman the news, adding that he was hard on the go for Burkeville, the railroad crossing
where he would block the route to Danville. If Lee got there first, he
told Sherman, "you will have to take care of him with the force you
have for a while," but if Lee lost the race and was thus obliged to keep
moving west toward Lynchburg, "there will be no special use in you
going any farther into the interior." In other words, the Army of the
Potomac would need no assistance in disposing of its four-year adversary, and two closing sentences reflected the pride Grant felt in what
had been achieved these past two days. "This army has now won a
most decisive victory and followed the enemy. This is all it ever wanted
to make it as good an army as ever fought a battle."

Back at City Point by sundown, Lincoln found a telegram Stanton
had sent that morning in response to the one informing him that the
President intended to visit Grant in Petersburg. "Allow me respectfully
to ask you to consider whether you ought to expose the nation to the
consequences of any disaster to yourself in the pursuit of a treacherous
and dangerous enemy like the rebel army. If it was a question concerning yourself only I should not presume to say a word. Commanding
Generals are in the line of their duty running such risks. But is the
political head of a nation in the same condition?" Amused by the
Secretary's alarm, and no doubt even more amused by the thought of
his reaction to what he now had in mind to do, Lincoln replied: "Yours
received. Thanks for your caution, but I have already been to Petersburg, staid with Gen. Grant an hour & a half, and returned here. It is
certain now that Richmond is in our hands, and I think I will go there
tomorrow. I will take care of myself."

He did "go there tomorrow," Tuesday, April 4, but the added promise to "take care" went unkept — indeed, could scarcely *be* kept: partly because of the inherently dangerous nature of the expedition, which was risky in the extreme, and partly because of unforeseen developments, which included the subtraction of all but a handful of the men assigned to guard him on the trip upriver and into the fallen capital itself. Still he went, and apparently would not have it otherwise. Once he learned at breakfast that the fire and the mob had been brought under control by the force in occupation since about that time the day before, he was determined to be off. "Thank God I have lived to see this," he told Porter. "It seems to me that I have been dreaming a horrid dream for four years, and now the nightmare is gone. I want to see Richmond."

So they set out, Lincoln and Tad and the White House guard on board the flagship with Porter, escorted by the *Bat*, which brought along a complement of marines detailed to accompany the President ashore. Approaching Dutch Gap by noon, they cleared the farthest upstream Union installation within another hour and entered a more dangerous stretch of river. Swept by now of floating and underwater mines, which lay along the banks like stranded fish, the channel was littered with charred timbers, the bloated, stiff-legged carcasses of horses, and other wreckage that made for cautious navigation. Past Chaffin's Bluff, under the spiked guns of Fort Darling, the admiral found the unremoved Confederate obstructions afforded too narrow passage for either the *Malvern* or the *Bat*, both sidewheelers. Accordingly, unwilling to wait on the tedious clearance operations, he unloaded a twelve-oared barge, commandeered a naval tug to tow him and his guests the rest of the way to Richmond, and put thirty of the marines aboard her to serve as guards when they arrived. Near the city, however, the tug ran hard aground, and Porter decided to proceed under oars, leaving the stuck vessel and the marines behind. Amused by this diminution of the flotilla, Lincoln told a story about "a fellow [who] once came to ask for an appointment as a minister abroad. Finding he could not get that, he came down to some more modest position. Finally he asked to be made a tide-waiter. When he saw he could not get that, he asked for an old pair of trousers. It is well to be humble."

Porter was more amused by the joke than he was by a situation whose difficulty grew obvious when he put in at Rocketts, on the outskirts of the city, to find not a single Federal soldier anywhere in sight. Apparently the occupation did not extend this far from the hilltop Capitol, visible through rifts in the smoke from the burned-out district between the river and Capitol Square, an air-line mile and a half to the northwest. Perturbed — as well he might be, with who knew how many diehard rebels and wild-eyed fanatics on the prowl in the toppled citadel of secession, wanting nothing on earth so much as they did a shot or a swing at the hated Yankee leader in his charge — the admiral landed ten of the twelve oarsmen, leaving two to secure the barge, and armed them with carbines to serve as presidential escorts, six in front and four behind, during the uphill walk toward the heart of town, where he hoped to find more adequate protection. They comprised a strange group in that setting, ten sailors in short jackets and baggy trousers, clutching their stubby, unfamiliar weapons; tall Abraham Lincoln in his familiar long black tailcoat, made even taller by contrast with the stocky Porter, whose flat-topped seaman's cap was more than a foot lower than the crown of the high silk hat beside him; the civilian guard holding Tad by the hand, and Tad himself, twelve years old today and looking somewhat possessively around him, as if his father had just given him Richmond for a birthday present. Before they could start they were set upon by a dozen jubilant Negroes, including one old white-haired man who rushed toward Lincoln shouting, "Bless the Lord, the great Messiah! I knowed him as soon as I seed him. He's been in my heart four long years, and he come at last to free his children from their bondage. Glory, hallelujah!" With that, he threw himself at the President's feet, as did the rest, much to Lincoln's embarrassment. "Don't kneel to me," he said. "That is not right. You must kneel to God only, and thank Him for the liberty you will enjoy hereafter." They responded with a hymn, "All Ye People, Clap Your Hands," and Lincoln and the others waited through the singing before they set out on their climb toward Capitol Square.

Behind them, as they trudged, the dozen celebrants were joined by many dozens more, and up ahead, as news of the Emancipator's coming spread, still larger clusters of people began to gather, practically all of them Negroes. The White House guard, whose name was William Crook, grew more apprehensive by the minute. "Wherever it was possible for a human being to gain a foothold there was some man or woman or boy straining his eyes after the President," he would recall. "Every window was crowned with heads. Men were hanging from tree-boxes and telegraph poles. But it was a silent crowd. There was something oppressive in those thousands of watchers, without a sound either of welcome or of hatred. I think we would have welcomed a yell of defiance. I stole a sideways look at Mr Lincoln. His face was set. It had the calm in it that comes over the face of a brave man when he is ready for whatever may come." Within half an hour they passed Libby Prison, empty now, still with its old ship chandler's sign attached. "We'll pull it down!" someone offered, but Lincoln shook his head. "No; leave it as a monument," he said. Skirting the burned district just ahead, the group began climbing Capitol Hill, and it occurred to Crook that he and his companions "were more like prisoners than anything else." Presently they saw their first evidence of welcome from anyone not black. A young white woman stood on the gallery spanning the street in front of the Exchange Hotel, an American flag draped over her shoulders. But she was the exception. A few blocks farther on, "one lady in a large and elegant building looked a while, then turned away her head as if from a disgusting sight." For the most part, such houses were shuttered, curtains drawn across the windows; but there were watchers in them as well, peering out unseen. "I had a good look at Mr Lincoln," one young matron wrote a friend next day. "He seemed tired and old — and I must say, with due respect to the President of the United States, I thought him the ugliest man I had ever seen."

By now they had encountered their first Union soldier, a cavalry-man idly sitting his horse and gawking like all the others in the crowd. "Is that Old Abe?" he asked Porter, who sent him to summon a mounted escort. Soon it came, and for the first time since the landing at Rocketts the group had adequate protection.

Lincoln continued to plod along with the shambling, flat-footed stride of a plowman, past the Governor's Mansion, then three more blocks out 12th Street to Weitzel's headquarters, the former Confederate White House. Sweaty and tired from his two-mile walk, he entered the study Davis had vacated two nights ago. Perhaps it was for this he had been willing to risk the danger — the likelihood, some would have said — of assassination in the just-fallen rebel capital: this moment of feeling, for the first time since his first inauguration, four years and one month ago today, that he now was President of the whole United States. One witness described him as "pale and haggard, utterly worn out," while another saw "a serious, dreamy expression" on his face. In any case, exhausted or bemused, he crossed the cream-colored rug and sank wearily into the chair behind his fugitive rival's desk. "I wonder if I could get a glass of water?" he inquired.

After a light midafternoon lunch, John A. Campbell, the only prominent member of the Confederate government remaining in Rich-mond, turned up to propose returning Virginia to the Union by means of an appeal to her elected officials, who knew as well as he did, he de-clared, that the war was lost and over. Lincoln had not been impressed by the Alabama jurist at Hampton Roads two months ago, but now that he came less as an envoy than as a supplicant, having reported his "sub-mission to the military authorities," his acceptability was considerably improved. "I speak for Virginia what would be more appropriate for a Virginian," he said, and quoted: "When lenity and cruelty play for a kingdom, the gentler gamester is the soonest winner." Lincoln liked the sound of that, along with the notion of Old Dominion soldiers — including, presumably, R. E. Lee — being removed, by authority of their own state government, from those rebel forces still arrayed against him. He told the former Assistant Secretary of War that he would be staying overnight in Richmond and would confer with him next morn-ing on the matter. Just now, though, he was joining Weitzel for a car-riage tour of the fallen capital.

He sat up front with one of the three division commanders Ord had left behind; Tad and Porter sat in back with Brigadier General George F. Shepley, Weitzel's chief of staff and the newly appointed military governor of Richmond, a post for which he had been schooled by service as Ben Butler's right-hand man in Louisiana. Weitzel himself — another Butler trainee, from New Orleans to Fort Fisher — rode alongside the carriage with a cavalcade of some two dozen officers, line and staff, who comprised a guard of honor for the sightseeing expedition. Their first stop was Capitol Square, where they pulled up east of Thomas Crawford's equestrian statue of the first President, posed gazing west, with one bronze arm extended majestically southward. "Washington is looking at me and pointing at Jeff Davis," Lincoln said. Refugees huddled about the Square, guarding the few household possessions they had managed to save from yesterday's fire, and the Capitol had been looted by vandals and souvenir hunters, military and civilian. From there the carriage rolled through the burned district, whose streets were choked with toppled masonry and littered with broken glass, on down Cary Street to Libby Prison, which Lincoln had passed earlier on his way uptown. It held captive rebels now, and in fact had had no Federal inmates since last May, when they were transferred to a new prison down in Georgia; but the thought of what it once had been caused one horseman to remark that Jefferson Davis should be hanged. Lincoln turned and looked at him. "Judge not, that ye be not judged," he said quietly. Soon afterwards Weitzel took the opportunity to ask if the President had any suggestions as to treatment of the conquered people in his charge. Lincoln replied that, while he did not want to issue orders on the subject, "If I were in your place I'd let 'em up easy; let 'em up easy."

Suddenly there was the boom of guns a mile downriver, which to everyone's relief turned out to be the *Malvern*; she had made it through the rebel obstructions to drop anchor at last off Rocketts, and was firing a salute in celebration. Porter was especially relieved. He still considered the President's welfare his responsibility, and he was in a state of dread from the risk to which he had let him expose himself today. Refusing to take no for an answer, he insisted that Lincoln sleep that night aboard the flagship, where he could be isolated from all harm. Weary from the strain of a long, exciting day, his charge turned in shortly after an early dinner, and presumably got another good night's sleep in the refurbished stateroom, this time with a guard posted outside his door.

One hundred miles to the north, few citizens of his own capital got any such rest, either that night or the one before. Washington was a blaze of celebration, and had been so ever since midmorning yesterday, when a War Department telegrapher received from Fort Monroe, for the first time in four years, the alerting message: "Turn down for Richmond," meaning that he was to relieve the tension on the armature spring of his instrument so that it would respond to a weak signal. He did, and the dit-dahs came through, distant but distinct. "We took Richmond at 8.15 this morning." Church bells pealed; fire engines clattered and clanged through the streets. Locomotives in the yards and steamboats on the river added the scream of their whistles to the uproar. Schools dismissed; clerks spilled out of government buildings; extras hit the stands. "Glory!!! Hail Columbia!!! Hallelujah!!! Richmond Ours!!!" the *Star* exulted. Army batteries fired an 800-gun salute that went on forever, three hundred for Petersburg, five hundred more for the fall of the rebel capital, while the Navy added another hundred from its biggest Dahlgrens, rattling windows all over town. "From one end of Pennsylvania Avenue to the other," a reporter noted, "the air seemed to burn with the bright hues of the flag. . . . Almost by magic the streets were crowded with hosts of people, talking, laughing, hurrahing and shouting in the fullness of their joy. Men embraced one another, 'treated' one another, made up old quarrels, renewed old friendships, marched arm-in-arm singing and chatting in that happy sort of abandon which characterizes our people when under the influence of a great and universal happiness. The atmosphere was full of the intoxication of joy." Stanton gave a solemn, Seward a light-hearted speech, both wildly cheered by the celebrants outside their respective offices: especially when the former read a dispatch from Weitzel saying Richmond was on fire. What should he reply? "Burn it, burn it! Let her burn!" the cry came up. "A more liquorish crowd was never seen in Washington than on that night," the newsman declared, and told of seeing "one big, sedate Vermonter, chief of an executive bureau, standing on the corner of F and 14th streets, with owlish gravity giving fifty-cent 'shin plasters' to every colored person who came past him, brokenly saying with each gift, 'Babylon has fallen.' "

That was Monday. The formal celebration — or "grand illumination," as it was called — was set for the following evening. All day Tuesday, while Lincoln walked and rode through the cluttered streets of Richmond, workmen swarmed over Washington's public buildings, preparing them for the show that would start at dusk. When it came it was altogether worth the waiting. "This is the Lord's doing; it is marvellous in our eyes" was blazoned in huge letters on a gaslighted transparency over the western pediment of the Capitol, which glittered from its basement to its dome. City Hall, the Treasury, the Post Office, the Marine Barracks, the National Conservatory, the prisons along First Street, even the Insane Asylum, lonely on its hill, burned like beacons in the night.

All Washington turned out to cheer and marvel at the candle-light displays, but the largest crowd collected in front of the Patent Office, where flaring gas jets spelled out U N I O N across the top of its granite pillars. A speaker's stand had been erected at their foot; for this was the Republican mass rally, opened by Judge David Cartter of the district supreme court, who got things off to a rousing start by referring in racetrack terms to Jefferson Davis as "the flying rascal out of Richmond," by way of a warm-up for the principal speaker, Andrew Johnson. He had been lying rather low since the inauguration, yet he showed this evening that he had lost none of his talent for invective on short notice. He too mentioned Davis early on, and when his listeners shouted, "Hang him! Hang him!" the Vice President was quick to agree: "Yes, I say hang him twenty times." Nor was the rebel leader the only one deserving of such treatment. Others like him were "infamous in character, diabolical in motive," and Johnson had a similar prescription for them all, including confiscation of their property. "When you ask me what *I* would do, my reply is — I would arrest them, I would try them, I would convict them, and I would hang them.... Treason must be made odious," he declared; "traitors must be punished and impoverished."

Other remarks, public and private — all in heady contrast to Lincoln's "Let 'em up easy," spoken today in the other capital after the interview in which Campbell described "the gentler gamester" as "the soonest winner" — followed as the celebration went on into and through the night. Long after the candles had guttered out and the flares had been extinguished, serenaders continued to make the rounds and corks kept popping in homes and hotel bars all over town.

Headaches were the order of the day in Washington by 10 o'clock Wednesday morning, April 5; at which time, as agreed on yesterday, the President received the Alabama jurist aboard the *Malvern*, riding at anchor off Rocketts Landing. Campbell brought a Richmond lawyer with him, Gustavus Myers, a member of the Virginia legislature, and their suggestion was that this body, now adjourned and scattered about the state, be reassembled for a vote withdrawing the Old Dominion from the Confederacy and formally returning her to her old allegiance. Weitzel, who was present, later summarized their proposal. "Mr Campbell and the other gentleman assured Mr Lincoln that if he would allow the Virginia Legislature to meet, it would at once repeal the ordinance of secession, and that then General Robert E. Lee and every other Virginian would submit; that this would amount to virtual destruction of the Army of Northern Virginia, and eventually to the surrender of all the other rebel armies, and would assure perfect peace in the shortest possible time."

Lincoln liked the notion, in part because it provided a way to get local government back in operation, but mainly because it offered at least a chance of avoiding that "last bloody battle" Grant and Sherman had told him would have to be fought before the South surrendered. Accordingly, he gave Campbell a document repeating his three Hampton

Roads conditions —"restoration of the national authority throughout all the states"; "no receding by the Executive on the slavery question"; "no cessation of hostilities short of an end to the war and the disbanding of all forces hostile to the government" — in return for which, confiscations of property would be "remitted to the people of any state which shall now promptly and in good faith withdraw its troops and other support from further resistance." In addition, though he declined to offer a general amnesty, he promised to use his pardoning power to "save any repentant sinner from hanging." Finally he agreed to reach an early decision in regard to permitting the Virginia legislators to reassemble.

This last he did next day, informing Weitzel that "the gentlemen who have acted as the legislature of Virginia, in support of the rebellion, may now desire to assemble at Richmond and take measures to withdraw the Virginia troops and other support from resistance to the general government. If they attempt it, give them permission and protection, until, if at all, they attempt some action hostile to the United States, in which case you will notify them and give them reasonable time to leave. . . . Allow Judge Campbell to see this, but do not make it public." Sending word to Grant of his decision, he added: "I do not think it very probable that anything will come of this, but I have thought it best to notify you, so that if you should see signs you may understand them," then closed with the familiar tactical warning: "Nothing I have done, or probably shall do, is to delay, hinder, or interfere with you in your work."

He was back at City Point by then, having steamed downriver at Porter's insistence as soon as the meeting with Campbell ended. Today — Thursday — made two full weeks he had been gone from Washington, and in response to a wire from Seward the day before, offering to come down for a conference on several matters "important and urgent in conducting the government but not at all critical or serious," he had informed the Secretary: "I think there is no probability of my remaining here more than two days longer. If this is too long come down." For one thing, he was awaiting the arrival next day of Mrs Lincoln. Having found her husband's dream of a White House fire a false alarm, she was returning with a number of distinguished visitors, all eager for a look at fallen Richmond. This might prolong his stay; or so he thought until bedtime Wednesday, when he received news that threatened to cut his vacation even shorter than he had supposed. Seward, he learned, had been thrown from his carriage that afternoon and had been so seriously injured, it was feared, that Lincoln might have to return to Washington at once. A follow-up wire from Stanton next morning, however, informed him that while the New Yorker's injuries were painful they were almost certainly not fatal; Lincoln could stay away as long as he chose. So he went down to the wharf at noon, this April 6, to meet his wife and the party of sightseers she had brought along on the boatride down the coast.

Irked to find that her husband had already been to the rebel capital and would not be going there again, Mrs Lincoln decided to make the trip herself on the *River Queen*, which would afford overnight accommodations for her guests, Senator and Mrs Harlan, Attorney General Speed and his wife, Charles Sumner and a young French nobleman friend, the Marquis de Chambrun. They left that afternoon and reached Richmond in time for a cavalry-escorted tour of the city before returning to sleep aboard the *Queen*, anchored in the James. Sumner was especially gratified by all he had seen, including the looted Capitol, where he asked in particular to examine the ivory gavel of the Congress. When it was brought he put it in his pocket — as a souvenir, or perhaps as further recompense for the caning he had suffered at the hands of Preston Brooks, nine years ago this spring — and brought it back with him to City Point next morning. Once more Lincoln was waiting on the dock, this time with an offer to take them by rail to Petersburg for a look at what ten months of siege and shelling had accomplished.

He was in excellent spirits, Harlan noted. "His whole appearance, pose, and bearing had marvelously changed. He was, in fact, transfigured. That indescribable sadness which had previously seemed to be an adamantine element of his very being had been suddenly changed for an equally indescribable expression of serene joy, as if conscious that the great purpose of his life had been attained." Partly this was the salutary effect of being removed for two full weeks from Washington and the day-in day-out frets that hemmed his White House office there, but a more immediate cause was a series of dispatches from Grant, all of them so encouraging to Lincoln that, in telling the general of his decision to let the Virginia legislature assemble, he remarked that Grant seemed to be achieving on his own, by "pretty effectually withdrawing the Virginia troops from opposition to the government," what he had hoped the legislators would effect by legal action. Not only had the blue pursuers won the race for Burkeville, thereby preventing Lee from turning south to combine with Johnston; they had also netted some 1500 grayback captives in the process. "The country is full of stragglers," Grant reported, "the line of retreat marked with artillery, burned or charred wagons, caissons, ambulances, &c." Gratifying as this was, he capped the climax with a wire sent late the night before, telling of a victory scored that afternoon by Humphreys, Wright, and Sheridan, some eight miles beyond Burkeville. Five rebel generals had been taken, including Richard Ewell and Custis Lee, along with "several thousand prisoners, fourteen pieces of artillery with caissons, and a large number of wagons." Such were the spoils listed by Sheridan in a message Grant passed along to Lincoln. "If the thing is pressed," the cavalryman urged his chief in closing, "I think Lee will surrender." Lincoln's enthusiasm soared, and he replied at 11 o'clock this Friday morning, about the time his wife and her guests returned from their overnight cruise to Richmond: "Sheridan says, 'If the thing is pressed I think that Lee will surrender.' Let the *thing* be pressed."

Two distractions, one slight and rather easily dismissed, the other a good deal more poignant in effect, broke into this three-day span of high good feeling. The first was a note from Andrew Johnson, who had come down on an army packet, now anchored nearby, and wanted to pay the President a visit before proceeding upriver for a tour of the fallen capital. Lincoln frowned, having read in the Washington papers of the Tennessean's call for all-out vengeance in his speech at the Republican mass rally Tuesday night. "I guess he can get along without me," he said distastefully, and did not reply to the note. That had been yesterday afternoon, and the second distraction followed that evening. He was taking the air after supper on the top deck of the *Malvern*, once more in a happy frame of mind, when he looked down from the rail and saw a group of rebel prisoners being loaded for shipment north aboard a transport moored alongside. The guard Crook, with him as usual, watched them too. "They were in a pitiable condition, ragged and thin; they looked half starved. When they were on board they took out of their knapsacks the last rations that had been issued to them before capture. There was nothing but bread, which looked as if it had been mixed with tar. When they cut it we could see how hard it was and heavy. It was more like cheese than bread." He watched, and as he did so he heard Lincoln groan beside him: "Poor fellows. It's a hard lot. Poor fellows." Crook turned and looked at his companion. "His face was pitying and sorrowful. All the happiness had gone."

Next morning's dispatch from the general-in-chief revived his genial spirits. "Let the *thing* be pressed," he replied, echoing Sheridan, and looked forward to the brightest news of all, which would be that Lee had at last been run to earth. Once that happened, he believed, commanders of other gray armies were likely to see the folly of further resistance on their part — if, indeed, they managed to survive that long. Developments elsewhere finally seemed to be moving at a pace that matched the stepped-up progress of events here in Virginia: particularly in South and Central Alabama. Canby had a close-up grip on Mobile's outer defenses, Spanish Fort and Fort Blakely, whose fall would mean the fall of the city in their rear, and he was preparing to assault, with results that were practically foregone, considering his better than four-to-one numerical advantage. Similarly — and incredibly, in the light of what had happened to those who tried it in the past — James Wilson, after crossing the Black Warrior, then the Cahaba, had driven Bedford Forrest headlong in the course of a two-day running skirmish, fifty miles in length, to descend on Selma, April 2, the day Richmond itself was abandoned. By now the all-important manufactories there were a mass of smoking rubble, and Wilson had his troopers hard on the go for Montgomery, where the Confederacy began. Neither Canby nor Wilson had started in time to be of much help to each other, as originally intended; nor had Stoneman crossed the Smokies in time to strike in Johnston's rear for Sherman's benefit. But now, in accordance with Grant's revised instructions, he turned his raiders north for Lynchburg, where Lee was apparently headed too.

No wonder, then, that Harlan found Lincoln "transfigured" as he stood on the dock at City Point to welcome his wife and her guests back from Richmond, or that he took increased encouragement from what he saw on the trip to Petersburg that afternoon. "Animosity in the town is abating," he told Chambrun; "the inhabitants now accept accomplished facts, the final downfall of the Confederacy and the abolition of slavery. There still remains much for us to do, but every day brings new reason for confidence in the future."

Aboard the *River Queen* that night — April 7; Good Friday was a week away — Elihu Washburne, en route to the front for another visit with Grant, whose rise he had done so much to promote through the first three years of a war that now had stretched to nearly four, called on Lincoln and found him "in perfect health and exuberant spirits," voluble in recounting for his guests the events of the past week, including his walk through the streets of Richmond. "He never flagged during the whole evening," the Illinois congressman would recall. Chambrun, however — a liberal despite his privileged heritage and the conservative domination of his homeland under the Second Empire — observed in his host contrasting traits often remarked by others in the past: Crook for one, just the night before, and Sherman at the conference held on this same vessel, ten days back. "He willingly laughed either at what was being said to him, or at what he said himself," the Frenchman later wrote. "But all of a sudden he would retire within himself; then he would close his eyes, and all his features would bespeak a kind of sadness as indescribable as it was deep. After a while, as though it were by an effort of his will, he would shake off this mysterious weight under which he seemed bowed; his generous and open disposition would again reappear. In one evening I happened to count over twenty of these alternations and contrasts."

Part of this intermittent sadness no doubt came from realization that he was approaching the end of the only real vacation he had taken in the past four years. All day Saturday preparations went forward for departure of the *Queen* that night, including a thorough check on the records of her crew, ordered by Porter in reaction to the belated fright he felt at the risk he had run in taking the President to and through the rebel capital, all but unescorted. That evening a military band came on board for a farewell concert. After several numbers, Lincoln requested the "Marseillaise," which he liked so well that he had it repeated. "You must, however, come over to America to hear it," he said wryly to the young marquis, knowing the Emperor had banned the piece in France. Then he called for "Dixie," much to the surprise of his guests and the musicians, as well as to listeners in the outer darkness on the docks and blufftop. "That tune is now Federal property," he told Chambrun. An hour before midnight, the *Queen* cast off and began to steam down the winding moonlit river, escorted by the *Bat*. Reaching Hampton Roads before dawn, she stopped long enough to board a pilot at Fort Monroe and was off again by sunrise, up Chesapeake Bay toward the mouth of the Potomac.

It was April 9; Palm Sunday. Eastward the sky was a glory of red, but the rising sun was presently dimmed by clouds rolling in from the sea with a promise of rain. The President and his guests rose early, and after breakfast went on deck to watch the gliding tableau of the ʳ' oreline. Soon after they entered the Potomac, paddle wheels churning ᵤgainst the current, they passed Stratford Hall, the birthplace of Robert Lee — presumably still in flight for his life, a hundred-odd miles to the southwest — and within the hour, on that same bank, saw the birth-sites too of Washington and James Monroe. Almost in view of the capital, as they steamed past Mount Vernon just at sundown, someone remarked that Springfield would someday be equally honored. Lincoln, who had been musing at the rail, came out of himself on hearing his home town mentioned. "Springfield!" he exclaimed. He smiled and said he would be happy to return there, "four years hence," and live in peace and tranquillity. Mainly though, according to Chambrun, "the conversation dwelt upon literary subjects." Lincoln read to the assembled group from what Sumner called "a beautiful quarto Shakespeare," mainly from *Macbeth*, perhaps his favorite, with emphasis on the scenes that followed the king's assassination.

> *"Duncan is in his grave;*
> *After life's fitful fever he sleeps well;*
> *Treason has done his worst: nor steel, nor poison,*
> *Malice domestic, foreign levy, nothing*
> *Can touch him further."*

He paused, then read the lines again, something in them responding to something in himself. After the reading he was again withdrawn, although presently when his wife spoke of Jefferson Davis—saying, as the staff officer had said five days ago in Richmond, "He must be hanged"—he replied, as he had then: "Judge not, that ye be not judged." Contradiction was risky in that direction, inviting "malice domestic" as it did, but he ventured to repeat it when they came within sight of the roofs of Washington and he heard her tell Chambrun, "That city is filled with our enemies." Lincoln made a gesture of impatience. "Enemies," he said, as if with the taste of something bitter on his tongue. "We must never speak of that."

Rain was coming down hard in the twilight by the time the steamer reached the wharf at the foot of Sixth Street. The President's carriage was waiting to take him to the White House, but he let Tad and Mrs Lincoln off there and went on alone to Seward's house, nearby on Franklin Square, where the Secretary lay recovering from the injuries he had suffered. They were extensive, the right shoulder badly dislocated, the jaw broken on both sides; the pain had been so great that he had been in delirium for three of the four days since his fall. Indeed, he was scarcely recognizable when his friend entered the upstairs bedroom to find him stretched along the far edge of the bed, his arm projected over the side to avoid pressure on the bruised socket, his face swathed in bandages, swollen and discolored, his jaw clamped in an iron frame for healing. "You are back from Richmond?" he said in a hoarse whisper, barely able to speak because of the damage and the pain. "Yes, and I think we are near the end at last," Lincoln told him. First he sat gingerly on the bed, then sprawled across it, resting on an elbow, his face close to Seward's while he described much that had happened down near City Point in the course of the past two weeks. He stayed half an hour, by which time the New Yorker had fallen into a feverish sleep. Then he came out, gesturing for silence in the hall, and tiptoed down the stairs to the front door, where his carriage was waiting to take him back to the White House.

Later that evening, undressing for sleep, he felt the familiar weariness all men feel on their first night home from a vacation. Then there came a knock, and he opened the bedroom door to find a War Department messenger in the hall with a telegram that made Lincoln forget that weariness had anything to do with living. It was from Grant and had been sent from a place called Appomattox Courthouse.

April 9, 1865 — 4.30 p.m.

Hon. E. M. Stanton,
Secretary of War:

General Lee surrendered the Army of Northern Virginia this afternoon upon terms proposed by myself. The accompanying additional correspondence will show the conditions fully.

U. S. Grant,
Lieutenant General.

⚹ 4 ⚹

What had begun as a retreat the previous Sunday night, when Lee abandoned Petersburg and Richmond with the intention of marching southwest beyond the Roanoke, developed all too soon into a race against Grant and starvation, which in turn became a harassed flight that narrowed the dwindling army's fate to slow or sudden death. For six days this continued, ever westward. Then on the seventh — April 9, Palm Sunday — Lee made his choice. The agony ended, as his opponent said in the bedtime telegram to Lincoln, "upon terms proposed by myself."

Few at the start, in the column he accompanied, apparently thought it would turn out so: least of all Lee himself, who told a companion when they took up the march on Monday morning: "I have got my army safely out of its breastworks, and in order to follow me, the enemy must abandon his lines and can derive no further benefit from his railroads or James River." Others felt a similar elation at their successful withdrawal across the Appomattox, unpursued, and the exchange of their cramped trenches for the spread-out landscape, where sunlight glittered on greening fields and new-fledged trees along the roadside. Whatever the odds, this was Chancellorsville weather, with its reminders of their old skill at maneuver. "A sense of relief seemed to pervade the ranks at their release from the lines where they had watched and worked for more than nine weary months," a staff brigadier would recall. "Once more in the open field, they were invigorated with hope, and felt better able to cope with their powerful adversary."

But that applied only to the central column, the 13,000 infantry under Longstreet and Gordon, Pendleton's 3000 cannoneers, and Mahone's 4000-man division on its way from Bermuda Hundred via Chesterfield Courthouse. Most of these 20,000 effectives had stood fast the day before, had conducted the nighttime withdrawal in good order, and had sustained their group identity in the process. It was different for the 6000 coming down from beyond the James with Ewell. Less than a third were veterans under Kershaw, while the rest — combined extemporaneously under Custis Lee, who had lately been promoted to major general though he had never led troops in action outside the capital defenses — were reservists, naval personnel, and heavy artillerymen, so unaccustomed to marching that the road in their rear was already littered with stragglers, footsore and blown from a single night on the go. Nor was their outlook improved by the view they had had, back over their shoulders the night before, of Richmond in flames on the far side of the river. Even so, they were in considerably better shape than the 3500 men with Anderson beyond the Appomattox, rattled fragments of the four divisions of Pickett, Johnson, Heth, and Wilcox, working their way west in the wake of Fitz Lee's 3500 jaded troopers on worse-than-jaded horses. Badly trounced at Five Forks, two days back, and scattered by yesterday's breakthrough on the right — which had now become the left — they had been whipped, and knew it. "There was an attempt to organize the various commands," a South

Carolina captain later said of this smallest and worst-off of the three infantry columns; "to no avail. The Confederacy was considered as 'gone up,' and every man felt it his duty, as well as his privilege, to save himself. I do not mean to say there was any insubordination whatever, but the whole left of the army was so crushed by the defeats of the past few days that it straggled along without strength and almost without thought. So we moved on in disorder, keeping no regular column, no regular pace. When a soldier became weary he fell out, ate his scanty rations — if, indeed, he had any to eat — rested, rose, and resumed the march when his inclination dictated. There were not many words spoken. An indescribable sadness weighed upon us. The men were very gentle toward each other, very liberal in bestowing the little of food that remained to them."

All that day, well into darkness, Anderson's fugitive survivors kept up their march northwest along the south bank of the Appomattox. Around midnight, when a halt was called at last, the weary captain watched as his men "fell about and slept heavily, or else wandered like persons in a dream. I remember, it all seemed to me like a troubled vision. I was consumed by fever, and when I attempted to walk I staggered about like a drunken man." A night's sleep helped, and Tuesday morning when they encountered Longstreet's veterans, crossing the river with Lee himself at the head of the central column, they were comforted to find that the rest of the army was by no means as badly off as they were. Small bodies of blue cavalry, attempting to probe their flank and interrupt the march, were driven off and kept at a respectful distance. "We revived rapidly from our forlorn and desolate feeling," the captain would recall.

Hunger was still a problem, to put it mildly, but there was also comfort for that; at any rate the comfort of anticipation. Amelia Courthouse lay just ahead on the Richmond & Danville, five miles west of the river, and Lee had arranged for meat and bread to be sent there from the 350,000 rations amassed in the capital in the course of the past two months. Or so he thought until he arrived, shortly before noon, to find a generous shipment of ordnance equipment — 96 loaded caissons, 200 crates of ammunition for his guns, and 164 boxes of artillery harness — waiting aboard a string of cars pulled onto a siding; but no food. His requisition had not been received, the commissary general afterwards explained, until "all railroad transportation had been taken up."

If Lee's face, as a cavalry staffer noted, took on "an anxious and haggard expression" at the news, it was no wonder. At the close of a march of nearly forty miles in about as many hours, with nothing to eat but what they happened to have with them at the outset or could scrounge along the way, he had 33,000 soldiers — the number to which his army, including reservists, had been reduced in the past ten days by

its losses at Fort Stedman and Five Forks and during the Sunday breakthrough, each of which had cost him just under or over 5000 men —
converging on a lonely trackside village where not a single ration could
be drawn. His only recourse was to call a halt while commissary details
scoured the countryside for such food as they could find. This they
soon began to do, armed with an appeal "To the Citizens of Amelia
County," signed R. E. Lee and calling on them "to supply as far as
each one is able the wants of the brave soldiers who have battled for
your liberty for four years."

    In point of fact, there would have been a delay in any case, since
nothing had yet been heard from Ewell, and the rest of the army could
not push on down the railroad until this laggard column was on hand.
Meantime, Lee got off a telegram to Danville, directing the immediate
rail shipment of rations from the stores St John had waiting for him
there, though whether the requisition would get through was doubtful,
the wires having been cut near Jetersville, a hamlet six miles down the
track and twelve miles short of Burkeville. After supper, a message
came from Ewell announcing that he had been delayed by flooded
bridges; he expected to cross the Appomattox tonight and would arrive
next morning. Lee could do nothing but wait for him and the commissary wagons, hopefully loaded with whatever food had been volunteered or impressed. Even so, he was aware that he had lost a good part
of the head start he had gained when he slipped away from Grant
two nights ago, and knowledge of this, together with the anguish he felt
for the hungry troops still hobbling in, was reflected in his bearing.
"His face was still calm, as it always was," an artillery sergeant major
later wrote, "but his carriage was no longer erect, as his soldiers had
been used to see it. The troubles of these last days had already plowed
great furrows in his forehead. His eyes were red as if with weeping, his
cheeks sunken and haggard, his face colorless. No one who looked
upon him, as he stood there in full view of the disastrous end, can ever
forget the intense agony written upon his features."

    Such distress was general that evening. While the wagon details
were out scouring the picked-over region for something the men or
animals could eat, the half-starved troops, bedded down in fields around
the rural county seat or still limping toward a concentration that should
have been completed before nightfall, evidenced a discouragement more
profound than any they had known in the darkest days of the siege
that now had ended. "Their strength was slowly drained from them," an
officer declared, "and despondency, like a black and poisonous mist,
began to invade the hearts before so tough and buoyant." Some were
taken with a restlessness, a sort of wanderlust that outweighed their
exhaustion: with the result that there were further subtractions from the
army's ranks. "Many of them wandered off in search of food, with no

thought of deserting at all. Many others followed the example of their government, and fled."

A hard shock followed next morning, April 5, when the foraging details came rattling back, their wagons all but empty. So thoroughly had Northrop's and St John's agents done their work these past ten months, impressing stock and grain to feed the trench-bound men at Petersburg, few of the farmers roundabout had anything left to give, even in response to a personal appeal from Robert Lee. Still, he had no choice except to keep moving. To stay where he was meant starvation, and every hour's delay was another hour's reduction of his head-start gain: if, indeed, there was any of it left. All the troops were up by now, and he had done what he could to ease the strain, including a culling of nearly one third of the 200 guns and 1000 wagons — which, fully spread out, covered more than twenty miles of road — to provide replacements for those draft animals exhaustion had subtracted from the teams needed to keep the other two thirds rolling; the culls were to be forwarded, if possible, by rail. A cold rain deepened the army's gloom when the fall-in sounded for still a third day of marching on empty stomachs. Longstreet took the lead, Gordon the rear-guard duty; Anderson and Ewell slogged between, while Fitz Lee's troopers ranged well to the front on their gaunt, weak-kneed horses, left and right of the railroad leading down to Danville, a hundred miles to the southwest.

Five of those miles from Amelia by early afternoon, the outriders came upon bluecoats intrenched in a well-chosen position just short of Jetersville, a dozen miles from Burkeville, where the Southside and the Danville railroads crossed. This was no surprise; enemy cavalry had been active in that direction yesterday. Longstreet shook out skirmishers, preparing to brush these vedettes from his path, but shortly before 2 o'clock, when Lee arrived, reports came back that the force in front amounted to a good deal more than cavalry. One corps of Union infantry was already on hand, in support of Sheridan's horsemen, and another was rapidly approaching. Lee's heart sank at the news. His adversary had won the race for the critical Burkeville crossing; he was blocked, and so were the rations he had ordered sent from Danville in hope of intercepting them en route. Regretfully he lowered his glasses from a study of the position, which he knew was too strong for an attack by his frazzled army, heavily outnumbered as it was by the three blue corps, with others doubtless hard on the way to join them. Rejecting the notion, if it crossed his mind, of going out in an Old Guard blaze of glory, he turned his thoughts to another plan of action — another route — still with the intention, or anyhow the hope, of combining with Joe Johnston somewhere to the south.

He would veer west, across the upper quadrant of the spraddled X described by the two railroads, to the vicinity of Farmville on the upper Appomattox, where rations could be sent to meet him, via the Southside line, from stores collected at Lynchburg by St John. Then, having fed his hungry men and horses, he would move south again, across the western quadrant of the X, bypassing the Burkeville inter-section — Grant's reported point of concentration — to resume his march down the Danville line for a combination with Johnston, beyond the Roanoke, before turning on his pursuers. Admittedly this was a long-odds venture, difficult at best. Farmville was five miles farther away than Burkeville, and he knew little of the roads he would have to travel, except that they were poor. Moreover, he was by no means sure that his half-starved troops and animals could manage a cross-country slog of perhaps twenty roundabout miles without food, especially since they would have to begin it with still another night march if he was to avoid being overtaken and overwhelmed, practically at the start. Here again, however, he had no choice but to attempt it or face the narrowed alternatives of surrender or annihilation. Accordingly, instructions for the westward trek went out; "the most cruel marching order the commanders had ever given the men in four years of fighting," a later observer was to say. As always, all that time, "Lee's miserables" re-sponded as best they could when the move began near sundown. "It is now a race for life or death," one wrote in his diary at the outset.

It was indeed. "Night was day. Day was night," a groggy can-noneer was to recall. "There was no stated time to sleep, eat, or rest, and the events of morning became strangely intermingled with the events of evening. Breakfast, dinner, and supper were merged into 'some-thing to eat,' whenever and wherever it could be found." Four miles out, a bridge collapsed into Flat Creek, stalling the guns and wagons for hours before it could be repaired, and though the infantry got over by fording, the discomfort of wet feet was added to those of hunger and exhaustion. Confusion and sleeplessness made the marchers edgy, quick to panic: as when a runaway stallion broke loose from a fence where he was tethered and came pounding down the road, the rail still tied to his rein. Abrupt and point-blank exchanges of fire by several units, in response to what they assumed was a night attack by Yankee cavalry, resulted in an undetermined number of casualties. Straggling was heavy, and many who kept going simply dropped their rifles as they hobbled along, too weak to carry them any farther, or else planted them by the roadside, bayonet down, each a small monument to determination and defeat.

Dawn showed the effects of this harrowing night, not only in the thinness of the army's ranks, but also in the faces of the survivors, the sullen lines of strain around their mouths, the red etchings of fatigue along their lower eyelids. Many staggered drunkenly, and some found, when they tried to talk, that their speech was incoherent. They had reached what later came to be called "poor old Dixie's bottom dollar," and for the most part they were satisfied that even that was spent. One of Longstreet's Deep South veterans put it strongest, dropping back toward the tail of the column as he struggled to keep up, tattered and barefoot, yet still with some vestige of the raucous sense of humor that had brought him this far along the four-year road he had traveled. "My shoes are gone; my clothes are almost gone. I'm weary, I'm sick, I'm hungry. My family has been killed or scattered, and may now be wandering helpless and unprotected." He shook his head. "I would die; yes, I would die willingly," he said, "because I love my country. But if this war is ever over, I'll be damned if I ever love another country!"

This was Grant's doing, the outcome of his steadiness and simplicity of purpose, designed to accomplish in short order the destruction of his opponent now that he had flushed him out of his burrow, into the open field, and had him on the run. He became again, in brief, the Grant of Vicksburg. "There was no pause, no hesitancy, no doubt what to do," a staff colonel afterwards declared. "He commanded Lee's army as much as he did ours; caused and knew beforehand every movement that Lee made, up to the actual surrender.... There was no let up; fighting and marching, and negotiating, all at once."

Mindful perhaps of Sherman's dictum, "A stern chase is a long one," the northern commander had decided at the outset that he stood to gain more from heading his adversary off than he did from pursuing him across the Appomattox. That way, once he was in his front, he could bag him entire, rather than engage in the doubtful and drawn-out process of attempting his piecemeal destruction by means of a series of attacks upon his rear, not to mention avoiding ambuscades at practically every step along the way. Moreover, a comparison of the two probable routes, Union and Confederate, showed clearly enough the advantage the former offered. Lee doubtless intended to assemble his army somewhere along the upper stretch of the Danville Railroad, with a march to follow down it, through Burkeville, for a combination with Johnston beyond the Carolina line. From all three of his starting points, Richmond, Bermuda Hundred, and Petersburg, the distance to Burkeville was just under sixty miles, and two of his three columns would have to make two time-consuming river crossings, one at the start and one near the end of the move toward concentration; whereas Grant's route, due west along the Southside Railroad, from Sutherland Station to Burkeville — blue chord of the gray arc — not only spanned no river, but was also twenty miles shorter; which in itself was enough to abrogate the head start Lee had gained by taking off at first-dark Sunday. Accordingly, before his meeting with Lincoln in Petersburg next morning, Grant issued orders for winning the race as he conceived it. Sheridan of course would lead, fanning out to the right to keep tabs on the graybacks still on the near side of the Appomattox, and

Griffin would press along in the wake of the troopers as fast as his men could manage afoot, under instructions to support them in any action that developed, whether defensive or offensive. Humphreys and Wright would follow Griffin, while Ord and Parke stuck to the rail-road, the latter repairing track as he went, thereby providing an all-weather supply line that led directly into the moving army's rear.

Speed was the main requirement, and the blue-clad veterans gave it willingly. "We never endured such marching before," a footsore private later wrote. As a result, they won the Monday-Tuesday race with time to spare. By Wednesday morning, April 5, when Lee began his delayed movement down the railroad from Amelia, Griffin was in position athwart his path, in close support of Sheridan's dug-in troopers; Humphreys was coming up fast in his rear, and Wright was expected before sundown. Confronted thus by twice his dwindled number, Lee called a halt that afternoon, just short of Jetersville, and Meade — who had traveled by ambulance for the past two days, a victim of wrought-up nerves and indigestion — decided that the army's best course would be to get some food and rest, including a good night's sleep, then pitch into the rebel host next morning. Sheridan fumed at this imposed restraint; rest was the last thing on earth he wanted at that stage, either for his own soldiers or anyone else's, blue or gray. "I wish you were here," he protested in a message to Grant, who was with Ord, some twelve miles off at Nottoway Courthouse. "I feel confident of capturing the Army of Northern Virginia if we exert ourselves. I see no escape for Lee."

In response to the summons, Grant undertook a cross-country ride over unfamiliar ground, with no more escort than a quartet of staff officers and a squad of cavalry, but arrived too late to overrule Meade, if in fact that was what he had had in mind when he set out. In any case, next morning's dawn proved Little Phil's concern well founded; Lee was gone. He had swung westward on a night march, scouts reported, apparently headed for Farmville, eighteen miles away on the upper Appomattox and the Southside Railroad, down which he could draw supplies from Lynchburg, then continue his getaway toward the fastness of the Blue Ridge, or turn back south in a renewal of his effort to combine with Johnston. Such disappointment as Grant felt at this loss of contact, this postponement of the showdown that was to have been his reward for winning the race to Burkeville, was more than offset by another consideration, stated later: "We now had no other objec-tive than the Confederate armies, and I was anxious to close the thing up at once." In other words, the race was now a chase — "a matter of legs," as the saying went — and he had confidence in the outcome, not only because he had had a chance to compare the legs of the two armies, these past three days on the march from Petersburg, but also because he understood the temper of his soldiers and the motive that impelled them. "They began to see the end of what they had been fighting four years for. Nothing seemed to fatigue them. They were ready to move without rations and travel without rest until the end. Straggling had entirely ceased, and every man was now a rival for the front."

Pursuit began without delay, and even before contact was reëstablished — first by Sheridan, whose horsemen lapped the rebel flank, probing for a gap, and then by Humphreys, whose lead division overtook the tail of the slow-grinding butternut column within a couple of hours of setting out — all the indications were that the course would not be long. Abandoned rifles and blanket rolls, cluttering the roadsides west of Amelia, testified to the weariness of the marchers who had carried them this far, while the roads themselves were clogged from point to point by broken-down or mud-stalled wagons, as well as by the creatures who had hauled them. "Dropped in the very middle of the road from utter exhaustion," one pursuer would recall, "old horses, literally skin and bones, [were] so weak as scarcely to be able to lift their heads when some soldier would touch them with his foot to see if they really had life." But the best, or worst, evidence in this regard was the condition of the stragglers encountered in increasing numbers as the chase wore on. Collapsed in ditches or staggering through the woods and sodden fields, near delirium from hunger and fatigue, they not only offered little resistance to being gathered up; they seemed to welcome capture as a comfort. For them at least the war was over, won or lost, and winning or losing made less difference than they had thought before they reached the end of their endurance. Not that all of them, even now, had abandoned the last vestige of that cackling sense of the ridiculous they had flaunted from the start, four years ago. A squad of well-clad, well-fed bluecoats, for example, descended on a tattered, barefoot North Carolina private who had wandered off, lone and famished, in search of food. "Surrender, surrender! We've got you!" they cried as they closed in with leveled weapons. "Yes, you've got me," the Tarheel scarecrow replied, dropping his rifle to raise his hands, "and a hell of a git you got."

Any army in this condition, more or less from top to bottom, was likely to stumble into some error that would cost it dearly, and that was what happened this April 6, known thereafter as the Black Thursday of the Confederacy. Longstreet, still in the lead, was under orders to march hard for Rice, a Southside station three miles short of the Appomattox, lest Ord's corps, reported to be on its way up the track from Burkeville, get there first and cut the hungry graybacks off from the rations St John had waiting for them at Farmville. Behind the First Corps train came Anderson, then Ewell, followed by the guns and wagons of the other three corps — so called, though none was larger than a division had been in the old days — including Gordon's, which had been fighting a rear-guard action against Humphreys since 8.30 that morning,

west of the Flat Creek crossing where the march had been delayed. By
then Old Peter had reached Rice at the head of his lead division, not
only in advance of Ord but also in time to send Rosser's horsemen in
pursuit of a flying column of 600 Federals who had just passed through
on their way north to burn the bridges the army would need if it was
to cross the river. This too was successful. Overtaken and surrounded,
outnumbered two to one, the raiders — two regiments of infantry, sent
forward by Ord with a squadron of cavalry — were killed or captured,
to a man, before they reached their objective. The bridges were saved,
along with the rations still awaiting the arrival of the half-starved troops
approaching from the south and, presumably, the east.

Lee's relief at this turn of events, which encouraged hope for a
successful getaway, was soon replaced by tension from a new development, one that left him in the dark as to what might have happened to
the other half of his army. Anderson, obliged to halt from time to time
to fight off mounted attacks on his flank, had lost touch with Longstreet's
rear; so that by noon, with three of the four First Corps divisions deployed near Rice to contest Ord's advance from the southeast, the gray
commander could only guess at what might have occurred or be oc-
curring rearward, beyond the gap Sheridan's troopers had created by
delaying Anderson. There was mean ground in that direction, as Lee
knew from just having crossed it: particularly between the forks of
Sayler's Creek, which combined to flow into the Appomattox half a
dozen miles below Farmville, athwart the westward march of all four
corps. Riding north, then east in an attempt to find out for himself, he
approached the point where the boggy little stream ran into the river,
and saw beyond it a skirmish in progress between Gordon's rear-guard
elements and heavy columns of blue infantry in pursuit. Not only was
this dire in itself; it also deepened the mystery of the disappearance of
Anderson and Ewell, supposedly on the march between Gordon and

Longstreet. Lee turned south and rode in search of them, only to encounter a staffer who informed him that enemy horsemen had struck
the unprotected train between the two branches of Sayler's Creek,
setting fire to wagons and creating panic among the teamsters. Eastward,
guns were booming in earnest now, and Lee still knew nothing as to the
fate or whereabouts of his two missing corps. "Where is Anderson?
Where is Ewell?" he said testily. "It is strange I can't hear from them."

It was worse than strange: far worse, he soon found out. Proceeding eastward with Mahone, whose division he summoned from its position in rear of Longstreet's other three near Rice, he topped a ridge
overlooking the valley of Sayler's Creek, and there he saw, spread out
below him and scrambling up the slope, the answer to his questions
about Anderson and Ewell. Union batteries were firing rapidly from a
companion ridge across the way, pounding the shattered remnant of
both gray corps as the fugitives streamed out of the bottoms where they
had met defeat; "a retiring herd," Mahone would later call them, made
up of "hurrying teamsters with their teams and dangling traces, infantry
without guns, many without hats — a harmless mob." Instinctively, Lee
straightened himself in the saddle at the sight. "My God!" he cried,
staring downhill at the worst Confederate rout he had seen in the thirty-
four months since Davis placed him in command amid the confusion
of Seven Pines. "Has the army been dissolved?"

That portion of it had at any rate, largely because of errors of
omission by the two corps commanders and the redoubled aggressiveness of the blue pursuers, mounted and afoot, once they became aware
of the resultant isolation of the graybacks slogging westward into the
toils of Sayler's Creek. Just as Anderson, in failing to notify Longstreet
of his need to stop and fight off cavalry attacks upon his flank, had
created the gap into which enemy troopers had plunged, so presently
had Ewell lost touch with Gordon through a similar oversight. Informed that the rear guard was heavily engaged, he too halted to let
part of the intervening train move on, then diverted the rest onto a
secondary road that led directly to High Bridge, where the railroad
crossed the Appomattox, three miles north of Rice, before looping back
to recross it at Farmville, four miles to the west. In resuming his march
to overtake Anderson, however, he neglected to tell Gordon of the
change: with the result that Gordon, still involved with the bluecoats
close in his rear, took the same route as the wagons he had been trailing
all along, unaware that he was alone, that his corps had become one of
three unequal segments into which Lee's army had been divided by this
double failure on the part of the two generals in charge of the central
segment. This was now the most gravely endangered of the three, though
neither of the two commanders knew it. Ewell, in fact, did not even
know that he had rear-guard duties until he came under fire from guns
of the VI Corps, which was coming up fast and massing for an assault

in conjunction with Sheridan's horsemen, still on Anderson's flank and cavorting among the burning wagons up ahead.

Sheridan had spotted the opportunity almost as soon as it developed. While Humphreys kept on after Gordon, pressing him back toward the crossing of the creek above the junction of its branches — this was the contest Lee had observed when he rode north from Rice in search of the missing half of his command — Little Phil sent word to Wright, whose corps was next in line, that together they could wipe out that portion of the rebel army stalled by his harassment of its flank and his probe of the resultant gap in front. Just then, about 2 o'clock, Anderson struck at Custer, who had made the penetration, and when Custer recoiled Sheridan threw in Devin to contain the drive. Then, hearing Wright's guns open against Ewell, a mile to the northeast, he committed Crook's division against Anderson's center, locked in position by Custer and Devin, front and rear. "Never mind your flanks," he shouted to his troopers as they dismounted for the assault. "Go through them! They're demoralized as hell."

He was right. Resistance by the jangled, road-worn survivors of the Petersburg breakthrough, four hungry days ago, was as brief and ineffectual as their commander later admitted when he reported that they "seemed wholly broken down and disheartened. After a feeble effort . . . they gave way in confusion." Only Wise's brigade of Virginians retired from the field as a military unit of any size. In all the rest it was more or less every man for himself, including those of highest rank; Anderson escaped on horseback, along with Pickett and Bushrod Johnson, but a solid half of the 3000 troops who had managed to stay with him this far on the retreat were killed or captured as they fled through the tangled brush and clumps of pine. Sheridan, leaving this roundup work to Custer, plunged on north with the other two divisions, intent on dealing with Ewell in much the same fashion. At Five Forks he had delivered the unhinging blow to Lee's army; now he was out to make Sayler's Creek the coup de grâce. And in fact that was what it came to, at least for that part of the bedraggled rebel host within his reach.

One-legged Ewell, strapped to the saddle to keep from falling off his horse, had his two undersized divisions facing east along the west side of the creek in an attempt to keep Wright from crossing before Anderson unblocked the road to Rice. Down to 3000 effectives as a result of the straggling by Custis Lee's reservists, he relied mainly on Kershaw's veterans in position on his right. Despite heavy shelling from the ridge across the way and mounting pressure from the three blue divisions in his front, he managed to hold his own until Kershaw's outer flank and rear were suddenly assailed by Sheridan's rapid-firing troopers, who had just overrun Anderson and came storming northward through the brush. "There's Phil! There's Phil!" the VI Corps infantrymen yelled as they splashed across the creek to join the attack being made by their old Valley comrades.

"On no battlefield of the war have I felt a juster pride in the conduct of my command," Joe Kershaw was to say, and Custis Lee was equally proud of what remained of his scratch division, though both saw clearly now that further resistance was useless. So did Ewell, who afterwards reported that "shells and even bullets were crossing each other from front and rear over my troops, and my right was completely enveloped. I surrendered myself and staff to a cavalry officer who came in by the same road General Anderson had gone out on." Some 200 of Kershaw's Georgians and Mississippians managed to escape in the confusion, but they were about all that got away. The rest were taken, along with their commanders at all levels. These 2800, combined with those lost earlier by Anderson, brought the total to 4300 graybacks snared in the fork of Sayler's Creek that afternoon. No wonder, then, that a Federal colonel visiting Sheridan's headquarters that evening found Richard Ewell "sitting on the ground hugging his knees, with his face bent down between his arms." Old Bald Head now bore little resemblance to the self he had been when he was Stonewall Jackson's mainstay, two years ago in the Shenandoah Valley. "Our cause is lost. Lee should surrender before more lives are wasted," he was reported to have told his captors. Watching him, the colonel remarked that "if anything could add force to his words, the utter despondency of his air would do it."

Sheridan provided a study in contrast. Elated, he got off a sundown message to Grant reporting the capture of one lieutenant general, two major generals, and three brigadiers, together with thousands of lesser prisoners, fourteen pieces of artillery, and an uncounted number of wagons. "I am still pressing on with both cavalry and infantry," he informed his chief, and added the flourish that would catch Lincoln's eye next morning: "If the thing is pressed I think Lee will surrender."

That might be, but Lee by then was in a better frame of mind than Sheridan supposed. Mahone, who was beside him on the western ridge when he exclaimed, in shock at what he saw in the valley down below, "My God! Has the army been dissolved?" replied stoutly, in reference to his division coming up behind: "No, General. Here are troops ready to do their duty." Lee at once recovered his composure, and turned his thoughts to preventing the enlargement of the disaster by the bluecoats in pursuit of the remnant of Anderson's corps streaming toward him up the hillside. "Yes, General," he said; "there are some true men left. Will you please keep those people back?"

Leaving Mahone to prepare a line of defense against "those people," he rode forward to meet and comfort his own. From somewhere, perhaps from the hand of a passing color bearer, or else from the ground where another had dropped it in flight, he secured a Confederate battle flag; with the result that Anderson's panicked fugitives, toiling uphill, saw him waiting astride Traveller near the crest, a gray general on a gray horse, over whose head the red folds of the star-crossed bunting caught the rays of the sun declining beyond the ridge. Some kept going, overcome by fear, while others stopped to cheer and cluster round him, though with more than a touch of delirium in their voices. "It's General Lee!" they cried. "Where's the man who won't follow Uncle Robert?" As at Gettysburg when they came limping back across the mile-wide valley from the carnage on Cemetery Hill, they found solace in his words and manner. Mahone's troops would cover their withdrawal, he said; they must go to the rear and form again. They did as he asked, most of them at any rate, and presently Mahone came forward to relieve him of the flag and escort him within the lines his veterans had drawn in case the Federals launched a follow-up assault.

No such attack ensued. Despite Sheridan's message assuring Grant that he was "pressing on," Custer had all he could handle in rounding up captives in the brush, as did Crook and Devin, a mile to the north; Wright went into bivouac, and Humphreys' clash with Gordon was still in progress near the Appomattox. Mahone remained in position till after dark, as Lee directed, then marched for High Bridge, four miles northeast, under instructions to cross and set it and an adjacent wagon span afire as soon as Gordon passed over with what remained of the three-corps train. Lee meantime had rejoined Longstreet at Rice for a night march to Farmville, where he too would cross the river and burn the bridges in his rear. A dispatch from Gordon, received soon after sundown, informed his chief that he was "fighting heavily" with Humphreys. "My loss is considerable," he reported, "and I am still closely pressed." By the time he was able to break contact, after nightfall, he had left some 1700 men behind as prisoners, together with a good part of the train. This brought the total to 6000 Confederates made captive today, with perhaps another 2000 killed, wounded, or otherwise knocked loose from their commands. Ewell's corps had been abolished, all but a couple of hundred survivors who made it through the lines that night. ("What regiment is that?" someone asked an officer at the head of the arriving column. "Kershaw's *division*," he replied.) Anderson's corps had been reduced by half, its units shattered except for one brigade, and Gordon's three divisions were cut to skeleton proportions, as Lee would see for himself when they came up next morning. "That half of our army is destroyed," he said of the troops engaged along Sayler's Creek this black Thursday.

Still, even though it was done at a cost of 8000 casualties — not half, but in any case a solid third of all that remained with the colors —

he had accomplished what he set out to do when he left Amelia the
day before. Old Peter's corps was intact, having had little trouble
holding off Ord's advance up the Southside Railroad. Moreover, rations
in plenty were waiting ahead at Farmville, and once there, with the
bridges burned behind him, he could put the swollen Appomattox between him and his pursuers, feed and rest his weary men, and perhaps,
by moving westward on the north side of the river, get enough of a
new head start to try again for a turn south to combine with Johnston
in North Carolina. Or, failing that, he might press on to gain the fastness
of the Blue Ridge Mountains, where he once had said he could hold out
"for years."

The night was cold, with flurries of snow reported in nearby
Burkeville next morning. Lee went ahead of Longstreet's men, who
trudged on a poor cross-country road, and got a few hours' rest in a
house at Farmville. When he rose at dawn, April 7, the First Corps
troops were filing through the town, their step quickened by the promise
of rations awaiting issue in boxcars parked on the northside tracks.
Anxious for some first-hand word of the Sayler's Creek survivors, who
were crossing downriver, with instructions to follow the railroad to
the vicinity of Farmville, he again doubled Old Peter's column and
proceeded eastward, beyond the Appomattox, until he encountered the
first of his missing veterans in the person of Henry Wise, who had
shared with him the rigors of his first campaign, out in western Virginia
in the fall of '61. Arriving on foot at the head of his brigade — the only
one to survive, as a unit more or less intact, Anderson's debacle of the
day before — the former governor presented an outlandish picture of
a soldier. He had lost not only his horse and baggage in yesterday's fight,
but also much else in the hurried withdrawal, including his headgear
and overcoat, which he had replaced with a jaunty Tyrolean hat,
acquired en route, and a coarse gray blanket held together in front by a
wire pin. His face, moreover, was streaked with red from having washed
it in a puddle. This gave him, as he later said, the appearance of an aged
Comanche brave. Lee thought so, too, and recovered a measure of his
accustomed good humor at the sight. "I perceive that you, at any rate,
have not given up the contest," he told his fellow Virginian, "as you are
in your warpaint this morning." Wise drew himself up, shoulders back;
he and Lee were of an age, just under two years short of sixty. "Ready
for dress parade," he responded proudly to a question about the condition of his command.

Other good news he had as well. Mahone was over the river, too,
in position to cover the downstream bridges; Gordon had crossed with
all that remained of the train, preceded by a number of Anderson's
stragglers, and Mahone was waiting for still others to get over before
he gave the engineers word to fire both spans; that is, unless the Yankees
came in sight beforehand, which they had not done by the time Wise

left at sunup. Encouraged, Lee rode back to where his staff had set up headquarters opposite Farmville. Here he was visited presently by the Secretary of War, who had come on horseback by a different route from Richmond and was off again for Danville as soon as he had conferred with the general-in-chief. In a wire sent to the President next day, while moving roundabout to join him, Breckinridge reported that Lee had been "forced across the Appomattox" to find "temporary relief" from the heavy columns of Federals in pursuit, but that he would "still try to move around [them] toward North Carolina," once he resumed his westward march up the left bank of the river shielding his flank. So he had said at any rate. A military man himself, however, the Kentuckian added his own appraisal of Lee's chances as he saw them: "The straggling has been great, and the situation is not favorable."

In point of fact the situation was considerably less favorable than he had known when the brief conference ended. He had no sooner left, around midmorning, than a courier reached headquarters with news of a development that threatened to undo all Lee's plans for his next move, if indeed there was to be one. Bluecoats were over the Appomattox in strength at High Bridge, four miles east, and were closing even now upon the famished graybacks filing into the fields across from Farmville to draw their first issue of rations in five days. Mahone, it seemed, had pulled out behind Wise and Gordon without giving the engineers orders to fire the two bridges, and the resultant delay, while an officer spurred after him and returned, brought a heavy enemy column in sight before a match was struck. High Bridge itself, an open-deck affair on sixty-foot trusses of brick and pine, burned furiously at once, dropping four of its dozen spans into the water; but the low wagon bridge alongside, built of hardwood, caught fire so slowly that the whooping Federals arrived in time to stamp out the flames. By 9 o'clock Humphreys had his lead division over the river and a second arriving to reinforce the bridgehead to a strength too great for Mahone to retake it, though he counter-marched and tried. As for Lee, when he got word of what had happened he lost his temper entirely. "He spoke of the blunder," a staffer observed, "with a warmth and impatience which served to show how great a repression he ordinarily exercised over his feelings."

His rage at this sudden removal of the advantage of having the swollen river between him and his pursuers — not to mention the loss of the anticipated rest halt, which was to have given his road-worn soldiers time to cook and eat their rations and perhaps even get some badly needed sleep before setting out once more to regain the head start that would enable them to turn south for Danville, across the front of the blue column, or anyhow win the race for Lynchburg, where St John had still more rations waiting just over forty miles away — was subdued by the need for devising corrective defensive measures, lest his approximately 20,000 survivors, effective and noneffective, suffer destruction at the hands of more than 80,000 Federals converging upon them from the east and south, on both sides of the Appomattox. Because of a deep bend in the river above Farmville, the Lynchburg pike ran north for about three miles before it turned west near Cumberland Church, where a road from High Bridge joined it. Lee's orders were for Mahone, falling back under pressure from Humphreys, to take up a position there and hold the enemy off until Gordon and Longstreet cleared the junction. At the same time, he summoned Brigadier General E. P. Alexander, the First Corps chief of artillery, and gave him the double task of sending a battalion of guns to support Mahone and of destroying the two bridges at Farmville, as soon as Old Peter's men and wagons finished crossing, to prevent the bluecoats in their rear from joining Humphreys in his attempt to end the campaign, and with it the Army of Northern Virginia, here and now.

Alexander, a Georgia-born West Pointer, not quite thirty and a veteran of nearly all the army's major battles, got the guns off promptly to Cumberland Church, where they presently were in action against the Federals arriving from High Bridge, and prepared the railroad and wagon spans for burning as soon as the last of the gray infantry on the march from Rice were safely over. There was time for that, but not for the horsemen covering their rear; Alexander was taking no chances on a repetition of what had happened earlier, four miles downstream. Closely pursued by Crook, whose division had been sent over by Sheridan after a good night's rest, Fitz Lee was obliged to turn and fight on the outskirts of Farmville in order to give the tail of Longstreet's column a chance to clear the bridges. By the time he was able to break off the action and retire under fire through the streets of the town, both spans were ablaze from end to end; Fitz had to veer west in a race for an upstream ford, which he hoped would not prove too deep for his bone-tired horses to cross before Crook overtook them and used his guns to bloody the waters at that point. His uncle, watching from the opposite bank, took alarm at the thought of his cavalry being cut off, as well as at the sight of the hard-driving VI Corps, which arrived just then from Sayler's Creek and appeared on the hills overlooking the river from the south. Displaying the first real agitation he had shown on the retreat, Lee rode to where Longstreet's earliest arrivers had begun to frizzle bacon and boil cornmeal over newly kindled fires. In response to his urgent orders, and despite Old Peter's remonstrance that Fitz and his troopers could look out for themselves, the issue of rations was discontinued, amid groans from men still waiting to receive them, and those that had been partly cooked were dumped from skillets and kettles which then were flung over the tailgates of wagons whose drivers were in a panic to be off. In a state of torment from the smell of food they had not gotten to eat, the First Corps veterans fell in for the march beyond Cumberland Church, where Mahone was making his stand.

When they got there they found the road still open to the west, but they were unable to take it because Mahone, hard pressed by Humphreys' flankers, had to be reinforced if he was to continue holding out against bluecoats whose attacks grew harder to withstand as more and more of them arrived from downriver, eager to make the most of the opportunity their rapid, dry-shod crossing had afforded them, first to bring the fleeing rebs to bay — which they had done already — and then to overrun them, while the rest of the blue army effected a crossing in their rear to cut them off and help complete their destruction. Neither of these two last things happened, however. Supported by Gordon and Longstreet when they came up, Mahone not only held firm, he also counterattacked with a fury that went far toward making up for this morning's lapse at High Bridge, which had brought on the present crisis. Longstreet, informed that the enemy was menacing the left, detached a brigade from Field's division "with orders to get around the threatening force and break it up. Mahone so directed them through a woodland," he later wrote, "that they succeeded in over-reaching the threatened march and took in some 300 prisoners, the last of our troubles for the day."

The sun by then was going down. When it had set, and the fighting sputtered into a silence broken only by the mewls and groans of the wounded trapped between the lines, Old Peter rode through the twilight to a cottage where Lee had set up headquarters near Cumberland Church. He found him in a much better frame of mind than when he last saw him that morning, agitated by the news of Humphreys' easy coup, which voided his plans for a rest halt and a shielded march up-river, as well as by the threat of having his cavalry overwhelmed by the superior force of blue troopers in a race for the perhaps unusable ford northwest of the bridges on fire at Farmville. As it happened, though their best pace was no more than a shaky gallop, Fitz Lee's horsemen not only effected their escape across the Appomattox; they also managed to turn the tables on their pursuers once they reached the other side. Crossing by the ford, hard on the heels of the gray riders, Crook's lead brigade soon came in sight of Longstreet's train, grinding northward on a poor road near the river, and sought to repeat its successful foray at Sayler's Creek the day before. Fitz saw his chance and prepared to take it. Posting his own division to block the attack by receiving it head on, he sent Rosser against the Union flank, which crumpled when he struck it. Surprised and routed, the former aggressors scurried hard for the ford they had crossed when the pursuit was in the opposite direction, roles reversed.

Lee's spirits rose as he watched his nephew's rousing counterstroke, and lifted again when he learned of Mahone's success in keeping Humphreys' flankers off his line of retreat near Cumberland Church. There still was fight in his diminished army, fight in the style that had won it fame, and while he could not react as he once would have done by going over to the offensive against a divided foe, he was much encouraged by what had been achieved in the course of a day that opened with threats of disaster, left and right, and closed with his forces reunited after inflicting heavier casualties than they suffered. Although it was clear that another night march would have to be undertaken — the third in a row, and the fourth since leaving Petersburg and Richmond — by sundown his trains were rolling westward on the Lynchburg turnpike, unmolested, and his still-hungry soldiers were preparing to follow after moonrise. "Keep your command together and in good spirits, General," he had told his son Rooney that afternoon. "Don't let them think of surrender. I will get you out of this."

★ ★ ★

Surrender. Though the word was spoken in buoyant reaction to his nephew's savage counterslash at Crook, Lee's use of it showed that he knew his weary, half-starved troops were thinking of that contingency: as indeed he himself was, if only to counsel rejection. Grant, by contrast, was thinking of it quite purposely by then — in reverse, of course — as a proposal to end the drawn-out agony of his adversary's retreat, which he perceived was doomed in any case, and as a duty he presently said he felt "to shift from myself the responsibility of any further effusion of blood."

He had arrived from Burkeville around midday, shortly after Wright's infantry topped the hills overlooking Farmville from the south, and established headquarters in the local hotel, a rambling brick structure on the main street, two blocks short of where the still-burning wreckage of the town's two bridges released twin plumes of smoke above the swollen Appomattox, now a barrier to pursuit of the Confederates, who apparently were free at last to take some badly needed rest on the far side. Couriers soon were coming and going, however, back and forth across the broad hotel veranda, and all the news was good. Yesterday's forays along Sayler's Creek, which had netted some 6000 butternut prisoners, had cost the attackers fewer than 1200 casualties, only 166 of them killed. Best of all, though, was the news that Humphreys was over the river, four miles below, and moving westward to deny the rebels the rest they thought they had won when they fired the bridges in their rear. He was, as Grant said later, "in a very hazardous position," but the sound of his guns, roaring nearer and nearer from the northeast, gave evidence that his boldness was paying off. Besides, he would not stay unsupported long; Grant told Wright to throw a footbridge over the Appomattox, tied to the charred pilings of the railroad span, and use it to reinforce Humphreys as soon as possible with his whole corps. Including Crook's troopers, who would cross by an upstream ford, close to 40,000 Federals would then be on the north bank of the river. That was twice the strength to which Lee by now had dwindled or been cut: surely enough for Wright and Humphreys to perform the task of simultaneously driving and delaying him when he continued (as he would be obliged to do, if he could get away to try) his efforts to move westward to Lynchburg, where rations were known to be waiting in abundance.

For all its heft, this northside push involved no more than half Grant's army, and only half his plan for Lee's undoing. The other half — exclusive of Parke's corps, which had been given the laborious non-combat chore of shifting one track of the Southside Railroad an inch and a half inward, all the way from Petersburg to Burkeville, to accommodate the narrower-gauged Union cars and locomotives and thus provide a high-speed supply line running close in the moving army's rear from the high-piled docks at City Point — would move south of the Appomattox, and also westward, unimpeded, to outmarch and cut the old fox off before he reached his goal. Sheridan, in fact, after sending Crook to support the convergence on Farmville, had already set out in that direction from Sayler's Creek this morning with his other two divisions, riding hard for Prince Edward Courthouse, a dozen miles west of Rice, on the chance that Lee might succeed in giving his pursuers the slip and pass through there, en route to Danville and a combination with Johnston. Nothing came of that, but presently a wire reached headquarters from the bandy-legged cavalry commander, who had covered better than twenty miles of winding road by early afternoon. He was moving instead to Appomattox Station, twenty-five miles out the Southside line from Farmville, to intercept eight supply trains loaded with rations Lee had ordered shipped from Lynchburg to feed his troops when they rounded the nearby headwaters of the Appomattox River. Grant was quick to act on this; indeed, had begun to act on it before he received the information, by sending Griffin after Sheridan with instructions to do all he could to keep up with the fast-riding horsemen then on their way to Prince Edward. Now he added Ord's corps to this southside interception force, with the difference that Ord was to move by a more direct route, due west out the railroad. This too would be a 40,000-man effort, and Grant himself would go along to see that everything went as planned, leaving to Meade the supervision of the march beyond the river, until such time as the two halves, slogging westward along its opposite banks, came together near its source, like upper and nether millstones, to grind between them whatever remained by then of Lee's bedraggled army.

That should occur by tomorrow evening, or Sunday morning at the latest. Meantime he had little to do but wait for Wright to complete his footbridge, just up the street from the hotel, and Ord to get started out the railroad; Griffin was already west of Rice, slogging after Sheridan, and Humphreys' guns were still booming aggressively, two or three miles beyond the river. Despite his mud-spattered clothes, which he had not been able to change since getting separated from his baggage on the twilight ride to Jetersville two nights back, Grant was in a pleasant frame of mind. "Let the *thing* be pressed," Lincoln had wired him this morning, and he was proceeding to do just that, being similarly convinced that the iron was hot for striking. He saw the end in sight at last. What was more, he believed that Lee must see it, too, outnumbered two-to-one as he was by each half of the well-fed and superbly equipped army that soon would be driving him westward up the opposite bank of the dwindling Appomattox. According to Wright, who had talked with him yesterday after his capture, even so stout a fighter as Dick Ewell had confessed that the Confederate cause was lost "and it was the duty of the authorities to make the best terms they could while they still had a right to claim concessions." To continue the conflict under present conditions, he added, "would be but very little better than murder."

Grant rather thought so, too, and presently said as much. Shortly before 5 o'clock, Ord and Gibbon came by headquarters for a final check with him before setting out westward, and as the conference drew to a close he suddenly fell silent, musing, then looked up, and in what Gibbon called "his quiet way," remarked: "I have a great mind to summon Lee to surrender." He seemed to have surprised himself almost as much as he surprised his listeners, but there was no doubt that he meant what he said, for he called at once for ink and paper and began to write accordingly.

> Headquarters Armies of the United States,
> April 7, 1865 — 5 p.m.
>
> General R. E. Lee,
> Commanding C. S. Army.
>
>   General: The results of the last week must convince you of the hopelessness of further resistance on the part of the Army of Northern Virginia in this struggle. I feel that it is so, and regard it as my duty to shift from myself the responsibility of any further effusion of blood by asking of you the surrender of that portion of the C. S. Army known as the Army of Northern Virginia.
>   Very respectfully, your obedient servant,
>
> U. S. GRANT, Lieutenant General,
> Commanding Armies of the United States.

Brigadier General Seth Williams, Grant's inspector general, charged with delivery of the message under a flag of truce, set out at once for High Bridge to cross the river there and make his way through Humphreys' lines to Lee's. He would have saved time, and spared himself and his orderly and their mounts two thirds of the roundabout nine-mile ride, if he had waited for the VI Corps engineers to complete their footbridge over the Appomattox. They did so by sundown, and Wright's lead division began crossing shortly afterwards, marching three abreast up the street in front of headquarters, where Grant came out and took a seat on the veranda to watch the troops swing past "with a step that seemed as elastic," a staffer observed, "as on the first day of their toilsome tramp." On that day he had called them "as good an army as ever fought a battle," and now they returned the compliment in kind. Passing thus in review, they spotted their rather stumpy, dark-bearded commander on the hotel porch, his cigar a ruby point of light in the deepening shadows, and cheered him lustily to show that whatever reservations they had felt in the past were as gone as his own. He left his chair and came to the railing, still quietly smoking his cigar, and they cheered louder at this reduction of the distance between them. When night fell, bonfires were kindled for illumination along both sides of the street. The effect was one of a torchlight parade as the men broke ranks to snatch brands from the fires, then fell back in to flourish them over-head, roaring the John Brown song while they slogged on toward the river and Lee's army on the other side.

Grant did not wait for the last of Wright's cheering veterans to march past the hotel. After finishing his smoke he turned in early, re-tiring to a room in which the manager falsely assured him Lee had slept the night before.

Three miles to the north, where Mahone still held his position near Cumberland Church, Captain H. H. Perry, adjutant of the brigade sent by Longstreet to reinforce the left, went forward around 9 o'clock to investigate a report that a flag of truce had been advanced by the enemy in front. He proceeded with caution, for there had been a similar inci-dent about an hour earlier, which ended when the butternut pickets, suspecting a Yankee trick, opened fire at the first hail from the twilit woods across the way. Now here were the truce-seekers back again, if that was what they had been in the first place. The young Georgia cap-tain picked his way carefully to a point some fifty yards in front of the lines, where he stopped amid a scattering of blue-clad dead and wounded, hit in the last assault, and called for the flag: if that was what it was. It was: for now there appeared before him, resplendent in the light of the rising moon, what he later described as "a very handsomely dressed Federal officer" who introduced himself as Brigadier General Seth Williams of Grant's staff. Highly conscious of the contrast they presented, no less in looks than in rank — "The truth is, I had not eaten two ounces in two days, and I had my coattail then full of corn, waiting to parch it as soon as the opportunity might present itself" — Perry said later, "I drew myself up as proudly as I could, and put on the appearance as well as possible of being perfectly satisfied with my personal exterior."

Williams measured up to the occasion. Formerly the "efficient and favorite" prewar adjutant at West Point, including a time while R. E. Lee was superintendent, he had served McClellan, Burnside, Hooker, and Meade in the same capacity, with emphasis on his ability to celebrate the amenities. Now, as Grant's I.G. and special envoy — despite the loss, an hour ago, of his orderly in the fire that greeted his first attempt to open communications — he demonstrated that same ability in the moon-lit clearing between the lines of Humphreys and Mahone. Once the formal introductions were concluded, he produced a handsome silver flask and remarked, as Perry afterwards recalled, "that he hoped I would not think it an unsoldierly courtesy if he offered me some very fine brandy." The Georgian, who had nothing to offer in return but the unparched corn in the tail of his coat, found himself in a dilemma. "I wanted that drink awfully," he said later. "Worn down, hungry and dis-pirited as I was, it would have been a gracious godsend if some old Confederate and I could have emptied that flask between us in that dreadful hour of misfortune. But I raised myself about an inch higher, if possible, bowed and refused politely, trying to produce the ridiculous appearance of having feasted on champagne and pound cake not ten minutes before." Williams — "a true gentleman," his then companion would declare — returned the flask unopened to his pocket, and for this Perry was most grateful down the years. "If he had taken a drink, and my Confederate olfactories had obtained a whiff of the odor of it, it is possible that I should have caved." Spared this disgrace, he received from Williams the letter from Grant to Lee, together with a request for its prompt delivery; after which the ragged captain and the well-groomed brigadier "bowed profoundly to each other and turned away," each toward his own lines.

A courier soon reached Lee's headquarters in the cottage near Cumberland Church. Longstreet, still with his chief though the time by now was close to 10 o'clock, watched as he studied the message. There was no emotion in his face, and he passed it to his lieutenant with-out comment. Old Peter read the surrender request, then handed it back. "Not yet," he said.

Lee made no reply to that, but he did to Grant's letter; first, to refuse acceptance of the responsibility therein assigned him for such blood as might still be shed, and second, to explore the possibility — however remote — that his adversary might be willing to reopen the Ord-Longstreet peace discussions he had broken off so abruptly the month before, disclaiming any "authority" in such matters. As soon as Old Peter went out into the night, rejoining his troops for the march that had begun to get under way at moonrise, Lee wrote his answer on a single sheet of paper and gave it to the courier to be sent across the lines.

7th Apl '65

Genl

I have recd your note of this date. Though not entertaining the opinion you express of the hopelessness of further resistance on the

part of the Army of N. Va. I reciprocate your desire to avoid useless effusion of blood, & therefore before considering your proposition, ask the terms you will offer on condition of its surrender.

Very respy your obt Svt
R. E. LEE, Genl

Lt Genl U. S. Grant,
Commd Armies of the U States.

Old Peter cleared his camps well before midnight, but presently,
in accordance with instructions to assume the more rigorous task of
guarding the rear, halted to let Gordon take the lead on the westward
march up the left bank of the Appomattox. The army thus had a head
and a tail, but no middle now that the other two corps had been "dissolved" in battle and by Lee; Wise's still sizeable brigade — practically
all that remained of Johnson's division — was assigned to Gordon, in
partial compensation for his losses at Sayler's Creek, while skeletal fragments of the other three divisions, under Pickett, Heth, and Wilcox,
were attached to Longstreet, thereby rejoining comrades they had not
seen since the Petersburg breakthrough sundered them, six days back.
That left Richard Anderson and Bushrod Johnson troopless, and George
Pickett not much better off with only sixty armed survivors; Lee solved
the problem by formally relieving all three of duty, with authorization
to return to their homes before reporting to the War Department.
Anderson and Johnson left that afternoon, but Pickett's orders apparently went astray. In any case he was still around, that day and the
next, still nursing grievances over rejection of a report in which he had
sought to fix the blame on others for his Gettysburg repulse. Lee may or
may not have known about the Five Forks shad bake, a week ago today,
but subsequently, when he saw his fellow Virginian ride by headquarters, ringlets jouncing, air of command intact, he reacted with dark
surprise. "I thought that man was no longer with the army," he remarked.

Otherwise, aside from continuing hunger and fatigue, there was
much that was pleasant about this sixth day's march, especially by contrast with the five that had gone before. Not only had the weather improved, the plodding graybacks noted when the sun came up this
Saturday morning, but so had the terrain, barely touched by war till
now. It was a day, one pursuing Federal wrote, "of uneventful marching; hardly a human being was encountered along the way. The country
was enchanting, the peach orchards were blossoming in the southern
spring, the fields had been peacefully plowed for the coming crops, the
buds were beginning to swell, and a touch of verdure was perceptible
on the trees and along the hillsides. The atmosphere was balmy and
odorous; the hamlets were unburnt, the farms all tilled." Best of all,
no roar of guns disturbed what a South Carolinian called "the soft airs,

at once warm and invigorating, which blew to us along the high ridges we traversed." Fitz Lee, whose horsemen trailed the column at a distance of two miles, reported the enemy infantry no closer to him than he was to his own, while the blue cavalry seemed equally disinclined to press the issue. Still, there was a driving urgency about the march, an apprehension unrelieved by the lack of direct pressure, and the need for it was evident from even a brief study of the map. On the left, the dwindling Appomattox soon would cease to be a barrier to whatever Union forces were in motion on the other side. A dozen miles beyond that critical point, westward across a watershed traversed by the Southside Railroad, the James River flowed northeast to reënter the tactical picture as a new barrier — one that was likely to be controlled by whichever army rounded the headwaters of the Appomattox first. If it was Lee's, he could feed his men from the supply trains he had ordered sent to Appomattox Station, then press on next day to take shelter behind the James. If on the other hand the Federals got there in time to seize his provisions and in strength enough to block his path across the twelve-mile watershed, the campaign would be over. Alexander, the First Corps artillerist, saw this clearly. Examining on the map the "jug-shaped peninsula between the James and the Appomattox," he noted that "there was but one outlet, the neck of the jug at Appomattox Station." Both armies were headed there now, north and south of the river that had its source nearby — and "Grant had the shortest road."

What was likely to come of this was plain enough to a number of high-ranking officers who had conferred informally about it the previous evening while waiting to set out on what they judged might well be their last march. Concluding that surrender would soon be unavoidable, they requested William Pendleton, the senior of the group, to communicate their view to Lee and thus, as Alexander put it, "allow the odium of making the first proposition to be placed upon them," rather than on him. Neither Longstreet nor Gordon took part in the discussion, and when Pendleton told them of it next morning, seeking their endorsement, both declined. Old Peter, in fact — saying nothing of the message from Grant, which he had read the night before — was quick to point out that the Articles of War provided the death penalty for officers who urged capitulation on their commanders. As for himself, he said angrily, "If General Lee doesn't know when to surrender until *I* tell him, he will never know."

Pendleton, who had been at West Point with Lee before leaving the army to enter the ministry, bided his time until midday, when he found his fellow graybeard resting in the shade of a large pine beside the road. Like Longstreet, after hearing him out, Lee said nothing of Grant's message — or of his own reply, in which, by requesting terms, he had already begun the negotiations Pendleton was recommending

— but rather expressed surprise at the proposal. "I trust it has not come to that," he said sternly, even coldly. "We certainly have too many brave men to think of laying down our arms."

Snubbed and embarrassed, convinced, in Alexander's words, that Lee "preferred himself to take the whole responsibility of surrender, as he had always taken that of his battles," Pendleton rejoined the troops slogging past on the road beside the river, which narrowed with every westward mile through the long spring afternoon. The going was harder now that this morning's hunger and exertion had been added to those of the past five days. Tailing the march, Longstreet observed that "many weary soldiers were picked up, and many came to the column from the woodlands, some with, some without, arms — all asking for food." There were also those who were too far gone for rescue, sitting as Ewell had sat two days ago, his arms on his knees, his head down between them. Others were even worse undone, "lying prone on the ground along the roadside, too much exhausted to march farther, and only waiting for the enemy to come and pick them up as prisoners, while at short intervals there were wagons broken down, their teams of horses and mules lying in the mud, from which they had struggled to extricate themselves until complete exhaustion forced them to wait for death to glaze their wildly staring eyes." A Virginia trooper saw them thus, but added: "Through all this, a part of the army still trudged on, with their faith still strong, only waiting for General Lee to say whether they were to face about and fight."

Fortunately, no such turnabout action was required before nightfall ended the march with the head of the column approaching Appomattox Courthouse, some three miles short of Appomattox Station. Part of the train was already parked in the fields around the county seat, and the reserve batteries, which had also gone ahead, were in position over toward the railroad. Lee was just dismounting to make camp beside the pike, about midway between Gordon and Longstreet, when a courier overtook him at last with a sealed message that had come through the lines earlier in the day. By the light of a candle held by an aide, he saw that it was Grant's reply to last night's request for his terms of surrender. "Peace being my great desire," the Union commander wrote, "there is but one condition I would insist upon — namely, that the men and officers surrendered shall be disqualified for taking up arms against the Government of the United States until properly exchanged." Not only was this a far cry from the "unconditional" demand that had won him his nom-de-guerre three years ago at Donelson, but Grant considerately added: "I will meet you, or will designate officers to meet any officers you may name for the same purpose, at any point agreeable to you, for the purpose of arranging definitely the terms upon which the surrender of the Army of Northern Virginia will be received."

Nothing of Lee's reaction showed in his face. "How would you answer that?" he asked the aide, who read it and replied: "I would answer no such letter." Lee mused again, briefly. "Ah, but it must be answered," he said, and there by the roadside, still by the flickering light of the candle, he proceeded to do so. Parole was infinitely preferable to imprisonment, but he had to weigh his chances of getting away westward, beyond the James, against the advantage of negotiating while surrender remained a matter of choice. Moreover, he still clung to the notion of resuming more general peace discussions that might lead to something less than total capitulation. "In mine of yesterday," he now told Grant, "I did not intend to propose the surrender of the Army of N. Va., but to ask the terms of your proposition. To be frank, I do not think the emergency has arisen to call for surrender of this Army, but as the restoration of peace should be the sole object of all, I desired to know whether your proposals would lead to that end. I cannot therefore meet you with a view to surrender the Army of N. Va.; but as far as your proposal may affect the C. S. forces under my command, and tend to the restoration of peace, I shall be pleased to meet you at 10 a.m. tomorrow on the old stage road to Richmond, between the picket lines of the two armies."

Soon after the courier set out rearward with this reply, a roar of guns erupted from over near the railroad, three miles off. It swelled and held, then subsided, and after a time — around 9 o'clock — Pendleton arrived from that direction to explain that he had ridden forward, a couple of miles beyond the courthouse village just ahead, to check on the reserve artillery, which had left Farmville with the train the day before. Sixty pieces were in park, awaiting resumption of the march tomorrow; all seemed well, he said, until a sudden attack by Union cavalry exploded out of the twilight woods, full in the faces of the lounging cannoneers. Two batteries were ordered to hold off the blue troopers while the rest pulled back, and there ensued what a participant called "one of the closest artillery fights in the time it lasted that occurred during the war. The guns were fought literally up to the muzzles. It was dark by this time, and at every discharge the cannon were ablaze from touchhole to mouth. There must have been six or eight pieces at work, and the small arms of some three or four hundred men packed in among the guns in a very confined space. It seemed like the very jaws of the infernal regions." Pendleton by then had left to help withdraw such pieces as might be saved, but narrowly avoided capture himself by enemy horsemen who came swarming up the wagon-crowded road. He feared perhaps half the guns had been lost, he told Lee, including those in the two batteries left behind, which soon fell silent in the darkness, three miles to the southwest.

As it turned out, two dozen of them were taken, there and on the road. But that was by no means the worst of the news, or the worst of its implications. Just beyond the overrun gun park was Appomattox

Station, where the supply trains had been ordered to await the arrival of the army. Most likely they had been captured too. If so, that meant still another rationless march tomorrow: if, indeed, a march could be made at all. No one could even guess at the number of Federals involved in the night attack across the way, and though they appeared to be cavalry, to a man — so far at least as anyone had been able to tell in the darkness and confusion — there was no way of knowing what other forces were at hand, including division after division of blue infantry near the end of their unhindered daylong westward tramp up the opposite bank of the river. One thing was certain in any case. If they were there in any considerable strength, corking the James-Appomattox jug, the way across the twelve-mile watershed was blocked and the campaign was over, all but the formal surrender on whatever terms Grant might require at the 10 o'clock meeting Lee had just requested.

Not even now, with the probable end in sight, did Lee show the mounting tension he had been under since the collapse of his flank at Five Forks, a week ago today. He did react swiftly to Pendleton's report, however, by summoning his two infantry corps commanders, as well as his nephew Fitz, who was told to alert his troopers for a shift from the tail of the column to its head. Before long, all three joined him at his camp, pitched near a large white oak on the last low ridge overlooking the north branch of the Appomattox, and the council of war began. Longstreet sat on a log, smoking his pipe; Gordon and Fitz shared a blanket spread on the ground for a seat. The new-risen moon, only two nights short of the full, lighted the scene while Lee, who stood by a fire that had been kindled against the chill, explained the tactical situation, so far as he knew it, and read them Grant's two letters, together with his replies. Then he did something he had not done, at least in this collective way, since the eve of the Seven Days, shortly after he took over as their leader. He asked for their advice. "We knew by our own aching hearts that his was breaking," Gordon was to say. "Yet he commanded himself, and stood calmly facing and discussing the long-dreaded inevitable."

So did they, and the decision accordingly reached was that the army would try for a breakout, a getaway westward beyond the glow of enemy campfires rimming the horizon on all sides except the barren north. While Fitz brought his horsemen forward to lead the attack out the Lynchburg pike, Gordon would prepare to move in support of the mounted effort. If successful in unblocking the road, they would then wheel left to hold it open for the passage of the train, which would be reduced to two battalions of artillery and the ammunition wagons, and Longstreet would follow, guarding the rear in case the pursuing Federals tried to interfere from that direction. It was a long-odds gamble at best; moreover, Gordon pointed out, "The utmost that could be hoped for was that we might reach the mountains of Virginia and Tennessee with a remnant of the army, and ultimately join General Johnston." Still it was no more, or less, than could be expected of men determined to keep fighting so long as a spark of hope remained. If the bluecoats could not be budged, if more than cavalry had arrived to bar the way, there would be time enough then, as Fitz Lee put it, "to accede to the only alternative left us."

While his lieutenants rode off to issue instructions for their share in the predawn movement, Lee prepared to take his last sleep under the stars. Before he turned in, however, a member of Gordon's staff returned to ask where the head of the column was to make camp next night on its westward march. The question was put as if there could be no doubt that the breakthrough would succeed, and Lee's reply, though grim and not without a touch of irony, was in much the same vein. "Tell General Gordon I should be glad for him to halt just beyond the Tennessee line," he said, much to the staffer's chagrin; for the Tennessee line was nearly two hundred miles away.

Grant too was bedded down by then, some fifteen miles to the east in an upstairs room of a deserted house beside the pike; but not to sleep. He had a splitting headache — on this of all days, which had opened with a spirit-lifting message from Lee requesting terms in response to last night's suggestion that he surrender. After stating them in a note that was soon on its way through the lines, Grant changed his mind about riding with the southside column, and crossed the river instead to be where Lee's reply could reach him with the least delay. "Hello, old fellow!" he greeted Meade, to the shock of both their staffs, when he overtook the grizzled Pennsylvanian, still confined to his ambulance by dyspepsia and the added discomfort of chills and fever. All through the bright warm morning the march continued without incident; Grant's spirits continued to mount. At the midday halt, aware that Lincoln was on his way up the coast, he got off an exuberant telegram to Stanton, briefing him on the tactical situation and concluding: "I feel very confident of receiving the surrender of Lee and what remains of his army tomorrow." His terms in this morning's note, he felt, were too generous for his opponent to decline them in his present condition, which was evident from the dolorous state of the stragglers Humphreys and Wright were gleaning while they pressed on westward in the littered wake of the butternut throng. All the same, as the day wore on and there still was no response to his predawn offer, sent forward some eight hours before, he began to wonder at the delay and at the ability of the half-starved graybacks to keep beyond reach of their pursuers. Then out of nowhere, just as the rim of the declining sun glittered below the brim of his hat, the blinding headache struck.

It struck and it kept striking, even after he stopped for the night in a large frame house beside the pike, a dozen miles from Farmville.

The pain was by no means lessened by the banging some aide was giving a piano in the parlor directly below Grant's upstairs bedroom, nor by assurances from another staffer that his migraine attacks were usually followed by good news. Indeed, the arrival of just such a dispatch from Sheridan around 10 o'clock failed to bring relief, although the news was about as good as even he could have hoped for. The cavalryman reported that he had reached Appomattox Station at dusk, ahead of the leading elements of Lee's army. Not only had he captured four and chased off the rest of the supply trains waiting there for the hungry rebels to arrive from Cumberland Church; he had also followed through with a night attack by Custer toward Appomattox Courthouse, which had netted him some two dozen guns, a considerable haul of prisoners and wagons, and — best of all — a dug-in position athwart the Lynchburg road, blocking Lee's escape in the only direction that mattered. Moreover, by way of assuring that the road stayed blocked, he had urged Ord and Griffin to press on westward with their six divisions in a forced-march effort to join him before daylight. "If [they] can get up tonight we will perhaps finish the job in the morning," he told Grant, adding suggestively: "I do not think Lee means to surrender until compelled to do so."

Presently Grant had cause to agree with this closing assessment, and what was more he received it from Lee himself in a message that arrived soon after Sheridan's. Denying that he had intended to propose surrender in his previous response, or that an emergency had arisen which called for him to adopt so drastic a course, the southern commander said only that he would be willing to meet between the lines for a general discussion that might "tend to a restoration of peace." Grant studied the note, more saddened than angered by what he discerned, and shook his head. "It looks as if Lee meant to fight," he said.

He was disappointed. But that was mild compared to the reaction of his chief of staff, with whom he was sharing the bed in the upstairs room. "He did not propose to surrender!" Rawlins scoffed, indignant. "Diplomatic, but not true. He did propose, in his heart, to surrender. . . . He now wants to entrap us into making a treaty of peace. You said nothing about that. You asked him to surrender. He replied by asking what terms you would give. You answered by stating the terms. Now he wants to arrange for peace — something beyond and above the surrender of his army; something to embrace the whole Confederacy, if possible. No, sir. No, sir. Why, it is a positive insult — an attempt, in an underhanded way, to change the whole terms of the correspondence." Grant demurred. "It amounts to the same thing, Rawlins. He is only trying to be let down easy. I could meet him as requested, in the morning, and settle the whole business in an hour." But Rawlins would not have it so. Listeners downstairs heard him shout that Lee had purposely shifted his ground "to gain time and better terms." He saw the Virginian as a sharper, a wriggler trying to squirm from under the retribution about to descend on his guilty head. "He don't think 'the emergency has arisen'! That's cool, but another falsehood. That emergency has been staring him in the face for forty-eight hours. If he hasn't seen it yet, we will soon bring it to his comprehension! He has to surrender. He shall surrender. By the eternal, it shall be surrender or nothing else."

Grant continued to defend his year-long adversary, protesting that in his present "trying position," the old warrior was "compelled to defer somewhat to the wishes of his government. . . . But it all means precisely the same thing. If I meet Lee he will surrender before I leave." At this, Rawlins was quick to remind his chief of last month's wire from Stanton, forbidding him to treat with the enemy on such matters. "You have no right to meet Lee, or anyone else, to arrange terms of peace. That is the prerogative of the President, or the Senate. Your business is to capture or destroy Lee's army." Obliged to admit the force of this, Grant yielded; "Rawlins carried his point," one downstairs listener was to say, "as he always did, when resolutely set." Grant yielded; but he insisted that he still must do Lee the courtesy of answering his letter, if only to decline the suggested meeting. "I will reply in the morning," he said.

That ended the discussion, but not the throb in his head. Before daybreak, a staff colonel found him pacing about the yard of the house, both hands pressed to his aching temples. At the colonel's suggestion, he tried soaking his feet in hot water fortified with mustard, then placed mustard plasters on his wrists and the back of his neck; to no avail. When dawn began to glimmer through he went over to Meade's headquarters, just up the road, and had a cup of coffee. Feeling somewhat better, though not much, he composed a sort of open-ended refusal of Lee's request for a meeting between the lines this Sunday morning. "Your note of yesterday is received," he wrote. "I have no authority to treat on the subject of peace; the meeting proposed for 10 a.m. today could lead to no good. I will state, however, General, that I am equally anxious for peace with yourself, and the whole North entertains the same feeling. The terms upon which peace can be had are well understood. By the South laying down their arms they will hasten that most desirable event, save thousands of human lives, and hundreds of millions of property not yet destroyed. Seriously hoping that all our difficulties may be settled without the loss of another life, I subscribe myself, &c. *U. S. Grant*, Lieutenant General."

After a sunrise breakfast he went forward to find Humphreys and Wright again on the march. Meade was still in his ambulance, but Grant declined the offer of one for himself, despite the headache that made jogging along on horseback a constant torture, apparently having decided to put up with the pain, much as he was putting up with the rumpled and muddy uniform he had been wearing ever since his baggage went astray near Burkeville. Up ahead, though contact had not yet been established with the rebel rear, guns were thumping faintly in the distance. What this meant, or what might come of it, he did not know. He decided, however, that the best way to find out would be to approach the conflict not from this direction, with the column in pursuit, but from the front with Sheridan, who was in position over beyond Appomattox Courthouse. Accordingly, he told Meade goodbye and doubled back, accompanied by his staff, for a crossing of the river and a fast ride west on the far side. So he intended; but there were delays. "We had to make a wide detour to avoid running into Confederate pickets, flankers, and bummers," a reporter who went with him would recall. "It proved to be a long rough ride, much of the way without any well-defined road, often through fields and across farms, over hills, ravines, and 'turned out' plantations, across muddy brooks and bogs of quicksand." Once they even got lost in a pathless stretch of woods, narrowly avoiding capture by a band of rebel stragglers on the roam there. All this time, the rumble of guns up ahead had been swelling and sinking, swelling and sinking, until finally it hushed; a matter for wonder, indeed, though it might well flare up again, as it had before. The sun was nearing the overhead when the riders stopped at last to rest their horses in a roadside clearing whose timber had been cut and heaped for burning. While they dismounted to light cigars from the fuming logs, the reporter later wrote, "someone chanced to look back the way we had come, and saw a horseman coming at full speed, waving his hat above his head and shouting at every jump of his steed."

Soon recognized as one of Meade's lieutenants — a young man well acquainted with army protocol, and observant of it even under the excitement of his current mission — the rider drew rein in front of the chief of staff, saluted stiffly, and presented him with a sealed envelope. Rawlins tore one end open slowly, withdrew the message, and read it deliberately to himself. Nothing in his manner revealed his feelings as he passed the single sheet to Grant, who read it with no more expression on his face, the reporter noted, "than in a last year's bird's nest." Handing it back, he said quietly: "You had better read it aloud, General." Rawlins did so, in a deep voice that by now was a little shaky with emotion.

> April 9th, 1865
>
> General: I received your note of this morning on the picket line, whither I had come to meet you and ascertain definitely what terms were embraced in your proposal of yesterday with reference to the surrender of this army. I now request an interview, in accordance with the offer contained in your letter of yesterday, for that purpose.
>
> Very respectfully, Your obt servt
> R. E. LEE.

The celebration that followed was unexpectedly subdued. "No one looked his comrade in the face," the reporter would declare years later. One staffer hopped on a stump, waved his hat, and called for three cheers; but the hurrahs were few and feeble. Most throats were too constricted for speech, let alone cheers. "All felt that the war was over. Every heart was thinking of friends — family — home."

Grant was the first to recover his voice: perhaps in happy reaction to finding his headache cured, as he afterwards testified, "the instant I saw the contents of the note." This time Lee had said nothing about a broad-scale discussion that might "tend to the restoration of peace." He spoke rather of "the surrender of this army," and sought, as he said, an interview "for that purpose." Negotiations were back on the track, and the track was Grant's.

"How will that do, Rawlins?" he asked, smiling as he recalled his friend's tirade in their upstairs bedroom, late the night before.

"I think *that* will do," the other said.

★ ★ ★

Lee had foreseen the outcome from the start, and showed it when he joined his staff around the campfire that morning, a couple of hours before daylight, dressed in a splendid new gray uniform. His linen was snowy, his boots highly polished, and over a deep red silken sash, gathered about his waist, he had buckled on a sword with an ornate hilt and scabbard. When Pendleton expressed surprise at finding him turned out in such unaccustomed finery, he replied: "I have probably to be General Grant's prisoner, and thought I must make my best appearance."

No considerable insight was required for this assessment of what was likely to come of today's effort. Including 2000 cannoneers available to serve the remaining 61 guns, he had by now some 12,500 effectives in his ranks — fewer, in all, than Sheridan had in bivouac just to the west and south, their horses tethered athwart his one escape route, and only about one third of the skeleton force that began its withdrawal from Richmond, Bermuda Hundred, and Petersburg, a week ago tonight. Nearly as many more were present or scattered roundabout in various stages of collapse from hunger and exhaustion, but that was the number still fit for fight and still with weapons in their hands. Closing on Fitz, whose 2400 troopers were assembled in the yards and lanes of the little courthouse hamlet up ahead, Gordon was down to no more than 2000 infantry, while Longstreet, in motion behind the train of creaking wagons, had barely 6000 to cover the rear. Lee could hear them shuffling past in the darkness, along the road and in the woods surrounding the low glow of his headquarters fire, where the staff was breakfasting on gruel heated in a single metal cup and passed from hand to hand, more or less in the order of rank. He did not share in this, but when the meal was over, such as it was, and daylight began to glimmer through, he mounted Traveller and rode forward to watch his nephew and Gordon try for the breakout that at best would mean that the long retreat would continue beyond the dawn of this Palm Sunday.

Eastward the rim of sky was tinged with red by the time Fitz sent his horsemen forward on the right of Gordon, whose three-division corps — not much larger now than a single good-sized brigade had been when Grant first crossed the Rapidan, just one month less than a year ago this week — attacked due west out the Lynchburg pike, where the Federals had thrown up a gun-studded line of fieldworks in the night. The volume of fire was heavy, but because of a dense ground fog, which the growing light seemed to thicken, Lee could see little from his position on a hill overlooking the town and the fields beyond. If he could have observed the action, screened from his view by the mist that filled the valley, his heart would have lifted, as it had done so often at the start of one of his pulse-quickening offensives. Infantry and cavalry alike, the gray veterans reached and overran the enemy works in a single rush, taking two brass Napoleons and screaming with their old savage delight as the bluecoats scattered rearward to avoid the onslaught. Gordon, exultant, wheeled his cheering men hard left to hold the road open for the passage of the train. All the enemy dead and wounded had on spurs, and he took this for assurance that the breakthrough would be sustained. But then, as he watched the outdone troopers scuttle left and right, across the fields on both sides of the road, it was as if a theater curtain parted to show what he least wanted to see in all the world. There in rear of the gap, rank on rank and growing thicker by the minute, stood long lines of Union infantry, braced and ready, facing the risen sun, their blue flags snapping in the breeze that by now was beginning to waft the fog away.

It was Ord and it was Griffin, with close to 15,000 men apiece. They had arrived at dawn, after an all-night march undertaken in response to the summons from Sheridan, and each had two of his three divisions in position by sunup — in time to hear the high-throated caterwaul of the rebels bearing down on the dismounted cavalry up front. "The sweetest music I ever heard," Stonewall Jackson had called what the Federals themselves variously referred to as "that hellish yell," scarcely human either in pitch or duration, apparently with no hint of brain behind it, and "nothing like a hurrah, but rather a regular wildcat screech." A Wisconsin soldier put it best, perhaps, without even trying for a description. "There is nothing like it this side of the infernal region," he declared, "and the peculiar corkscrew sensation that it sends down your backbone under these circumstances can never be told. You have to *feel* it, and if you say you did not feel it, and heard the yell, then you have never *been* there." They heard it now, through the mist ahead, and for them too, as the cavalry scuttled rearward and sideways, the effect was one of a curtain parting on dread. There stood the butter-

nut infantry, full in front, their regiments so diminished by attrition that
their flags took the breeze not in intersticed rows, as in the old days,
but in clusters of red, as if poppies or roses had suddenly burst into
crowded bloom amid the smoke of their rapid-firing batteries. "We
grew tired and prostrated," a blue veteran said of the hard six-day
pursuit, "but we wanted to be there when the rebels found the last ditch
of which they had talked so much." Now here it was, directly before
them, and they were not so sure. Persuaded last night to press on westward out the railroad for the sake of getting a hot breakfast at Appomattox Station, they instead found graybacks in their front, scarecrow thin
and scarecrow ragged, but still about as dangerous, pound for pound,
as so many half-starved wolves or panthers. It might be the end, as
some were saying, yet nobody wanted to be the last man to fall. "We
were angry at ourselves," one candidate for that distinction later wrote,
"to think that for the sake of drawing rations we had been foolish
enough to keep up and, by doing so, get in such a scrape." It was not so
much the booming guns they minded, he explained; "We dreaded the
moment when the infantry should open on us."

Such dread was altogether mutual. Fitz Lee recoiled, and while
the other two blue divisions came up to extend the triple Union line
to a width of about three miles — 10,000 men to the mile, afoot —
Sheridan remounted and alerted his troopers for an all-out strike at the
rebel left as soon as the infantry started forward. "Now smash 'em, I
tell you; smash 'em!" he was urging his subordinates, and Gordon knew
only too well that, given the opportunity at hand, this was what Little
Phil would be saying. Exposed to attack on both flanks and his center,
the Georgian perceived that he had to pull back if he was to avoid being
cut off and annihilated. He kept his sharpshooters active and stepped up
the fire of his batteries, hoping at best to effect a piecemeal withdrawal
that would discourage a swamping rush by the Federals in his front.
Just then — about 8 o'clock — a staff colonel arrived from the fog-
bound army command post to inquire how things were going. Gordon
gave him a straight answer. "Tell General Lee I have fought my corps to
a frazzle and I fear I can do nothing unless I am heavily supported by
Longstreet."

Blind on his hilltop, Lee received the message without flinching,
though he saw clearly enough what it meant. If so stalwart a fighter as
Gordon could "do nothing" without the help of Longstreet, who had
just been warned that Humphreys and Wright had resumed their advance and soon would pose as grave a threat to his rear as Ord and
Griffin now presented in his front, he had lost all choice in the matter.
What was more he admitted as much, however regretfully, in the
presence of his staff. "Then there is nothing left me to do but go and
see General Grant," he said, "and I would rather die a thousand deaths."

It was by now about 8.30. With more than an hour to wait before setting out for the meeting he had suggested in last night's letter across the lines, Lee returned to his headquarters beside the pike and sent for Longstreet. Leaving Field in charge of the rear guard, which had halted behind the stalled train and was digging in to confront the two blue corps reported to be advancing from the east, Longstreet brought Mahone and Alexander along, apparently in the belief that their advice would be helpful at the council of war he thought had been called to determine the army's next move. As it turned out, however, he had not been summoned for that purpose, but rather to give his opinion on the question of surrender. Countering with a question of his own, he asked whether the sacrifice of the Army of Northern Virginia would in any way help the cause elsewhere. Lee said he thought not. "Then your situation speaks for itself," Old Peter told him. Mahone felt the same. A slight, thin man in a long brown linen duster — so thin, indeed, that his wife, once informed that he had received a flesh wound, replied in alarm: "Now I know it is serious, for William has no flesh whatever" — he was shivering, and he wanted it understood that this was from the chill of the morning, not from fear. All the same, he too could recommend nothing but surrender under the present circumstances. Alexander disagreed. Ten years younger than Mahone, who was crowding forty, he proposed that the troops take to the woods, individually and in small groups, under orders to report to the governors of their respective states. That way, he believed, two thirds of the army would avoid capture by the Yankees; "We would be like rabbits or partridges in the bushes, and they could not scatter to follow us." Lee heard the young brigadier out, then replied in measured tones to his plan. "We must consider its effect on the country as a whole," he told him. "Already it is demoralized by the four years of war. If I took your advice, the men would be without rations and under no control of officers. They would be compelled to rob and steal in order to live. They would become mere bands of marauders, and the enemy's cavalry would pursue them and overrun many sections they may never have occasion to visit. We would bring on a state of affairs it would take the country years to recover from. And as for myself, you young fellows might go bushwhacking, but the only dignified course for me would be to go to General Grant and surrender myself and take the consequences of my acts." Alexander was silenced, then and down the years. "I had not a single word to say in reply," he wrote long afterwards. "He had answered my suggestion from a plane so far above it that I was ashamed of having made it."

Nothing much had been accomplished by all this, but at least Lee had managed to get through the better part of a hard hour: which had probably been his purpose in sending for Longstreet in the first place. Now the time was at hand, and he prepared to set out for the 10 o'clock meeting, rearward between the lines, with his young adjutant, Walter Taylor, and Lieutenant Colonel Charles Marshall, his military secretary; Sergeant George Tucker — Hill's courier, who had attached himself to Lee after the fall of his chief, a week ago this morning — would go along as bearer of the flag of truce. They rode eastward, the four of them, through the cheering ranks of First Corps troops waiting beside the road, and on beyond a stout log barricade under construction for reception of the enemy, due to arrive at any moment. Reaching the picket line, they paused for Tucker to break out the white flag — a soiled handkerchief, tied by one corner to a stick — then continued, half a mile or so, until they saw blue skirmishers approaching. They drew rein, and Marshall rode out front with Tucker, expecting to encounter Grant and his staff. Instead, a single Federal officer appeared, also a lieutenant colonel and also accompanied by an orderly with a flag of truce. He introduced himself as a member of Humphreys' staff, but said that he knew nothing about any meeting, here or elsewhere. All he knew was that he had been given a letter to deliver through the lines, together with instructions to wait for an answer, if one was made. Marshall took the envelope, which was addressed to Lee, and trotted back to hand it to him.

Lee broke it open and read the note Grant had written at Meade's headquarters before sunup, declining the proposed conference on grounds that he had "no authority to treat on the subject of peace," and declaring that hostilities could only be ended "by the South laying down their arms." It was, then, to be "unconditional" surrender; Grant had reverted to type, and Lee had no choice except to repeat his request for a meeting, this time in accordance with whatever preconditions were required. Accordingly, he dictated the message Rawlins would read aloud two hours later, on the far side of the Appomattox. Marshall took it back to the waiting colonel, told him of its contents, and asked that fighting be suspended on this front until it could be delivered and replied to. The Federal turned and rode back through the line of halted skirmishers. While waiting, Lee sent a note to Gordon, through Longstreet, authorizing him to request a similar truce of the enemy moving against him from the opposite direction.

A cease-fire, even a brief one, was likely to prove a good deal easier to ask for than to receive from either direction: especially westward, where Sheridan might have a voice in the matter. And so it was. "Damn them," the cavalryman said angrily on learning that a white flag had come out from Gordon, whose troops by then had fallen back through the town in their rear, "I wish they had held out an hour longer and I would have whipped hell out of them." Suspecting a trick, he wanted no let-up until he bagged the lot. "I've got 'em; I've got 'em like that!" he cried, and he brandished a clenched fist. But Ord outranked and overruled him, and the guns fell silent along the rebel front. Meade, however, reacted much as Sheridan did. Four miles to the east, coming up in the rear of the stalled gray army, he was for pressing the advantage he had worked so hard to gain, flat on his back though he was with chills and fever. "Hey! What?" he exclaimed, emerging from his ambulance when Humphreys' truce-flag colonel delivered Lee's request. "I have no authority to grant such a suspension. General Lee has already refused the terms of General Grant. Advance your skirmishers, Humphreys, and bring up your troops. We will pitch into them at once." He sent the colonel back to inform Lee that Grant had left that part of the field some hours ago; the letter could not reach him in time to stop the attack.

Marshall's reply was that if Meade would read Lee's note to Grant he would surely agree that a truce was in order, but even as the staffer rode back to deliver this suggestion the blue skirmishers resumed their advance. Lee held his ground, determined to do all he could to prevent unnecessary bloodshed, and when another white-flag officer emerged to warn him to withdraw, he responded — over Meade's head, so to speak — with a second message to Grant: "I ask a suspension of hostilities pending the adjustment of the terms of the surrender." Still the skirmishers came on, along and on both sides of the road where Lee and his three companions sat their horses. Only when the bluecoats were within one hundred yards, and he was peremptorily informed that their advance could not be halted, did he turn Traveller's head and ride back up the road, past his own pickets and beyond the now finished barricade. Longstreet was there, bracing his troops for the attack that seemed about to open. Instead — it was close to 11 o'clock by then — the Federal colonel reappeared with a note from Meade, agreeing to an informal one-hour truce and suggesting that Lee might be able to get in touch with Grant more quickly through some other part of the line. Lee accordingly rode on toward the front, which Gordon had established on the near side of the north fork of the Appomattox, and dismounted in a roadside apple orchard to compose his third message of the day to Grant, repeating his request for "an interview, at such time and place as you may designate, to discuss the terms of the surrender of this army."

He was weary from the strain of the long morning. After the messenger set out — this time through Gordon's lines, in accordance with Meade's suggestion — he lay down on a blanket-covered pile of fence rails in the shade of one of the trees. Longstreet presently joined him, and when Lee expressed concern that Grant was stiffening his terms, replied that he did not think so. Well acquainted with the northern commander for years before the war, he believed he would demand nothing that Lee would not demand if the roles were reversed. Lee still had doubts, however, and continued to express them until shortly after noon, when they saw riding toward them, from the direction of Gordon's lines, a well-mounted Federal officer under escort. Presuming that he had been sent by Grant to summon Lee to the meeting requested in one of his earlier notes, Old Peter told his chief: "Unless he offers us honorable terms, come back and let us fight it out." Lee sat up, squaring his shoulders, and Longstreet observed that "the thought of another round seemed to brace him."

Dismounting, the blue-clad emissary saluted and introduced himself as Lieutenant Colonel Orville Babcock of Grant's staff, then presented a note the Union commander had scribbled in his order book half an hour ago, five miles southeast of Appomattox Courthouse, in reply to Lee's first message that morning — the one that Rawlins had finally said would "do." Not mentioning terms or conditions, Grant merely wrote that he would "push forward to the front for the purpose of meeting you. Notice sent to me on this road where you wish the interview to take place will meet me."

Lee only delayed his departure to attend to two comparatively minor matters. One was to have Grant's aide send a dispatch to Meade, directing him to extend the truce until further orders, and the other was to grant a plea from his young adjutant, Walter Taylor, to be spared the heartbreak of attending the surrender. Then he set out, riding alongside Babcock and preceded by Marshall and Tucker, who led the way through Gordon's thin and silent line of battle, down the slope to the creek-sized north branch of the Appomattox. Here he paused to let Traveller drink, then continued his ride toward the courthouse village less than half a mile beyond the stream. Remembering at last that his adversary had left it to him to appoint a meeting place, he sent Marshall ahead, along with the flag-bearing sergeant, to select a proper house for the occasion.

By then it was close to 1 o'clock. Within half an hour Grant arrived from the southeast to find Sheridan waiting for him on the outskirts of town, still eager, as he said later, "to end the business by going in and forcing an absolute surrender by capture." Though this was the first time they had met since the start of the pursuit, a week ago tomorrow, the greetings exchanged were casual.

"How are you, Sheridan?"

"First rate, thank you. How are you?"

"Is Lee up there?"

"Yes, he is in that brick house."

"Very well. Let's go up."

The house Sheridan pointed out belonged to a man named Wilmer McLean, who had agreed to let it be used when Marshall rode in ahead of Lee in search of a place for the meeting with Grant. By the oddest of chances, McLean had owned a farm near Manassas Junction, stretching along the banks of Bull Run, at the time of the first of the two battles fought there. In fact, a shell had come crashing through one of his windows during the opening skirmish, and after that grim experience he had resolved to find a new home for his family, preferably back in the rural southside hill country, "where the sound of battle would never reach them." He found what he wanted at Appomattox Courthouse — a remote hamlet, better than two miles from the railroad and clearly of no military value to either side — only to discover, soon after midday on this fateful Palm Sunday, that the war he had fled was about to end on his doorstep; indeed in his very parlor, where Lee and Marshall waited a long half hour until Babcock, watching beside a window for his chief's arrival, saw him and his staff turn in at the gate, then crossed the room and opened the door into the hall.

Grant entered and went at once to Lee, who rose to meet him. They shook hands, one of middle height, slightly stooped, his hair and beard "nut-brown without a trace of gray," a little awkward and more than a little embarrassed, as he himself later said, mud-spattered trouser legs stuffed into muddy boots, tunic rumpled and dusty, wearing no side arms, not even spurs, and the other tall and patrician-looking, immaculately groomed and clad, with his red sash and ornate sword, fire-gilt buttons and polished brass, silver hair and beard, demonstrating withal, as one observer noted, "that happy blend of dignity and courtesy so difficult to describe." Fifteen years apart in age — the younger commander's forty-third birthday was just over two weeks off — they presented a contrast in more than appearance. Surprised at his own reaction to the encounter, Grant did not know what to make of Lee's at all. "As he was a man of much dignity, with an impassable face," he afterwards declared, "it was impossible to say whether he felt inwardly glad that the end had finally come, or felt sad over the result and was too manly to show it. Whatever his feelings they were entirely concealed from my observation; but my own feelings, which had been quite jubilant on the receipt of his letter, were sad and depressed. I felt like anything rather than rejoicing at the downfall of a foe who had fought so long and valiantly, and had suffered so much for a cause, though that cause was, I believe, one of the worst for which a people ever fought."

Lee resumed his seat, while Marshall remained standing beside him, leaning against the mantel over the unlighted fireplace. Grant took a chair near the middle of the room. Meantime his staff officers were filing in, as one would note, "very much as people enter a sick chamber where they expect to find the patient dangerously ill." Some found seats, but most stood ranged along one wall, looking intently at the old gray fox — the patient — cornered at last and seated across the room from them in his fine clothes. Grant tried to relieve the tension. "I met you once before, General Lee," he said, recalling a time in Mexico when the Virginian had visited his brigade. "I have always remembered your appearance and I think I should have recognized you anywhere." Lee nodded. "Yes, I know I met you on that occasion," he replied, "and I have often thought of it and tried to recollect how you looked. But I have never been able to recall a single feature." If this was a snub Grant did not realize it, or else he let it pass. He went on with his Mexican recollections, warming as he spoke, until Lee, feeling the strain of every dragging moment, broke in at the first pause to say: "I suppose, General Grant, that the object of our present meeting is fully understood. I asked to see you to ascertain upon what terms you would receive the surrender of my army." Grant's response was made with no change of expression, either on his face or in his voice. "The terms I propose are those stated substantially in my letter of yesterday — that is, the officers and men surrendered to be paroled and disqualified from taking up arms again until properly exchanged, and all arms, ammunition, and supplies to be delivered up as captured property." Inwardly, Lee breathed a sigh of vast relief: Longstreet had been right about Grant, and his own worst fears had been groundless. Now, though, it was his turn to mask his emotion, and he did so. "Those are about the conditions I expected would be proposed," he said quietly.

Grant spoke then of a possible "general suspension of hostilities," which he hoped would follow shortly throughout the land, but Lee, anxious to end the present surrender ordeal, once more cut him short, albeit courteously. "I would suggest that you commit to writing the terms you have proposed, so that they may be formally acted upon," he said, and the other replied: "Very well, I will write them out." He called for his order book, bound sheets of yellow flimsy with alternate carbons, and opened it flat on the small round marble-topped table before him. "When I put my pen to the paper," he later declared, "I did not know the first word I should make use of in writing the terms. I only knew what was in my mind, and I wished to express it clearly so that there could be no mistaking it." He succeeded in doing just that. Rapidly and in fewer than two hundred words, he stipulated that officers would "give their individual paroles not to take up arms against the Government of the United States until properly exchanged," that unit commanders would "sign a like parole for the men of their commands," and that "the arms, artillery and private property [were] to be parked and stacked and turned over to the officer appointed by me to receive them." He paused, looking briefly at Lee's dress sword, then added the two last sentences. "This will not embrace the side arms of the officers, nor their private horses or baggage. This done, each officer and man will be allowed to return to their homes, not to be disturbed by the United States authority so long as they observe their paroles and the laws in force where they may reside."

Lee made something of a ritual of examining the document now passed to him. No doubt in an effort to master his nerves, he placed the book on the table before him — small and marble-topped like Grant's, but square — took out his steel-rimmed spectacles, polished them very carefully with a handkerchief, crossed his legs, set the glasses deliberately astride his nose, and at last began to read. Nothing in his expression changed until he reached the closing sentences. Having read them he looked up at Grant and remarked in a warmer tone than he had used before: "This will have a very happy effect on my army." When his adversary said that he would have a fair copy made for signing, "unless you have some suggestions in regard to the form in which I have stated the terms," Lee hesitated before replying. "There is one thing I would like to mention. The cavalrymen and artillerists own their own horses in our army. Its organization in this respect differs from that of the United States. I would like to understand whether these men will be permitted to retain their horses." Grant overlooked what he later called "this implication that we were two countries," but said flatly: "You will find that the terms as written do not allow this." Lee perused again the two sheets of yellow flimsy. He was asking a favor, and he did not enjoy the role of supplicant. "No," he admitted regretfully, "I see the terms do not allow it. That is clear." Then Grant relented. Perhaps recalling his own years of hardscrabble farming near St Louis before the war — or Lincoln's remark at City Point, less than two weeks ago, that all he wanted, once the time came, was "to get the men composing the Confederate armies back to their homes, at work on their farms or in their shops" — he relieved Lee of the humiliation of having to plead for a modification of terms already generous. "Well, the subject is quite new to me," he mused, feeling his way as he spoke. "Of course I did not know that any private soldiers owned their animals, but I think this will be the last battle of the war — I sincerely hope so — and that the surrender of this army will be followed soon by all the others, and I take it that most of the men in the ranks are small farmers, and as the country has been so raided by the two armies it is doubtful whether they will be able to put in a crop to carry themselves and their families through the next winter without the aid of the horses they are now riding, I will arrange it this way; I will not change the terms as now written, but I will instruct the officers I shall appoint to receive the paroles to let all the men who claim to own a horse or mule take the animals home with them to work their little farms." Lee's relief and appreciation were expressed in his response. "This will have the best possible effect upon the men," he said. "It will be very gratifying, and will do much toward conciliating our people."

Grant passed the document to his adjutant for copying, and while this was in progress Lee had Marshall draft a letter of acceptance. In the wait that followed, the northern commander introduced his staff, together with Ord and Sheridan. Shaking hands with those who offered theirs, the Virginian bowed formally to the others, but spoke only to Seth Williams, his former West Point associate, and even then, for all his studied courtesy, could not manage a smile in response to a pleasantry of the old days. The introductions over, he informed Grant that he had a number of Federal prisoners he would like to return to their own lines as soon as it could be arranged, "for I have no provisions for them. I have, indeed, nothing for my own men. They have been living for the last few days principally on parched corn, and are badly in need of both rations and forage." Grant said he wanted his troops back as soon as possible, and would be glad to furnish whatever food the surrendered army needed. "Of about how many men does your present force consist?" Lee scarcely knew; casualties and straggling had been heavy, he admitted. "Suppose I send over 25,000 rations. Do you think that will be a sufficient supply?" "Plenty, plenty; an abundance," Lee replied.

Marshall having completed his draft of the brief acceptance, Lee made a few corrections — "Don't say, 'I have the honor to acknowledge receipt of your letter.' He is here. Just say, 'I accept the terms' " — and while he waited for the finished copy, Grant, whose appearance Marshall would charitably describe as "rather dusty and a little soiled" — in contrast to a quip by one of his own staffers, who remarked that he "looked like a fly on a shoulder of beef" — came over again and apologized for his rumpled clothes and lack of side arms. His baggage had gone astray, he said, "and I thought you would rather receive me as I was than be detained." Lee replied that he was much obliged; "I am very glad you did it that way." He signed the completed fair copy of his letter of acceptance, which Marshall then sealed and handed to Grant's adjutant, receiving in turn the signed and sealed terms of surrender. Lee broke the envelope open and read them through for the third time, but Grant did not bother with reading the letter to him just yet, later explaining that Lee's spoken acceptance of the terms was surety enough for him, without the formality of words set down on paper.

It was close to 4 o'clock by now, and all that protocol required had been performed. After nearly three hours in the McLean parlor — half of one spent waiting and the rest in what could scarcely be called negotiation, since his adversary had freely given all he asked and more than he had hoped for: including immunity, down the years, from prosecution on any charge whatever in connection with the war — Lee was free to go. He rose, shook hands with Grant again, bowed to the others, and passed from the room, followed by Marshall. Out on the porch, several blue-clad officers came to attention and saluted as he emerged. He put on his hat to return their salute, then crossed to the head of the steps leading down to the yard. There he drew on his gauntlets, distractedly striking the fist of one hand three times into the palm of the other as he looked out across the valley to where the men of his army were waiting to learn that they had been surrendered. "Orderly! Orderly!" he called hoarsely, not seeing Tucker close by with Traveller, whose bit had been slipped to let him graze. "Here, General, here," Tucker replied, and Lee came down the steps to stand by the horse's head while he was being bridled. A cavalry major, watching from the porch, noted that "as the orderly was buckling the throat latch, the general reached up and drew the forelock out from under the brow band, parted and smoothed it, and then gently patted the gray charger's forehead in an absent-minded way, as one who loves horses, but whose thoughts are far away, might all unwittingly do." Mounted, Lee waited for Marshall and Tucker, then started at a walk across the yard. Grant had come out of the house and down the steps by then, also on his way to the gate where his own horse was tethered. Stopping, he removed his hat in salute, as did the staff men with him. Lee raised his own hat briefly in return, and passed out through the gate and up the road. Presently, northward beyond the dwindled, tree-lined Appomattox, listeners on the porch heard cheers, and then a poignant silence.

Indoors behind them, as they watched him go and heard the choked-off yells subside beyond the tree line, scavengers were at work. "Relic-hunters charged down upon the manor house," a staff colonel would recall, "and began to bargain for the numerous pieces of furniture." Ord paid forty dollars for Lee's table, and Sheridan gave half as much for Grant's — though 'bargain' and 'paid' were scarcely words that applied to either transaction; Wilmer McLean, not wanting to sell his household possessions, threw the money on the floor or had it flung there when he declined to accept it. No matter; the rest of the furniture was quickly snapped up, beginning with the chairs the two commanders had sat in. Sheridan's brother Michael, a captain on his staff, made off with a stone inkstand, and an enterprising brigadier secured two brass candlesticks for ten dollars. Once these and other prize items were gone, mainly to persons whose rank had placed them early on the scene, what remained was up for grabs, and something close to pandemonium set in. "Cane-bottomed chairs were ruthlessly cut to pieces," a reporter was to write, "the cane splits broken into pieces a few inches long and parceled out among those who swarmed around. Haircloth upholstery, cut from chairs and sofas, was also cut into strips and patches and carried away." McLean was left surveying a Tacitean wilderness his enemies called peace. They made off with their spoils, exulting as they went, and a few years later — with still more rank, and again with the advantage of working close to the man in charge — some of them would try their hand at doing much the same thing to the country at large, with considerable success.

Grant knew nothing of this, of course, just as he would know little or nothing of their later endeavors along that line. He rode on toward his headquarters tent, which had been found at last, along with his baggage, and pitched nearby. He had not gone far before someone asked if he did not consider the news of Lee's surrender worth passing on to the War Department. Reining his horse in, he dismounted and sat on a large stone by the roadside to compose the telegram Lincoln would receive that night. By the time he remounted to ride on, salutes were beginning to roar from Union batteries roundabout, and he sent word to have them stopped, not only because he feared the warlike racket might cause trouble between the victors and the vanquished, both of them still with weapons in their hands, but also because he considered it unfitting. "The war is over," he told his staff. "The rebels are our countrymen again."

Lee by then was back in the apple orchard he had left four hours ago. The yells that greeted him as he reëntered Gordon's lines had come in part by force of custom; the troops, for all their cumulative numbness from hunger, weariness, and stress, cheered him as they had always done when he moved among them. Moreover, despite the grinding week-long retreat and its heavy losses, more from straggling than in combat — despite last night's red western glow of enemy campfires and this morning's breakout failure; despite the coming and going of couriers, blue and gray, and his own outward passage through their line of battle, accoutered for something more solemn even than church on this Palm Sunday — many of them were still not ready to believe the end had come. One look at his face as he drew near, however, confirmed what they had been unwilling to accept. They broke ranks and crowded round him. "General, are we surrendered? Are we surrendered?" they began asking.

Hemmed in, Lee removed his hat and spoke from horseback to a blurred expanse of upturned faces. "Men, we have fought the war together, and I have done the best I could for you. You will all be paroled and go to your homes until exchanged." Tears filled his eyes as he tried to say more; he could only manage an inaudible "Goodbye." Their first stunned reaction was disbelief. "General, we'll fight 'em yet," they told him. "Say the word and we'll go in and fight 'em yet." Then it came home to them, and though most responded with silence, one man threw his rifle down and cried in a loud voice: "Blow, Gabriel, blow! My God, let him blow, I am ready to die!"

Grief brought a sort of mass relaxation that let Traveller proceed, and as he moved through the press of soldiers, bearing the gray commander on his back, they reached out to touch both horse and rider, withers and knees, flanks and thighs, in expression of their affection. "I love you just as well as ever, General Lee!" a ragged veteran shouted, arms held wide above the crowd. At the orchard he drew rein, dismounted, and walked through the trees to one well back from the road, and there began pacing back and forth beneath its just-fledged branches, too restless to sit down on this morning's pile of fence rails. "He seemed to be in one of his savage moods," a headquarters engineer declared, "and when these moods were on him it was safer to keep out of his way." His own people knew to let him alone, but Federal officers kept arriving, "mostly in groups of four or five and some of high rank. It was evident that they came from curiosity, or to see General Lee as friends in the old army." He had small use for any of them just now though, whether they were past acquaintances or strangers. Coming up to be presented, they removed their hats out of deference and politeness, but he did not respond in kind, and sometimes did not even touch his hatbrim in return to their salutes. When he saw one of his staff approach with another group of such visitors, "he would halt in his pacing, stand at attention, and glare at them with a look which few men but he could assume." Finally, near sundown, when the promised rations began arriving from the Union lines, he remounted and rode back to a less exposed position, under the white oak tree on the ridge where he had slept the night before.

This second ride was through the ranks of the First Corps, and Longstreet saw him coming. "The road was packed by standing troops as he approached," Old Peter was to write, "the men with hats off, heads and hearts bowed down. As he passed they raised their heads and looked at him with swimming eyes. Those who could find voice said goodbye; those who could not speak, and were near, passed their hands gently over the sides of Traveller." From point to point there were bursts of cheers, which the dark-maned gray acknowledged by arching his neck and tossing his head, but Longstreet observed that Lee had only "sufficient control to fix his eyes on a line between the ears of Traveller and look neither to the right nor left." He too had his hat off, and tears ran down his cheeks into his beard. Back on the white oak ridge he stood for a time in front of his tent — "Let me get in. Let me bid him farewell," the men were crying as they thronged forward — then went inside, too choked for speech. Later he came out and sat by the fire with his staff. He told Marshall to prepare an order, a farewell to the army, but he had little heart for talk and turned in early, weary from the strain of perhaps the longest and no doubt the hardest day he had ever known.

A cold rain fell next morning. He kept mainly to his tent until shortly after 9 o'clock, when word came that Grant, on the way to see him, had been stopped by pickets who had been put out yesterday to prevent the troops of the two armies from engaging in possible squabbles. Embarrassed, Lee set out at a gallop and found his distinguished visitor waiting imperturbably on a little knoll beside the road, just south of the north branch of the Appomattox. He lifted his hat in greeting, as did the other; then they shook hands, sitting their horses in the rain while their aides retired beyond earshot, and began to talk. Grant had come to ask Lee to use his influence — "an influence that was supreme," he later said — to help bring the war to an early end by advising his subordinates, in command of the other armies of the South, to lay down their arms under the terms he himself had received the day before. Lee replied, in effect, that he agreed that further resistance was useless, but that he felt obliged as a soldier to leave all such matters to his Commander in Chief; in any case, he could do nothing without conferring with him beforehand. Grant did not persist — "I knew there was no use to urge him to do anything against his ideas of what was right" — but he deeply regretted the refusal, he declared long afterward, because "I saw that the Confederacy had gone a long way beyond the reach of President Davis, and that there was nothing that could be done except what Lee could do to benefit the Southern people. I was anxious to get them home and have our armies go to their homes and fields."

He was also anxious to get himself to Burkeville, where, thanks to the hard-working IX Corps, he could take the cars for City Point and get aboard a fast packet for Washington. By now the war was costing four million dollars a day, and he wanted to get back to the capital and start cutting down on expenses. So the two parted, Grant to set out for Burkeville and Lee to return to his own lines. Within them, the latter encountered Meade, who had recovered from his indisposition and ridden over to see him. Lee at first did not recognize his old friend. Then he did, but with something of a shock. "What are you doing with all that gray in your beard?" he asked, and his Gettysburg opponent replied genially: "You have to answer for most of it." As they rode together toward headquarters, the soldiers camped along the road began to cheer, and Meade, not wanting to misrepresent himself, told his color bearer, who had the flag rolled up: "Unfurl that flag." The bearer did, and drew a sharp retort. "Damn your old rag!" a butternut veteran called from beside the road. "We are cheering General Lee."

Back in his tent Lee talked for a time with Meade, then turned to the writing of his report on the campaign that now was over. "It is with pain that I announce to Your Excellency the surrender of the Army of Northern Virginia," the document began. Walter Taylor did most of the work on this, as he had on all the others, but Lee also conferred with Charles Marshall, whom he had instructed to draw up an order bidding the troops farewell. Marshall, a former Baltimore lawyer and grandnephew of the illustrious Chief Justice, had delayed preparing the address — because all the coming and going around headquarters had left him no time, he said, but also because of a certain reluctance, a feeling of inadequacy for the task. "What can I say to those people?" he asked a friend this morning, still avoiding getting down to putting pen to paper. Lee settled this by ordering the colonel to get into his ambulance, parked nearby with a guard on duty to fend off intruders, and stay there until he finished the composition. Marshall, his writer's block effectively broken, soon emerged with a penciled draft. Lee looked it over and made a few changes, including the deletion of a paragraph he thought might "tend to keep alive the feel-

ing existing between the North and South"; after which the Marylander returned to the ambulance, wrote out the final version of the
order, and turned it over to a clerk for making inked copies which
Lee then signed for distribution to the corps commanders and ranking
members of his staff.

Having signed his parole he might have left then, as Grant had
done by noon on this rainy Monday; yet he did not. The formal surrender ceremony was set for Wednesday — the required turning over
of all "arms, artillery and public property," in accordance with the
terms accepted — and he stayed on, not to take an active role as a
participant, but simply to be on hand, if not in view, when his men
faced the sad ritual of laying down their shot-torn flags and weapons.
He continued to keep to his tent, however, through most of the waiting
time, while all around him, despite the pickets both sides had posted
to discourage fraternization, blue-clad visitors of all ranks drifted
through the camps for a look at their one-time enemies. For the most
part they were received without animosity; "Success had made them
good-natured," one grayback uncharitably observed. A Federal colonel
noted that the Confederates "behaved with more courtesy than cordiality," and it was true. "Affiliation was out of the question; we were
content with civility," one explained. Union troops, on the other hand,
were friendly and outgoing; "in fact almost oppressively so," a butternut declared. "We've been fighting one another for four years. Give
me a Confederate five-dollar bill to remember you by," a bluecoat
said, and his hearers found nothing offensive in his manner. Sometimes,
though, a discordant note would be struck and would bring on a fiery
answer — as when a Federal major, seeking a souvenir to take home,
asked a Confederate staff captain for the white towel he had carried
as a flag of truce on Sunday. "I'll see you in hell first!" the angered staffer
replied. "It is humiliating enough to have had to carry it and exhibit it;
I'm not going to let you preserve it as a monument of our defeat."
Similarly, when a visiting sergeant tried to open a friendly discussion
by remarking: "Well, Johnny, I guess you fellows will go home now
to stay," he found that he had touched a nerve. The rebel was in no
mood to be gloated over. "You *guess*, do you?" he said hotly. "Maybe
we are. But don't be giving us any of your impudence. If you do, we'll
come back and lick you again."

Much of Tuesday, with rain still murmurous on the canvas overhead, Lee spent working on his last report. He finished and signed it
next morning, April 12, while his veterans, in Longstreet's words,
"marched to the field in front of Appomattox Courthouse, and by
divisions and parts of divisions deployed into line, stacked their arms,
folded their colors, and walked empty-handed to find their distant,
blighted homes." The weather having faired, they made as brave a show
as their rags and sadness would permit; "worn, bright-eyed men," a

Federal brigadier would call them. They seemed to him "purged of the mortal, as if knowing pain or joy no more," and he asked himself as he watched them pass before him "in proud humiliation . . . thin, worn, and famished, but erect, and with eyes looking level into ours . . . Was not such manhood to be welcomed back into a Union so tested and assured?" They had been whipped about as thoroughly as any American force had ever been or ever would be, short of annihilation, but it was part of their particular pride that they would never admit it, even to themselves. "Goodbye, General; God bless you," a ragged private told his brigadier commander over a parting handshake at the close of the surrender ceremony. "We'll go home, make three more crops, and try them again."

They left in groups, dispersing by routes as varied as their destinations, and one of the smallest groups was Lee's. He rode with Taylor and Marshall northeast into Buckingham County, bound for Richmond, and stopped for the night, some twenty miles out, in a strip of woods beside the road. To his surprise he found Longstreet there before him, likewise headed for a reunion with his family. Once more they shared a campsite, then next morning diverged to meet no more. The burly Georgian was assailed by mixed emotions, partly as a result of having encountered his friend Grant on Monday, shortly before the blue commander's departure for Burkeville. "Pete, let's have another game of brag to recall the old days," Grant had said, and though there was no time for cards he gave him a cigar, which Longstreet said "was gratefully received." Moved by the reunion, he later wondered: "Why do men fight who were born to be brothers?" and remarked, not without bitterness, that the next time he fought he would be sure it was necessary.

But that was by no means a reaction characteristic of the veterans now trudging the roads in all directions from the scene of their surrender. They were content with "the satisfaction that proceeds from the consciousness of duty faithfully performed." The words were part of Lee's final behest they took with them from the farewell issued two days ago, near Appomattox Courthouse.

Headquarters Army of N. Va.
April 10, 1865

General Orders⎫
   No. 9 ⎭

    After four years of arduous service marked by unsurpassed courage and fortitude, the Army of Northern Virginia has been compelled to yield to overwhelming numbers and resources.

    I need not tell the brave survivors of so many hard fought battles, who have remained steadfast to the last, that I have consented to this result from no distrust of them. But feeling that valor and devotion could accomplish nothing that could compensate for the loss that must have attended the continuance of the contest, I determined to avoid the useless sacrifice of those whose past services have endeared them to their countrymen.

By the terms of the agreement, officers and men can return to their homes and remain until exchanged. You will take with you the satisfaction that proceeds from the consciousness of duty faithfully performed, and I earnestly pray that a merciful God will extend to you His blessing and protection.

With an unceasing admiration of your constancy and devotion to your Country, and a grateful remembrance of your kind and generous consideration for myself, I bid you all an affectionate farewell.

R. E. LEE
General.

In addition to the copies made by Marshall's clerk for normal distribution, others were transcribed and taken to the general for his signature, and these remained for those who had them the possession they cherished most. One such was Henry Perry, the young infantry captain who had refused a drink from Seth Williams' silver flask three nights before, near Cumberland Church. Later he told how he got it and how he felt, then and down the years, about the man who signed it. "I sat down and copied it on a piece of Confederate paper," he recalled, "using a drumhead for a desk, the best I could do. I carried this copy to General Lee, and asked him to sign it for me. He signed it and I have it now. It is the best authority, along with my parole, that I can produce why after that day I no longer raised a soldier's hand for the South. There were tears in his eyes when he signed it for me, and when I turned to walk away there were tears in my own eyes. He was in all respects the greatest man who ever lived, and as a humble officer of the South, I thank heaven I had the honor of following him."

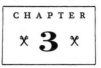

Lucifer in Starlight

★ ✗ ☆

GUNS BOOMED THE NEWS OF APPOMATTOX as dawn broke over Washington next morning, April 10, one week after a similar uproar hailed the fall of Richmond. If the reaction now was less hysterical, if many loyal citizens were content to remain abed, counting the five hundred separate thuds of the salute — as compared to nine hundred the Monday before — that was not only because of the earlier drain on their emotions, it was also because of rain drumming hard on their bedroom windows and mud slathered more than shoetop-deep outside. Still, a carousing journalist observed, the streets were soon "alive with people singing and cheering, carrying flags and saluting everybody, hungering and thirsting for speeches." They especially wanted a speech from Lincoln, whose presence in town, after his return from down the coast last evening, was in contrast to his absence during the previous celebration. At the Treasury Department, for example, when the clerks were told they had been given another holiday, the same reporter noted that they "assembled in the great corridor of their building and sang 'Old Hundredth' with thrilling, even tear-compelling effect," then trooped across the grounds to the White House, where, still in excellent voice, they serenaded the President with the national anthem.

He was at breakfast and did not appear, but a night's sleep had done nothing to diminish the excitement he felt on reading Grant's wire at bedtime. "Let Master Tad have a Navy sword," he directed in a note to Welles, and added in another to the Secretary of War (omitting the question mark as superfluous on this day of celebration): "Tad wants some flags. Can he be accommodated." Stanton evidently complied in short order, for when a procession arrived from the Navy Yard a couple of hours later, dragging six boat howitzers which were fired as they rolled up Pennsylvania Avenue, the boy stood at a second-story window and flaunted a captured rebel flag, to the wild applause of a crowd that quickly swelled to about three thousand. Presently Lincoln himself appeared at the window, and the yells redoubled. "Speech! Speech!" men cried from the lawn below. But he put them off. He would speak tonight, or more likely tomorrow, "and I shall have nothing to say if you dribble it all out of me before." As the laughter subsided he took up a notion that had struck him. "I see you have a band of music with you," he said, and when a voice called up: "We have two or three!" he proposed closing the interview by having the musicians play "a particular tune which I will name.... I have always thought 'Dixie' one of the best tunes I ever heard. Our adversaries over the way attempted to appropriate it, but I insisted yesterday that we fairly captured it. I presented the question to the Attorney General and he gave it as his legal opinion that it is now our lawful prize. I now request the band to favor me with its performance."

The band did, to roars of approval from the crowd, then followed the irreverent rebel anthem with a lively rendition of "Yankee Doodle," after which Lincoln called for "three good hearty cheers for General Grant and all under his command." These given, he requested "three more cheers for our gallant navy," and when they were over he retired, as did the rollicking crowd. Near sundown, a third crew of celebrants turned up, to be similarly put off on grounds that he had to be careful what he said at times like this. "Everything I say, you know, goes into print. If I make a mistake it doesn't merely affect me nor you, but the country. I therefore ought at least to try not to make mistakes. If, then, a general demonstration be made tomorrow evening, and it is agreeable, I will endeavor to say something and not make a mistake without at least trying carefully to avoid it."

Next night he was back, as promised, and they were there to hear him in their thousands, packed shoulder to shoulder on the White House lawn and looking up at the same window. Off in the drizzly distance, Arlington House — R. E. Lee's former home, long since commandeered by the government he had defied — glittered on its hillside beyond the Potomac, illuminated tonight along with all the other public buildings, while nearer at hand, gilded with light from torches and flares, the Capitol dome seemed to float like a captive balloon in a gauzy mist that verged on rain. To one observer yesterday, seeing him for the first time, Lincoln "appeared somewhat younger and more off-hand and vigorous than I should have expected. His gestures and countenance had something of the harmless satisfaction of a young politician at a ratification meeting after his first election to the Legislature. He was happy, and glad to see others happy." Tonight, though, he was different. Appearing after Tad had once more warmed the crowd by flourishing the Confederate banner, he seemed grave and thoughtful, and he had with him, by way of assuring that he would "not make a mistake without

at least trying carefully to avoid it," a rolled-up manuscript he had spent
most of the day preparing. What he had in mind to deliver tonight was
not so much a speech as it was a closely written document, a state paper
dealing less with the past, or even the present, than with the future; less
with victory than with the problems victory brought. The crowd below
did not know this yet, however, and Noah Brooks — a young newsman
who was slated to replace one of his private secretaries — saw "something terrible in the enthusiasm with which the beloved Chief Magis-
trate was received. Cheers upon cheers, wave after wave of applause
rolled up, the President patiently standing quiet until it was over."

"Fellow Citizens," he said at last. Holding a candle in his left
hand to light the papers in his right, he waited for new cheers to subside, and then continued. "We are met this evening not in sorrow but in
gladness of heart. The evacuation of Petersburg and Richmond, and
the surrender of the principal insurgent army, give hope of a righteous
and speedy peace whose joyous expression cannot be restrained."
Cheered again, he sought relief from the difficulty of managing both the
candle and his manuscript by signaling to Brooks, who stood behind one
of the window drapes beside him, with what the journalist called "a
comical motion of his left foot and elbow, which I construed to mean
that I should hold his candle for him." With both hands free to grip
the sheaf of papers, and Brooks extending the light from behind the
curtain, he went on with his speech, dropping each read page as he
began the next. Unseen by the crowd, Tad scrambled about on the
balcony floor to catch the sheets as his father let them flutter down.
"Another, another," he kept saying impatiently all through the reading,
heard plainly because of a hush that soon descended on the celebrants
on the lawn below.

Referred to afterwards by Brooks as "a silent, intent, and perhaps
surprised multitude," they were in fact both silent and surprised, but
they were more confused than they were intent. Until Lincoln began
speaking they had not supposed tonight was any occasion for mentioning sadness, even to deny it, and as he continued along other lines,
equally unexpected at a victory celebration, their confusion and discomfort grew. After this brief introduction, scarcely fitting in itself,
he spoke not of triumphs, but rather of the problems that loomed with
peace; in particular one problem. "By these recent successes," he read
from the second of the sheets that fell fluttering to his feet, "the reinauguration of the national authority — reconstruction — which has
had a large share of thought from the first, is pressed much more closely
upon our attention. It is fraught with great difficulty. Unlike the case
of a war between independent nations, there is no authorized organ for
us to treat with — no one man has authority to give up the rebellion
for any other man. We simply must begin with, and mold from, dis-

organized and discordant elements. Nor is it a small additional embarrassment that we, the loyal people, differ among ourselves as to the
mode, manner, and means of reconstruction."

This then was his subject — "the mode, manner, and means of
reconstruction" — and he stayed with it through Tad's retrieval of the
last dropped sheet, addressing himself less to his listeners, it seemed,
than to the knotty problem itself, and in language that was correspondingly knotty. For example, in dealing with the claim that secession, while
plainly illegal, had in fact removed from the Union certain states which
now would have to comply with some hard-line requirements before
they could be granted readmission, he pronounced it "a merely per-
nicious abstraction," likely to "have no effect other than the mischievous
one of dividing our friends" left and right of the stormy center. "We all
agree that the seceded states, so called, are out of their proper practical
relation with the Union, and that the sole object of the government,
civil and military, in regard to those states, is to again get them into
that proper practical relation. I believe it is not only possible, but in fact
easier, to do this without deciding or even considering whether these
states have even been out of the Union, than with it. Finding themselves
safely at home, it would be utterly immaterial whether they had ever
been abroad. Let us all join in doing the acts necessary to restoring
the proper practical relations between these states and the Union, and
each forever after innocently indulge his own opinion whether, in doing
the acts, he brought the states from without into the Union, or only gave
them proper assistance, they never having been out of it."

In regard to the new state government in Louisiana, which had
the support of only ten percent of the electorate, he acknowledged the
validity of criticism that it was scantly based and did not give the
franchise to the Negro. All the same, though he himself wished its
constituency "contained fifty, thirty, or even twenty thousand [voters]
instead of only twelve thousand, as it does," and though he preferred to
have the ballot extended to include the blacks — at least "the very
intelligent" and "those who serve our cause as soldiers" — he did not
believe these shortcomings invalidated the present arrangement, which
in any case was better than no arrangement at all. "Concede that the
new government of Louisiana is only to what it should be as the egg is
to the fowl, we shall sooner have the fowl by hatching the egg than
by smashing it." For one thing, the state legislature had already voted
to ratify the 13th Amendment, and the sooner its authority was recognized by Congress, the sooner all men would be free throughout the
land. He had thought long and hard about the problem, as well as
about various proposals for its solution, "and yet so great peculiarities
pertain to each state, and such important and sudden changes occur in
the same state, and withal, so new and unprecedented is the whole case,
that no exclusive and inflexible plan can safely be prescribed as to details

and collaterals. . . . In the present 'situation,' as the phrase goes, it may be my duty to make some new announcement to the people of the South. I am considering, and shall not fail to act when satisfied that action will be proper."

That was the end, and he let it hang there, downbeat, enigmatic, inconclusive, as perfunctory and uncertain, even in its peroration, as the applause that followed when his listeners finally understood that the speech — if that was what it had been — was over. Tad gathered up the last sheet of manuscript, and as Lincoln stepped back into the room he said to Brooks, still holding the candle out from behind the window drape: "That was a pretty fair speech, I think, but you threw some light on it." Down on the lawn, the misty drizzle had turned to rain while he spoke, and the crowd began to disperse, their spirits nearly as dampened as their clothes. Some drifted off to bars in search of revival. Others walked over to Franklin Square to serenade Stanton, who might do better by them.

Not that there were no repercussions. There were, and they came fast — mostly from disaffected radicals who contended that secession had been a form of suicide from which no state could be resurrected except on conditions imposed by them at the end of the struggle now drawing rapidly to a close. Differing from Lincoln in this, or at any rate on what those terms should be, they believed they saw clearly enough what he was up to. Congress would not meet again until December, and he had it in mind to unite the people behind him, between now and then, and thus confront his congressional opponents with an overwhelming majority of voters whom he would attract to his lenient views by a series of public appeals, such as the one tonight from the high White House window or last month's inaugural, adorned with oratorical phrases as empty as they were vague. "Malice toward none" had no meaning for them, as here applied, and "charity for all" had even less; for where was the profit in winning a war if then you lost the peace? They asked that with a special urgency now that they had begun to suspect the Administration of planning to neglect the Negro, who was in fact what this war had been about from start to finish. Lincoln's reference tonight to a possible limited extension of the franchise to include those who were "very intelligent" only served to increase their apprehension that the cause of the blacks was about to be abandoned, possibly in exchange for the support of certain reactionary elements in the reunited country — not excluding former Confederates — in putting together a new and powerful coalition of moderates, unbeatable at the polls for decades to come. One among those perturbed was Chase, who had written this day to his former chief of his fears in regard to that neglect. The most acceptable solution, he said, was "the reorganization of state governments under constitutions securing suffrage to all citizens. . . . This way is recommended by its simplicity, facility, and, above all, justice," the Chief Justice wrote. "It will be hereafter counted equally a crime and a folly if the colored loyalists of the rebel states shall be left to the control of restored rebels, not likely in that case to be either wise or just, until taught both wisdom and justice by new calamities."

Lincoln found the letter on his desk when he came into the office next morning, and Chase followed it up with another, that same Wednesday, midway of Holy Week, suggesting an interview "to have the whole subject talked over." Others had the same notion; Charles Sumner, for example. He had not heard the speech last night, but his secretary reported that it was "not in keeping with what was in men's minds. The people had gathered, from an instructive impulse, to rejoice over a great and final victory, and they listened with respect, but with no expressions of enthusiasm, except that the quaint simile of 'the egg' drew applause. The more serious among them felt that the President's utterances on the subject were untimely, and that his insistence at such an hour on his favorite plan was not the harbinger of peace among the loyal supporters of the government." The Massachusetts senator felt this, too, and regretted it, his secretary noted; "for he saw at hand another painful controversy with a President whom he respected, on a question where he felt it his duty to stand firm." Already his mail was filled with urgings that he do just that. "Magnanimity is a great word with the disloyal who think to tickle the President's ear with it," a prominent New Yorker wrote. "Magnanimity is one thing. Weakness is another. I know you are near the throne, and you must guard its honor." A Boston constituent knew where to fix the blame: on Lincoln, whose reconstruction policy was "wicked and blasphemous" in its betrayal of the cause of freedom by his failure to take the obvious next step after emancipation. "No power but God ever has or could have forced him up to the work he has been instrumental of, and now we see the dregs of his backwardness."

Mainly these were old-line abolitionists, men with a great capacity for wrath. Ben Wade, for one, expressed the hope that such neglect would goad the southern blacks to insurrection. "If they could contrive to slay one half of their oppressors," he asserted, "the other half would hold them in the highest regard, and no doubt treat them with justice." But even this was mild compared to the reaction that followed disclosure that Lincoln had authorized John A. Campbell to reassemble the Virginia legislature, composed in part of the very men who had withdrawn the Old Dominion from the Union in the first place. As it happened, the Joint Committee on the Conduct of the War was down at Richmond now, aboard the steamer *Baltimore*, and one of its members went ashore this morning to get the daily papers. He came back, much excited, with a copy of the Richmond *Whig*, which carried an Address to the People of Virginia by some of the legislators then about to assemble. Moreover, Weitzel had indorsed it, and Wade went into a frenzy at this evidence of official sanction for the outrage. Fuming, he declared — "in substance, if not in exact words," a companion afterwards testified — "that there had been much talk of the assassination of Lincoln; that if he authorized the approval of that paper . . . by God, the sooner he was assassinated the better!" Others felt as strongly about this development, which seemed to them to undo all they had worked for all these years. Zachariah Chandler, according to the same report, "was also exceedingly harsh in his remarks," and none of the other members took offense at the denunciations.

In Washington, the Secretary of War was apparently the first to get the news. He went at once to Lincoln, then to Sumner, who wrote Chase: "I find Stanton much excited. He had a full and candid talk with the President last eve, and insisted that the proposed meeting at Richmond should be forbidden. He thinks we are in a crisis more trying than any before, with the chance of losing the fruits of our victory. He asks if it was not Grant who surrendered to Lee, instead of Lee to Grant. He is sure that Richmond is beginning to govern Washington."

But Lincoln by then had revoked his authorization for the Virginians to assemble. At a cabinet meeting the day before, he had found Stanton and Speed vehement in their opposition, and none of the rest in favor of creating a situation in which, as Welles pointed out, "the so-called legislature would be likely to propose terms which might seem reasonable, but which we could not accept." To these were added the protests of various other advisers, by no means all of them die-hard radicals. Lincoln considered the matter overnight — aside, that is, from the time he spent delivering his speech from the balconied window — and though, as he said, he rather fancied the notion of having the secessionists "come together and undo their own work," at 9 o'clock Wednesday morning he telegraphed Weitzel a question and a suggestion: "Is there any sign of the rebel legislature coming together on the basis of my letter to you? If there is any sign, inform me of what it is; if there is no such sign you may as [well] withdraw the offer."

Although it was true he had no wish just now for a knockdown drag-out fight with either wing of his party, his decision to revoke what he called his 'offer' was in fact less political than it was practical in nature. The conditions under which it had been extended no longer obtained; the gains sought in exchange had since been won. His purpose in approving Campbell's proposal, just under a week ago, had been to encourage Virginia's legislators, in return for certain "remissions" on his part, to withdraw her troops from the rebel armies and the state itself from the Confederacy. Grant had accomplished the first of these objectives on Palm Sunday — the formal surrender ceremony was getting under way at Appomattox Courthouse even as Lincoln's telegram went over the wire to Weitzel — and the second scarcely mattered, since there was no longer any sizeable body of armed graybacks within the borders of the Old Dominion. So much for that. As for the problem of keeping or breaking his promise to Campbell, that was merely personal; which was only another way of saying it didn't count. "Bad promises are better broken than kept," he had said in his speech the night before, with reference to assurances he had given those who set up the provisional Louisiana government. "I shall treat this as a bad promise, and break it, whenever I shall be convinced that keeping it is adverse to the public interest." And so it was in this case; he simply labeled the promise 'bad' — meaning profitless — and broke it.

When he heard from Weitzel that afternoon that "passports have gone out for the legislators, and it is common talk that they will come together," Lincoln wired back a definite order that their permission to assemble be revoked. He prefaced this, however, with some lawyerly explication of the events leading up to his decision, which he said was based on statements made by Campbell in a letter informing certain of the prospective legislators what their task would be in Richmond. He had talked the matter over with the President on two occasions, the Alabama jurist declared, and both conversations "had relation to the establishment of a government for Virginia, the requirement of oaths of allegiance from the citizens, and the terms of settlement with the United States." Lincoln flatly denied this in his sundown wire to Weitzel. "[Judge Campbell] assumes, as appears to me, that I have called the insurgent legislature of Virginia together, as the rightful legislature of the state, to settle all differences with the United States. I have done no such thing. I spoke of them not as a legislature, but as 'the gentlemen who have *acted* as the Legislature of Virginia in support of the rebellion.' I did this on purpose to exclude the assumption that I was recognizing them as a rightful body. I dealt with them as men having power *de facto* to do a specific thing; to wit, 'to withdraw the Virginia troops and other support from resistance to the general government.' . . . I meant this and no more. Inasmuch however as Judge Campbell misconstrues this, and is still pressing for an armistice, contrary to the explicit statement of the paper I gave him, and particularly as Gen. Grant has since captured the Virginia troops, so that giving a consideration for their withdrawal is no longer applicable, let my letter to you and the paper to Judge Campbell both be withdrawn, or countermanded, and he be notified of it. Do not allow them to assemble; but if any have come, allow them safe-return to their homes."

Word of this revocation spread rapidly over Washington and out across the land, to the high delight of those who lately had seethed with indignation: particularly the hard-war hard-peace Jacobins, who saw in the action near certain proof that, in a crunch, the President would always come over to their side of the question — provided, of course, the pressure was kept on him: which it would be. James Speed, who had no sooner been confirmed as Attorney General than he went over to the radicals all-out, presently wrote to Chase that Lincoln "never seemed so near our views" as he did now, with Holy Week drawing rapidly toward a close.

★　★　★

Davis by then was in Greensboro, North Carolina, just under fifty miles south of the Virginia line. Once more "a government on wheels," he and his cabinet had left Danville late Monday night in a driving rainstorm that only added to the depression and confusion brought on by the arrival of simultaneous reports, no less alarming for being unofficial and somewhat vague, that Lee had surrendered to Grant the day before, near Appomattox Courthouse, and that a heavy column of enemy cavalry was approaching from the west. Nothing more was heard for a time about the extent of Lee's removal from the war — that is, whether all or only part of his army had been surrendered — but the other report was soon confirmed by word that a detachment from the column of blue troopers, some 4000 strong under Stoneman, had burned the Dan River bridge a few hours after the fugitive President's train rattled across it and on into Carolina. Informed of his narrow escape from capture, Davis managed a smile of relief. "A miss is as good as a mile," he remarked, and his smile broadened.

Such pleasure as he took from this was soon dispelled by the coolness of his reception when the train crept into Greensboro next morning. Though news of his coming had been wired ahead, no welcoming group of citizens turned out to greet him or even acknowledge his presence, which made their town the Confederacy's third capital in ten days. For the most part, like many in this Piedmont region of the Old North State, they had never been enthusiastic about the war or its goals, and their pro-Union feeling had been considerably strengthened by reports, just in, that Stoneman's raiders were headed in their direction and that Sherman had begun his advance from Goldsboro the day before, first on Raleigh, with Johnston known to be falling back, and then on them. Fearing reprisal for any courtesy offered Davis and his party, they extended none — except to the wealthy and ailing Trenholm; he and Mrs Trenholm were taken in by a banker who, it was said, hoped to persuade the Secretary to exchange some gold from the treasure train for his Confederate bonds. Davis himself would have had no place to lay his head if an aide, John T. Wood — former skipper of the *Tallahassee* and the President's first wife's nephew — had not had his family refugeeing in half of a modest Greensboro house. Despite protests from the landlord, who feared that his property would go up in flames as soon as Stoneman or Sherman appeared, Wood's wife had prepared a small upstairs bedroom for the Chief Executive. While Trenholm was being made comfortable in the banker's mansion across town, the rest of the cabinet adapted themselves as best they could to living in the dilapidated coaches, which had been shunted onto a siding near the depot.

Beauregard and his staff were similarly lodged in three boxcars parked nearby. He had arrived the previous night, en route to Danville in response to a summons from the Commander in Chief, and now he crossed the tracks to report aboard the presidential coach. Davis greeted him cordially, eager for news of the situation around Raleigh. Dismayed, the Creole told of Johnston's hurried evacuation of Smithfield, under pressure from Sherman, and of his present withdrawal toward the state capital, which he did not plan to defend against a force three times his size. In short, Beauregard said, the situation was hopeless. Davis disagreed. Lee's surrender had not been confirmed; some portion of his army might have escaped and could soon be combined with Johnston's, as originally intended. The struggle would continue, whatever the odds, even if it had to be done on the far side of the Mississippi. Beauregard was amazed, but by no means converted from his gloom, when Davis got off a wire instructing Johnston to come at once to Greensboro for a strategy conference. "The important question first to be solved is what point of concentration should be made," the President declared. He had no intention of giving up the war, and he wanted the Virginian to be thinking of his next move before they met, though he was frank to admit that "your more intimate knowledge of the data for the solution of the problem deters me from making a specific suggestion on that point."

Johnston arrived next morning — Wednesday, April 12 — and took up quarters in one of Beauregard's boxcars. Yesterday in Raleigh, Zeb Vance had warned him that Davis, "a man of imperfectly constituted genius, . . . could absolutely *blind himself* to those things which his prejudices or hopes did not desire to see." Johnston readily agreed, having observed this quality often in the past. But he had never seen it demonstrated more forcefully than he did today, when he and his fellow general entered the presidential coach for the council of war to which he had been summoned from his duties in the field. "We had supposed that we were to be questioned concerning the military resources of our department in connection with the question of continuing or terminating the war," he later wrote. Instead, "the President's object seemed to be to give, not obtain information." Quite as amazed as his companion had been the day before, he listened while Davis spoke of raising a large army by rounding up deserters and conscripting men who previously had escaped the draft. Both generals protested that those who had avoided service in less critical times were unlikely to come forward now, and when Johnston took the occasion to advise that he be authorized to open a correspondence with Sherman regarding a truce that might lead to a successful conclusion of the conflict, this too was rejected out of hand. Any such effort was sure to fail, he was informed, and "its failure would have a demoralizing effect on both the troops and the people, neither of [whom]" — as Davis later summed up his reply — "had shown any disposition to surrender, or had any reason to suppose that their government contemplated abandoning its trust."

There was a pause. All three men sat tight-lipped, brooding on the impasse they had reached. Davis at last broke the silence by remarking that Breckinridge was expected to arrive at any moment from Virginia with definite information about the extent of Lee's disaster, and he suggested that they adjourn until the Secretary got there. The two generals were glad to retire from a situation they found awkward in the extreme — something like being closeted with a dreamy madman — although the encounter was not without its satisfactions for them both, convinced as they were, not only that they were right and he was wrong about the military outlook, but also that he would presently be obliged to admit it; if not to them, then in any case to Grant and Sherman.

In point of fact, they were righter than they would have any way of knowing until reports came in from close at hand and far afield. On this fourth anniversary of the day Beauregard opened fire on Sumter, Lee's men — not part: all — were formally laying down their arms at Appomattox Courthouse, just over a hundred miles away, and James Wilson, after visiting destruction upon Selma, even now was riding unopposed into Montgomery, the Confederacy's first capital, in bloodless celebration of the date the shooting war began. Nor was that all by any means. Canby marched this morning into Mobile, which Maury had abandoned in the night to avoid encirclement and capture; while here in North Carolina itself, some eighty miles to the east, Sherman was closing on Raleigh, whose occupation tomorrow would make it the ninth of the eleven seceded state capitals to feel the tread of the invader; all, that is, but Austin and Tallahassee, whose survival was less the result of their ability to resist than it was of Federal oversight or disinterest. Even nearer at hand — but unaware that Jefferson Davis was a prize within their reach — Stoneman's raiders had bypassed Greensboro to strike today at Salisbury, fifty of the ninety miles down the railroad to Charlotte, rounding up 1300 prisoners and putting the torch to supplies collected in expectation that Lee would move that way from Burkeville. Also taken were 10,000 stands of small arms and 14 pieces of artillery, the latter commanded by Lieutenant Colonel John C. Pemberton, who had surrendered Vicksburg, three months under two years ago, as a lieutenant general. Enlarging his destruction to include the railway bridges for miles in both directions before he swung west from Salisbury to return to Tennessee, Stoneman, though still uninformed of its proximity, ensured that when the fugitive rebel government resumed its flight — Meade and Ord hovered northward;

Sherman was advancing from the east — Davis and his ministers would no longer have the railroad as a means of transportation, swift and tireless and more or less free of the exigencies of weather, but would have to depend on horses for keeping ahead of the fast-riding bluecoats who soon would be hard on their trail.

Arriving that evening after his roundabout ride from Richmond by way of Farmville, Breckinridge knew even less of most of this than Johnston and Beauregard did. He did know, however, that Lee's surrender included the whole of his army, and this in itself was enough to convince the two generals that any further attempt to continue the conflict "would be the greatest of crimes." Johnston said as much to the Secretary when he called on him that night, adding that he wanted the opportunity to tell Davis the same thing, if Davis would only listen. Breckinridge assured him he would have his chance at the council of war, which he had been informed would be resumed next morning in the house John Wood had provided across town.

When the two generals entered the small upstairs room at 10 o'clock Thursday morning the atmosphere was grim. "Most solemnly funereal," Reagan later called it; for he and his fellow cabinet members, Benjamin, Mallory, and George Davis — Trenholm, still ailing, was absent — had just concluded a session during which Breckinridge presented his report, and "it was apparent that they had to consider the loss of the cause." Only the President and the imperturbable Benjamin seemed unconvinced that the end was at hand. Davis in fact not only did not believe that Lee's surrender meant the death of Confederate hopes for survival; he began at once, after welcoming Johnston and Beauregard, a further exposition of his views that resistance could and must continue until the northern people and their leaders grew weary enough to negotiate a peace that acknowledged southern independence. "Our late disasters are terrible," he admitted, "but I do not think we should regard them as fatal. I think we can whip the enemy yet, if our people will turn out." After a pause, which brought no response, he turned to the senior of the two field commanders. "We should like to hear your views, General Johnston."

The Virginian had been told he would have his chance, and now he took it. In a tone described by Mallory as "almost spiteful" he spoke directly to the man he had long considered his bitterest enemy, North or South. "My views are, sir, that our people are tired of the war, feel themselves whipped, and will not fight." Overrun by greatly superior Union forces, the Confederacy was "without money, or credit, or arms, or ammunition, or means of procuring them," he said flatly, driving home the words like nails in the lid of a coffin. "My men are daily deserting in large numbers. Since Lee's defeat they regard the war as at an end." There was, he declared in conclusion, no choice but surrender. "We may perhaps obtain terms which we ought to accept."

Davis heard him out with no change of expression, eyes fixed on a small piece of paper which he kept folding, unfolding, and folding. After the silence that followed Johnston's declaration of defeat, he asked in a low even tone: "What do you say, General Beauregard?" The Creole too had his moment of satisfaction. "I concur in all General Johnston has said," he replied quietly. Another silence followed. Then Davis, still holding his eyes down on the paper he kept folding and refolding, addressed Johnston in the same inflectionless voice as before: "You speak of obtaining terms. . . ." The general said he would like to get in touch with Sherman to arrange a truce during which they could work out the details required for surrender. All those present except Benjamin agreed that this was the thing to do, and Davis accepted their judgment, but not without a reservation he considered overriding. "Well, sir, you can adopt this course," he told Johnston, "though I am not sanguine as to ultimate results." At the general's insistence, he dictated a letter to Sherman for Johnston's signature. "The results of the recent campaign in Virginia have changed the relative military condition of the belligerents," it read. "I am, therefore, induced to address you in this form the inquiry whether, to stop the further effusion of blood and devastation of property, you are willing to make a temporary suspension of active operations . . . the object being to permit the civil authorities to enter into the needful arrangements to terminate the existing war."

Tomorrow was Good Friday; Davis spent it preparing to continue his flight southward. Others might treat for peace, not he. Nor would he leave the country. He had, he said when urged to escape to Mexico or the West Indies by getting aboard a ship off the Florida coast, "no idea whatever of leaving Confederate soil as long as there are men in uniform to fight for the cause." Fortunately, the treasure train had been sent ahead to Charlotte before Stoneman wrecked the railroad above and below Salisbury, but Davis and his party would have to take their chances on the muddy roads and byways. Nothing in his manner showed that he had any doubt of getting through, however, any more than he doubted the survival of the nation he headed. Only in private, and only then in a note he wrote his wife that same Good Friday, did he show that he had anything less than total confidence in the outcome of a struggle that had continued unabated for four years and was moving even now into a fifth.

"Dear Winnie," he wrote to her in Charlotte, employing her pet name before signing with his own, "I will come to you if I can. Everything is dark. You should prepare for the worst by dividing your baggage so as to move in wagons. . . . I have lingered on the road to little purpose. My love to the children and Maggie. God bless, guide and preserve you, ever prays Your most affectionate Banny."

★   ★   ★

There was a ceremony that same holy day in Charleston Harbor, held in accordance with War Department instructions which Stanton himself had issued back in March. "*Ordered.* That at the hour of noon on the 14th day of April, 1865, Brevet Major General Anderson will raise and plant upon the ruins of Fort Sumter the same United States flag which floated over the battlements of that fort during the rebel assault, and which was lowered and saluted by him and the small force of his command when the works were evacuated on the 14th day of April, 1861."

At first there was only minor interest in the occasion, even when it was given out that Henry Ward Beecher, the popular Brooklyn minister, would be the principal speaker. Presently, however, the fall of Richmond, followed within the week by Lee's surrender, placed the affair in a new light, one in which it could be seen as commemorating not only the start but also the finish of the war, in the same place on the same date, with precisely four years intervening between the hauling down and running up of the same flag. People began to plan to attend from all directions, especially from Boston and Philadelphia, where abolitionist sentiment ran strong, as well as from the sea islands along the Georgia and Carolina coasts, where uplift programs had been in progress ever since their occupation. Prominent men were among them, and women too, who for decades had been active in the movement. "Only listen to that — in Charleston's streets!" William Lloyd Garrison marveled, tears of joy brimming his eyes as a regimental band played "John Brown's Body" amid the ruins created by the long bombardment, which another visitor noted "had left its marks everywhere, even on gravestones in the cemeteries." So many came that the navy was hard put, this mild Good Friday morning, to provide vessels enough to ferry them from the Battery wharves out to the fort. More than four thousand were on hand, including a number of blacks from nearby plantations, though it was observed that there were scarcely a dozen local whites in the throng pressed close about the platform where the dignitaries awaited the stroke of noon.

Except for the bunting draped about the rostrum, the polished brass of army and navy officers, and the colorful silks on some of the women, the scene was bleak enough. Sumter, a Union soldier declared at the time it was retaken, "was simply an irregular curved pile of pulverized masonry, which had with enormous labor been industriously shoveled back into place as fast as we knocked it out of shape, and was held up on the inside by gabions and timber work. So many tons of projectiles had been fired into it that the shot and shell seemed to be mixed through the mass as thick as plums in a pudding." Somewhere in the pudding mass of the central parade, where the crowd gathered, was the grave of Private Daniel Hough, who had died in a flare-back while firing the fifty-gun salute of departure, four years ago today, and thus had been the first to fall in a war that by now had cost well over 600,000 lives. What was more, the man generally credited with firing from nearby Cummings Point the first shot of that war — white-haired Edmund Ruffin, past seventy and still hating, as he said in a farewell note this week, "the perfidious, malignant and vile Yankee race" — was dead too now from a bullet he put through his head when he heard the news from Appomattox.

Few if any were thinking of either Hough or Ruffin, however, as noon approached and Robert Anderson arrived with Quincy Gillmore, the department commander. Two months short of sixty, Anderson looked much older; sickness had worn him down and deprived him, except for a brief period of command in his native Kentucky, of any part in the struggle that followed the bloodless two-day bombardment in Charleston Harbor, which had turned out to be the high point in his life. He carried himself with military erectness, but he appeared somewhat confused: perhaps because, as a journalist would report, he "could see nothing by which to recognize the Fort Sumter he had left four years ago."

Still, this was another high point, if not so high as the one before, and as such had its effect both on him and on those who watched from in front of the canopied platform, where a tall new flagstaff had been erected. After a short prayer by the chaplain who had accompanied the eighty-odd-man force into the fort on the night after Christmas, 1860 — six days after South Carolina left the Union — and a responsive reading of parts from several Psalms, selected for being appropriate to the occasion — "When the Lord turned again the captivity of Zion, we were like them that dream" — a sergeant who was also a veteran of the bombardment stepped forward, drew from a leather pouch the scorched and shot-ripped flag Anderson had kept for use as a winding sheet when the time came, and began to attach it to the rope that would run it up the pole.

"We all held our breath for a second," a young woman from Philadelphia was to write many years later, "and then we gave a queer cry, between a cheer and a yell; nobody started it and nobody led it; I never heard anything like it before or since, but I can hear it now." Then, as she watched, "General Anderson stood up, bareheaded, took the halyards in his hands, and began to speak. At first I could not hear him, for his voice came thickly, but in a moment he said clearly, 'I thank God that I have lived to see this day,' and after a few more words he began to hoist the flag. It went up slowly and hung limp against the staff, a weather-beaten, frayed, and shell-torn old flag, not fit for much more work, but when it had crept clear of the shelter of the walls a sudden breath of wind caught it, and it shook its folds and flew straight out above us, while every soldier and sailor instinctively saluted."

What happened next was confused in her memory by the emotion of the moment. "I think we stood up; somebody started 'The Star-Spangled Banner,' and we sang the first verse, which is all that most people know. But it did not make much difference, for a great gun was fired close to us from the fort itself, followed, in obedience to the President's order, 'by a national salute from every fort and battery that fired upon Fort Sumter.' The measured, solemn booming came from Fort Moultrie, from the batteries on Sullivan and Folly Islands, and from Fort Wagner.... When the forts were done it was the turn of the fleet, and all our warships, from the largest — which would look tiny today — down to the smallest monitor, fired and fired in regular order until the air was thick and black with smoke and one's ears ached with the overlapping vibrations."

All this was prelude, so to speak, to the main event, the address to be delivered by the reverend Mr Beecher, the fifty-two-year-old younger brother of the author of *Uncle Tom's Cabin*, whom Lincoln was said to have greeted once as "the little lady who started this great war." Beecher's specialty was flamboyance: as when, some years before, he staged in his church a mock auction of a shapely mulatto who stood draped in white beside the pulpit, her loosened hair streaming down her back. "How much am I bid? How much am I bid for this piece of human flesh?" he intoned, and men and women in their enthusiasm removed their jewelry and unhooked their watches for deposit in the collection baskets which then were passed. There was no such heady reaction here today, however, perhaps because, as another Philadelphia visitor noted, the Brooklyn pastor "spoke very much by note, and quite without fire. [He] *read* his entire oration." His performance was also cramped by the wind, which rose briskly, once the flag was aloft, and presented him with some of the problems Lincoln had had at the White House window, two nights back, in trying to manage a candle at the same time he delivered a quite different kind of speech. Beecher's problem, while the stiff breeze off the ocean whipped his hair and threatened to scatter his manuscript broadcast, was his hat. His solution was to clap it firmly on his head and jam it down tight against his ears, thus freeing both hands to grip the wind-fluttered leaves of his text.

Even so, a measure of the old fiery rhetoric came through the awkwardness of his disadvantaged performance. For though he predicted that the common people North and South would soon unite to rule the country, he entertained no notion of forgiveness for those "guiltiest and most remorseless traitors," the secessionist aristocrats. They were the villains; "polished, cultured, exceedingly capable and wholly unprincipled," they were the ones who had "shed this ocean of blood," and he foresaw eternal agony for them on the Day of Judgment, when they would be confronted by their victims. "Caught up in black clouds full of voices of vengeance and lurid with punishment,

[they] shall be whirled aloft and plunged downward forever and forever in endless retribution." He paused for a brief rest and a drink of water, then passed on to the subject of reconstruction, which he believed posed no problems not easily solved. *"One nation, under one government, without slavery*, has been ordained, and shall stand.... On this base, reconstruction is easy, and needs neither architect nor engineer." In closing, though he had been one of Lincoln's harshest critics throughout the war — "Not a spark of genius has he; not an element for leadership. Not one particle of heroic enthusiasm" — Beecher wound up his address by offering the President "our solemn congratulations that God has sustained his life and health under the unparalleled burdens and sufferings of four bloody years, and permitted him to behold this auspicious confirmation of that national unity for which he has waited with so much patience and fortitude, and for which he has labored with such disinterested wisdom."

Robert Anderson, having performed what he called "perhaps the last act of my life, of duty to my country," had a somewhat let-down feeling as the ceremony ended and he and the rest got aboard boats to return to Charleston. At the outset he had urged Stanton to keep the program brief and quiet, but it had turned out to be neither. What was more, he faced still another speaking ordeal that night at a formal dinner Gillmore was giving for him and other guests of honor, including the old-line abolitionist Garrison, who had been hanged and burned in effigy on a nearby street corner, thirty-odd years before, in reaction to the Nat Turner uprising in Virginia. Garrison spoke, as did Beecher again — impromptu this time, and to better effect — and John Nicolay, who had been sent from Washington to deliver the Chief Executive's regrets that he himself was unable to attend. Others held forth at considerable length, interrupted from time to time by the crump and crackle of a fireworks display being staged in the harbor by Dahlgren's fleet, with Battery wharves and rooftops nearly as crowded as they had been for a grimmer show of pyrotechnics, four years ago this week. In the banquet hall of the Charleston Hotel the evening wore on as speaker after speaker, not sharing Anderson's aversion to exposure, had his say. At last, the various orators having subsided, the Kentuckian's turn came round.

He rose, glass in hand, and haltingly, with no mention of Union victory or Confederate defeat, of which so much had already been said by the others, proposed a toast to "the man who, when elected President of the United States, was compelled to reach the seat of government without an escort, but a man who now could travel all over our country with millions of hands and hearts to sustain him. I give you the good, the great, the honest man, Abraham Lincoln."

★ ★ ★

The man to whom the celebrants raised their glasses down in Charleston this Good Friday evening was seated in a box at Ford's Theater, attentive to the forced chatter of a third-rate farce which by then was into its second act. Apparently he was enjoying himself, as he generally did at the theater, even though he had come with some reluctance, if not distaste, and more from a sense of obligation than by choice. "It has been advertised that we will be there," he had said that afternoon, "and I cannot disappoint the people. Otherwise I would not go. I do not want to go."

In part this was because of a last-minute withdrawal by Grant, who earlier had accepted an invitation for him and his wife to come along, and whose presence, as the hero of Appomattox, would have lent the presidential box a glitter that outdid anything under limelight on the stage. Besides, Lincoln had looked forward to the general's company as a diversion from the strain of the daily grind, which the advent of peace had not made any less daily or less grinding. Today, for example, he was in his office by 7 o'clock as usual, attending to administrative matters in advance of the flood of supplicants who would descend on him later. After issuing a call for a cabinet meeting at 11, he went back upstairs for breakfast with Mrs Lincoln and their two sons. Robert, just up from Virginia, brought with him a photograph of R. E. Lee which he presented to his father at the table, apparently as a joke. Lincoln did not take it so. He polished his glasses on a napkin, studied the portrait, then said quietly: "It's a good face. I am glad the war is over."

This last was repeated in varied phrasings through the day. Returning to his office he conferred first with Speaker Colfax, who was slated for a cabinet post — probably Stanton's, who more than anything wanted a seat on the Supreme Court as soon as one became vacant — and then with Senator John Creswell, who had done much to keep Maryland in the Union during the secession furor. "Creswell, old fellow," Lincoln hailed him, "everything is bright this morning. The war is over. It has been a tough time, but we have lived it out. Or some of us have." His face darkened, then lightened again. "But it is over. We are going to have good times now, and a united country." He approved a number of appointments, granted a military discharge, sent a messenger over to Ford's on 10th Street to reserve the State Box for the evening performance — not forgetting to inform the management that Grant would be a member of his party, which would help to increase the normally scant Good Friday audience — and wrote on a card for two Virginians requesting passes south: "No pass is necessary now to authorize anyone to go and return from Petersburg and Richmond. People go and return just as they did before the war." Presently, as the hour approached for the cabinet meeting he had called, he walked over to the War Department, hoping for news from Sherman of Johnston's surrender. There was nothing, but he was not discouraged. He said later at the meeting that he was convinced some such news was on the way, and soon would be clicking off the wire, because of a dream he had had the night before.

Grant was there by special invitation, having arrived from City Point just yesterday. Welcomed and applauded as he entered the cabinet room, he told of his pursuit of Lee and the closing scene at Appomattox, but added that no word had come from Carolina, where a similar campaign was being mounted against Joe Johnston, hopefully with similar results. The President said he was sure they would hear from Sherman soon, for he had had this dream the night before. What sort of dream? Welles asked. "It relates to your element, the water," Lincoln replied, and told how he had been aboard "some singular, indescribable vessel" which seemed to be "floating, floating away on some vast and indistinct expanse, toward an unknown shore." The dream was not so strange in itself, he declared, as in the fact that it was recurrent; that "each of its previous occurrences has been followed by some important event or disaster." He had had it before Sumter and Bull Run, he said, as well as before such victories as Antietam, Stones River, Gettysburg, Vicksburg, and Wilmington. Grant — who seldom passed up a chance to take a swipe at Rosecrans — remarked that Stones River was no victory; he knew of no great results it brought. In any case, Lincoln told him, he had had this dream on the eve of that battle, and it had come to him again last night. He took it as a sign that they would "have great news very soon," and "I think it must be from Sherman. My thoughts are in that direction."

After a brief discussion of dreams and their nature, the talk returned to Appomattox. Grant's terms there had assured that no member of the surrendered army, from Lee on down, would ever be prosecuted by the government for treason or any other crime, so long as he observed the conditions of his parole and the laws in force where he resided. Lincoln's ready approval of this assurance gave Postmaster General William Dennison the impression that he would like to have it extended to the civilian leaders — a number of whom by now were fugitives, in flight for their lives amid the ruins of the rebellion — if only some way could be found to avoid having them hauled into court. "I suppose, Mr President," he half-inquired, half-suggested, "that you would not be sorry to have them escape out of the country?" Lincoln thought it over. "Well, I should not be sorry to have them out of the country," he replied, "but I should be for following them up pretty close to make sure of their going." Having said as much he said still more to others around the table. "I think it is providential that this great rebellion is crushed just as Congress has adjourned and there are none of the disturbing elements of that body to hinder and embarrass us. If we are wise and discreet we shall reanimate the states and get their governments in successful operation, with order prevailing and the Union reëstablished before Congress comes together in December." Returning to the question of what should be done with the rebel leaders, he became more animated both in speech and gesture. "I hope there will be no persecution, no bloody work after the war is over. No one need expect me to take any part in hanging or killing these men, even the worst of them. Frighten them out of the country; open the gates; let down the bars." He put both hands out, fluttering the fingers as if to frighten sheep out of a lot. "Shoo; scare them off," he said; "enough lives have been sacrificed."

It was for this, the consideration of reconstruction matters and incidentals preliminary to them, that the cabinet had been assembled in the first place, midway between its regular Tuesday gatherings. In the absence of Seward — still on his bed of pain, he was represented at the meeting by his son Frederick — Stanton had come armed with a plan, drawn up at the President's request, for bringing the states that had been "abroad" back into what Lincoln, in his speech three nights ago, had called "their proper practical relation with the Union." The War Secretary's notion was that military occupation should precede readmission, and in this connection he proposed that Virginia and North Carolina be combined in a single district to simplify the army's task. Welles took exception, on grounds that this last would destroy the individuality of both states and thus be "in conflict with the principles of self-government which I deem essential." So did Lincoln. After some earnest discussion, back and forth across the green-topped table, he suggested that Stanton revise his plan in this regard and provide copies for the other cabinet members to study between now and their next meeting, four days off. Congress would no doubt have its say when it returned in December, but as for himself he had already reached certain bedrock conclusions. "We can't undertake to run state governments in all these southern states. Their own people must do that — though I reckon that at first some of them may do it badly."

By now it was close to 2 o'clock, and the meeting, nearly three hours long, adjourned. Grant however remained behind to talk with Lincoln: not about army matters, it turned out, but to beg off going to the theater that night. His wife, he said, was anxious to catch the late-afternoon train for Philadelphia, en route to a visit with their young sons in Burlington, New Jersey. Lincoln started to press him, but then refrained, perhaps realizing from the general's embarrassed manner that the real reason was Julia Grant, who was determined not to expose herself to another of Mary Lincoln's tirades, this time in full view of the audience at Ford's. Disappointed, Lincoln accepted the excuse — reinforced just then by a note from Mrs Grant, reminding her husband not to be late for their 6 o'clock departure — and went upstairs for lunch, faced with the unpleasant job of informing his wife that the social catch of the season would not be going with them to the theater that evening. If he also told her, as he would tell others between now and curtain time, that he too no longer wanted to go, it made no difference; Grant or no Grant, she was set on attending what the papers were calling the "last appearance of Miss Laura Keene in her celebrated comedy of *Our American Cousin*."

He was back in his office by 3 o'clock, in time for an appointment with the Vice President, the first since the scandalous scene at his swearing in. They talked for twenty minutes or so, and though neither left any record of what was said, witnesses noted that Lincoln called him "Andy," shaking him vigorously by the hand, and that Johnson seemed greatly relieved to find himself greeted cordially after nearly six weeks of pointed neglect. This done, Lincoln attended to some paper work, including an appeal on behalf of a soldier convicted for desertion. So far in the war he had approved 267 death sentences for military offenses, but not this one. "Well, I think the boy can do us more good above ground than under ground," he drawled as he fixed his signature to a pardon. Before setting out on a 4.30 carriage ride with his wife — "Just ourselves," he had said at lunch when she asked if he wanted anyone else along — he walked over to the War Department, in hope that some word had come at last from Sherman. Again there was nothing, which served to weaken his conviction that the news of "some important event or disaster" would shake the capital before the day was over. Time was running out, and he was disappointed. It was then, on the way back from the telegraph office, that he told his bodyguard Crook that he did not want to go to the theater that night, and would not go, except for notices in the papers that he would be there. Crook was about to go off shift, and when they reached the White House door Lincoln paused for a moment and turned to face him. He seemed gloomy, depressed. "Goodbye, Crook," he said, to the guard's surprise. Always before, it had been "Good night, Crook," when they parted. Now suddenly it was goodbye; "Goodbye, Crook."

Still, by the time the carriage rolled out of the driveway a few minutes later, on through streets that glittered with bright gold April sunshine, he had recovered his spirits to such an extent that he informed his wife: "I never felt better in my life." What was more — even though, just one month ago today, he had been confined to his bed with what his doctor described as "exhaustion, complete exhaustion" — he looked as happy as he said he felt. The recent City Point excursion, his first extended vacation of the war, had done him so much good that various cabinet members, after observing him at the midday meeting — in contrast to the one a month ago, when they gathered about his sickbed — remarked on the "expression of visible relief and content upon his face." One said that he "never appeared to better advantage," while another declared that "the weary look which his face had so long worn . . . had disappeared. It was cheerful and happy." They were glad to see him so. But Mary Lincoln, whose moods were quite as variable as his own, had a different reaction when he told her he had never felt better in his life. "Don't you remember feeling just so before our little boy died?" she asked. He patted her hand to comfort her, and spoke of a trip to Europe as soon as his term was up. After that they would return to Springfield, where he would resume the practice of law and perhaps buy a farm along the Sangamon. "We must both be more cheerful in the future," he told her. "Between the war and the loss of our darling Willie, we have both been very miserable."

The good mood held. Seeing two old friends just leaving as the open barouche turned into the White House driveway an hour later, he stood up and called for them to wait. They were Richard Oglesby, the new governor of Illinois, and his adjutant general Isham Haynie, a combat brigadier who had left the army to work for him and Lincoln in the recent campaign. Lincoln led the way inside, where he read to them from the latest collection of "Letters" by Petroleum V. Nasby, a humorist he admired so much that he once said he would gladly swap his present office for the genius to compose such things. "Linkin rides into Richmond!" he read from the final letter. "A Illinois rale-splitter, a buffoon, a ape, a goriller, a smutty joker, sets hisself down in President Davis's cheer and rites dispatchis! . . . This ends the chapter. The Confederasy hez at last consentratid its last consentrate. It's ded. It's gathered up its feet, sed its last words, and deceest. . . . Farewell, vane world." The reading went on so long — four letters, with time out for laughter and thigh-slapping all around — that supper was delayed, as well as his departure for the theater. Even so, with the carriage waiting, he took time to see Colfax, who called again to ask if a special session of Congress was likely to interrupt a Rocky Mountain tour he was planning. The President said there would be no special session, and they went on talking until Mrs Lincoln appeared in the office doorway. She wore a low-necked evening dress and was pulling on her gloves, by way of warning her husband that 8 o'clock had struck.

He excused himself and they started out, only to be interrupted by two more men, a Massachusetts congressman and a former congressman from Illinois, both of whom had political favors to collect. One wanted a hearing for a client who had a sizeable cotton claim against the government; Lincoln gave him a card that put him first on tomorrow's list of callers. What the other wanted no one knew, for he whispered it into the presidential ear. Lincoln had entered and then backed out of the closed carriage, cocking his head to hear the request. "Excuse me now," he said as he climbed in again beside his wife. "I am going to the theater. Come and see me in the morning."

Stopping en route at the home of New York Senator Ira Harris to pick up their substitute guests, the senator's daughter Clara and her fiancé, Major Henry Rathbone, the carriage rolled and clopped through intersections whose streetlamps glimmered dimly through the mist. It was close to 8.30, twenty minutes past curtain time, when the coachman drew rein in front of Ford's, on 10th Street between E and F, and the two couples alighted to enter the theater. Inside, about midway of Act I, the performance stopped as the President and his party came down the side aisle, and the orchestra struck up "Hail to the Chief" as they entered the flag-draped box to the right front. A near-capacity crowd of about 1700 applauded politely, masking its disappointment at Grant's absence. Clara Harris and Rathbone took seats near the railing; the First Lady sat a little behind them, to their left, and Lincoln slumped into a roomy, upholstered rocker toward the rear. This last represented concern for his comfort and was also the management's way of expressing thanks for his having been here at least four times before, once to see Maggie Mitchell in *Fanchon the Cricket,* once to see John Wilkes Booth in *The Marble Heart* — "Rather tame than otherwise," John Hay had complained — and twice to see James Hackett play Falstaff in *Henry IV* and *The Merry Wives of Windsor.* Tonight's play resumed, and Lincoln, as was his habit, at once grew absorbed in the action down below: though not so absorbed that he failed to notice that the major was holding his fiancée's hand, for he reached out and took hold of his wife's. Pleased by the attention he had shown her on their carriage ride that afternoon, and now by this further expression of affection, Mary Lincoln reverted to her old role of Kentucky belle. "What will Miss Harris think of my hanging onto you so?" she whispered, leaning toward him. Lincoln's eyes, fixed on the stage, reflected the glow of the footlights. "Why, she will think nothing about it," he said, and he kept his grip on her hand.

Act I ended; Act II began. Down in Charleston the banqueters raised their glasses in response to Anderson's toast, and here at Ford's, in an equally festive mood, the audience enjoyed *Our American Cousin* with only occasional sidelong glances at the State Box to see whether Grant had arrived. He might have done so without their knowledge, for though they could see the young couple at the railing and Mrs Lincoln half in shadow behind them, the President was screened from view by the box curtains and draped flags. Act II ended; Act III began. Lincoln, having at last released his wife's hand and settled back in the horsehair rocker, seemed to be enjoying what was happening down below. In the second scene, which opened shortly after 10 o'clock, a three-way running dialogue revealed to Mrs Mountchessington that Asa Trenchard, for whom she had set her daughter's cap, was no millionaire after all.

— No heir to the fortune, Mr Trenchard?
— Oh, no.
— What! No fortune!
— Nary a red. . . .

Consternation. Indignation.

— Augusta, to your room.

— Yes, ma. The nasty beast!

— I am aware, Mr Trenchard, that you are not used to the manners of good society, and that alone will excuse the impertinence of which you have been guilty.

Exit Mrs Mountchessington, trailing daughter. Trenchard alone.

— Don't know the manners of good society, eh? Wal, I guess I know enough to turn you inside out, you sockdologizing old mantrap!

Then it came, a half-muffled explosion, somewhere between a boom and a thump, loud but by no means so loud as it sounded in the theater, then a boil and bulge of bluish smoke in the presidential box, an exhalation as of brimstone from the curtained mouth, and a man coming out through the bank and swirl of it, white-faced and dark-haired in a black sack suit and riding boots, eyes aglitter, brandishing a knife. He mounted the ledge, presented his back to the rows of people seated below, and let himself down by the handrail for the ten-foot drop to the stage. Falling he turned, and as he did so caught the spur of his right boot in the folds of a flag draped over the lower front of the high box. It ripped but offered enough resistance to bring all the weight of his fall on his left leg, which buckled and pitched him forward onto his hands. He rose, thrust the knife overhead in a broad theatrical gesture, and addressed the outward darkness of the pit. "Sic semper tyrannis," he said in a voice so low and projected with so little clarity that few recognized the state motto of Virginia or could later agree that he had spoken in Latin. "Revenge for the South!" or "The South is avenged!" some thought they heard him cry, while others said that he simply muttered "Freedom." In any case he then turned again, hobbled left across the stage past the lone actor standing astonished in its center, and vanished into the wings.

Barely half a minute had passed since the jolt of the explosion, and now a piercing scream came through the writhing tendrils of smoke — a full-voiced wail from Mary Lincoln. "Stop that man!" Rathbone shouted, nursing an arm slashed by the intruder, and Clara Harris, wringing her hands, called down from the railing in a tone made falsely calm by shock: "Water. Water." The audience began to emerge from its trance. "What is it? What happened?" "For God's sake, what is it?" "What has happened?" The answer came in a bellow of rage from the curtained orifice above the spur-torn flag: "He has shot the President!" Below, men leaped from their seats in a first reaction of disbelief and denial, not only of this but also of what they had seen with their own eyes. "No. For God's sake, no! It can't be true." But then, by way of reinforcement for the claim, the cry went up: "Surgeon! A surgeon! Is there a surgeon in the house?"

The young doctor who came forward — and at last gained admission to the box, after Rathbone removed a wooden bar the intruder had used to keep the hallway door from being opened while he went about his work — thought at first that he had been summoned to attend a dead man. Lincoln sat sprawled in the rocker as if asleep, knees relaxed, eyes closed, head dropped forward so that his chin was on his chest. He seemed to have no vital signs until a closer examination detected a weak pulse and shallow breathing. Assuming that he had been knifed, as Rathbone had been, the doctor had him taken from the chair and laid on the floor in a search for a stab wound. However, when he put his hands behind the patient's head to lift it, he found the back hair wet with blood from a half-inch hole where a bullet had entered, three inches to the right of the left ear. "The course of the ball was obliquely forward," a subsequent report would state, "toward the right eye, crossing the brain in an oblique manner and lodging a few inches behind that eye. In the track of the wound were found fragments of bone driven forward by the ball, which was embedded in the anterior lobe of the left hemisphere of the brain." The doctor — Charles A. Leale, assistant surgeon, U.S. Volunteers, twenty-three years old and highly familiar with gunshot wounds — did not know all this; yet he knew enough from what he had seen and felt, here in the crowded box for the past five minutes, as well as in casualty wards for the past year, to arrive at a prognosis. Everything was over for Abraham Lincoln but the end. "His wound is mortal," Leale pronounced. "It is impossible for him to recover."

Two other surgeons were in the box by then, both senior to Leale in rank and years, but he remained in charge and made the decision not to risk a removal to the White House, six cobblestone blocks away. "If it is attempted the President will die before we reach there," he replied to the suggestion. Instead, with the help of four soldier volunteers, the three doctors took up their patient and carried him feet first down the stairs and aisle, out onto 10th Street — packed nearly solid with the curious and grieving, so that an infantry captain had to draw his sword to clear a path for the seven bearers and their awkward burden, bawling excitedly: "Out of the way, you sons of bitches!" — up the front steps, down a narrow hall, and into a small back ground-floor bedroom in one of a row of modest houses across the way. Let by the night by its owner, a Swedish tailor, the room was mean and dingy, barely fifteen by nine feet in length and width, with a threadbare rug, once Turkey red, and oatmeal-colored paper on the walls. The bed itself was too short for the long form placed diagonally on the cornshuck mattress; Lincoln's booted feet protruded well beyond the footboard, his head propped on extra pillows so that his bearded chin was on his chest, as it had been when Leale first saw him in the horsehair rocker, back at

Ford's. By then the time was close to 11 o'clock, some forty-five minutes after the leaden ball first broke into his skull, and now began a
painful, drawn-out vigil, a death watch that would continue for another
eight hours and beyond.

Three more doctors soon arrived, Surgeon General Joseph Barnes,
his chief assistant, and the family physician, who did what he could for
Mary Lincoln in her distress. Barnes took charge, but Leale continued
his ministrations, including the removal of the patient's clothing in a
closer search for another wound and the application of mustard plasters
in an attempt to improve his respiration and heartbeat. One did as little
good as the other; for there was no additional wound and Lincoln's
condition remained about the same, with stertorous breathing, pulse a
feeble 44, hands and feet corpse-cold to the wrists and ankles, and both
eyes insensitive to light, the left pupil much contracted, the right dilated
widely. Gideon Welles came in at this point and wrote next day in his
diary of "the giant sufferer" as he saw him from his post beside the bed.
"He had been stripped of his clothes. His large arms, which were occasionally exposed, were of a size which one would scarce have expected
from his spare appearance. His slow, full respiration lifted the bedclothes with each breath that he took. His features were calm and
striking. I had never seen them appear to better advantage than for the
first hour, perhaps, that I was there." Presently, though, their calm
appearance changed. The left side of the face began to twitch, distorting
the mouth into a jeer. When this desisted, the upper right side of the
face began to darken, streaked with purple as from a blow, and the eye
with the ball of lead behind it began to bulge from its socket. Mary
Lincoln screamed at the sight and had to be led from the room, while a
journalist noted that Charles Sumner, "seated on the right of the President's couch, near the head, holding the right hand of the President in
his own," was about equally unstrung. "He was sobbing like a woman,
with his head bowed down almost on the pillow of the bed on which the
President was lying."

By midnight, close to fifty callers were in the house, all of
sufficient prominence to gain entrance past the guards and most of them
wedged shoulder to shoulder in the death chamber, at one time or
another, for a look at the final agony of the man laid diagonally on the
bed in one corner. Andrew Johnson was there — briefly, however,
because his presence was painful to Mrs Lincoln, who whimpered at
the sight of her husband's imminent successor — as were a number of
Sumner's colleagues from the House and Senate, Robert Lincoln and
John Hay, Oglesby and Haynie again, a pair of clergymen — one
fervent, the other unctuous — and Laura Keene, who claimed a star's
prerogative, first in the box at the theater, where she had held the
President's bleeding head in her lap, and now in the narrow brick house
across the street, where she helped Clara Harris comfort the distraught

widow-to-be in the tailor's front parlor, what time she was not with her in the crowded bedroom toward the rear. All members of the cabinet were on hand but the Secretary of State, and most of the talk that was not of Lincoln was of him. He too had been attacked and grievously wounded, along with four members of his household, by a lone assassin who struck at about the same time as the one at Ford's: unless, indeed, it was the same man in rapid motion from one place to the other, less than half a mile away. Seward had been slashed about the face and throat, and he was thought to be dying, too, except that the iron frame that bound his jaw had served to protect him to some extent from the knife. "I'm mad, I'm mad," the attacker had said as he ran out into the night to vanish as cleanly as the other — or he — had done when he — or the other — leaped from the box, crossed the stage, entered the wings, and exited into the alley behind Ford's, where he — whoever, whichever he was — mounted his waiting horse and rode off in the darkness.

In this, as in other accounts concerning other rumored victims — Grant, for one, and Andrew Johnson for another, until word came that the general was safe in Philadelphia and the Vice President himself showed up unhurt — there was much confusion. Edwin Stanton undertook on his own the task of sifting and setting the contradictions straight, in effect taking over as head of the headless government. "[He] instantly assumed charge of everything near and remote, civil and military," a subordinate observed, "and began issuing orders in that autocratic manner so superbly necessary to the occasion." Among other precautions, he stopped traffic on the Potomac and the railroads, warned the Washington Fire Brigade to be ready for mass arson, summoned Grant back to take charge of the capital defenses, and alerted guards along the Canadian border, as well as in all major eastern ports, to be on the lookout for suspicious persons attempting to leave the country. In short, "he continued throughout the night acting as president, secretary of war, secretary of state, commander in chief, comforter, and dictator," all from a small sitting room adjacent to the front parlor of the tailor's house on 10th Street, which he turned into an interrogation chamber for grilling witnesses to find out just what had happened in the theater across the street.

From the outset, numbers of people who knew him well, including members of his profession, had identified John Wilkes Booth as Lincoln's attacker, and by now the twenty-six-year-old matinee idol's one-shot pocket derringer had been found on the floor of the box where he had dropped it as he leaped for the railing to escape by way of the stage and the back alley. Identification was certain. Even so, and though a War Department description eventually went out by wire across the land — "height 5 feet 8 inches, weight 160 pounds, compact build; hair jet black, inclined to curl, medium length, parted behind; eyes black, heavy dark eyebrows; wears a large seal ring on little finger; when talking inclines head forward, looks down" — Stanton was intent on larger game. Apparently convinced that the President could not have been shot by anyone so insignificant as an actor acting on his own, he was out to expose a full-scale Confederate plot, a conspiracy hatched in Richmond "and set on foot by rebels under pretense of avenging the rebel cause."

So he believed at any rate, and though he gave most of his attention to exploring this assumption — proceeding with such misdirected and disjointed vigor that he later aroused revisionist suspicions that he must have wanted the assassin to escape: as, for instance, by his neglect in closing all city bridges except the one Booth used to cross into Maryland — he still had time for periodic visits to the small back room, filled with the turmoil of Lincoln's labored breathing, and to attend to such incidental administrative matters as the preparation of a message giving Johnson formal notice that the President had died. His purpose in this, with the hour of death left blank to be filled in later, was to avoid delay when the time came, but when he read the rough draft aloud for a stenographer to take down a fair copy he produced a premature effect he had not foreseen. Hearing a strangled cry behind him, he turned and found Mary Lincoln standing in the parlor doorway, hands clasped before her in entreaty, a stricken expression on her face. "Is he dead? Oh, is he dead?" she moaned. Stanton tried to explain that what she had heard was merely in preparation for a foreseen contingency, but she could not understand him through her sobbing and her grief. So he gave it up and had her led back into the parlor, out of his way; which was just as well, an associate declared, for "he was full of business, and knew, moreover, that in a few hours at most she must be a widow."

It was by then about 1.30; Good Friday was off the calendar at last, and Mary Lincoln was into what everyone in the house, doctors and laymen alike, could see would be the first day of her widowhood. At intervals, supported on either side by Clara Harris and Laura Keene, she would return to the crowded bedroom and sit or stand looking down at her husband until grief overcame her again and the two women would half-guide half-carry her back to the front parlor, where she would remain until enough strength returned for her to repeat the process. She made these trips about once an hour, and each was more grueling than the last, not only because of her own cumulative exhaustion, but also because of the deteriorating condition of the sufferer on the bed, which came as a greater shock to her each time she saw him. Earlier, there had been a certain calm and dignity about him, as if he were in fact aboard "some singular, indescribable vessel . . . floating, floating away on some vast and indistinct expanse, toward an unknown shore." Now this was gone, replaced by the effects of agony. The dream ship had become a rack, and the stertorous uproar of his breathing, interspersed with drawn-out groans, filled the house as it might have filled a torture chamber. "Doctor, save him!" she implored first one and then another of the attending physicians, and once she said in a calmer tone: "Bring Tad. He will speak to Tad, he loves him so." But all agreed that would not do, either for the boy or for his father, who was beyond all knowledgeable contact with anything on earth, even Tad, and indeed had been so ever since Booth's derringer crashed through the laughter in the theater at 10.15 last night. All the while, his condition worsened, especially his breathing, which not only became increasingly spasmodic, but would stop entirely from time to time, the narrow chest expanded between the big rail-splitter arms, and then resume with a sudden gusty roar through the fluttering lips. On one such occasion, with Mrs Lincoln leaning forward from a chair beside the bed, her cheek on her husband's cheek, her ear near his still, cyanotic mouth, the furious bray of his exhalation — louder than anything she had heard since the explosion in the box, five hours ago — startled and frightened her so badly that she shrieked and fell to the floor in a faint. Stanton, interrupted in his work by the piercing scream, came running down the hall from his improvised Acting President's office up front. When he saw what it was he lost patience entirely. "Take that woman out," he ordered sternly, thrusting both arms over his head in exasperation, "and do not let her in again."

He was obeyed in this as in all his other orders, and she remained in the front parlor until near the very end. Meantime dawn came through, paling the yellow flare of gas jets. A cold rain fell on the people still keeping their vigil on the street outside, while inside, in the dingy room made dingier by daylight, Lincoln entered the final stage of what one doctor called "the saddest and most pathetic deathbed scene I ever witnessed." Interruptions of his breathing were more frequent now, and longer, and whenever this happened some of the men about the bed would take out their watches to note the time of death, then return them to their pockets when the raucous sound resumed. Robert Lincoln — "only a boy for all his shoulder straps," the guard Crook had said — "bore himself well," according to one who watched him, "but on two occasions gave way to overpowering grief and sobbed aloud, turning his head and leaning on the shoulder of Senator Sumner." At 7 o'clock, with the end at hand, he went to bring his mother into the room for a last visit. She tottered in, looked at her husband in confusion, saying nothing, and was led back out again. Stanton was there full-time now, and strangely enough had brought his hat along, standing motionless with his chin on his left hand, his right hand holding the hat and supporting his left elbow, tears running down his face into his beard.

By this time Lincoln's breathing was fast and shallow, cheeks pulled inward behind the closed blue lips. His chest heaved up in a last deep breath, then subsided and did not rise again. It was 7.22; the nine-hour agony was over, and his face took on what John Hay described as "a look of unspeakable peace." Surgeon General Barnes leaned forward, listened carefully for a time to the silent chest, then straightened up, removed two silver half-dollars from his pocket, and placed them carefully on the closed eyes. Observing this ritual, Stanton then performed one of his own. He stretched his right arm out deliberately before him, clapped his hat for a long moment on his head, and then as deliberately removed it, as if in salute. "Now he belongs to the ages," he said, or anyhow later saw to it that he was quoted as having said. "Let us pray," one of the parsons intoned, and sank to his knees on the thin red carpet beside the bed.

Soon thereafter Mary Lincoln was brought back into the room. "Oh, why did you not tell me he was dying?" she exclaimed when she saw her husband lying there with coins on his eyes. Then it came home to her, and her grief was too great to be contained. "Oh my God," she wailed as she was led out, weeping bitterly, "I have given my husband to die!" Presently she was taken from the house, and the other mourner witnesses picked their way through the wet streets to their homes and hotels near and far.

Bells were tolling all over Washington by the time Lincoln's body, wrapped in a flag and placed in a closed hearse, was on its way back to the White House, escorted (as he had not been when he left, twelve hours before) by an honor guard of soldiers and preceded by a group of officers walking bareheaded in the rain. He would lie in state, first in the East Room, then afterwards in the Capitol rotunda, preparatory to the long train ride back to Springfield, where he would at last be laid to rest. "Nothing touches the tired spot," he had said often in the course of the past four years. Now Booth's derringer had reached it.

At 10 o'clock that Saturday morning, less than three hours after Lincoln died in the tailor's house two blocks away, Andrew Johnson took the oath of office in the parlor of his suite at the Kirkwood House, just down Pennsylvania Avenue from the mansion that was soon to be his home. After kissing the Bible held out to him by Chase, he turned and made a short speech, a sort of extemporaneous inaugural, to the dozen senators and cabinet members present, all with faces that showed the strain of their all-night vigil. "Gentlemen," he said, "I have been almost overwhelmed by the announcement of the sad event which has so recently occurred." Other than this he made no reference to his predecessor, and as for any policy he would adopt, "that must be left for development as the Administration progresses. . . . The only assurance I can now give of the future is reference to the past. Toil, and an honest advocacy of the great principles of free government, have been my lot. The duties have been mine; the consequences are God's."

If this sounded at once conventional and high-handed, if some among the new President's hearers resented his singular omission of any reference to the old one — "Johnson seemed willing to share the glory of his achievements with his Creator," a New Hampshire senator observed, "but utterly forgot that Mr Lincoln had any share of credit in the suppression of the rebellion" — there were those beyond reach of his voice just then who were altogether delighted with the change, as they saw it, from a soft- to a hard-peace Chief of State. Back from Richmond that same day, most of the members of the Joint Committee on the Conduct of the War spent the afternoon at a caucus held to consider "the necessity of a new cabinet and a line of policy less conciliatory than that of Mr Lincoln." They had been upset by a number of things, including his recent speech from the White House window, and Julian of Indiana complained that "aside from his known tenderness to the rebels, Lincoln's last public avowal, only three days before his death, of adherence to the plan of reconstruction he had announced in December 1863, was highly repugnant." All in all, "while everybody was shocked at his murder," Julian declared, "the feeling was nearly universal that the accession of Johnson to the Presidency would prove a godsend to the country."

Sure enough, when they requested through their chairman a meeting with the new President — himself a member of the committee until he left the Senate, three years ago, to take up his duties as military governor of Tennessee — he promptly agreed to see them the following day, not at the White House, which was in a turmoil of preparation for the funeral, but next door at the Treasury Department. It was Easter Sunday, and Ben Wade, as chairman, got things off to a rousing start. "Johnson, we have faith in you," he said. "By the gods, there will be no trouble *now* in running the government."

Lincoln's life had ended, so to speak, in a tailor shop; Johnson's could be said to have begun in one, plying needle and thread while his wife taught him to read. Since then, he had come far — indeed, all the way to the top — with much of his success attributable to his skill as a stump speaker whose specialty was invective. Nor did he disappoint his Jacobin callers now in that regard. One year older and half a foot shorter than his predecessor, he thanked Wade for the warmth of his greeting and launched at once into a statement of his position on the burning issue of the day, repeating, with some expansion and adjustment of the words, what he had said on the steps of the Patent Office, twelve days back. "I hold that robbery is a crime; rape is a crime; murder is a crime; *treason* is a crime — and crime must be punished. Treason must be made infamous, and traitors must be impoverished." The impression here was as strong as the one produced at the Republican rally, two days after the fall of Richmond, and it was also encouraging to learn that the text under his lips when he kissed the Bible held out to him by Chase the day before, open to the lurid and vengeful Book of Ezekiel, carried a similar burden of blame and retribution: *And I will give them one heart, and I will put a new spirit within you; and I will take the stony heart out of their flesh, and will give them an heart of flesh: That they may walk in my statutes, and keep mine ordinances, and do them: and they shall be my people, and I will be their God. But as for them whose heart walketh after the heart of their detestable things and their abominations, I will recompense their way upon their own heads, saith the Lord God.* Although he made them no commitment as to changes in the cabinet he had inherited — not even regarding dismissal of the twice-injured Seward, whom they detested — they did not expect that; not just yet. It was enough, for the present, that he was with them. They knew him of old; he was *of* them, a long-time colleague, and they counted on him to come down stronger on their enemies all the time. They knew, as their chairman had said at the outset, there would be no trouble in running the government now.

Anyhow they thought they knew, and when Johnson presently issued a proclamation offering rewards that ranged from $100,000 to $10,000 for the capture of Jefferson Davis and certain of his "agents," on charges of having conspired to incite the murder of Abraham Lincoln, their cup nearly ran over. Zachariah Chandler, for one, was pleased with the prospect brought about by the assassination, and he said as much in a letter he wrote his wife in Michigan, one week after the Easter meeting. "Had Mr Lincoln's policy been carried out, we should have had Jeff Davis, Toombs, etc. back in the Senate at the next session of Congress, but now their chances to stretch hemp are better. . . . So mote it be."

❌ 2 ❌

Escorted by a small band of Tennessee cavalry, Davis and his official family left Greensboro on the morning Lincoln died, April 15, all on horseback except the ailing Trenholm, accompanied in his ambulance by Adjutant General Samuel Cooper, crowding seventy years of age, and Judah Benjamin, for whom a saddle was an instrument of torture. While they toiled southwest over clay roads made slippery by recent heavy rains, Joe Johnston waited in his Hillsboro headquarters, forty miles northwest of Union-occupied Raleigh, for a reply to his request, sent through the lines the day before — Good Friday; Lincoln had been right, after all, about good news in the offing — for "a temporary suspension of active operations . . . to permit the civil authorities to enter into the needful arrangements to terminate the existing war." Reluctant to have the overture made, even though he himself, under pressure from his advisers, had written the message the Virginian signed, Davis had said he was not "sanguine" as to the outcome. But the response, received by Johnston on Easter Sunday, showed Sherman to be a good deal more receptive to the notion than the departed President had expected. "I am fully empowered," the Ohioan replied, "to arrange with you any terms for the suspension of further hostilities between the armies commanded by you and those commanded by myself, and will be willing to confer with you to that end." He proposed surrender on the same terms Grant had given Lee, a week ago today, and spoke in closing of his "desire to save the people of North Carolina the damage they would sustain by the march of this army through the central or western parts of the state."

In point of fact, Sherman was even more pleased than he sounded: not only because, as he later said, "the whole army dreaded the long march to Charlotte" and beyond, "back again over the thousand miles we had just accomplished," but also because of his own fear that Johnston, overtaken, might "allow his army to disperse into guerrilla bands" and thereby cause the war to be "prolonged indefinitely." Surrender of course would obviate both of these unwanted eventualities, and Sherman, with Grant's example before him — "Glory to God and our country," he had exclaimed in a field order passing the news of Appomattox along to his troops, "and all honor to our comrades in arms, toward whom we are marching! A little more labor, a little more toil on our part, the great race is won, and our Government stands regenerated after four long years of war" — fairly leaped at the invitation thus extended. Accordingly, after assuring Washington that he would "be careful not to complicate any points of civil policy" in the terms he planned to offer, he arranged with Johnston to meet at noon on Monday, April 17, midway between the picket lines of the two armies.

That would be somewhere between the Confederate rear at Hillsboro and his own advance at Durham Station, twenty-odd miles up the track from Raleigh. Monday morning, as he was boarding the train that would take him and his staff to the midday meeting, a telegrapher came hurrying down the depot stairs with word that a coded message from the War Department, sent by steamer down the coast, was just coming over the wire from Morehead City. Sherman waited nearly half an hour for it to be completed and decoded, then took it from the operator, who came running back much excited. It was from Stanton and it had been nearly two days in transit. "President Lincoln was murdered about 10 o'clock last night in his private box at Ford's Theatre in this city, by an assassin who shot him through the head by a pistol ball." Seward too had been gravely hurt, and Andrew Johnson was about to take over even as Stanton wrote the final words of the message: "I have no time to add more than to say that I find evidence that an assassin is also on your track, and I beseech you to be more heedful than Mr Lincoln was of such knowledge."

Sherman thrust the sheet of flimsy into his pocket and said nothing of it to anyone but the telegrapher, whom he swore to secrecy. Aboard the train as it chuffed along he sat tight-lipped all the way to Durham,

where he and his staff changed to horses for the flag-of-truce ride toward
Hillsboro to meet Johnston. They encountered him and his party about
five miles out, also under a flag of truce, and here, midway between
their lines of battle, the two generals met for the first time in person: although, as Sherman put it afterwards, looking back on the hundred-mile
minuet they had danced together in North Georgia from early May
through mid-July, "We knew enough of each other to be well acquainted at once." Riding side by side — forty-five-year-old "Uncle
Billy," tall and angular, and his spruce, spare companion, thirteen years
his senior, "dressed in a neat gray uniform," a blue staffer noted, "which
harmonized gracefully with a full beard and mustache of silvery white-
ness, partly concealing a genial and generous mouth" — they led the
small blue-gray column to a roadside house owned by a farmer named
James Bennett, whose permission they asked for its use, and then went
in, leaving their two staffs in the yard. Once they were alone Sherman
took the sheet of flimsy from his pocket and handed it over without
comment. As Johnston read it, "perspiration came out in large drops on
his forehead," his companion observed, and when he had finished he
denounced the assassination as "the greatest possible calamity to the
South," adding that he hoped Sherman did not connect the Confederate
government with the crime. "I told him," the red-head would recall, "I
could not believe that he or General Lee, or the officers of the Confederate army, could possibly be privy to acts of assassination; but I
would not say as much for Jeff Davis . . . and men of that stripe."

Johnston made no reply to this, and the two proceeded at once
to the subject arranged beforehand. Both agreed that any resumption
of the fighting would be "the highest possible crime," the Virginian —
outnumbered four to one by enemy troops in the immediate vicinity,
and ten to one or worse by others who could be brought to bear within
a week — even going so far as to define the crime as "murder." All the
same, they soon reached an apparent impasse. For while Sherman rejected any proposal designed to lead to negotiations between the civil
authorities, Davis had consented to the meeting only if it was to be conducted on that basis; which, incidentally, was why he had not been
"sanguine as to ultimate results." Johnston, however, stepped over the
barrier by proposing that he and Sherman "make one job of it," then
and there, by settling "the fate of all armies to the Rio Grande." Taken
aback, the Ohioan questioned whether his companion's authority was
that broad. Johnston replied that it was, or anyhow could be made so
by the Secretary of War, whose orders would be obeyed by Taylor,
Forrest, Maury, and all the others with forces still under arms, including
Kirby Smith beyond the Mississippi. In fact, he said, he could send a
wire requesting Breckinridge to join them overnight. Sherman demurred;
he could not deal with a member of the rebel cabinet, no matter how desirable the outcome. However, when Johnston pointed out that the

Kentuckian was also a major general, and could be received on that basis, Sherman agreed. They would meet tomorrow, same time, same place, soldier to soldier, and work out the details, all of which would of course be dependent on approval by his Washington superiors, civil as well as military.

They parted "in extreme cordiality," Johnston later declared, he to wait near Greensboro for Breckinridge to arrive from Salisbury, which Davis and his party had reached by then, and Sherman to face the problem of how to go about informing his troops of Lincoln's death. So far, the occupation of the North Carolina capital had been orderly and forbearing; "Discipline was now so good that the men didn't know themselves," an Illinois infantryman observed. But their commander, nursing his bombshell of news on the trainride back to Raleigh, was aware that "one single word by me would have laid the city in ashes and turned its whole population homeless upon the country, if not worse." Accordingly, he ordered all units back to their camps before releasing a bulletin in which he was careful to exonerate the Confederate army from complicity in the assassination. It seemed to work. At least there was no violent reaction within the guarded bivouacs. However: "The army is crazy for vengeance," a private wrote home, remarking that "if we make another campaign it will be an awful one." Some even went so far as to hope that Johnston would not surrender; in which case they planned to turn loose with both hands. "God pity this country if he retreats or fights us," the soldier closed his letter.

From what he had heard today in the roadside farmhouse Sherman believed there was little chance of that; Johnston, he knew, was eager to surrender, and he intended to give him every chance. He would do so in part because of his soldier's pride in being generous to a disadvantaged foe who asked for mercy. "The South is broken and ruined and appeals to our pity," he would tell Rawlins before the month was out. "To ride the people down with persecutions and military exactions would be like slashing away at the crew of a sinking ship." There was that, and there was also his reaction to the Good Friday assassination, which was quite the opposite of the angered private's hope that Old Joe would not surrender. Lincoln's death brought Lincoln himself into sharper focus in Sherman's memory: particularly as he had come to know him at City Point, three weeks ago. Remembering his concern for avoiding "this last bloody battle," his eagerness "to get the men composing the Confederate armies back to their homes, at work on their farms and in their shops," he was resolved, as he set out for the second meeting Tuesday morning, "to manifest real respect for his memory by following after his death that policy which, if living, I felt certain he would have approved." Grant had removed from the contest the most feared and admired of the rebel armies; now Sherman would remove all the rest by taking Johnston up on his soldier-to-soldier proposal that they "make one job of it," here and now in the Bennett farmhouse, and settle "the fate of all armies to the Rio Grande."

He arrived first and went in alone, his saddlebags over one arm. They contained writing materials, together with something else he mentioned when Johnston entered the room with Breckinridge. "Gentlemen, it occurred to me that perhaps you were not overstocked with liquor, and I procured some medical stores on my way over. Will you join me before we begin work?" Johnston afterwards described his companion's expression — till now "rather dull and heavy" — as "beatific" when he heard these words. For some days the Kentuckian had been deprived of his customary ration of bourbon and had had to make do with tobacco, which he was chewing vigorously with a steady sidewise thrust of his jaw beneath the outsized mustache of a Sicilian brigand. When the bottle appeared, along with a glass, he tossed his quid into the fireplace, rinsed his mouth with water, and "poured out a tremendous drink, which he swallowed with great satisfaction. With an air of content he stroked his mustache and took a fresh chew of tobacco," while Sherman returned the bottle to his saddlebags. Thus refreshed, the three generals then got down to business, and Johnston observed that the former Vice President "never shone more brilliantly than he did in the discussions which followed. He seemed to have at his tongue's end every rule and maxim of international and constitutional law." Indeed, he cited and discoursed with such effect that Sherman — "confronted by the authority, but not convinced by the eloquence" — pushed his chair back from the table and registered a complaint. "See here, gentlemen," he protested. "Who is doing this surrendering anyhow? If this thing goes on, you'll have me sending a letter of apology to Jeff Davis."

Certain of his superiors would presently accuse him of having done just about that in the "Memorandum, or Basis of Agreement" arrived at in the course of the discussion. He wrote it himself, after rejecting a draft of terms prepared that morning in Greensboro by John Reagan — who had also come up from Salisbury but was not admitted to the conference because of his nonmilitary status — as "too general and verbose." Having said as much, he settled down to composing one of his own, more soldierly and direct, based on Reagan's and the agreements reached with Johnston yesterday and the silver-tongued Kentuckian today. As he worked he grew increasingly absorbed, until at one point, pausing to arrange his thoughts, he stopped writing, rose from the table, walked over to his saddlebags, and fumbled absentmindedly for the bottle. Seeing this, Breckinridge removed his quid in anticipation of another treat. But that, alas, was not to be. Still preoccupied, the Ohioan poured himself a couple of fingers of whiskey, recorked the bottle and returned it to the bag, then stood gazing abstractedly out of a window, sipping the drink while he got his thoughts in order; which done, he set the empty glass down, still without so much as a sidelong glance at his companions, and returned to his writing. In a state of near shock, his face taking on what Johnston called "an injured, sorrowful look," the Kentuckian solaced himself as best he could with a new chew of tobacco. Finally Sherman completed his draft of the terms and passed it across the table, saying: "That's the best I can do."

It was enough, perhaps indeed even more than enough from the rebel point of view. In seven numbered paragraphs, the memorandum provided that the present truce would remain in effect pending approval by superior authorities on both sides; that the troops in all Confederate armies still in existence would be "disbanded and conducted to their several state capitals, there to deposit their arms and public property in the state arsenals"; that federal courts would be reëstablished throughout the land; that the U.S. President would recognize existing state governments as soon as their officials took the required oath of loyalty, and would guarantee to all citizens "their political rights and franchises, as well as their rights of person and property, as defined by the Constitution," pledging in addition that neither he nor his subordinates would "disturb any of the people by reason of the late war, so long as they live in peace and quiet, abstain from acts of armed hostility, and obey the laws in force at the place of their residence." Such, in brief, were the terms set forth, and though Sherman knew that they went far beyond those given Lee, and knew too that he had violated his promise "not to complicate any points of civil policy," he felt more than justified by the assurance, received in return, that all the surviving gray armies — not one of which had been brought to bay, let alone hemmed in, as Lee's had been at Appomattox — would disband en masse, rather than fragment themselves into guerilla bands which might disrupt and bedevil the nation for years to come. In any case, nothing he had promised would be given until, and unless, it was approved by his superiors. Moreover, even if all he had written was rejected — which, on second thought, seemed possible, and on third thought seemed likely — he still would be the gainer by the provisional arrangements he had made. "In the few days it would take to send the papers to Washington, and receive an answer," he rather slyly pointed out, "I could finish the railroad up to Raleigh, and be the better prepared for a long chase."

Once he and Johnston had signed the copies then drawn up, Sherman shouldered his saddlebags and walked out into the gathering dusk, convinced that he had found a simple, forthright, soldierly solution to the multifarious problems of reconstruction by declaring, in effect, that there would be no reconstruction; at any rate none that would involve the politicians. They might not be willing to go along with the instrument which achieved this — the "Memorandum, or Basis of Agreement" — but he believed he knew a solution to that, too. "If you will get the President to simply indorse the copy and commission me to carry out the terms," he told Grant in a letter sent north by courier with the document next morning, "I will follow them to the conclusion."

Johnston too seemed in good spirits as he walked out of the Bennett house and across the yard with his fellow Confederate, who, on the other hand, had reverted to the "full and heavy" condition that preceded the one drink he had been offered before their host recorked the bottle and stuffed it back into his saddlebag. Hoping to divert him, and perhaps dispel the gloom, the Virginian asked his companion what he thought of Sherman. Breckinridge glowered. "He is a bright man, a man of great force," he replied. "But, General Johnston" — his voice rose; his face took on a look of intensity — "General Sherman is a hog. Yes, sir, a hog. Did you see him take that drink by himself?" Johnston suggested that the Ohioan had merely been absent-minded, but Breckinridge had been offended past endurance. He could overlook charges of pillage and arson; not this, which he found quite beyond the pale. "No Kentucky gentleman would ever have taken away that bottle," he said hotly. "He knew we needed it, and needed it badly."

There was a five-day wait, both armies remaining in position as agreed, and then on April 24 the staff courier sent to Washington returned, accompanied — much to Sherman's surprise — by Grant, who had come down the coast to say in person that the proposed "agreement" wouldn't do; wouldn't do at all, in fact, from several points of view.

He himself had seen as much in a single hurried reading when the document first reached him, late in the afternoon three days ago, and got in touch at once with Stanton to have the President call a meeting of the cabinet that night. This was done, and when he read them what Sherman had written, the reaction of the assembled dignitaries was even more vehement than he had expected. Lincoln's body, on display for the past three days in the East Room of the White House and the Capitol rotunda, had been put aboard a crepe-draped train that morning for the burial journey back to Illinois; now, hard in the wake of that emotional drain — that sense of loss which swept over them as they watched the train fade down the track, the smell of cinders fading too — came this documentary evidence that one of the nation's top generals wanted to end the war by reproducing the conditions that began it. Not only was there no mention of the Negro in any of the seven numbered paragraphs Grant read, but the provision for home-bound rebel soldiers to deposit their arms in state arsenals sounded suspiciously like a plan for keeping them ready-stacked for re-rebellion once the men who had carried them for the past four years grew rested enough to try their hand again at tearing the fabric of the Union. Hard to take, too, was the suggested exculpation of all Confederates from all blame, which contrasted strongly with the new President's post-inaugural statement lumping treason with rape and murder as a crime that "must be punished." Johnson was particularly angered by this attempt to override his bedrock pronouncement on the issue of guilt. Angriest of all, however, was the Secretary of War, who saw Sherman's so-called "memorandum" as a bid for the "Copperhead nomination for President" three years hence — if, indeed, he was willing to wait that long and was not planning a military coup when he marched north. Speed, "prompted by Stanton, who seemed frantic," according to Welles, "expressed fears that Sherman, at the head of his victorious legions, had designs upon the government" right now.

Grant defended his friend as best he could; defended his motives, that is, even though he agreed that what they had led to "could not possibly be approved." Nor was he displeased with instructions from his superiors to go in person down to Raleigh and inform his out-of-line subordinate that, his plan having been rejected, he was to "notify General Johnston immediately of the termination of the truce, and resume hostilities against his army at the earliest moment." Their notion was that he should be there in case the red-head attempted defiance of the order, whereas his own purpose was to be on hand to blunt the sting of the rebuke; which was also why he kept the trip a secret, thereby avoiding speculation and gossip about his mission, as well as embarrassment for the man he was going to see. He left at midnight, steaming away from the 6th Street wharf, and two mornings later, after a trainride from the coast, was with Sherman at his headquarters in the North Carolina capital.

Actually, when told of the disapproval of his plan for bringing peace "from the Potomac to the Rio Grande," the Ohioan was not as shocked as Grant expected him to be. Just yesterday he had received a bundle of newspapers reflecting anger throughout the North at the shock of Lincoln's murder, and he sent them along to Johnston with the comment: "I fear much the asassination of the President will give such a bias to the popular mind, which, in connection with the desires of the politicians, may thwart our purpose of recognizing 'existing local governments.'" This last, in fact, was what Grant chose to stress as the principal reason for disapproval of the terms proposed. Making no mention of Johnson's or Stanton's fulminations, he produced a copy of the War Department telegram he had received in early March while still in front of Petersburg. "You are not to decide, discuss, or confer upon any political question," he had been told. "Such questions the President holds in his own hands; and will submit them to no military conference or conventions." Sherman read the dispatch through, then remarked that he wished someone had thought to send him a copy at the time. "It would have saved a world of trouble," he said dryly, and promptly notified Johnston that Washington had called off their agreement. "I am instructed to limit my operations to your immediate command and not to attempt civil negotiations," he wrote, serving notice that hostilities would resume within forty-eight hours unless the Virginian surrendered before that time, "on the same terms as were given General Lee at Appomattox on April 9, instant, purely and simply."

This was plainly an ultimatum; events had taken the course predicted by Davis even as he approved the now repudiated "Basis of Agreement." Dismayed, Johnston wired Breckinridge for instructions, but when these turned out to be a suggestion that he fall back toward Georgia with his cavalry, light guns, and such infantry as could be mounted on spare horses, he replied that the plan was "impracticable," and instead got in touch with Sherman to arrange a third meeting and work out the details for surrender in accordance with the scaled-down terms. Two days later — April 26; Grant, still concerned with avoiding any show of interference, did not attend — they met again in the Bennett farmhouse and the matter was soon disposed of, including an issue of ten days' rations for 25,000 paroled graybacks, offered by Sherman "to facilitate what you and I and all good men desire, the return to their homes of the officers and men composing your army." Johnston replied that "the enlarged patriotism manifested in these papers reconciles me to what I previously regarded as the misfortune of my life — that of having had you to encounter in the field." On this high note of mutual esteem they parted to meet no more, though Johnston would die some twenty-six years later from the effects of a severe cold he contracted in New York while standing bareheaded in raw February weather alongside the other pallbearers at Sherman's funeral. "General, please put on your hat," a friend urged the eighty-four-year-old Virginian; "you might get sick." Johnston refused. "If I were in his place," he said, "and he were standing here in mine, he would not put on his hat."

But that would be a full generation later. Just now all the talk was of surrender, at any rate in the Federal camps; for though a Confederate staffer had remarked on "the eagerness of the men to get to their homes" through these past ten days of on-and-off negotiations, another observed that on the day when the actual news came down, "they scarcely had anything to say." Such dejection was offset by the elation of the bluecoats in their bivouacs around Raleigh. One wrote home of how the birds woke him that morning with their singing — four years and two weeks, to the day, since the first shot was fired in Charleston harbor. "I never heard them sing so sweetly, and never saw them flit about so merrily," he declared, adding that "the green groves in which we were camped had a peculiar beauty and freshness, and as the sun rose above the steeples, it seemed as if we could float right up with it."

Presently there was other news, to which reactions also varied. On that same April 26, about midway between Washington and Richmond, Lincoln's assassin, run to earth at last, was shot and killed by a platoon of New York cavalry. After a week spent hiding in the woods and swamps of southeast Maryland, suffering all the while from pain in the leg he had broken in his leap from the box at Ford's, Booth and an associate succeeded in crossing the Potomac near Port Tobacco on April 22, then two days later made it over the Rappahannock, some twenty miles below Fredericksburg, only to be overtaken the following night on a farm three miles from the river. Surrounded by their pursuers they took refuge in a tobacco shed, and though his companion surrendered when ordered out (and was carried back to the capital next day to stand trial along with seven other alleged conspirators, including one who had made the knife attack on Seward and another who had been slated to dispose of the Vice President but had lacked the nerve to try) Booth himself refused to emerge, even after the tinder-dry structure was set afire. The troopers could see him in there, a crippled figure with a crutch and a carbine, silhouetted against the flames. Then one fired and he fell, dropped by a bullet that passed through his neck, "perforating both sides of the collar." He was still breathing when they dragged him out of the burning shed and onto the porch of a nearby house, but he was paralyzed below the point where his spinal cord had been struck. Two weeks short of his twenty-seventh birthday, he was so much the worse for wear — and the loss of his mustache, which he had shaved off the week before — that he scarcely resembled the darkly handsome matinee idol he had been before his ordeal of the past eleven days. "I thought I did for the best," he managed to say. Just at sunup he asked to have his hands lifted so he could see them, and when this was done he stared at them in despair. "Useless, useless," he muttered. Then he died.

So tight a grip had been kept on official news of the assassination — particularly southward, where Stanton believed the plot had been hatched and where such information might be of use to the conspirators in their flight from justice — most citizens did not know of the murder, except as one more piece of gossip among many that were false, until the murderer himself had been dispatched. Down in rural Georgia, for example, a full week after Lincoln's death and four days before Booth's, a young woman wrote in her diary: "None of our people believe any of the rumors, thinking them as mythical as the surrender of General Lee's army." Presently though, when the truth came out, there were those who reacted with a bitterness nurtured by four long years of a war that now was lost. Another Georgian, an Augusta housewife, writing to her mother-in-law on the last day of April, saw the northern leader's violent fall as a "righteous retribution," a minor comfort in a time of shock. "One sweet drop among so much that is painful is that he at least cannot raise his howl of diabolical triumph over us," she declared. Some in Johnston's army, waiting around Greensboro for the details of their surrender to be worked out, reacted initially in much the same fashion; that is, until Beauregard heard them whooping outside his tent. An aide later testified that this was the only time he saw Old Bory lose his temper all the way. "Shut those men up," he said angrily. "If they won't shut up, have them arrested. Those are my orders."

For the most part, however, even those celebrations that went unchecked lasted only about as long as it took the celebrants to turn their thoughts to Andrew Johnson, who was now in a position to exact the vengeance he had been swearing all along. Jefferson Davis perceived this from the outset. In Charlotte on April 19, when he learned from Breckinridge of his war-long adversary's sudden removal from the scene, he saw in the Tennessean's elevation a portent of much woe. "Certainly I have no special regard for Mr Lincoln," he remarked, "but there are a great many men of whose end I would rather hear than his. I fear it will be disastrous to our people, and I regret it deeply."

That was his first reaction, and he held to it down the years. Though, like Beauregard, he was quick to silence those in his escort who cheered the news, he never engaged in pious homilies over the corpse of his chief foe, but rather stressed his preference for him over the "renegade" who replaced him. "For an enemy so relentless in the war for our subjugation, we could not be expected to mourn," he wrote afterwards; "yet, in view of its political consequences, [Lincoln's assassination] could not be regarded otherwise than as a great misfortune to the South. He had power over the Northern people, and was without personal malignity toward the people of the South; [whereas] his successor was without power in the North, and [was] the embodiment of malignity toward the Southern people, perhaps the more so because he had betrayed and deserted them in the hour of their need."

★   ★   ★

As long ago as late September, before Hood set out on the northward march that turned his fine-honed army into a skeow — "s-k-e-o-w, bubble, bubble, s-k-e-o-w, bust" — Richard Taylor had told Davis that "the best we could hope for was to protract the struggle until spring." Now spring had come, and all he had left for the defense of his Department of Alabama, Mississippi, and East Louisiana were some 10,000 troops under Forrest and Maury, recently flung out of Selma and Mobile, plus something under half that number in garrisons scattered about the three-state region west of the Chattahoochee. Clearly enough, the time was at hand "for statesmen, not soldiers, to deal with the future." Accordingly, when he learned of the week-old "Basis of Agreement" worked out by Sherman, Johnston, and Breckinridge near Durham Station on April 18, he got in touch at once with Canby to arrange a similar armistice here in the western theater, pending approval by the civil authorities of terms that would, in Sherman's words, "produce peace from the Potomac to the Rio Grande." Canby — who knew no more than Taylor did of Washington's quick rejection of those terms — was altogether willing, and a meeting was scheduled for the last day in April, twelve miles up the railroad from Mobile.

Magee's Farm, the place was called. Canby, waiting at the appointed hour beside the tracks, had a full brigade drawn up as a guard of honor, along with a band and a brassy array of staffers, all turned out in their best. The effect, when Taylor at last pulled in, was anticlimactic to say the least. Arriving from Meridian on a handcar — practically the only piece of rolling stock left unwrecked by Wilson's raiders — he had been "pumped" down the line by two Negroes and was accompanied by a single aide whose uniform was as weathered as his own. Nothing daunted, for all his awareness that "the appearance of the two parties contrasted the fortunes of our respective causes," he then retired with the Federal commander to a room prepared in a nearby house, where they promptly agreed to observe a truce while awaiting ratification by their two governments of the terms given Johnston twelve days ago by Sherman, copies of which had been forwarded to them both. This done, they came out into the yard to share an al fresco luncheon that included a number of bottles of champagne, the drawing of whose corks provided what the Louisianian said were "the first agreeable explosive sounds I had heard for years." Presently, when the musicians struck up "Hail, Columbia," Canby ordered a quick switch to "Dixie," but Taylor, not to be outdone, suggested that the original tune continue, the time having come when they could "hail Columbia" together, as in the old days.

Back in Meridian next day he heard from Canby that the Sherman-Johnston agreement had been disavowed; that fighting would resume within forty-eight hours unless he surrendered — as Johnston had done, five days ago — on the terms accorded Lee at Appomattox, three weeks back. Taylor had neither the means nor the inclination to continue the struggle on his own; his task as he saw it, now that the Confederacy had crumbled, was "to administer on the ruins as residuary legatee," and he said as much in his reply, May 2, accepting Canby's scaled-down offer. Two days later they met again, this time at Citronelle, also on the Mobile & Ohio, twenty miles north of Magee's Farm, where, as Taylor later put it, "I delivered the epilogue of the great drama in which I had played a humble part." In Alabama, Mississippi, and East Louisiana, as had already been done in Virginia, North and South Carolina, and Georgia, all butternut survivors were to lay down their arms in exchange for assurance by the victors that they were not to be "disturbed" by the U.S. government "so long as they continue to observe the conditions of their parole and the laws in force where they reside." Although Sherman's proposal for restoring peace "from the Potomac to the Rio Grande" had been rejected, more or less out of hand, the arrangement that replaced it — commander to individual army commander, blue and gray, after the pattern set by Grant and Lee — achieved as much, in any case, for all of that region east of the Mississippi.

Or did it? Would it? Some, indeed many, believed it would not: including Sherman. "I now apprehend that the rebel armies will disperse," he had written Grant the week before, "and instead of dealing with six or seven states, we will have to deal with numberless bands of desperadoes, headed by such men as Mosby, Forrest, Red Jackson, and others who know not and care not for danger and its consequences."

One at least of these, despite the Ohioan's assertion that "nothing is left for them but death or highway robbery," had already proved him wrong. On April 21, soon after learning of Lee's capitulation, John Mosby formally disbanded his Rangers and presently — remarking, as if in specific response to Sherman: "We are soldiers, not highwaymen" — made official application for parole in order to hang up his shingle and resume the life he had led before the war. So much then for baleful predictions as to the postsurrender activities of Virginia's leading partisan, who soon was practicing law in the region where he and his men had given the blue authorities so much trouble for the past two years. As for Forrest and his red-haired subordinate, W. H. Jackson, there was considerable doubt, even in their own minds, as to what course they would follow. Between Taylor's final meeting with Canby, May 4 at Citronelle, and the issuance of paroles four days later, a staff colonel would recall, "all was gloom, broken only by wild rumors." This was especially the case in Forrest's camps around Gainesville, Alabama, fifty miles northeast of Meridian. There was much talk of "going to Mexico" as an alternative to surrender, and the general himself was said to be turning the notion over in his mind.

He was in fact in a highly disgruntled state, one arm in a sling from his fourth combat wound, suffered during a horseback fight with a young Indiana captain at Ebenezer Church, just north of Selma on the day before Wilson overran him there. The Federal hacked away at the general's upraised arm until Forrest managed to draw his revolver and kill him. "If that boy had known enough to give me the point of his saber instead of the edge," he later said, "I should not have been here to tell about it." Instead the Hoosier captain became his thirtieth hand-to-hand victim within a four-year span of war that also saw twenty-nine horses shot from under him, thereby validating his claim that he was "a horse ahead at the close." What rankled worse, despite the mitigating odds, was the drubbing Wilson had given him in what turned out to be his last campaign. Unaccustomed to defeat, this only soldier on either side who rose from private to lieutenant general had no more fondness for surrender now than he had had when he rode out of Donelson, nearly forty months ago. Mexico seemed preferable — at any rate up to the day before the one on which he and his troopers were scheduled to lay down their arms. That evening he and his adjutant set out on a quiet, thoughtful ride. Neither spoke until they drew rein just short of a fork in the road. "Which way, General?" his companion asked, and Forrest replied glumly: "Either. If one road led to hell and the other to Mexico, I would be indifferent which to take." They sat their horses in the moonlight for a time, the adjutant doing most of the talking, which had to do with the duty they owed their native land, whether in victory or defeat: particularly Forrest, who could lead into the ways of peace the young men who had followed him in war. "That settles it," the general said, and turned back toward camp.

As usual, once he made up his mind to a course of action, he followed it all-out: as did his men, who dropped all talk of Mexico when they learned that he had done so before them. Whatever doubt they had of this was dispelled by the farewell he addressed to them at Gainesville on May 9, soon after they furled their star-crossed flags and gave their parole to fight no more against the Union he and they rejoined that day.

SOLDIERS:

By an agreement made between Lieutenant General Taylor, commanding the Department of Alabama, Mississippi, and East Louisiana, and Major General Canby, commanding U.S. forces, the troops of this department have been surrendered. I do not think it proper or necessary at this time to refer to the causes which have reduced us to this extremity, nor is it now a matter of material consequence as to how such results were brought about. That we are beaten is a self-evident fact, and any further resistance on our part would be justly regarded as the height of folly and rashness. . . . Reason dictates and humanity demands that no more blood be shed. Fully realizing and feeling that such is the case, it is your duty and mine to lay down our arms, submit to the "powers that be," and aid in restoring peace and establishing law and order throughout the land. The terms upon which you were surrendered are favorable, and should be satisfactory and acceptable to all. They manifest a spirit of magnanimity and liberality on the part of the Federal authorities which should be met on our part by a faithful compliance with all the stipulations and conditions therein expressed. . . .

Civil war, such as you have just passed through, naturally engenders feelings of animosity, hatred, and revenge. It is our duty to divest ourselves of all such feelings, and, so far as it is in our power to do so, to cultivate feelings toward those with whom we have so long contested and heretofore so widely but honestly differed. Neighborhood feuds, personal animosities, and private differences should be blotted out, and when you return home a manly, straightforward course of conduct will secure the respect even of your enemies. Whatever your responsibilities may be to government, to society, or to individuals, meet them like men. The attempt made to establish a separate and independent confederation has failed, but the consciousness of having done your duty faithfully and to the end will in some measure repay for the hardships you have undergone. . . . I have never on the field of battle sent you where I was unwilling to go myself, nor would I now advise you to a course which I felt myself unwilling to pursue. You have been good soldiers, you can be good citizens. Obey the laws, preserve your honor, and the government to which you have surrendered can afford to be and will be magnanimous.

N. B. FORREST,
Lieutenant General.

★ ★ ★

On April 26, the day of Booth's death and Johnston's renegotiated surrender, Davis met for the last time with his full cabinet and decided to end his week-long stay in Charlotte by pressing on at once to the southwest. He had not been surprised at Washington's rejection of the Sherman-Johnston "Basis of Agreement," which he himself had approved two days before, since his opinion of the new northern leader and "his venomous Secretary of War," as he said afterwards, did not permit him to expect "that they would be less vindictive after a surrender of the army had been proposed than when it was regarded as a formidable body defiantly holding its position in the field." What did surprise and anger him, some time later, was the news that Johnston, ignoring the suggestion that he fall back with the mobile elements of his army to draw Sherman after him, had laid down his arms without so much as a warning note to superiors he knew were in flight for their lives. Davis's indignation was heightened all the more when he learned that the Virginian, in his last general order, had blamed "recent events in Virginia for breaking every hope of success by war." Lee had fought until he was virtually surrounded and a breakout attempt had failed; whereas Johnston not only had not tried for the getaway suggested and expected, but had also, by a stroke of the pen, ended all formal resistance in three of the states through which his fugitive superiors would be traveling in their attempt to reach Dick Taylor or Kirby Smith, on this or the far side of the Mississippi River.

Hope for escape by that route had been encouraged by a series of dispatches from Wade Hampton, who did not consider himself or his troopers bound by the surrender negotiations then in progress. "The military situation is very gloomy, I admit," he wrote Davis on the day after the Sherman-Johnston-Breckinridge meeting near Durham Station, "but it is by no means desperate, and endurance and determination will produce a change." His notion was that the struggle should continue wherever there was ground to stand on, in or out of the country, whatever the odds. "Give me a good force of cavalry and I will take them safely across the Mississippi, and if you desire to go in that direction it will give me great pleasure to escort you.... I can bring to your support many strong arms and brave hearts — men who will fight to Texas, and who, if forced from that state, will seek refuge in Mexico rather than in the Union." Hoping to confer with the President in Salisbury, he reached Greensboro three days later, April 22, and found that the government had been transferred to Charlotte. "My only object in seeing you," he declared in a follow-up message, "was to assure you that many of my officers and men agree with me in thinking that nothing can be as disastrous to us as a peace founded on the restoration of the Union. A return to the Union will bring all the horrors of war, coupled with all the degradation that can be inflicted on a conquered people.... If I can serve you or my country by any further fighting you have only to tell me so. My plan is to collect all the men who will stick to their colors, and to get to Texas. I can carry with me quite a number, *and I can get there.*"

Heartened by this stalwart reassurance from the South Carolina grandee, whose views — delusions, some would say — were in accordance with his own, Davis took time out next day for the first real letter he had had a chance to write his wife since he left Richmond, three weeks back. In it were mingled the hopes expressed by Hampton and the private doubts that surfaced when he shifted his attention from his duty to his country, as the symbol of its survival, to his concern for the welfare of his four children and their mother. Threatened by Stoneman's descent on Salisbury, they had left Charlotte ten days ago, six days before he got there, and were now in Abbeville, South Carolina, down near the Georgia line. He spoke first of the difficulty of his position in deciding whether to urge his people to continue their resistance to what he saw as subjugation. "The issue is one which it is very painful for me to meet," he told Varina. "On one hand is the long night of oppression which will follow the return of our people to the 'Union'; on the other, the suffering of the women and children, and carnage among the few brave patriots who would still oppose the invader, and who, unless the people would rise en masse to sustain them, would struggle but to die in vain. I think my judgment is undisturbed by any pride of opinion, [for] I have prayed to our Heavenly Father to give me wisdom and fortitude equal to the demands of the position in which Providence has placed me. I have sacrificed so much for the cause of the Confederacy that I can measure my ability to make any further sacrifice required, and am assured there is but one to which I am not equal — my wife and my children.... For myself," he added, "it may be that a devoted band of cavalry will cling to me and that I can force my way across the Mississippi, and if nothing can be done there which it will be proper to do, then I can go to Mexico, and have the world from which to choose a location." That such a choice would come hard for him was shown by the emotion that swept over him when, having faced the prospect of spending the rest of his life in exile, he closed his letter. "Dear Wife, this is not the fate to which I invited [you] when the future was rose-colored to us both; but I know you will bear it even better than myself, and that, of us two, I alone will ever look back reproachfully on my past career. . . . Farewell, my dear. There may be better things in store for us than are now in view, but my love is all I have to offer, and that has the value of a thing long possessed, and sure not to be lost."

Three days later, in reaction to the news that Sherman's terms had been rejected, Davis and his advisers — fugitives in a profounder sense now that the new enemy President had branded them as criminals not eligible for parole — concluded that the time had come to press on southward, out of the Old North State. This was the last full cabinet meeting, for it was no sooner over than George Davis submitted his resignation on grounds that his motherless children required his attention at Wilmington. Concerned as he was about his own homeless family up ahead, Jefferson Davis had sympathy for the North Carolinian's view as to where his duty lay, and the Confederacy — which had never had any courts anyhow, Supreme or otherwise — no longer had an Attorney General by the time its government pulled out of Charlotte that same afternoon. At Fort Mill two mornings later, just over the South Carolina line, Trenholm also resigned, too ill to continue the journey even by ambulance. Davis thanked the wealthy Charlestonian for his "lofty patriotism and personal sacrifice," then shifted John Reagan to the Treasury Department, leaving the postal service headless and the cabinet score at two down, four to go.

"I *cannot* feel like a beaten man," he had remarked before setting out, and now on the march his spirits rose. In part this was because of his return to the field, to the open-air soldier life he always fancied. Four more cavalry brigades — so called, though none was as large as an old-style regiment, and all five combined totaled only about 3000 men — had turned up at Charlotte, fugitive and unattached, in time to swell the departing column to respectable if not formidable proportions. Breckinridge took command of the whole, and Davis had for company three military aides, all colonels, John Wood, Preston Johnston — son of his dead hero, Albert Sidney Johnston — and Francis Lubbock, former governor of Texas. Like Judah Benjamin, who had an apparently inexhaustible supply of wit and prime Havanas, these were congenial traveling companions. Moreover, progress through this section of South Carolina, which had been spared the eastward Sherman torch, was like a return to happier times, the crowds turning out to cheer their President and wish him well. This was the homeland of John C. Calhoun, and invitations poured in for one-night stays at mansions along the way. Davis responded accordingly. "He talked very pleasantly of other days," Mallory would recall, "and forgot for a time the engrossing anxieties of the situation." He spoke of Scott and Byron, of hunting dogs and horses, in a manner his fellow travelers found "singularly equable and cheerful" throughout the six-day ride to Abbeville, which they reached on May 2.

Mrs Davis and the children were not there, having moved on into Georgia three days ago. "Washington will be the first point I shall 'unload' at," she informed her husband in a note brought by a courier who met him on the road. That was less than fifty miles off, the closest they had been to one another in more than a month, and though she planned to "wait a little until we hear something of you," she urged him not to risk capture by going out of his way to join her, saying: "Let me beseech you not to calculate upon seeing me unless I happen to cross your shortest path toward your bourne, be that what it may." Stragglers and parolees from Lee's and Johnston's armies had passed through in large numbers, she also cautioned, and "not one has talked fight. A stand cannot be made in this country; do not be induced to try it. As to the Trans-Mississippi, I doubt if at first things will be straight, but the spirit is there and the daily accretions will be great when the deluded on this side are crushed out between the upper and nether millstone."

Speed then was the watchword, lest he be gathered up by blue pursuers or victimized by butternut marauders, hungry alike for the millions in treasury bullion he was rumored to have brought with him out of Richmond. At 4 o'clock that afternoon he summoned Breckinridge and the brigade commanders to a large downstairs parlor in the house where his family had stayed while they were here. Through a large window opening westward the five could see a rose garden in full bloom, and one among them later remarked that he had "never seen Mr Davis look better or show to better advantage. He seemed in excellent spirits and humor, and the union of dignity, graceful affability, and decision, which made his manner usually so striking, was very marked in his reception of us." After welcoming and putting them at ease, as was his custom at such meetings — even when the participants were familiars, as these were not; at least not yet — he passed at once to his reason for having called them into council. "It is time that we adopt some definite plan upon which the further prosecution of our struggle shall be conducted. I have summoned you for consultation. I feel that I ought to do nothing now without the advice of my military chiefs." He smiled as he said this last: "rather archly," according to one hearer, who observed that while "such a term addressed to a handful of brigadiers, commanding altogether barely 3000 men, by one who so recently had been the master of legions, was a pleasantry; yet he said it in a way that made it a compliment." What followed, however, showed clearly enough how serious he was. "Even if the troops now with me be all that I can for the present rely on," he declared, "3000 brave men are enough for a nucleus around which the whole people will rally when the panic which now afflicts them has passed away."

A tense silence ensued; none of the five wanted to be the first to say what each of them knew the other four were thinking. Finally one spoke, and the rest chimed in. What the country was undergoing wasn't panic, they informed their chief, but exhaustion. Any attempt to prolong the war, now that the means of supporting it were gone, "would be a cruel injustice to the people of the South," while for the soldiers the consequences would be even worse; "for if they persisted in a conflict so hopeless they would be treated as brigands and would forfeit all chance of returning to their homes." Breaking a second silence, Davis asked why then, if all hope was exhausted, they still were in the field. To assist in his escape, they replied, adding that they "would ask our men to follow us until his safety was assured, and would risk them in battle for that purpose, but would not fire another shot in an effort to continue hostilities." Now a third silence descended, in which the gray leader sat looking as if he had been slapped across the face by a trusted friend. Recovering, he said he would hear no suggestion that had only to do with his own survival, and made one final plea wherein, as one listener said, "he appealed eloquently to every sentiment and reminiscence that might be supposed to move a Southern soldier." When he finished, the five merely looked at him in sorrow. "Then all is indeed lost," he muttered, and rose to leave the room, deathly pale and unsteady on his feet. He tottered, and as he did so Breckinridge stepped forward, hale and ruddy, and offered his arm, which Davis, aged suddenly far beyond his nearly fifty-seven years, was glad to take.

Now it was flight, pure and simple — flight for flight's sake, so to speak — with no further thought of a rally until and unless he reached the Transmississippi. That was still his goal, and all agreed that the lighter he traveled the better his chances were of getting there. One encumbrance was the treasury hoard, which had got this far by rail, outracing Stoneman, but could go no farther. Of this, $39,000 had been left in Greensboro for Johnston to distribute among his soldiers (which he did; all ranks drew $1.15 apiece to see them home) and now the balance was dispersed, including $108,000 in silver coins paid out to troopers of the five brigades, the cadet guards, and other members of the presidential party; officers and men alike drew $26.25 each. Transferred to wagons, $230,000 in securities was sent on to a bank in Washington, just beyond the Georgia line, for deposit pending its return to Richmond and the banks that owned it, while $86,000 in gold was concealed in the false bottom of a carriage and started on its way to Charleston, there to be shipped in secrecy to England and drawn on when the government reached Texas. That left $30,000 in silver bullion, packed in trunks and stored in a local warehouse, and $35,000 in gold specie, kept on hand to cover expenses on the journey south and west. Relieved at last of their burden and "detached," the cadets promptly scattered for their homes.

Before leaving-time, which was midnight that same May 2, others expressed their desire to be gone, and one of these was Stephen Mallory. Pleading "the dependent condition of a helpless family," he submitted his resignation as head of the all-but-nonexistent C. S. Navy. He would leave soon after they crossed the Savannah River into Georgia, he said, and join his refugee wife and children in La Grange. That would bring the cabinet tally to three down, three to go. Or rather, four down, two to go; for by then still another member had departed. Plump and chafed, Judah Benjamin took off informally the following night, after a private conversation with his chief. His goal was the Florida coast, then Bimini, and he set out disguised variously as a farmer and a Frenchman, with a ramshackle cart, a spavined horse, and a mismatched suit of homespun clothes. Davis wished him well, but again declined an offer from Mallory, when the Floridian parted from him in Washington on May 4, of a boat then waiting up the Indian River to take him to Cuba or the Bahamas. He said, as he had said before — unaware that, even as he spoke, Dick Taylor was meeting with Canby at Citronelle to surrender the last gray army east of the Mississippi — that he could not leave Confederate soil while a single Confederate regiment clung to its colors.

Here again, as at Abbeville two days ago, he found that his family, fearful of being waylaid by marauders, had moved on south. "I dread the Yankees getting news of you so much," his wife had written in a note she left behind. "You are the country's only hope, and the very best intentioned do not calculate upon a stand this side of the river. Why not cut loose from your escort? Go swiftly and alone, with the exception of two or three. . . . May God keep you, my old and only love," the note ended.

He had it in mind to do just that, or anyhow something close, and accordingly instructed Breckinridge to peel off next day with the five brigades of cavalry, leaving him only an escort company of Kentucky horsemen; which, on second thought — for they were, as he said, "not strong enough to fight, and too large to pass without observation" — he ordered reduced to ten volunteers. He would have with him after that, in addition to a handful of servants and teamsters, only these men, his three military aides, and John Reagan. The Texan had been with him from the start and was determined to stick with him to the finish, which he hoped would not come before they reached his home beyond the Mississippi and the Sabine. Davis was touched by this fidelity, as he also was by a message received when he took up the march next morning. Robert Toombs lived in Washington, and though none of the party had called on him, or he on them, he sent word that all he had was at the fugitive President's disposal. "Mr Davis and I have had a quarrel, but we have none now," he said. "If he desires, I will call all my men around here to see him safely across the Chattahoochee at the risk of my life." Davis, told of this, replied: "That is like Bob Toombs. He always was a whole-souled man. If it were necessary, I should not hesitate to accept his offer."

No such thoughts of another Georgia antagonist prompted a side trip when he passed within half a dozen miles of Liberty Hall, the Vice President's estate near Crawfordville; nor did he consider getting in touch with Joe Brown at Milledgeville, twenty-five miles to the west, when he reached Sandersville, May 6. Pressing on — as if aware that James Wilson had issued that day in Macon, less than fifty miles away, a War Department circular announcing: "One hundred thousand dollars Reward in Gold will be paid to any person or persons who will apprehend and deliver JEFFERSON DAVIS to any of the military authorities of the United States. Several millions of specie reported to be with him will become the property of the captors" — the now fast-moving column of twenty men and three vehicles made camp that evening on the east side of the Oconee, near Ball's Ferry. Their intention was to continue southwest tomorrow for a crossing of the Chattahoochee "below the point where the enemy had garrisons," but something Preston Johnston learned when he walked down to the ferry before supper caused a sudden revision of those plans. Mrs Davis and the children, escorted by Burton Harrison, had crossed here that morning, headed south, and there was a report that a group of disbanded soldiers planned to attack and rob their camp that night. Hearing this, Davis remounted his horse. "I do not feel that you are bound to go with me," he told his companions, "but I must protect my family."

What followed turned out to be an exhausting all-night ride beyond the Oconee. Though the escort horses finally broke down, Davis and his better-mounted aides kept on through the moonlit bottoms until shortly before dawn, near Dublin, close to twenty miles downstream, they came upon a darkened camp beside the road. "Who's there?" someone called out in an alarmed, determined voice which Davis was greatly relieved to recognize as Harrison's. He and his wife and children were together again for the first time since he put them aboard the train in Richmond, five weeks back.

Having rested their mounts, the escort horsemen arrived in time for breakfast, and the two groups — with Davis so bone-tired that he agreed for the first time to ride in an ambulance — pushed on south together to bivouac that night some twenty miles east of Hawkinsville, where 3000 of Wilson's raiders were reported to be in camp. Alarmed, Mrs Davis persuaded her husband to proceed without her the following day, May 8. Once across the Ocmulgee at Poor Robin Bluff, however, he heard new rumors of marauders up ahead, and stopped on the outskirts of Abbeville to wait for her and the children, intending to see them through another day's march before turning off to the southwest. They arrived that night, and next morning the two groups, again combined, continued to move south. Lee had surrendered a month ago today; tomorrow would make a solid month that Davis had been on the go from Danville, a distance of just over four hundred miles, all but the first and last forty of which he had spent on horseback; he was understandably weary. Yet the arrangement, when they made camp at 5 o'clock that afternoon in a stand of pines beside a creek just north of Irwinville, was that he would take some rest in his wife's tent, then press on with his escort after dark, presumably to see her no more until she rejoined him in Texas.

Outside in the twilight, seated with their backs against the boles of trees around the campfire, his aides waited for word to mount up and resume the journey. They too were weary, and lately they had been doubtful — especially during the two days spent off-course because of Davis's concern for the safety of his wife and children — whether they would make it out of Georgia. But now, within seventy miles of the Florida border, they felt much better about their chances, having come to believe that Breckinridge, when he peeled off near Washington with the five brigades, had decoyed the Federals onto his track and off theirs. In any case, the President's horse was saddled and waiting, a brace of pistols holstered on its withers, and they were waiting, too, ready to move on. They sat up late, then finally, receiving no call, dozed off: unaware that, even as they slept and dawn began to glimmer through the pines, two regiments of Union cavalry — 4th Michigan and 1st Wisconsin, tipped off at Hawkinsville that the rebel leader and his party had left Abbeville that morning, headed for Irwinville, forty-odd miles away — were closing in from opposite sides of the camp, one having circled it in the darkness to come up from the south, while the other bore down from the northwest. The result, as the two mounted units converged, was the last armed clash east of the Mississippi. Moreover, by way of a further distinction, all the combatants wore blue, including the two killed and four wounded in the rapid-fire exchange. "A sharp fight ensued, both parties exhibiting the greatest determination," James Wilson presently would report, not without a touch of pride in his men's aggressiveness, even when they were matched against each other. "Fifteen minutes elapsed before the mistake was discovered."

All was confusion in the night-drowsed bivouac. Wakened like the others by the sudden uproar on the fringes of the camp — he had lain down, fully dressed, in expectation of leaving before midnight, but had slept through from exhaustion — Davis presumed the attackers were butternut marauders. "I will go out and see if I can't stop the firing," he told his wife. "Surely I will have some authority with Confederates." When he lifted the tent flap, however, he saw high-booted figures, their uniforms dark in the pearly glow before sunrise, dodging through the woods across the creek and along the road on this side. "Federal cavalry are upon us!" he exclaimed. Terrified, Varina urged him to flee while there was time. He hesitated, then took up a lightweight sleeveless rain-coat — which he supposed was his own but was his wife's, cut from the same material — and started out, drawing it on along with a shawl she threw over his head and shoulders. Before he had gone twenty paces a Union trooper rode up, carbine at the ready, and ordered him to halt. Davis paused, dropping the coat and shawl, and then came on again, directly toward the trooper in his path. "I expected, if he fired, he would miss me," he later explained, "and my intention was in that event to put my hand under his foot, tumble him off on the other side, spring into his saddle, and attempt to escape." It was a trick he had learned from the Indians, back in his early army days, and it might have worked except for his wife, who, seeing the soldier draw a deliberate bead on the slim gray form advancing point-blank on him, rushed forward with a cry and threw her arms around her husband's neck. With that, all chance for a getaway was gone; Davis now could not risk his life with-out also risking hers, and presently other blue-clad troopers came riding up, all with their carbines leveled at him and Varina, who still clung to him. "God's will be done," he said in a low voice as he turned away and walked slowly past the tent to take a seat on a fallen tree beside the campfire.

Elsewhere about the camp the struggle continued on various levels of resistance. Four days ago, a wagon had gone south from Sandersville with most of the $35,000 in gold coin; the remaining $10,000, kept for travel expenses between there and the Gulf, was distributed among the aides and Reagan, who carried it in their saddlebags; as the bluecoats now discovered. Reagan, with his own and the President's portion of the burden — some $3500 in all — turned it over with no more than a verbal protest, but his fellow Texan Lubbock hung onto his in a tussle with two of the soldiers, despite their threats to shoot him if he did not turn loose. "Shoot and be damned!" he told them. "You'll not rob me while I'm alive and looking on." They did, though, and Preston Johnston lost his share as well, along with the pistols his father had carried when he fell at Shiloh. Only John Wood was successful in his resistance, and that was by strategy rather than by force. Knowing that he would be charged with piracy for his work off the New England coast last August, the former skipper of the *Tallahassee* took one of his captors aside, slipped him two $20 gold pieces, and walked off unnoticed through the pines — eventually to make it all the way to Cuba with Breckinridge, whom he encountered down in Florida two weeks later, determined like himself to leave the country rather than stay and face charges brought against him by the victors in their courts.

But that was later. For the present, all Wood's friends knew was that he was missing, and only one of his foes knew even that much. Besides, both groups were distracted by the loud bang of a carbine, followed at once by a shriek of pain. Convinced that the reported millions in coin and bullion must be cached somewhere about the camp, one unfortunate trooper had used his loaded weapon in an attempt to pry open a locked trunk, and the piece had discharged, blowing off one of his hands. Others took over and got the lid up, only to find that all the trunk contained was a hoop skirt belonging to Mrs Davis. Despite their disappointment, the garment turned out to have its uses, being added to the cloak and shawl as evidence that the rebel chieftain had tried to escape in women's clothes. Three days later, Wilson would inform the War Department that Davis, surprised by the dawn attack, "hastily put on one of Mrs Davis' dresses and started for the woods, closely pursued by our men, who at first thought him a woman, but seeing his boots while running suspected his sex at once. The race was a short one, and the rebel President soon was brought to bay. He brandished a bowie knife of elegant pattern, and showed signs of battle, but yielded promptly to the persuasion of Colt revolvers without compelling our men to fire." This was far too good to let pass unexploited, providing as it did a counterpart to the story of Lincoln's passage through Baltimore four years ago, similarly clad in a Scotch-plaid garment borrowed from his wife, on the way to his first inauguration. "If Jefferson Davis was captured in his wife's clothes," Halleck recommended after reading Wilson's dispatch, "I respectfully suggest that he be sent North in the same habiliments."

That too would come later, along with the many jubilant cartoons and a tableau staged by Barnum to display the Confederate leader in flight through brush and briers, cavorting in hooped calico and brandishing a dagger. Just now his worst indignity came from having to look on powerless while the treasure-hungry bluecoats rifled his and Varina's personal luggage, tossing the contents about and only pausing to snatch from the fire and gulp down the children's half-cooked breakfast. "You are an expert set of thieves," he told one of them, who replied: "Think so?" and kept on rifling. Presently the Michigan colonel approached and stood looking down at the Mississippian, seated on his log beside the campfire. "Well, old Jeff, we've got you at last," he declared with a grin. Davis lost his temper at this and shouted: "The worst of it all is that I should be captured by a band of thieves and scoundrels!" Stiffening, the colonel drew himself up. "You're a prisoner and can afford to talk that way," he said.

Davis knew well enough that he was a prisoner. What was more, in case it slipped his memory during the three-day trip to Wilson's headquarters at Macon, the soldiers took pains to keep him well reminded of the fact. "Get a move on, Jeff," they taunted him from time to time. He rode in an ambulance with his wife and a pair of guards, while her sister Margaret followed in another with the children, all four of whom were upset by her weeping. The other captives were permitted to ride their own horses, which were "lent" them pending arrival. There was a carnival aspect to the procession, at least among the troopers riding point. "Hey, Johnny Reb," they greeted paroled Confederates by the roadside, "we've got your President!" That was good for a laugh each time save one, when an angered butternut replied: "Yes, and the devil's got yours." A supposed greater shock was reserved for Davis along the way, when he was shown the proclamation Andrew Johnson had issued charging him with complicity in Lincoln's assassination. He took it calmly, however, remarking that there was one man who knew the document to be false — "the one who signed it, for he at least knew that I preferred Lincoln to himself."

After a night spent in Macon, May 13, he and his wife, together with Margaret Howell and the children, Reagan, Lubbock, and Preston Johnston, were placed in a prison train for an all-day roundabout journey to Augusta, where they were driven across town to the river landing and put on a tug waiting to take them down the Savannah to the coast. Already aboard, to his surprise, were two distinguished Confederates, now prisoners like himself. One was Joe Wheeler, who had been captured five days ago at Conyer Station, just east of Atlanta, frustrated in his no-surrender attempt to reach the Transmississippi with three members of his staff and eleven privates. The other was Alexander Stephens, picked up last week at Liberty Hall after Davis passed nearby. Pale and shaken, the child-sized former Vice President looked forlorn in the greatcoat and several mufflers he wore despite the balmy late-spring weather. Davis gave him a remote but courteous bow, which was returned in kind. At Port Royal, on the morning of May 16, the enlarged party transferred to an ocean-going steamer, the side-wheeler *William P. Clyde*. Presumably, under escort by the multigunned warship *Tuscarora*, she would take them up the coast, into Chesapeake Bay, then up the Potomac to the northern capital.

So they thought. But three days later, after a stormy delay while rounding Hatteras, the *Clyde* dropped anchor off the eastern tip of the York-James peninsula, and there she lay for three more days, under the guns of Fort Monroe, "the Gibraltar of the Chesapeake," whose thirty-foot granite walls, close to a hundred feet thick at their base, had sheltered its Union garrison throughout the four years of the war. Next day, May 20, Stephens and Reagan were transferred to the *Tuscarora* for delivery to Fort Warren in Boston harbor. The day after that, Wheeler, Lubbock, and Johnston were sent on their way to Fort Delaware, downriver from Philadelphia. Then on May 22 came Davis's turn, though he had nothing like as far to go. His destination was there at hand, and the delay had been for the purpose of giving the fort's masons time to convert a subterranean gunroom into a prison cell: strong evidence that, for him as for the others gone before, the charges and the trial to follow would be military, not civil.

"In leaving his wife and children," a witness informed Stanton,

"Davis exhibited no great emotion, though he was violently affected." This last was clearly true, in spite of the prisoner's efforts to conceal what he was feeling. "Try not to cry. They will gloat over your grief," he told Varina as he prepared to board the tug that would take him ashore. She managed to do as he asked, but then, having watched him pass from sight across the water, rushed to her cabin and gave way to weeping. It was as if she had read what tomorrow's New York *Herald* would tell its readers: "At about 3 o'clock yesterday, 'all that is mortal' of Jeff'n Davis, late so-called 'President of the alleged Confederate States,' was duly, but quietly and effectively, committed to that living tomb prepared within the impregnable walls of Fortress Monroe.... No more will Jeff'n Davis be known among the masses of men. He is buried alive."

✗ 3 ✗

On May 10, unaware that the Confederate leader had been captured before sunup down in Georgia, Andrew Johnson issued a proclamation declaring that "armed resistance to the authority of this Government in the said insurrectionary States may be regarded as virtually at an end." This was subsequently taken by some, including the nine Supreme Court justices, to mark the close of the war, and it was followed twelve days later — the day Davis entered the granite bowels of Fort Monroe — by another presidential edict announcing that all the reunited nation's seaports would be open to commerce, with the exception of Galveston and three others along the Texas coast, and that civilian trade in all parts of the country east of the Mississippi would be resumed without restrictions.

That was May 22, and this second pronouncement, like the first, not only reflected the widespread public hope for a swift return to the ways of peace, but also served to clear the Washington stage for still another victory celebration, a two-day Grand Review planned for tomorrow and the next day, larger in scale, and above all in panoply, than the other two combined. Meade's and Sherman's armies had come north from Appomattox and Raleigh, and by then were bivouacked around the capital; which gave rise to a number of problems. In addition to the long-standing rivalry between paper-collar Easterners and roughneck Westerners, the latter now had a new burden of resentment to unload. Soon after the Administration's rejection of the original Durham Station terms, the papers had been full of Stanton's denunciation of the red-haired general who composed them, including charges that he was politically ambitious, with an eye on the Copperhead vote, and quite possibly had been seduced by Confederate gold, slipped to him out of the millions the fugitive rebel leader carried southward when Sherman obligingly called a halt to let him pass across his front. Angered by the slander of their chief, western officers no sooner reached the capital than they began leaping on saloon bars to call for "three groans for the Secretary of War," and the men in the ranks provoked fistfights with the Potomac veterans, whom they saw as allied with Stanton if only because of proximity. Eventually Grant solved the problem, in part at least, by having the two armies camp on opposite sides of the river; yet the bitterness continued.

The showdown would come tomorrow and the following day, not in a direct confrontation — though by now large numbers of men in the ranks of both might have welcomed such a test — but rather in a tandem display, whereby the public would judge their respective merits in accordance with their looks, their martial demeanor as they swung up Pennsylvania Avenue toward a covered stand erected in front of the White House for the President and his guests, including Grant and other dignitaries, civil as well as military. By prearrangement, the Army of the Potomac would parade on May 23 and the Westerners would take their turn next day. Sherman had qualms about the outcome: as well he might, for close-order marching was reported to be the chief skill of the bandbox Easterners, who moreover would be performing on home turf to long-term admirers, whereas his own gangling plowboys, though they had slogged a thousand roundabout miles through Georgia and the Carolinas, then north across Virginia, had done scarcely any drilling since they set out south from Chattanooga, a year ago this month. Then too there was the matter of clothes and equipment, another comparative disadvantage for members of the Armies of the Tennessee and the Cumberland. Their uniforms had weathered to "a cross between Regulation blue and Southern gray," a New England soldier observed, and the men inside were no less outlandish in his eyes. "Their hair and beards were uncut and uncombed; huge slouched hats, black and gray, adorned their heads; their boots were covered with the mud they had brought up from Georgia; their guns were of all designs, from the Springfield rifle to a cavalry carbine." That was how they looked to him on their arrival, three days before the start of the Grand Review. Sherman, with only that brief span for preparation, could only order such intensified drill instruction as there was time for, between hours of refurbishing dingy leather and dull brass, and hope meanwhile for the best; or in any case something better than the worst, which would be to have his veterans sneered or laughed at by people along the route of march or, least bearable of all, by those in the reviewing stand itself.

Washington — midtown Washington anyhow; the outlying sections were practically deserted — had never been so crowded as it was on the day when the first of more than 200,000 blue-clad victors, up from Virginia and the Carolinas, stepped out for the start of their last parade. In brilliant sunshine, under a cloudless sky, bleachers lining the avenue from the Capitol, where the march began, overflowed with citizens dressed this Tuesday in their Sunday best to watch the saviors of the Union swing past in cadence, twelve abreast. All the national flags were at full staff for the first time since April 15, and the crepe had been removed from public buildings as a sign that nearly six weeks of mourning for Lincoln were to be rounded off with two days of rejoicing for the victory he had done so much to win but had not lived to see completed. Meade led the column of march today, and after saluting Johnson and Grant, who stood together against a frock-coated backdrop of dignitaries massed in the stand before the White House, dismounted and joined them to watch his troops pass in review. Zouaves decked in gaudy clothes, Irish units with sprigs of greenery in their caps, engineers with ponderous equipment, artillerists riding caissons trailed by big-mouthed guns, all lent their particular touches to a show dominated in the main by close-packed throngs of infantry, polished bayonets glittering fiery in the sunlight, and seven unbroken miles of cavalry, steel-shod hoofs clopping for a solid hour past any given point. Spectators marveled at the youth of many commanders: especially Custer, whose "sunrise of golden hair" rippled to his shoulders as if in celebration of his latest promotion, one week after Appomattox. Barely four years out of West Point, not yet twenty-six and already a major general of volunteers, he came close to stealing the show when his horse, spooked by a wreath tossed from the curb, bolted just short of the White House. "Runaway!" the crowd shrieked, frightened and delighted. A reporter, watching the general's hat fly off and "his locks, unskeined, stream a foot behind him," was put in mind — more prophetically than he knew — of "the charge of a Sioux chieftain." The crowd cheered as Custer brought the animal under control, though by then he had passed the grandstand and, as Sherman said, "was not reviewed at all."

Wedged among the politicians, diplomats, and other honc.ed guests, the red-haired Ohioan studied today's parade with all the intentness of an athletic coach scouting a rival team. His eye was peeled for shortcomings, and he found them. Observing for example that the Potomac soldiers "turned their heads around like country gawks to look at the big people on the stand," he would caution his ranking subordinates tonight not to let their men do that tomorrow. "I will give [them] plenty of time to go to the capital and see everything afterwards," he promised, "but let them keep their eyes fifteen feet to the front and march by in the old customary way." Still, for all his encouragement, he decided he would do well to register a disclaimer in advance, and accordingly, as today's review wore toward a close, he found occasion to remark to Meade: "I am afraid my poor tatterdemalion corps will make a poor appearance tomorrow when contrasted with yours." The Pennsylvanian, pleased with his army's performance today, was sympathetic in response. People would make allowances, he assured him.

Hopeful, but still deeply worried about what kind of showing his Westerners would manage now that their turn had come, Sherman rose early next morning to observe his six corps as they filed out of their Virginia camps — a march likened by one journalist to "the uncoiling of a tremendous python" — first across the Potomac, then on to the assembly area back of Capitol Hill. There they formed, not without a good deal of confusion, and there at 9 o'clock a cannon boomed the starting signal. He was out front on a handsome bay, hat in hand, sunlight glinting coppery in his close-cropped hair, and though the tramp of Logan's XV Corps marchers sounded solid and steady behind him during breaks in the cheers from the bleachers on both sides, he lacked the nerve to glance rearward until he topped the rise beside the Treasury Building, where a sharp right would bring into view the stand in front of the White House. Then at last he turned in the saddle and looked back. What he saw down the long vista, a full mile and a half to the Capitol shining on its hilltop, brought immeasurable relief. "The sight was simply magnificent. The column was compact, and the glittering muskets looked like a solid mass of steel, moving with the regularity of a pendulum." So he later wrote, adding: "I believe it was the happiest and most satisfactory moment of my life." Now, though, he was content to grin as he released his bated breath. "They have swung into it," he said.

They had indeed swung into it, and the crowd responded in kind. A reporter noted "something almost fierce in the fever of enthusiasm" roused by the sight of these lean, sunburnt marchers, all "bone and muscle and skin under their tattered battle flags." Risking fiasco, their commander had decided to go with their natural bent, rather than try for the kind of spit-and-polish show their rivals had staged the day before, and the gamble paid off from the moment the first of them set out, swinging along the avenue with a proud, rolling swagger, their stride a good two inches longer than the mincing twenty-two inches required by regulations, and springier as well. "They march like the lords of the world!" spectators exclaimed, finding them "hardier, knottier, weirder" than yesterday's prim, familiar paraders. Moreover, they provided additional marvels, reminders of their recent excursion across Georgia, some grim, others hilarious in effect. Hushes came at intervals when ambulances rolled past in the wake of each division, blood-stained stretchers strapped to their sides, and there was also laughter — rollicksome, however: not the kind Sherman had feared — when the crowd found each corps trailed by a contingent of camp followers, Negro men and women and children riding or leading mules alongside wagons filled with tents and kettles, live turkeys and smoked hams. Pet pigs trotted on leashes and gamecocks crowed from the breeches of cannon, responding to cheers. "The acclamation given Sherman was without precedent," the same reporter wrote. "The whole assemblage raised and waved and shouted as if he had been the personal friend of each and every one of them."

He had approached the White House stand by then, delivered his salute, dismounted, and walked over to take his guest-of-honor place among the reviewers, intent on securing a satisfaction only slightly less rewarding than the one he had experienced when he turned in the saddle, a few minutes ago, and thrilled at the compact, rhythmic beauty of the column stretching all the way back to the marble Capitol. The men who composed it had already protested, in their hard-handed way, the recent slanders directed at their chief — and so, now that the time had come, would Sherman himself, in person. He had Edwin Stanton in mind, up there in the stand, and he was resolved, as he said later, not only "to resent what I considered an insult," but also to do so "as publicly as it was made." Accordingly, after shaking hands with the President he moved on to Stanton, who was standing with his hand out, next in line. "Sherman's face was scarlet and his red hair seemed to stand on end," one among the startled watchers noted, as he drew himself up, glared at the Secretary for a couple of baleful seconds, then stepped deliberately past him to shake hands with the other cabinet members before returning to take his post on the left of Johnson. For more than six hours his long-striding troops surged by, applauded enthusiastically by everyone who saw them. "On the whole, the grand review was a splendid success," he afterwards declared, "and was a fitting conclusion to the campaign and the war."

It was also, in its way, a valedictory. "In a few weeks," another journalist was to write, "this army of two or three hundred thousand men melted back into the heart of the people from whence it came, and the great spectacle of the Grand Army of the Republic ... disappeared from sight." In point of fact, a considerable portion of that army had already disappeared — or "melted back," as the reporter put it — in the course of the four years leading up to this and other last parades at various assembly points throughout the beaten South. A total of just over 110,000 northern soldiers had died on the field of battle or from wounds received there; which meant that, for every two men who marched up Pennsylvania Avenue on both days of the Grand Review, the ghost of a third marched with them. There were indeed skeletons at that feast, at any rate for those along the route who remembered this army of the fallen, equal in number to the survivors who swung past the grandstand, twelve abreast, for six long hours on either day.

One among the last to have joined this ghostly throng — later, even, than Abraham Lincoln, and like him the victim of a northern bullet — was a young V Corps lieutenant, George H. Wood, a line officer in a regiment from Maine. On the march north from Appomattox, two weeks back, his unit made camp one night just outside Fredericksburg, surrounded by memories of corpses lying frozen where they had been dropped in trying to reach the rebel-held sunken road at the base of Marye's Heights, and next morning, while the lieutenant and his platoon were getting ready to depart, a teamster accidentally fired a round from a carbine he was handling. It passed through several tents, then struck Wood. He had seen too much of death these past three years, as a veteran of all the major battles of the Army of the Potomac within that span, to find anything exceptional in his own, which the surgeons now informed him was at hand. His regret was not so much that he was dying, but rather that he had spent the past three years as he had done. A devout young man, he doubted that what he had been engaged in was the work of the Lord, and in this connection, hoping fervently for mercy in the hereafter, he expressed a further wish to the minister who was with him when the end drew near. "Chaplain," he said, "do you suppose we shall be able to forget anything in heaven? I would like to forget those three years."

Another veteran, of considerably higher rank, also missed the Grand Review: not as the result of any mishap — no piece of flying metal ever so much as grazed him, though it had been his practice, throughout an even longer war career, to go where there was least room between bullets — but rather because of last-minute orders that took him elsewhere. This was Sheridan. Arriving in Washington on May 16, one week before he and his seven miles of horsemen were scheduled to clop up Pennsylvania Avenue, he was informed next day by Grant that he was to proceed without delay to the Transmississippi and take charge of operations designed to restore West Louisiana and Texas to the Union. Although he would command a force of better than 50,000 seasoned effectives — Canby's army from Mobile, already alerted for the move, plus one corps each from Ord and Thomas at City Point and Nashville — Little Phil did not covet an assignment that would deny him a role in next week's big parade and separate him, permanently perhaps, from his hard-riding troopers. Moreover, while the Transmississippi would be the scene of what little fighting there was left, it did not seem to him to offer much in the way of a chance for distinction, especially by contrast with all he had achieved in the past year. As he had done on the eve of the Appomattox campaign, when the plan had been to send him down to Sherman, he protested for all he was worth at being shifted from stage center, out of the limelight.

Now as then, Grant explained that there was more to these new orders than met the eye, "a motive not explained by the instructions themselves." In addition to the task of closing down Kirby-Smithdom, there was also the problem of ending defiance of the Monroe Doctrine by the French in Mexico, where their puppet Emperor had been on the throne for a full year, usurping the power of the elected leader, President Benito Juárez. Maximilian had been pro-Confederate from the outset, Juárez pro-Union, and the time had come to persuade or compel the French "to quit the territory of our sister republic." The State Department — meaning Seward, who by now was on the mend from the slashing he had received on assassination night, just over a month ago — was "much opposed to the use of our troops along the border in any active way that would involve us in a war with European powers." Grant however went on to say that he did not think it would come to that; the French would remain in Mexico no longer than it took them to find that he had sent his most aggressive troop commander to patrol the border with 50,000 of the hardest-handed soldiers the world had known since Napoleon's illustrious uncle retired to Saint Helena. Flattered, Sheridan was more amenable to the shift, which he now perceived might involve him in still another war, despite his superior's confidence that his presence would serve rather to prevent one. Though he complained that he could not see why his departure could not be delayed a couple of days, so he could ride up the avenue at the head of his column of troopers, he later declared that, "under the circumstances, my disappointment at not being permitted to participate in the review had to be submitted to, and I left Washington without an opportunity of seeing again in a body the grand Army of the Potomac."

Whatever might come of the projected border venture, he soon discovered that he had been right to suspect that little or no additional glory awaited him for subduing what remained of the Confederacy beyond the Mississippi. Leaving the capital on May 21, two days short of the start of the Grand Review, he learned before he reached New Orleans, where he planned to confer with Canby on the upcoming campaign, that Kirby Smith had already agreed to surrender on the terms accepted earlier by Taylor, Johnston, and Lee.

Smith in fact had had little choice in the matter. Credited with 36,000 troops on paper, he commanded practically none in the flesh, and even these few, as he complained, were "deaf alike to the dictates of duty, reason, and honor." Price's ill-starred Missouri raid, from August through November, had used up their hope along with their dash. Such things as they did now were done on their own, usually under enemy compulsion: for example, a two-day engagement at Palmito Ranch, May 12–13, on the east bank of the Rio Grande near Brownsville, down at the very tip of Texas. Andrew Johnson's May 10 declaration that armed resistance was "virtually at an end" had thus been premature, but only by three days; for this was the last sizeable clash of arms in the whole war. Two Union regiments of white and colored infantry, plus one of cavalry, marched upriver from Brazos Santiago to attack the rebel camp. At first they were successful. Then they were driven back. Next day they tried again, and again succeeded, only to be repulsed when the defenders once more rallied and drove them from the ranch with a loss of 115 killed, wounded, and missing. It was Wilson's Creek all over again, reproduced in miniature and stretched out over a period of two days. When it was done, the Federals withdrew downriver to the coast. They had gained nothing except the distinction of having made the last attack of the four-year conflict, as well as the last retreat.

Ironically, this last fight, like the first, was a Confederate victory; yet the news was scarcely noticed in the excitement over the outcome of a conference held at the opposite end of the state while the second day of battle was in progress. Responding to a call from the department commander, the exiled governors of Louisiana, Arkansas, and Missouri met that day in Marshall, forty miles west of Shreveport, to assess the current situation, political as well as military, so far as it affected the four Transmississippi states, including Texas, whose ailing chief executive sent a spokesman in his place. Lee's surrender had been known for about three weeks now, together with the southward flight of the government from Richmond. Kirby Smith informed the assembled heads of states that he considered himself duty bound to hold out "at least until President Davis reaches this department, or I receive some definite orders from him." The governors, for all their admiration of his soldierly commitment, did not agree. Speaking for their people, whose despair they understood and shared, they considered it "useless for the Trans-Mississippi Department to undertake to do what the Cis-Mississippi Department had failed to do," and accordingly recommended an early surrender — if liberal, or anyhow decent, terms could be secured. In line with this, they appointed one of their number, Governor Henry W. Allen of Louisiana, to go to Washington and confer with the Federal authorities to that end.

But there was nothing like time enough for that. Returning to Shreveport with the threats of bitter-enders ringing in his ears — Jo Shelby, for one, wanted to turn him out if he so much as thought of capitulation — Smith rejected on May 15 terms proposed by an emissary from John Pope in Missouri, who presented him with a choice between outright surrender and "all the horrors of violent subjugation." Pope, as usual, overplayed his hand. Speaking for himself as well as his country, Smith replied that he could not "purchase a certain degree of immunity from devastation at the expense of the honor of its army." So he said. Yet he had no sooner done so than news of a series of disasters began arriving from beyond the Mississippi: first, that Johnston and Sherman had come to terms, and then that Taylor and Canby had followed suit. He now commanded, such as it was, the Confederacy's only unsurrendered department, and in reaction he ordered his headquarters moved from Shreveport to Houston, where he would be less vulnerable to attack in the campaign he knew was about to be launched against him. Before he could make the shift, however, word came that Davis himself had been captured in South Georgia. That did it. Convinced at last that he no longer had anything left to hope for, let alone fight for, Smith decided to reopen negotiations: not with Pope, up in Missouri, but with Canby, who was en route from Mobile to New Orleans. Rather than go himself he sent his chief of staff, Lieutenant General Simon Buckner, with full authority to accept whatever terms were offered. That was fitting. At Donelson, three years and three months ago, the Kentuckian had surrendered the first Conferedate army to lay down its arms. Now he was charged with surrendering the last.

His mission was soon accomplished. Steaming under a flag of truce, first down the Red and then the Mississippi, he reached New Orleans on May 25, the same day Canby got there. They conferred, and next morning, having accepted the terms afforded Lee and Johnston and Taylor, Buckner signed the surrender agreement with Peter Osterhaus, Canby's own chief of staff. One week later, on June 2, Kirby Smith came down to Galveston, boarded the Federal steamer *Fort Jackson* out in the harbor, and fixed his signature to the document brought from New Orleans for that purpose. Before he left Houston he had already issued his farewell to such troops as were still with him, if only on paper. "Your present duty is plain," he told them. "Return to your families. Resume the occupations of peace. Yield obedience to the laws. Labor to restore order. Strive both by counsel and example to give security to life and property. And may God, in his mercy, direct you aright and heal the wounds of our distracted country."

Thus the final place of refuge within the vanished Confederate borders passed from being, no longer a goal for die-hards such as Wheeler, who had been trying to get there when he was taken near Atlanta, three weeks back. Similarly, four days ago at Natchez, unaware that Buckner had come to terms with Canby a couple of hundred winding miles downstream, John B. Hood and two aides were picked up by Federal patrollers before they could get across the river. He had stopped off in South Carolina long enough for Sally Preston to break her engagement to him, and then, aggrieved, had ridden on, intent on reaching his adoptive Texas. Paroled on May 31, the day after his capture, he continued his journey, no longer as a general in search of recruits for the army he had promised Jefferson Davis he would raise there, but rather as one more one-legged civilian who had to find some way to make a living.

Thousands of others in the region had that problem, too, and only a handful solved it without changing the life style they had known for the past four years. These exceptions came mainly from the ranks of the guerillas, some of whom enlisted in the Union army, thereby avoiding government prosecution, while others simply moved on west and resumed on the frontier such wartime activities as bank and stagecoach robbery, with cattle rustling thrown in for a sideline. One among them was W. C. Quantrill, except that he went east, not west, bent on bringing off a coup that would outdo in notoriety even his sacking of Lawrence, Kansas, late in the summer of '63. Back in Missouri after Price retreated, Quantrill assembled some two dozen followers, including Frank James and Jim Younger — but not George Todd or Bill Anderson, who had been killed within a month of the Centralia massacre — and set out for a crossing of the Mississippi on New Year's Day, just north of Memphis, at the head of a column of blue-clad horsemen he identified as a platoon from the nonexistent 4th Missouri Cavalry, U.S. His plan, announced at the outset, was to proceed by way of Kentucky and Maryland to Washington, and there revive Confederate hopes by killing Abraham Lincoln. He took up so much time en route, however, that he never got there. In the Bluegrass by mid-April he learned that J. Wilkes Booth had beat him to the act. Still in Kentucky three weeks later, he was wounded in a barnyard skirmish on May 10, thirty miles southeast of Louisville. Like Booth he was struck in the spine and paralyzed, though he lived for nearly a month in that condition. Recognizing one of the physicians at his bedside, he asked if he had not treated him previously, in another part of the state. "I am the man. I have moved here," the doctor replied. "So have I," Quantrill said, enigmatic to the end, which came on June 6.

By that time Kirby Smith had returned from Galveston; the last outlying remnants of organized resistance were submitting or departing. On June 23 at Doaksville, near Fort Towson in the Indian Territory, Brigadier General Stand Watie, a Cherokee chief who had held out with a third of his people when the other two thirds renewed their allegiance to the Union, surrendered and disbanded his battalion of Cherokees, Creeks, Seminoles, and Osages, all proscribed as tribal outlaws for refusing to repudiate the treaty made with Richmond in the early days of the war. Close to sixty, a veteran of Wilson's Creek, Elkhorn Tavern, Prairie Grove, and a hundred lesser fights — not to mention the long march out the "trail of tears" from Georgia, nearly thirty years ago — Watie, his gray-shot hair spread fanwise on his shoulders, was the last Confederate general to lay down his arms.

One who did not surrender was Jo Shelby, who had sworn he never would. When news of the Buckner-Smith capitulation reached him he assembled his division on the prairie near Corsicana, Texas, for a speech. "Boys, the war is over and you can go home. I for one will not go home. Across the Rio Grande lies Mexico. Who will follow me there?" Some two hundred of his veterans said they would, and next morning, after parting with comrades who chose to stay behind, set out southward. Proceeding through Waco, Austin, and San Antonio, they picked up recruits along the way, together with a number of dignitaries in and out of uniform: John Magruder and Sterling Price, for instance, as well as Henry Allen of Louisiana and Texas Governor Pendleton Murrah, who rose from his sickbed to join the horsemen riding through his capital, five hundred strong by then. Finally, beyond San Antonio, Kirby Smith himself caught up with the column. He was bound for Mexico, like all the rest, but not as a soldier, having discovered for the first time since he left West Point, twenty years ago this month, "the feeling of lightness and joy experienced by me when I felt myself to be plain Kirby Smith, relieved from all cares and responsible only for my own acts."

Clearing Eagle Pass by the last week in June, Shelby paused to weight his tattered battle flag with stones and sink it in the Rio Grande before crossing into Mexico. At Monterrey the column lost most of its distinguished civilian hangers-on, who scattered variously for Cuba, Brazil, and other regions where ex-Confederates were reported to be welcome. But Shelby and his body of troopers, grown by now to the size of a small brigade, kept on for Mexico City, having decided — such was their proclivity for lost causes — to throw in with Maximilian, rather than Juárez. The Emperor, whose subjects already were showing how much they resented his foreign support, knew better than to enlist the help of *gringo* mercenaries. Still, he was friendly enough to offer them a plot of land near Vera Cruz for colonization. Most declined and went their several ways, being far from ready to settle down to the farming life they had left four years ago, but Shelby and a few others accepted and even sent for their families to join them; which they did, though not for long. The settlement — dubbed Carlota, in honor of the Empress — scarcely outlasted Maximilian, who fell in front of a firing squad two Junes later, after the troops supporting Juárez rushed into the vacuum left by the departing French. Grant had been right about Napoleon's reaction, once Sheridan reached the Texas border and bristled along it, much as he had done in the old days up and down the Shenandoah Valley.

★　★　★

Afloat, whether on salt water or fresh, the wind-down of the rebellion seemed likely to prove a good deal more erratic and explosive than on land, depending as it would on the attitude and nature of the individual skipper operating on his own, as so many did in the Confederate navy, up lonely rivers or far out to sea. "Don't give up the ship" — a proud tradition sometimes taken to irrational extremes: as in duels to the death, with eight-inch guns at ranges of eight feet — might apply no less at the finish than at the start. A case in point was Lieutenant Charles W. Read, whose handling of the steam ram *William H. Webb* in a late-April dash for freedom down the Red and the Mississippi provided a possible forecast of instances to come.

A twenty-four-year-old Mississippian, Read had finished at Annapolis in 1860, one year ahead of his Union counterpart William Cushing, and like him had had a colorful war career. He fought with distinction against Farragut below New Orleans, then again at Vicksburg as a gunnery officer on the *Arkansas*, and next aboard the *Florida* in her great days, when Maffitt gave him a captured brig, along with a crew of twenty and one boat howitzer, and set him up as an independent raider. In twenty-one days, cruising the Atlantic coast from Norfolk to New England, he took twenty-one prizes before he himself was taken, off Portland, Maine, in June of 1863, and confined at Fort Warren. Exchanged in October of the following year, he was assigned to duty with the James River squadron below Richmond until March of 1865, when Mallory chose him to command the *Webb*, languishing in far-off Louisiana for the past two years. Reported to be "the fastest thing afloat," she had seen no substantial action since her sinking of the monster ironclad *Indianola*, back in the early spring of '63, and it was Mallory's belief that she could be put to highly effective use against Yankee merchantmen and blockaders, if Read could only get her out into the open waters of the Gulf of Mexico.

Arriving by the end of the month he found the 206-foot sidewheel steamer tied up eighty miles below Shreveport, "without a single gun on board, little or no crew, no fuel, and no small arms save a few cutlasses." Undaunted, he took her up to department headquarters and secured from the army a 30-pounder Parrott rifle, which he mounted on her bow, and two 12-pounder smoothbores, one for each broadside, as well as fifty-one soldier volunteers and sixteen officers. Back at Alexandria, while training his new green crew, he put carpenters to work constructing a rough bulwark around the *Webb*'s forecastle and loaded close to two hundred bales of cotton for use as a shield for her machinery until he reached Cuba and could exchange them for a longer-burning fuel than the pine knots he now had stacked about her decks. By that time, news had come of Lee's surrender and the government's flight south. He knew he would have to hurry, and on April 22, as he prepared to cast off down the Red, he learned of Lincoln's assassination, which might or might not add to the confusion he hoped to encounter during his run past Baton Rouge and New Orleans and the warships on patrol above and below them both. "As I will have to stake everything upon speed and time," he wrote Mallory that day, "I will not attack any vessel in the passage unless I perceive a possibility of her arresting my progress. In this event I am prepared with five torpedoes . . . one of which I hold shipped on its pole on the bows."

He left that evening and reached the mouth of the river about 8.30 the following night, the first Sunday after Easter. Displaying the lights of a Federal transport and running slow to reduce the engine noise, he hoped to sneak past the blue flotilla on patrol there, which included two ironclads and a monitor. For a time it seemed the *Webb* was going to steam by undetected, but then a rocket swooshed up from the deck of one of the blockaders, giving the signal: "Strange vessel in sight, positively an enemy." Read shouted, "Let her go!" and the engineer opened the throttle all the way. As the ram shot forward, whistles screamed and drums rolled beat-to-quarters along the line of warships dead ahead. "Keep for the biggest opening between them," Read told the pilot. Out in the moonless night, the monitor *Manhattan* swung her big guns in their turret and hurled two 11-inch shells at the rebel churning past. Both missed, and the *Webb* was soon out of range, driving hard as she began her intended 300-mile run down the Mississippi to the Gulf. Unpursued by anything that had even an outside chance of overtaking him, Read tied up to the east bank and sent a detail ashore to cut the telegraph wires, then set out again, gliding past Baton Rouge in the darkness, unseen or unrecognized, and on to Donaldsonville by daylight, still carrying the signals of a Union transport. Here too the ram passed unchallenged, though some who saw her booming along with the midstream current later testified that she was making a good 25 knots as she went by. That may well have been; for by 1 o'clock that afternoon, April 24, the church spires of low-lying New Orleans came in view.

Read hoisted the U.S. flag at half mast, brought his boiler pressure up to maximum, and began his run past the Crescent City. No warning message had got through, thanks to the cutting of the wires the night before; lookouts here, like those at Donaldsonville that morning, took the *Webb* to be a friendly transport, mourning with her lowered colors the death of Abraham Lincoln. They did, that is, until about midway through the run, when a bluejacket who had fought against her, a couple of years ago upriver, recognized her and gave the alarm, setting off a din of bells and drums and whistles, soon punctuated by the roar of guns. Most of the shots went wild, but three struck the ram before she cleared the fleet, one through her chimney, one into a bale of cotton, and one just above the waterline at her bow, damaging the torpedo mechanism so badly that the explosive had to be jettisoned. Stopping to accomplish this, Read took down the half-staffed Union emblem, ran up to the peak his true Confederate colors, and continued downriver at full speed, bound for the open waters of the Gulf.

Behind him New Orleans was abuzz with rumors that Jeff Davis and John Wilkes Booth were aboard the ram, headed for South America with millions in gold bullion. Read knew nothing of this, of course, but he did know that the two fastest gunboats in the enemy flotilla, *Hollyhock* and *Florida*, were churning downstream after him. Confident that he could outrun them, the young Mississippian was alarmed only so far as their pursuit might interfere with his plan for not reaching Forts Jackson and St Philip, sixty winding miles away, before night came down to help screen him from the plunging crossfire of guns on both sides of the river. He considered stopping to dispose of them, despite their superior armament, but up ahead just then, twenty-five miles below the city, he saw something that commanded all his attention. It was the veteran screw sloop *Richmond*, mounting twenty-one guns, anchored for engine repairs and now being cleared for action. He studied her briefly, regretting the loss of his spar torpedo, then told the pilot: "Make straight for the *Richmond*'s bow, and ram." "I can't reach her bow because of a shoal," the pilot replied, "but I can come in under her broadside." Read shook his head at that suggestion. "I've been under the *Richmond*'s broadside before, and don't wish to try it again," he said. He assembled all hands on the foredeck and informed them of what he knew he had to do. "It's no use. The *Richmond* will drown us all — and if she doesn't, the forts below will, as they have a range of three miles each way up and down the river, and they know by this time that we are coming." He turned to the helmsman. "Head for shore," he told him.

Fifty yards from bank the *Webb* struck bottom, and while most of the crew began climbing down ropes thrown over the bow, others went about dousing the deck and cabins with turpentine before they too abandoned ship. Read started fires with a lighted match, then went over the side, the last to leave the flaming ram. He and his men lay in waiting in the brush till they heard her magazine explode, after which they broke into groups and scattered. By daybreak, half of them had been rounded up, including Read, who suffered the indignity of being placed on public display in New Orleans; but not for long. Presently he and the rest were paroled and allowed to return to their homes. At a cost of one man wounded, and of course the *Webb* herself, he had given the victors notice of what they might expect in the way of naval daring between now and the time the final curtain fell.

Whatever might come of such fears as this aroused, a river mishap of far bloodier proportions occurred six hundred miles upstream in the early morning hours of April 27, the day Read was put on display in New Orleans. En route for Cairo with an outsized cargo of surplus army mules and discharged soldiers who had crowded aboard at Vicksburg and Helena after their release from Deep South prison camps, the sidewheel steamer *Sultana*, one of the largest on the Mississippi, blew her boilers near Paddy's Hen and Chickens, north of Memphis two hours before dawn. Although her authorized capacity was less than 400 passengers, she had about six times that number packed about her decks and in her hold — mostly Ohio, Illinois, and Indiana veterans, men who had fought perhaps the hardest war of all, sweating out its finish in stockades beyond reach of the various columns of invasion. So sudden was the blast and the fire that followed, those who managed to make it over the side had to dive through flames into muddy water running swift and cold as any millstream. A body count put the official death toll at 1238, but there was really no way of telling how many troops had been aboard or were consumed by shrimp and gars before all those hundreds of other blue-clad corpses bobbed up downstream in the course of the next month. Estimates ran as high as 1800 dead and presumed dead, with 1585 as the figure most generally agreed on. That was more than the number killed on both sides at First Bull Run and Wilson's Creek combined, and even by the lowest count the loss of the *Sultana* went into the books as the greatest marine disaster of all time. Just under one month later, as if to emphasize the shock that came with sudden peace, on May 25 — the day after the Grand Review up Pennsylvania Avenue ended, and the day before Simon Buckner surrendered to Canby in New Orleans for his chief — a warehouse on the Mobile waterfront, stocked with some twenty tons of surrendered ammunition, blew up and "shook the foundations" of the city. An estimated 300 people were killed outright, and the property loss was reckoned at $5,000,000.

By way of consolation for these subtractions — unexpected and all the more tragic because they were self-inflicted, so to speak — fears regarding those other losses, anticipated because of the example set by Read in his abortive downstream dash, turned out to be quite groundless. Joe Johnston's capitulation, followed within two weeks by Richard Taylor's — the former on the day before the *Sultana* blew her boilers above Memphis — brought about the surrender of the few surviving rebel warships east of the Mississippi, bloodlessly and practically without fanfare. On May 10, four that had taken refuge up the Tombigbee almost a month ago, after the evacuation of Mobile, struck their colors in accordance with a commitment by the flotilla captain to hand over to the Federals "all public property yet afloat under his command." On May 27, down in West Florida, the gunboat *Spray* was the last to go. Stationed up the St Marks River to cover the water approaches to Tallahassee, her skipper agreed to surrender when he learned that the troops defending the capital in his rear had laid down their arms the week before. Then came Kirby Smith's formal capitulation at Galveston, and next day, June 3, the *Webb*'s one-time consorts up the Red hauled down their flags. One among them was the ironclad *Missouri*, completed at Shreveport in late March and taken down to Alexandria, not in time to fight, but at any rate in time to be handed over with the rest. "A most formidable vessel," one Union officer pronounced her, though after a closer look he added an assessment that might have served as an epitaph for all the improvised warships knocked together by backwoods carpenters and blacksmiths, here and elsewhere throughout the South: "She is badly built of green lumber, caulked with cotton, leaks badly, and is very slow."

By that time, too, the gravest of all the Union navy's current fears had been allayed. These concerned still another ironclad, a seagoing armored ram described by those who had seen her as the most powerful thing afloat. Built not by amateur shipwrights in the rebel hinterland, but rather by French craftsmen at Bordeaux, she was commissioned the C.S.S. *Stonewall* — "an appellation not inconsistent with her character," the purchasing agent proudly declared — and in mid-January set out down the European coast on the first leg of a voyage across the Atlantic, under instructions to lift the blockade at Wilmington and elsewhere by sinking the blockaders: an assignment considered by no means beyond her capability, since in addition to her defensive attributes, which reportedly made her unsinkable, she featured such dread offensive devices as a protruding underwater beak, heavy enough to drive through the flank and bottom of any rival, wood or metal, and a 300-pounder Armstrong rifle mounted on her bow. Damaged by rough weather, she put into Ferrol, Spain, for repairs. By the time these were made, two multigunned U.S. frigates were on station outside the harbor, apparently waiting to take her on when she emerged. When she did so, however, on March 24, both refrained and stood aside to let her go, one blue skipper afterwards explaining that "the odds in her favor were too great and too certain, in my humble judgment, to admit of the slightest hope of being able to inflict upon her even the most trifling injury."

As it turned out, that one negative triumph, achieved by a bluff for whose success the Federal commander was court-martialed, was the *Stonewall*'s only contribution to the struggle whose tide of victory her purchasers had hoped she would reverse. After filling with coal at Lisbon, down the coast, she set out across the ocean on March 28, still unchallenged. Obliged to make another refueling stop in the Canaries, she did not reach Nassau until May 6. Not only had she made poor time; her bunkers were nearly empty again, and her skipper, Captain T. J. Page, a Virginian in his middle fifties, was shaking his head at her lumbering performance and the sharpness of French salesmen. "You must not expect too much of me," he wrote his superiors; "I fear the power and effect of this vessel have been much exaggerated." On May 11 he dropped anchor at Havana. News had not yet arrived of the capture of Jefferson Davis the day before, but he soon learned that both Lee and Johnston had surrendered their armies. While he pondered what to do, word came that Taylor had followed suit, ending all possibility of resistance east of the Mississippi. By now, moreover, Union warships of all types were assembling outside the harbor from all directions, including the monitors *Canonicus* and *Monadnock*, veterans of Fort Fisher and the first of their type to leave home waters. "*Canonicus* would have crushed her, and the *Monadnock* could have taken her beyond a doubt," the admiral in command of the blue flotilla later said of the holed-up *Stonewall*. No one would ever know for sure, however. On May 19, having reached his decision, Page turned over to the Captain

General of Cuba, for a decision by Spain as to her eventual disposition, the only ironclad ever to fly the Confederate flag on the high seas.

That flag still flew on the high seas, but only at one ever-moving point, the peak of the cruiser *Shenandoah*. "An erratic ship, without country or destination," Gideon Welles quite accurately described her, urging his otherwise unemployed frigate captains to locate and run down this last Confederate raider, which lately had been reported raising havoc in the South Pacific. By now, though, she was elsewhere; Welles was warm, yet far from hot, in the game of hide-and-seek the rebel privateer was playing with his men-of-war. James Waddell had sailed her north from Melbourne in mid-February, intent on "visiting," as his instructions put it, "the enemy's distant whaling grounds." He had no luck in that regard until April 1, when he approached Ascension Island in the eastern Carolines and found a quartet of the blubber-laden vessels anchored in Lea Harbor like so many sitting ducks. After putting the crews ashore he set all four afire and continued northward, past Japan, into the northwest reaches of the Sea of Okhotsk, where he took one more prize during the final week in May. So far, the pickings had been rather slim, but now he had accurate, up-to-date whaling charts, as well as a number of volunteers from the captured ships, to show him where to go: south, then north, around the Kamchatka Peninsula, into the Bering Sea. There the forty-year-old North Carolinian found what he had been seeking all along.

Off Cape Navarin on June 22 he came upon two whalers, one of which — a fast bark out of New Bedford, aptly named the *Jerah Swift* — tried to make a run for it. *Shenandoah* gave chase, dodging ice floes as she went, and after a hard three-hour pursuit, drew close enough to put a round from a 32-pounder Whitworth rifle across her bow; whereupon her captain "saw the folly of exposing the crew to a destructive fire and yielded to his misfortunes with a manly and becoming dignity." So Waddell later wrote, unaware at the time — as, indeed, he would remain for weeks to come — that he had just fired the last shot of the American Civil War. He burned the two ships, then started after more. Next day he took a trading vessel, only two months out of San Francisco, and found aboard her a newspaper dated April 17, containing the latest dispatches from the eastern theater. Lee had surrendered: Richmond had fallen: the Government had fled. Shaken though he was by this spate of disasters, he also read that Johnston had won a victory over Sherman in North Carolina, back in March, and that the President, resettled with his cabinet in Danville, had issued a proclamation announcing "a new phase of the struggle," which he urged all Confederates to wage with "fresh defiance" and "unconquered and unconquerable hearts." Waddell took his cue from that, and was rewarded three days later when he steamed into a cluster of six whalers lying becalmed off St Lawrence Island. Five he burned; the sixth he ransomed to take on board the crews of all the rest. Two days later, on June 28, he made his largest haul near the narrows of Bering Strait, where he fell in with a rendezvous of eleven whalers. He put all the crews aboard two of these, bonded as before, and set the other nine ablaze in a single leaping conflagration, rivaling with its glow of burning oak and sperm oil, reflected for miles on the ice that glittered round-about, the brilliance of the Aurora Borealis. In nine months of sailing close to 40,000 miles, the *Shenandoah* now had taken an even two dozen whalers, along with 1053 prisoners and another 14 merchant vessels, destroying all but six of the 38, whose total value Waddell placed at $1,361,983. Wanting still more, he steamed next day into the Arctic Ocean.

But there were no more. He discovered, after searching, that he had abolished the whaling trade, so far at least as his one-time fellow countrymen were concerned. Narrowly escaping getting ice-bound, he turned back and passed once more between the outpost capes of Asia and North America. Propeller triced up to save coal, he crowded on all sail and set out for the coast of Baja California, intending to make prizes of the clippers plying between Panama and San Francisco. By July 4 he was clear of the chain of the Aleutians and back into the ice-free waters of the North Pacific. For a month he held his southward course, sailing well out of sight of land, and then on August 2 en-countered the English bark *Barracouta*, less than two weeks out of Frisco. Newspapers on her told of Kirby Smith's capitulation, two months ago today; Jefferson Davis was in prison, and the Confederacy was no longer among the nations of earth. Despite earlier indications, the news came hard for those on board the *Shenandoah*. "We were bereft of ground for hope or aspiration," her executive officer wrote in his journal that night, "bereft of a cause for which to struggle and suffer." Waddell now was faced with the problem of what to do with his ship and his people: a decision, he said, "which involved not only our personal honor, but the honor of the flag entrusted to us which had walked the waters fearlessly and in triumph." Though he ordered the battery struck below and the crew disarmed, he was de-termined to avoid capture if possible. Accordingly, after rejecting the notion of surrendering at some port close at hand, where treatment might be neither fair nor unprejudiced, he decided to make a nonstop run, by way of Cape Horn, for England.

The distance was 17,000 miles, very little of it in sight of land, and required three full months of sailing, never speaking another vessel from start to finish lest the *Shenandoah*'s whereabouts became known to Federal skippers who by now were scouring the seas under orders to take or sink her. Rounding the Horn in mid-September, she was driven off course by a northeast gale and did not cross the equator until October 11. Then she took the trades, with smooth going all the way to the western coast of England. "I believe the Divine will directed and protected that ship in all her adventures," her captain was to say. On November 5 she reached St George's Channel and dropped anchor to wait for a pilot, then steamed next morning up the Mersey to Liverpool, the Stars and Bars flying proudly at her peak. She had covered better than 58,000 miles, circumnavigated the globe, visited all its oceans except the Antarctic, and taken in the course of her brief career more prizes than any other Confederate raider except the *Alabama*. Anchored beside a British ship-of-the-line, she lowered her abolished country's last official flag and was turned over to the port authorities for adjudication. Two days later, Waddell and his crew were unconditionally released to go ashore for the first time since they left Melbourne, almost nine months ago. Looking back with pride and satisfaction on all the *Shenandoah* had accomplished in her thirteen months at sea, he later wrote: "I claim for her officers and men a triumph over their enemies and over every obstacle.... For myself," he added, "I claim having done my duty."

★　★　★

By that time, no more than a handful of Confederates remained in Federal custody, locked up awaiting trial or other disposition of their cases. On May 27, the day after Canby's provisional acceptance of the surrender of the last armed grayback in the Transmississippi, Andrew Johnson had ordered the discharge, with but few exceptions, of all persons imprisoned by military authorities. Two days later a presidential Proclamation of Amnesty offered pardon to all who had participated, directly or indirectly, in "the existing rebellion," with full restitution of property rights — except of course slaves — on the taking of an oath by such people that they would "henceforth" support and defend the Constitution and abide by the laws of the reunited land. In this latter instance, however, so many exceptions were cited that the document was about as much a source of alarm as it was of solace. Among those excluded were all who held civil or diplomatic offices in the secessionist regime and the governors of its member states; former U.S. congressmen, senators, and judges; West Pointers, Annapolis men, and members of the armed forces who had resigned or deserted to join the South; those engaged in the destruction of commerce or mistreatment of prisoners, officers above the rank of army colonel or navy lieutenant, and finally all "voluntary" participants with taxable property worth more than $20,000. The list ran on, and though it was stated that even those ineligibles could apply directly to the President for pardon, with assurance that "such clemency will be liberally extended as may be consistent with the facts of the case and the peace and dignity of the United States," few took much consolation in that provision, knowing as they did the views of Johnson with regard to treason and its consequences, which he had proclaimed so often in the course of the past four years. Kirby Smith, for example, no sooner read the offer than he rode off after Jo Shelby, bound for Mexico, as he informed his wife, in order "to place the Rio Grande between myself and harm."

Some measure of his concern, and that of others in flight from northern justice, was aroused by the savagery with which the eight accused of complicity with Booth in his assassination plot were being prosecuted at the time. Shackled at their trial, as no prisoner had been in an English-speaking court for more than a hundred and fifty years, they were kept hooded in their cells, with thick cotton pads over eyes and ears, lest they see or hear each other or their guards, and two small slits in the canvas for the admission of food and air. The military trial, presided over by nine high-ranking army officers in Washington's Arsenal Penitentiary, began on May 10 and ended June 30, when verdicts were returned. Johnson approved them on July 5, and two days later they were carried out. All eight had been found guilty. Four were soon on their way to the Dry Tortugas, three with life sentences, including a Virginia doctor who had set Booth's broken leg, and one, a stagehand at Ford's, with a six-year term for having allegedly helped the actor leave the theater. The other four got death: Lewis Paine, an ex-Confederate soldier who had made the knife attack on Seward, George Atzerodt, an immigrant carriage-maker who had lacked the nerve to attempt his assignment of killing the Vice President, David Herald, a slow-witted Maryland youth who had served as a guide for the fugitive in his flight, and Mary E. Surratt, the widowed proprietor of a boarding house where Booth was said to have met with some of the others in planning the work only he carried out in full. All were in their twenties except Mrs Surratt, who was forty-five and whose principal offense appeared to be that her twenty-year-old son had escaped abroad before he could be arrested for involvement in the crime. Some objections arose to the execution of a woman, but not enough to prevent her being one of the four who were hanged and buried in the yard of the penitentiary where Booth had been buried in secret, under the dirt floor of a cell, ten weeks before.

Despite this evidence of how ruthless the government — mainly Stanton, who had engineered the trial — could be in pursuit and removal of those it was determined to lay hands on, Johnson proved quite as liberal in granting clemency as he had said he would be in his amnesty proclamation. By mid-October, not only had all the arrested secessionist governors been released on their application for pardon, but so too had such once high-placed rebels as John Reagan and George Trenholm, John A. Campbell, and even Alexander Stephens. In November there was one sharp reminder of the claws inside the velvet Federal glove, when Captain Henry Wirz, the Swiss-born commandant of Andersonville, was convicted on trumped-up testimony of deliberate cruelty to the prisoners in his care. He was tried in violation of his parole, as well as of other legal rights, but Stanton had more or less assured a guilty verdict by appointing Lew Wallace president of the court; Wallace had consistently voted against the accused in the trial of the Lincoln conspirators, and Wirz was duly hanged on November 10, four days after the *Shenandoah* lowered the last Confederate flag. Meantime, Johnson continued granting amnesty to ex-rebels. By April 2 of the following year, when he declared the insurrection officially "at an end," Stephen Mallory had been relieved of long-pending charges of having promoted the willful destruction of commerce. Two weeks later Raphael Semmes was similarly released, along with Clement C. Clay, another Alabamian, who had been detained all this time on suspicion of having "incited, concerted, and procured" Lincoln's assassination from his post as a special commissioner in Canada. Now only Jefferson Davis remained behind bars in his cell at Fort Monroe.

Clay's release on April 17 resulted in a good deal of speculation about his former chief, who was being held on the same charge. Nothing came of that, for the present, but just over two weeks later, on May 3 — one week less than a year after his capture down in Georgia — Varina Davis was permitted to see her husband for the first time since they parted aboard the vessel that brought them up the coast to Hampton Roads. She was conducted past three lines of sentries, each requiring a password, then through a guardroom, until at last she approached and saw him beyond the bars of his quarters, moving toward her. His "shrunken form and glassy eyes" nearly caused her to collapse from shock, she later said. "His cheek bones stood out like those of a skeleton. Merely crossing the room made his breath come in short gasps, and his voice was scarcely audible."

He had had a harder time than she or anyone else not in the fort with him for the past year could know. What was more, it had begun in deadly earnest before the end of his first full day of incarceration. Near sundown, he looked up from reading his small-print Bible, the only possession allowed him except the clothes he wore, and saw that a guard captain had entered the casemate, accompanied by two men who seemed to be blacksmiths. One of them held a length of chain with a shackle at each end, and suddenly he knew why they were there, though he still could not quite believe it. "My God," he said. "You don't intend to iron me?" When the captain replied that those were indeed his orders, the prisoner rose and protested for all he was worth. "But the war is over; the South is conquered. For the honor of America, you cannot commit this degradation!" Told again that the orders were peremptory, Davis met this as he had met other challenges in the past, whatever the odds. "I shall never submit to such an indignity," he exclaimed. "It is too monstrous. I demand that you let me see the commanding general."

Here a certain irony obtained, unknown as yet to the captive in his cell. For it was the fort commander, Brigadier General Nelson A. Miles, who, in prompt response to a War Department directive authorizing him "to place manacles and fetters upon the hands and feet of Jefferson Davis...whenever he may think it advisable in order to render [his] imprisonment more secure," had made the decision to shackle him forthwith, not for the reason stated, but rather because he was eager to give his superiors what they wanted. Miles was cruel, in this as in other instances to follow, not so much by nature as by design. Not yet twenty-six, a one-time Massachusetts farm boy who had left the farm to clerk in a Boston crockery shop, he had achieved a brilliant record in the war, suffering four wounds in the course of his rise from lieutenant to brigadier, with the prospect of still another promotion if he did well at his current post, to which he had been assigned in part because of his lack of such West Point and Old Army ties as were likely to make him stand in awe of the prisoner in his charge. That he felt no such awe he quickly demonstrated, beginning with Davis's first full day in his care, and his reward would follow. By October he would be a major general. In a couple of years he would marry a niece of Sherman's, and before the century was out he would succeed Grant, Sherman, and Sheridan as general-in-chief; William McKinley, himself a former sergeant, would make him a lieutenant general, and he would live until 1925, when he died at a Washington circus performance and was buried at Arlington in a mausoleum he had built some years before. His was an American success story—Horatio Alger in army braid and stars—and part of the story was the time he spent as Jefferson Davis's jailer, giving his superiors what he saw they wanted, including the fetters now about to be applied.

Davis subsided after registering his protest, and the guard captain supposed him resigned to being ironed. "Smith, do your work," he said. But when the man came forward, kneeling to attach the shackles, the prisoner unexpectedly grabbed and flung him across the room. Recovering, the smith charged back, hammer lifted, and would have struck his assailant if the captain had not stopped him. One of the two armed sentries present cocked and leveled his rifle, but the captain stopped him too, instructing the four men "to take Mr Davis with as little force as possible." The struggle was brief, though it took more force than they had thought would be required; Davis, the captain later reported, "showed unnatural strength." While his helper and the sentries pinned the frail gray captive to the cot, the blacksmith riveted one clasp in place and secured its mate around the other ankle with a large brass lock, "the same as is in use on freight cars." The struggle ceased with the snap of the lock; Davis lay motionless, flat on his back, as the smith and his helper retired, their job done. Looking over his shoulder as he left, the captain saw the prisoner sit up, turn sideways on the cot, and with a heavy effort drop both feet to the stone floor. The clank of the chain was followed by unrestrained weeping, and the departing captain thought it "anything but a pleasant sight to see a man like Jefferson Davis shedding tears."

Mercifully, this particular humiliation was brief. Within five days, vigorous private and public objections — first by the post surgeon, who protested that the captive was being denied even such limited exercise as he could get from pacing up and down his cell, and then by a number of northern civilians who, though willing to keep on hating the former Confederate leader, disapproved of tormenting him in this fashion — caused the removal of the shackles. Other hardships continued in force, however, including the constant presence of two sentries under orders to keep tramping back and forth at all hours, a lamp that burned day and night, even while he slept or tried to, and the invariable dampness resulting from the fact that the floor of his cell was below the level of the water in the adjacent moat. Davis's health declined and declined, from neuralgia, failing eyesight, insomnia, and a general loss of vitality. Passing his fifty-seventh birthday in early June, he had to wait until late July, more than two months after his arrival, to be permitted an hour's daily exercise on the ramparts, and still another month went by before he was allowed to read the first letter from his wife. In October he was moved from the casemate to a second-story room in the fort's northwest bastion, but it was mid-December, after nearly seven months of seeing no one but the surgeon and his guards — including Miles, who sneered at him and called him Jeff — before he received his first visitor, his wartime pastor, who came down from Richmond to give him Communion and found him changed in appearance by long confinement, but not in spirit. "His spirit could not be subdued," the minister later wrote, "and no indignity, angry as it made him at the time, could humiliate him."

By that time, prominent Northerners — especially those in the legal profession — had seen the weakness of the government's case against Davis and the handful of Confederates yet being held. One who saw it was the Chief Justice who would rule on their appeal in the event that one was needed, which he doubted. "If you bring these leaders to trial it will condemn the North," Chase had warned his former cabinet colleagues in July, "for by the Constitution secession is not rebellion." As for the rebel chieftain, the authorities would have done better not to apprehend him. "Lincoln wanted Jefferson Davis to escape, and he was right. His capture was a mistake. His trial will be a greater one. We cannot convict him of treason. Secession is settled. Let it stay settled." Charles O'Conor, the distinguished New York attorney who had volunteered his services in Davis's behalf, was convinced that he would eventually be freed. "No trial for treason on any like offense will be held in the civil courts," he predicted, and as for his client's chances of being railroaded by the army, as Wirz and Mrs Surratt had been, "the managers at Washington are not agreed as to the safety of employing military commissions to color a like outrage upon any eminent person." Horace Greeley had come over, early on, and was saying in the *Tribune* that Davis should either be tried or turned loose without delay. Even so stalwart an Abolitionist as the philanthropist Gerrit Smith, a backer of John Brown, was persuaded that an injustice was in progress and was willing to sign a petition to that effect, as were others who wanted liberty for all men, black and white, by due process of law.

Clement Clay's release in mid-April, 1866, showed clearly enough the government's abandonment of the charge that he and Davis had been instigators of the assassination, but it also permitted total concentration on what was left of the case against the one prisoner still held. Stanton and Judge Advocate General Joseph Holt were determined, as Schuyler Colfax put it, to see the Mississippian "hanging between heaven and earth as not fit for either." Despite the Chief Justice's opinion, given in private nine months ago, that no such accusation could be sustained, they fell back on a vague charge of "treason," and persisted in it even after the distinguished jurist Francis Lieber, handed all the War Department evidence to study for recommendations on procedure, told them flatly: "Davis will not be found guilty and we shall stand there completely beaten." All the same, in early May an indictment was handed down by the U.S. Circuit Court, District of Virginia. "Jefferson Davis, yeoman," it began, "not having fear of God before his eyes, nor weighing the duty of his said allegiance, but being moved and seduced by the institution of the devil, and wickedly devising against the peace and tranquillity of the United States to subvert and to stir, move, and incite insurrection, rebellion, and war — " There was more, much more, but this alone was enough to rally support all over the South for its fallen leader. "That such a creature should be allowed to dispense justice is a perfect farce," Mrs R. E. Lee remarked of the judge presiding. "I think his meanness and wickedness have affected his brain."

By then Varina Davis was with her husband and had even begun to get accustomed to the change in his looks and condition, which had shocked her at first sight. Given quarters in the fort, and allowed to visit with him once a day, she could tell him of the growth of affection in the hearts of many who had turned blameful while the war was on the down slope. Recently she had written from New Orleans: "It is impossible to tell you the love which has been expressed here for you — the tenderness of feeling for you. People sit and cry until I am almost choked with the effort to be quiet. But it is a great consolation to know that a nation is mourning your suffering with me, and to be told hourly how far above reproach you are — how fair your fame. I am overwhelmed by the love which everything of your name attracts." Now that feeling had been extended and enlarged by the harsh indictment and the passing of the anniversary of his capture. To many of his former fellow countrymen it seemed that he alone was undergoing punishment for them all, and presently still another measure was added to the debt they felt they owed him. In late May, Mrs Davis secured an appointment with the President in Washington to plead for her husband's release. To her surprise, Johnson informed her that he was on her side. "But we must wait," he said. "Our hope is to mollify the public to Mr Davis." Meantime, he suggested, the prisoner's best course would be to make application for a pardon. Varina replied that she felt certain he would never do so, and she was right. When she returned to Fort Monroe and told Davis of Johnson's advice, he declined it on grounds that to ask for pardon would be to confess a guilt he did not feel. In this he resembled Robert Toombs, who, having gone abroad to avoid arrest, was counseled by northern friends to apply for pardon. "Pardon for what?" he said with an unreconstructed glare. "I have not pardoned you-all yet." So it was with Davis, and when word got round of his refusal, the growing affection for him grew still more. So long as he declined to ask forgiveness, it was as if they too had never humbled their pride. It was even as if they had never been defeated — except in fact, which mattered less and less as time wore on.

Reassured by such reports from the home front, so to speak, as well as by his attorneys, with whom he now was permitted to confer, Davis suffered a legal setback on June 5, two days after his fifty-eighth birthday, when his plea for an early trial was declined by the Richmond court on grounds that he had never been in its custody, despite the indictment recently handed down, but rather was being held as a State Prisoner "under order of the President, signed by the Secretary of War." A follow-up motion for his release on bail was also disallowed, but it was more or less clear by then that Stanton and Holt were fighting a holding action, with scarcely a hope of securing a conviction. They scheduled a trial for early October, overriding O'Conor's protest at the delay.

All Davis could do was wait. He found this easier, however, now that he had his wife to comfort him, unrestricted access to his mail, and a steady stream of visitors, including ex-President Franklin Pierce, Richard Taylor, and Wade Hampton. August brought two encouraging developments. One was the petition signed by Gerrit Smith and other prominent Northerners, addressed to Johnson in his behalf, and the other was a presidential order removing Nelson Miles as fort commander, after fifteen months of personal abuse. Miles's replacement soon gave the State Prisoner freedom of the post and better quarters, which he and Varina shared. A second Christmas came and went, the trial having been postponed; New Year's 1867 was far different from the one before.

The plan now was to force his release by a writ of habeas corpus, and among those willing to put up $25,000 each for bail were Horace Greeley and Cornelius Vanderbilt.

Spring came on, greening the York-James peninsula from the Chickahominy bottoms to its tip at Old Point Comfort, where "the world's most famous prisoner" was lodged. On the first Monday in May, the trial having been postponed again, an aide left for Richmond to secure the signature of the District Court clerk, as required by law, to the writ O'Conor and his associates had prepared. He returned to Fort Monroe on Friday, May 10 — the second anniversary of the then President's capture in South Georgia — to deliver the authenticated document to the fort commander, who was directed "to present the body of Jefferson Davis" in court three days later. Packed and ready, the State Prisoner and his wife set out upriver the following day. Still under guard, but hopefully not for long now, he saw from the rail that clusters of people had gathered at plantation landings along the James to salute him as he passed, and when the boat approached the capital that Saturday afternoon the wharves and streets along the rebuilt waterfront were so jammed that it seemed all Richmond had assembled to pay him its respects. Men removed their hats as he came ashore, and women fluttered handkerchiefs from balconies and windows along the route his carriage followed toward the heart of town. At the Spotswood, he and Varina were given the same rooms he had occupied when he arrived from Montgomery, six years back, and some declared that a greater number of people turned out to greet him now than had done so when he first arrived to take up his duties in the new capital. "I have never seen this city in such a state of pleased excitement," a visitor wrote home, "except upon the news of a Confederate victory. Men and women in tears was a common sight, and the ladies say they are very much afraid they will have to love the Yankees a little."

On Sunday the Davises kept to their rooms except for a secret trip to Hollywood Cemetery to lay flowers on the grave where their son Joe had lain since his fall from the White House balcony in that other fateful spring, three years ago. After church, old friends came by the hotel, some bringing daughters and nieces who had emerged from girlhood during the past two years, and it was noted that while Davis kissed them all on arrival, "he kissed the prettiest again on their departure." Still, the tension was unmistakable. Tomorrow he would appear before Judge John C. Underwood, who had composed the scabrous charge under which he had been indicted the previous May, and it was feared that he would no sooner have escaped the clutches of the military than Underwood would have him jailed on some new civil pretext of his own.

Next morning, leaving his wife to wait and pray at the hotel, he rode down Main Street — heavily thronged, especially for a Monday, with townspeople and others who had come in hope of witnessing his deliverance — to the old Customs House, where the hearing would be held, and went inside to join his lawyers — six of them, three northern and three southern — seated at a table within the bar. After the first shock of recognition, those watching in the close-packed chamber were pleased to see that the change he had undergone was mainly on the surface. "He wears a full beard and mustache," a reporter had observed in the *Enquirer* the day before, "but his countenance, although haggard and careworn, still preserves the proud expression and the mingled look of sweetness and dignity for which it was ever remarkable. His hair is considerably silvered, but his eye still beams with all the fire that characterized it in the old time." Now one among the spectators, watching him enter the courtroom "with his proud step and lofty look," was convinced that "a stranger would have sworn that he was the judge and Underwood the culprit."

What followed was not only brief and to the point; it also proved yesterday's fears to be groundless. Presented with "the body of Jefferson Davis," as he had required in response to the writ, Underwood declared that the prisoner had passed from the control of martial law to the custody of the local U.S. marshal. O'Conor then requested a trial without delay, and when the district attorney replied that the case could not be heard at the present term, the judge received and granted a motion for bail, which he fixed at $100,000. Horace Greeley was there, along with other one-time enemies who had agreed to give their bond for that amount, and while they came forward to sign the necessary papers, one among the applauding spectators crossed to a window and shouted down to the crowd below on Main Street: "The President is bailed!" A roar came up in response to the news, and those inside the courtroom could hear the cry being passed from street to street, all over Richmond and its seven hills: "The President is bailed!"

They still called him that, and always would: thanks in part to Stanton and his subordinates, whose harshness had recovered for him an affection and devotion as profound as any he had received when the title was his in fact. Presently, when he came out of the Customs House and got into his carriage, the roar of approval grew shrill with the weird halloo of the rebel yell, loosed by veterans who had been waiting two years now to give it. This continued vociferously all the way to the Spotswood, where a crowd of about 5000 had gathered. Then a strange thing happened. When the coachman pulled up in front of the entrance a grave hush came down, as if everyone in the throng had suddenly felt too deeply moved for cheers. "Hats off, Virginians!" a voice rang out. All uncovered and stood in silence as Davis stepped from the carriage, free at last, and entered the hotel where his wife was waiting.

ℵ 4 ℵ

All things end, and by ending not only find continuance in the whole, but also assure continuance by contributing their droplets, clear or murky, to the stream of history. Anaximander said it best, some 2500 years ago: "It is necessary that things should pass away into that from which they are born. For things must pay one another the penalty and compensation for their injustice according to the ordinance of time." So it was with the Confederacy, and so one day will it be for the other nations of earth, if not for earth itself. Appomattox was one of several endings; Durham Station, Citronelle, Galveston were others; as were Johnson's mid-May proclamation and the ratification of the 13th Amendment, which seven months later freed the slaves not freed in the course of a four-year struggle that reunited the nation Lincoln's election had split asunder. But at what cost — if not in suffering, which was immeasurable, then at any rate in blood — had the war been won and lost?

In round numbers, two million blue-clad soldiers and sailors were diminished by 640,000 casualties — more than a fourth — while the 750,000 in gray, all told, lost 450,000 — well over half. Of the former, 110,000 had been killed in battle, as compared to 94,000 of the latter. Death from diseases (dysentery, typhus, malaria, pneumonia, smallpox, measles, tuberculosis) or mishaps out of combat (murder, suicide, drowning, sunstroke, execution, adjunctive to a host of unstated causes) raised these totals to 365,000 and 256,000 respectively, and the addition of the wounded — 275,000 Federals, 194,000 Confederates — yielded the figures quoted above. Minimal computations (deceptive in their specificity, for they too were little more than educated guesses, especially with regard to the southern forces) showed a North-South total of 623,026 dead and 471,427 wounded. The butcher's bill thus came to no less than 1,094,453 for both sides, in and out of more than 10,000 military actions, including 76 full-scale battles, 310 engagements, 6337 skirmishes, and numerous sieges, raids, expeditions, and the like. For the most part, having fewer troops on any given field, the rebels lost fewer in the fighting, but in at least one category the ratio was reversed and extended. Out of 583 Union generals, 47 were killed in action; whereas, of the 425 Confederate generals, 77 fell — roughly one out of twelve, as compared to one out of five. Moreover, much the same awesome ratios obtained when applied to the number slain or maimed out of the total number available for conscription on each side. Approximately one out of ten able-bodied Northerners was dead or incapacitated, while for the South it was one out of four, including her noncombatant Negroes. Some notion of the drain this represented, as well as of the poverty the surrendered men came home to, was shown by the fact that during the first year of peace the state of Mississippi allotted a solid fifth of its revenues for the purchase of artificial arms and legs for its returning veterans.

Few wars — western wars, that is; for in China the Tai-ping Rebellion, which began in 1850 and ended only a year before our own, cost an estimated twenty million lives — had been so proportionately expensive, either in money or in blood. And yet, for all the hard-earned cynicism that prompted them to echo Bill Arp, saying: "I've killed as many of them as they have of me. I'm going home," veterans on both sides knew that, even as they headed for their farms and shops and the girls they left behind, something momentous was passing from them, something that could never be recaptured. "I have no idea that many of them will ever see as happy times as they have had in the army," Rutherford Hayes wrote his wife from West Virginia as he watched his discharged troops depart. They would no doubt have hooted at this, eager for home as they were just then, although some among them already had experienced intimations of nostalgia. "None of us were fond of war," an Indiana infantryman would recall, looking back on the farewell review Thomas staged in Nashville, "but there had grown up between the boys an attachment for each other they never had nor ever will have for any other body of men." For others, there were doubts and fears about the future; a future now at hand. "I do feel so idle and lost to all business," an Iowa cavalryman told his diary on the eve of the Grand Review, "that I wonder what will become of me. Can I ever be contented again? *Can I work?* Ah! how doubtful — it's raining tonight."

Among the shocks awaiting homebound northern soldiers, especially those who had been gone the longest, was the fact that while wages had been rising 43 percent in the course of the war, the cost of living had gone up 117 percent. "Democracies are prone to war, and war consumes them," Seward had said, fifteen years before, and doubtless that was part of what he meant. In any case, demobilization proceeded apace. Within six months of Kirby Smith's surrender, the Union army had declined from just over a million men to 183,000. By the end of the following year it was down to 54,000, and would continue to decline for thirty years. For Southerners there was of course no waiting to be mustered out; a man's parole was his discharge, and he started home as soon as he received it. What awaited him there, particularly if home was a place Sherman or Wilson had given their passing attention, had little or nothing to do with wages. All too often there were no wages, and the cost of living was measured less in dollars than in sweat. Some notion of the waiting desolation was given by a former Georgia slave, who recalled his own departure: "The master had three boys to go to war, but there wasn't one come home. All the children he had was killed. Master, he lost all his money, and the house soon begun dropping away to nothing. Us niggers one by one left the old place, and the last time I seed the home plantation I was standing on a hill. I looked back on it for the last time through a patch of scrub pine, and it looked so lonely. There wasn't but one person in sight, the master. He was a-setting in a wicker chair in the yard looking out over a small field of cotton and corn. There was four crosses in the graveyard on the side lawn where he was setting. The fourth one was his wife."

Whatever else the veterans brought or failed to bring home with them, and whether they returned to snugness or dilapidation, with or without back pay, bonuses, and pensions, they had acquired a sense of nationhood, of nationality. From the outset Lincoln had had the problem of uniting what remained of his divided country if he was to recover by conquest the segment that had departed, and though he succeeded well enough in this to achieve his immediate purpose, true fulfillment came after his death, after the victory that brought the soldiers home. They knew now they had a nation, for they had seen it; they had been there, they had touched it, climbed its mountains, crossed its rivers, hiked its roads; their comrades lay buried in its soil, along with many thousands of their own arms and legs. Nor did this apply only to those whose return was northward, above the Mason-Dixon line. Below it, too, men who never before had been fifty miles from their places of birth now knew, from having slept and fought in its fields and woods and cane brakes, gawked at its cities, such as they were, and trudged homeward through its desolation, that they too had had a country. Not secession but the war itself, and above all the memories recurrent through the peace that followed — such as it was — created a Solid South, more firmly united in defeat than it had been during the brief span when it claimed independence. Voided, the claim was abandoned, but the pride remained: pride in the segment reabsorbed, as well as in the whole, which now for the first time was truly indivisible. This new unity was best defined, perhaps, by the change in number of a simple verb. In formal as in common speech, abroad as well as on this side of its oceans, once the nation emerged from the crucible of that war, "the United States *are*" became "the United States *is*."

It would continue so, but toward what goal? Walt Whitman, for one, believed he saw what was to come of this forged unity. "I chant the new empire, grander than before. I chant commerce opening!" he exulted. John Sherman was more specific, telling his soldier brother: "The truth is, the close of the war with our resources unimpaired gives an elevation, a scope to the ideas of leading capitalists, far higher than anything ever undertaken before. They talk of millions as confidently as formerly of thousands." Soon the nation was into a raucous era whose inheritors were Daniel Drew, Jay Gould, Jim Fisk, and others of that stripe, operating in "a riot of individual materialism, under which," as Theodore Roosevelt was to say, "complete freedom for the individual . . .

turned out in practice to mean perfect freedom for the strong to wrong the weak." The big fish ate the little fish, and once the little fish got scarce or learned to hide among the rocks, the big fish ate each other. *Laissez faire* meant *laissez nous faire*, and free enterprise reached its symbolic apogee with the attempt by a gang of thieves, one night late in 1876, to steal and ransom for $200,000 the body of Abraham Lincoln. They made it into his Springfield tomb and had begun removing the casket from its sarcophagus when they were caught.

Freedom then was variously interpreted, and these differences of stance and opinion — especially as they applied to the Negro in the procedure for getting the seceded states back into what Lincoln had called "their proper practical relation with the Union" — lay at the knotty heart of Reconstruction, the four-year war's lurid twelve-year epilogue. It was in fact a sequel, a drama in three acts, of which the first was much the shortest and the mildest. Johnson, in the remaining six months of the 1865 congressional recess, put into operation his predecessor's lenient plan for allowing the defeated rebels to form their own state governments and return to their old allegiance, on condition that they pledge obedience to the national laws and promise to deal fairly with their former slaves. Summer and fall wore by; Johnson declared the process of reconstruction all but complete. Then in December Congress reassembled for Act Two, the longest and quite the rowdiest of the three. Indignant over what had been done in their absence — particularly southward, where ex-Confederates were demonstrating their notion that the black man's preparation for freedom, after two hundred years of bondage, should include an indefinite interlude of peonage — the Republican majority repudiated the new state governments and declined to seat their elected senators and representatives. Vengeance-minded, the hard-war men were out for blood. "As for Jeff Davis," George Julian told the House, "I would indict him, I would convict him and hang him in the name of God. As for Robert E. Lee, unmolested in Virginia, hang him too. And stop there? Not at all. I would hang liberally while I had my hand in."

They were above all out to get Johnson, who had jumped as it were from their pocket, where he himself had assured them he was lodged, and betrayed them while their backs were turned. The battle, promptly joined, raged through the year that followed, beginning with the passage, over the President's veto, of the first civil rights bill. That was on the anniversary of Appomattox, and two months later came the 14th Amendment, which, together with other legislation barreled through, assured full citizenship to former slaves and disqualified former Confederate leaders from holding office or casting ballots in local or national elections. Victory at the polls in November having increased the close-knit, radical-dominated Republican majority to better than two thirds in both houses, Congress then was ready to move in for the kill. Impeached by the House in February 1868 for "high crimes and misdemeanors," chief among which was his "usurpation of power," Johnson avoided conviction in May by one vote in the upper chamber. Disappointed at not having replaced him with one of their own — Ben Wade, president pro tempore of the Senate — the Jacobins concentrated on winning the fall election, and got something even better for their pains. They got U. S. Grant; which was another way of saying they got their way through most of the next eight years. Grant, with his profound mistrust of intellectuals and reformers — "narrow headed men," he called them, with eyes so close-set they could "look out of the same gimlet hole without winking" — provided the perfect foil by which the Vindictives could secure what they were after. He admired their forthrightness, as he did that of certain high-powered businessmen, who also profited from his trust; with the result that the country would wait more than fifty years for an administration as crooked in money matters, and a solid hundred for one as morally corrupt.

In the end it was the sum of these excesses that brought down the second-act curtain and moved the drama into Act Three. Shock and indignation paled to boredom as news of the scandals grew, and this, combined with the effects of the financial panic of 1873, alienated enough voters to give the Democratic candidate, Samuel J. Tilden of New York, a substantial majority of the ballots cast in the presidential election three years later. Tilden did not get into the White House, though. An engineered deal, whereby the Republicans agreed to withdraw the last Union troops from occupation of the South in exchange for the electoral votes of Louisiana and Florida, put Rutherford Hayes — three times governor of Ohio by then — into office by an electoral count of 185 to 184. All this time the play had been winding down anyhow, as state after state reëstablished "home rule": Tennessee in 1869, Virginia and North Carolina in 1870, Georgia in 1871, Arkansas, Alabama, and Texas in 1874, and Mississippi in 1875. Now with the departure in 1877 of the occupation forces, Louisiana, Florida, and South Carolina also threw off the Federal yoke, and the final curtain fell. Reconstruction, so called, was over.

Home rule, as both sides knew, meant white supremacy. The Negro, then, was bartered: or his gains were, which came to the same thing. "Bottom rail on top!" he had cried in 1870 when Hiram Revels of Mississippi, the first black man to become a member of the U.S. Senate, took Jefferson Davis's former seat. After Revels came Blanche K. Bruce, also of Mississippi. He was the second Negro senator, and the last for ninety years. In 1883 the Supreme Court would invalidate the Civil Rights Act of 1875, and would follow through, before the turn of the century, by approving racial segregation on condition that "separate" accommodations also be "equal," which they seldom were. Bottom rail was back on bottom. The 14th and 15th Amendments remained as legacies of Reconstruction, along with greatly expanded free school facilities for both races, but until the government and the courts were ready again to take the Constitution at its word, the Negro — locked in a caste system of "race etiquette" as rigid as any he had known in formal bondage — could repeat, with equal validity, what an Alabama slave had said in 1864 when asked what he thought of the Great Emancipator whose proclamation went into effect that year. "I don't know nothing bout Abraham Lincoln," he replied, "cep they say he sot us free. And I don't know nothing bout that neither."

It so happened that the year that marked the end of Reconstruction, 1877, was also the watershed year in which the United States, well on its way toward becoming a — and, ultimately, the — major industrial power, began regularly exporting more than it imported. Simultaneously, the invention of what seemed at first to be little more than toys, together with their eventual mass production, was about to change the way of life, first of its own people, then the world's. Just the year before, Alexander Bell had sent the first telephone message; this year Thomas Edison had a phonograph playing, and within another two years George B. Selden would apply for a patent for a "gasoline carriage." Change was at hand, and there were those who observed its coming with mingled approval and apprehension. "I tell you these are great times," young Henry Adams had written his brother from London during the war. "Man has mounted science, and is now run away with. I firmly believe that before many centuries more, science will be the master of man. The engines he will have invented will be beyond his strength to control. Some day science may have the existence of mankind in its power, and the human race commit suicide by blowing up the world. Not only shall we be able to cruise in space, but I see no reason why some future generation shouldn't walk off like a beetle with the world on its back, or give it another rotary motion so that every zone should receive in turn its due portion of heat and light."

North and South, the veterans were part of this, but mainly as observers rather than participants, and least of all as profiteers. Few or no tycoons had served in the northern armies, and southern talents seemed not to lie in that direction, except for a prominent few who lent their names for use on letterheads. Well into what passed for middle age by then, they had something of the studied indifference of men who had spent their lives in another world. Visiting regions where they had fought, ten, then twenty, then thirty years ago, they found the distances not as great as they remembered, but the hills a good deal steeper. Certain tags of poetry had a tendency to hang in their minds, whether from a dirge by Whitman:

> *Beautiful that war and all its deeds of carnage*
> *must in time be utterly lost,*
> *That the hands of the sisters Death and Night*

incessantly softly wash again,
and ever again, this soil'd world —

or, more likely, a snatch from a rollicking cavalry tune, sung in time
with hoofbeats pounding the moon-drenched highways of their youth:

He who has good buttermilk aplenty,
And gives the soldiers none,
Shan't have any of our buttermilk
When his buttermilk is gone.

Time played its tricks, distorting and subtracting. The rebel yell, for
instance — "shrill, exultant, savage," a one-time blue infantryman recalled, "so different from the deep, manly, generous shout of the Union
soldiers" — would presently be lost to all who had never heard it on the
field of battle. Asked at the close of a U.D.C. banquet to reproduce it,
a Tennessee veteran explained that the yell was "impossible unless made
at a dead run in full charge against the enemy." Not only could it not
be given in cold blood while standing still; it was "worse than folly to
try to imitate it with a stomach full of food and a mouth full of false
teeth." So it perished from the sound waves. Wildcat screech, foxhunt
yip, banshee squall, whatever it had been, it survived only in the fading
memories and sometimes vivid dreams of old men sunning themselves on
public benches, grouped together in resentment of the boredom they
encountered when they spoke of the war to those who had not shared
it with them.

Once a year at least — aside, that is, from regimental banquets and
mass reunions, attended more and more sparsely by middle-aged, then
old, then incredibly ancient men who dwindled finally to a handful of
octogenarian drummer boys, still whiskered for the most part in a clean-
shaven world that had long since passed them by — these survivors got
together to honor their dead. Observed throughout the North on May
30, Memorial Day hopscotched the calendar in the South, where individual states made their choice between April 26, May 10, and June 3.
In any case, whenever it came, this day belonged to the veterans and
their fallen comrades, and they made the most of it, beginning with their
choice of a speaker, always with the hope that he would rival the "few
appropriate remarks" Lincoln had uttered at Gettysburg on a similar
occasion. None ever did, but one at least came close at Keene, New
Hampshire, in 1884, twenty years after that day on the outskirts of
Washington when he yelled at the since-martyred leader, high on the
parapet of Fort Stevens: "Get down, you damn fool!" Young Captain
Holmes, thrice gravely wounded in three years of service, was forty-
three by now, not halfway into a distinguished life that would continue
through more than a third of the approaching century. He would deliver,
in the course of his ninety-four years, many speeches highly admired for
their pith and felicity of expression, yet he never spoke more to the

point, or more to the satisfaction of his hearers, than he did on this Memorial Day in his native New England.

He began by expressing his respect, not only for the veterans gathered to hear him, but also for the men they had fought, and he told why he felt it. "You could not stand up day after day, in those indecisive contests where overwhelming victory was impossible because neither side would run as they ought when beaten, without getting at last something of the same brotherhood for the enemy that the north pole of a magnet has for the south, each working in an opposite sense to the other, but unable to get along without the other." Such scorn as he felt he reserved for those who had stood aside when the call came for commitment. "I think that, as life is action and passion, it is required of a man that he should share the passion and action of his time at peril of being judged not to have lived." Memorial Day was for him and his listeners "the most sacred of the year," and he believed it would continue to be observed with pride and reverence. "But even if I am wrong, even if those who are to come after us are to forget all that we hold dear, and the future is to teach and kindle its children in ways as yet unrevealed, it is enough for us that to us this day is dear and sacred. . . . For one hour, twice a year at least — at the regimental dinner, where the ghosts sit at table more numerous than the living, and on this day when we decorate their graves — the dead come back and live with us. I see them now, more than I can number, as once I saw them on this earth." He saw them, and he saw what they stood for, even now in the midst of what Mark Twain had dubbed the Gilded Age. "The generation that carried on the war has been set aside by its experience. Through our great good fortune, in our youth our hearts were touched with fire. It was given to us to learn at the outset that life is a profound and passionate thing. While we are permitted to scorn nothing but indifference, and do not pretend to undervalue the worldly rewards of ambition, we have seen with our own eyes, beyond and above the gold fields, the snowy heights.of honor, and it is for us to bear the report to those who come after us."

No wonder, then, if they looked back on that four-year holocaust — which in a sense was begun by one madman, John Brown, and ended by another, J. Wilkes Booth — with something of the feeling shared by men who have gone through, and survived, some cataclysmic phenomenon; a hurricane or an earthquake, say, or a horrendous railway accident. Memory smoothed the crumpled scroll, abolished fear, leached pain and grief, and removed the sting from death. "Well," a former hospital steward testified, recalling the moribund patients in his ward, "they would see that the doctor gave them up, and they would ask me about it. I would tell them the truth. I told one man that, and he asked how long? I said not over twenty minutes. He did not show any fear — they never do. He put his hand up, so, and closed his eyes with his own fingers, then stretched himself out and crossed his arms over his breast. 'Now, fix me,' he said. I pinned the toes of his stockings together; that was the way we laid corpses out; and he died in a few minutes. His face looked as pleasant as if he was asleep, and smiling. Many's the time the boys have fixed themselves that way before they died." In time, even death itself might be abolished. Sergeant Berry Benson, a South Carolina veteran from McGowan's brigade, Wilcox's division, A. P. Hill's corps, Army of Northern Virginia — he had enlisted three months before Sumter, aged eighteen, and served through Appomattox — saw it so when he got around to composing the Reminiscences he hoped would "go down amongst my descendants for a long time." Reliving the war in words, he began to wish he could relive it in fact, and he came to believe that he and his fellow soldiers, gray and blue, might one day be able to do just that: if not here on earth, then afterwards in Valhalla. "Who knows," he asked as his narrative drew toward its close, "but it may be given to us, after this life, to meet again in the old quarters, to play chess and draughts, to get up soon to answer the morning roll call, to fall in at the tap of the drum for drill and dress parade, and again to hastily don our war gear while the monotonous patter of the long roll summons to battle? Who knows but again the old flags, ragged and torn, snapping in the wind, may face each other and flutter, pursuing and pursued, while the cries of victory fill a summer day? And after the battle, then the slain and wounded will arise, and all will meet together under the two flags, all sound and well, and there will be talking and laughter and cheers, and all will say: Did it not seem real? Was it not as in the old days?"

★ ★ ★

By then they had nearly all come round, both sides having entered into a two-way concession whereby the victors acknowledged that the Confederates had fought bravely for a cause they believed was just and the losers agreed it was probably best for all concerned that the Union had been preserved. The first step lay in admission of defeat, and one of the first to take it publicly was Joe Johnston. Aboard a Chesapeake Bay steamer, not long after his surrender, the general heard a fellow passenger insisting that the South had been "conquered but not subdued." Asked in what command he had served, the bellicose young man — one of those stalwarts later classified as "invisible in war and invincible in peace" — replied that, unfortunately, circumstances had made it impossible for him to be in the army. "Well, sir, I was," Johnston told him. "You may not be subdued, but I am."

Similarly, R. E. Lee encouraged all who sought his advice to take the loyalty oath required by the President's amnesty proclamation as a prerequisite to recovery of their rights as citizens, and even did so himself, barely two months after Appomattox, though nothing came of it then or later; he would go to his grave disfranchised. However, news that he had "asked for pardon" spread rapidly through the South, producing consternation, which was followed for the most part, even among those who had been die-hards up till then, by prompt acceptance and emulation. "You have disgraced the family, sir!" Ex-Governor Henry Wise sputtered when he learned that one of his sons had taken the oath. "But, Father," the former captain said, "General Lee advised me to do it." Taken aback, Wise paused only a moment before he replied: "That alters the case. Whatever General Lee advises is right."

Neither of these attitudes or reactions — Johnston's admission that he had been "subdued," Lee's willingness to pledge loyalty to a government he had sought to overthrow — was acceptable to Jefferson Davis in his own right. He did not object intrinsically to their view, so long as they applied it to themselves, but as the symbolic leader of a nation, even one that had been abolished by force of arms, he had other factors to consider. For him, the very notion of subdual was something to be rejected out of hand, if acceptance, as he conceived it, meant abandoning the principles of constitutional government. The war had been lost beyond denial, but not the cause. Nothing would ever bend him from that. He clung to the views he had held in 1861, and indeed ever since he entered public life some twenty years before. As for anything resembling an apology — which he believed was what he would be offering if he took the oath required — he would say repeatedly, first and last: "I have no claim to pardon, not having in any wise repented." No wonder, then, that Andrew Johnson referred to him as Lucifer incarnate, "the head devil of them all."

To his own people he was something else, in part because of all he had suffered, first in the granite bowels of Fort Monroe — where Miles, acting on Stanton's orders, martyred him about as effectively as Booth had martyred Lincoln — and then through much of the decade following his release on bail, a time referred to by his wife as one spent "floating uprooted." From Richmond, his trial having been put off until November, he went to Canada, where the two older of his four children were in school, then came back by way of Cuba for his health's sake, his trial having been postponed again till March of 1868, then still again until the following February. Impeachment was heading up by now in Washington, and the danger loomed of Johnson's being replaced by bluff Ben Wade, who was not above Star Chamber proceedings. On the advice of his attorneys, Davis and his family planned to sail for Europe, and did so in July, though Wade by then had been kept from becoming President by one senatorial vote. In England the former State Prisoner was entertained by high-born sympathizers and had the pleasure of dining with his old companion Judah Benjamin, fast on the rise as a distinguished member of the bar. A visit to France at the end of the year also gave him the satisfaction of declining an audience with

Napoleon and Eugénie, who, he said, had "played us false" at a time when the need for friends was sore.

He had by now had more than enough of "floating," and his pride would not allow him to accept indefinitely from admirers the financial help he was obliged to live on while his trial was pending. Then suddenly it no longer was. Early in 1869, with the indictment quashed at last, he was free to come home and accept employment as president of the Carolina Life Insurance Company, headquartered in Memphis. He returned without his family, got settled in the business, and went back to England in late summer, 1870, for his wife and children. Docking at Baltimore in mid-October he learned that Robert Lee had died that week. "Virginia has need of all her sons," the general had replied when asked by veterans what he thought of their going elsewhere to escape the strictures of poverty and Reconstruction, and he himself had set them an example by serving, at a salary of $1500 a year, as president of Washington College, a small, all but bankrupt institution out in the Shenandoah Valley. He aged greatly in the five years left him after Appomattox, suffering from the heart ailment which his doctors now could see had been what plagued him through much of the war, when the symptoms were diagnosed as rheumatism. Stricken in late September, he lingered till October 12. Back in battle toward the end, like Stonewall before him, he called in his delirium on A. P. Hill: "Tell Hill he must come up." Then he quieted, as Jackson too had done before he crossed the river. "Strike the tent," he said, and then he died.

"Of the man, how shall I speak? His moral qualities rose to the height of genuis," Davis declared at a memorial service held in Richmond in early November. It was his first public address since the end of the war, and though he was encouraged by the fervor of his reception in the one-time national capital, the passing of the great Confederate captain was the signal for the onset of a series of reversals for his former chief, the heaviest of which came two years later with the death of one of his two surviving sons. Eleven-year-old Billy, conceived in Montgomery during the secession furore and born after the removal of the government to Virginia, fell victim to diphtheria in Memphis. Settled in a house of his own for the first time in six years, and released at last, as he thought, from the life his wife described as "floating uprooted," Davis suffered this sudden deprivation only to have it followed by still another during the financial panic of '73, precipitated by the failure of Jay Cooke & Company in New York, which had marketed the huge war loans of the Federal government. Carolina Life went under, too, a chip among the flotsam, taking with it his last $15,000 and the only job he had ever had. Afloat again, he sought other ventures, some involving trips to Europe in search of backers, but nothing came of them. Though he kept his home in Memphis, even managing the expense of a wedding for his daughter Maggie in 1875, the result was that he again found himself floating rootless, his life no longer a career, but rather an existence.

When at last he found the answer, a way out of this dilemma, it was neither in Memphis nor in business. Ever since his release from prison he had had it in mind to write a personal history of the war, and even as early as his stay in Canada he had begun to look through such papers as were then available for his purpose, including duplicates of messages sent commanders in the field. One of the first he examined, however — a telegram he had addressed to Lee from Danville on the day of Appomattox, unaware that the surrender was in progress — put an end to this preliminary effort. "You will realize the reluctance I feel to leave the soil of Virginia," he had wired, "and appreciate my anxiety to win success north of the Roanoke." Mrs Davis, who was there to help him sort the documents, saw a stricken look come on his face at the memories the words called up. He pushed the papers away. "Let us put them by for a while. I cannot speak of my dead so soon," he told her. That had been nearly ten years ago, and he had not returned to them since, despite the urging of such friends as Preston Johnston, who admonished him: "I do not believe any man ever lived who could dare to tell in the light more fully what was done in the dark, than you can. It seems to be a friendly duty to warn you not to forget your design." Davis did not forget, but he was fully occupied by the insurance business: until it vanished, that is, along with what little he had left in the way of funds. Failure freed him to return to his old design; failure and necessity, and something else as well. Recently, old comrades who had shared the glory and pain of battles won and lost — ex-Confederates for the most part, though the victors also had their differences in public — had begun to turn on each other, quarreling over what they considered a proper distribution of praise and blame, especially the latter. One of the hottest of these arguments had to do with Gettysburg; Fitzhugh Lee and Jubal Early crossed swords with Longstreet, who had compounded their enmity by going over to the Republicans and his old friend Grant. Davis stayed well out of it, reserving his ire for a long-time adversary, Joseph E. Johnston, who had brought out in 1874 his *Narrative of Military Operations Directed During the Late War Between the States*, much of it devoted to unburdening himself of grievances against his former superior. "The advance sheets exhibit his usual malignity and suppression of the truth when it would affect his side of the case unfavorably," Davis informed his wife by way of warming up for the counteroffensive he now had it in mind to launch. He would write his own account, quartering much of the same ground, of course, and accordingly signed a contract with Appleton's of New York, who agreed to cover such expenses as he required for secretarial assistance.

Bustling Memphis, hot in summer, cold in winter — the scene of his loss, moreover, of the third of his four sons — seemed unconducive to

the peace he believed he needed for such work. Who could write anything there, let alone a full-fledged two- or three-volume history of the
war? He had found the atmosphere he wanted on a trip to the Mississippi Coast the previous November, when he wrote his wife that "the
moaning of the winds among the pines and the rolling waves of the
Gulf on the beach gave me a sense of rest and peace which made me
wish to lay me down and be at home." Midway between New Orleans
and Mobile was "Beauvoir," an estate belonging to Sarah E. Dorsey, a
wealthy, recently widowed childhood friend of Varina's; "a fine place,"
Davis called it, with a "large and beautiful house" set among spreading
live oaks "and many orange trees yet full of fruit." Receiving him now
as a visitor, Mrs Dorsey offered him the use of a cottage on the grounds,
"a refuge without encumbrances" in which to write his book. He quickly
accepted, on condition of paying board, and by February 1877 he and
a body servant had moved in. Quarters were found nearby for Major
W. T. Walthall, his research assistant, and work began at once, with
the added help of Sarah Dorsey herself. She had written four novels
under the nom de plume "Filia," and was delighted to serve as an
amanuensis, having long admired her house guest as "the noblest man she
had ever met on earth."

Varina, who had never enjoyed the notion of sharing Jefferson
Davis with anyone — least of all another woman, childhood friend or
not — was considerably less pleased with this outcome of his quest for
domestic tranquillity. She had been in Germany most of the past eight
months, getting twelve-year-old Winnie settled in a girls' school in
Carlsruhe, and despite urgings from her husband and Mrs Dorsey that
she join them on the Coast, she remained in Europe for another eight,
determined not to be a party to any such *ménage à trois* arrangement.
Finally in October she returned, not to Beauvoir but to Memphis, where
twenty-year-old Jeff Junior, after an unsatisfactory year at V.M.I., had
accepted a place in a bank with his sister Maggie's husband. Davis himself came up at once, hoping to take her back with him, but she refused.
She was pleased, however, to see him looking well, absorbed in his work
and eager to get back to it. A new urgency was on him, caused in part
by the recent passing of some of the principal characters in the story he
was attempting to retell. Braxton Bragg, for example, had dropped dead
on the street in Galveston last year, and Raphael Semmes had been
buried only the month before in Mobile. Another great raider, Bedford
Forrest, was dying in Memphis even now, wasted by diabetes to a scant
one hundred pounds. "I am completely broke up," he confessed to
friends. "I am broke in fortune, broke in health, broke in spirit." Davis
sat by his bedside the day before he died, then served as a pallbearer at
his funeral on the last day of October. In the carriage, en route to
Elmwood Cemetery, a companion remarked on Forrest's greatness as
a soldier. "I agree with you," the former President said. "The trouble

was that the generals commanding in the Southwest never appreciated him until it was too late. Their judgment was that he was a bold and enterprising raider and rider. I was misled by them, and never knew how to measure him until I read the reports of his campaign across the Tennessee River in 1864. This induced a study of his earlier reports, and after that I was prepared to adopt what you are pleased to name as the judgment of history." Someone mentioned Brice's Crossroads, and Davis replied as before: "That campaign was not understood in Richmond. The impression made upon those in authority was that Forrest had made another successful raid. . . . I saw it all after it was too late."

He returned alone to Beauvoir, Sarah Dorsey, and his work. Varina was willing to help by mail, amplifying his recollections with her own, but not in person. "Nothing on earth would pain me like living in that kind of community," she had written from Europe, and she still felt that way about it. At any rate she did for another eight months before she relented, in part because of the heat of a Memphis summer, but mainly because her husband by then had offered to give up his present living arrangement if she would join him elsewhere. Apparently it was this she had been waiting for all along, for he no sooner made the offer than she consented to join him where he was. She arrived in July, 1878, and at once took over the job of amanuensis. Indignant at the unrelenting vindictiveness of Washington in excluding Davis from the benefits of a pension bill for veterans of the Mexican War, they settled down to work amid reports of a yellow fever epidemic moving upriver from New Orleans. Memphis and other cities and towns were still under quarantine in October when a wire reached Beauvoir to inform them that Jeff Junior had come down with the disease. Then five days later another arrived to tell them he had rallied and then died. Davis had lost the fourth of his four sons; Samuel, Joseph, William, and now Jeff. "I presume not God to scorn," he wrote a kinsman, "but the many and humble prayers offered before my boy was taken from me are hushed in the despair of my bereavement."

Work was the answer, as much for Varina as for her husband, and they got on with it, sometimes into the small hours of the night. In February the domestic strain was relieved by Mrs Dorsey, who sold Beauvoir to Davis for $5500, to be paid in three installments, then went to New Orleans to consult a physician for what turned out to be cancer. By July she was dead. Childless, she left Beauvoir to Davis, absolving him from making the other two payments. Nor was that all. "I hereby give and bequeath all my property, wherever located and situated, wholly and entirely, without hindrance or qualification," her will read, "to my most honored and esteemed friend, Jefferson Davis, ex-President of the Confederate States, for his sole use and benefit, in fee simple forever. . . . I do not intend," she had said in closing, "to share in the ingratitude of my country towards the man who is in my eyes the highest and noblest in existence." He was now the master of Beauvoir, along with much else, including three plantations in Louisiana, and Varina was its mistress.

The work went on. Reconstruction was over, but Davis still fought the war, landing verbal blows where armed strokes had failed. Soon the first of what were to be two large volumes was ready for the printer. *Rise and Fall of the Confederate Government*, he would call it: not *Our Cause*, as he had originally intended. He moved into and steadily through the second volume. On an afternoon in April, 1881, he took a long nap, then at 8 o'clock that evening resumed dictation. Speaking slowly and distinctly, so that Varina would not miss a word, he tugged firmly on the drawstrings of his logic for a final explication of his thesis that the North, not the South, had been the revolutionary party in the struggle, malevolent in its effort to subvert, subjugate, and destroy, respectively, the states, the people, and the Union as it had been till then. "When the cause was lost, what cause was it?" he asked, and answered: "Not that of the South only, but the cause of constitutional government, of the supremacy of law, of the natural rights of man." It was by then well past midnight, and only the rhythmic plash of waves on the beach came through the stillness of the dark hours before dawn. He kept on, launched now onto the last of nearly 1500 pages, restating his conviction "that the war was, on the part of the United States Government, one of aggression and usurpation, and, on the part of the South, was for the defense of an inherent, unalienable right." He paused, then continued.

> In asserting the right of secession, it has not been my wish to incite to its exercise: I recognize the fact that the war showed it to be impracticable, but this did not prove it to be wrong. And now that it may not be again attempted, and that the Union may promote the general welfare, it is needful that the truth, the whole truth, should be known, so that crimination and recrimination may forever cease, and then, on the basis of fraternity and faithful regard for the rights of the States, there may be written on the arch of the Union, *Esto perpetua.*

He leaned back, sighed, and closed his eyes against the glare of lamplight. It was 4 o'clock in the morning and he was within two months of being seventy-three years old. Her pen poised above the paper, Varina looked up, ready for the next sentence. "I think I am done," he said with a tired smile.

He was done, and the book — already in type, except these final pages — came out in June. In the South it was hailed and praised. No home that could afford them was without the two thick volumes, often bound in calf, on a parlor table. The trouble was, so few could afford them, and in the North the book was largely ignored, save in a few grudging magazine reviews. Financially, it was a failure; Appleton's lost money, and Davis himself made little, despite a drawn-out lawsuit with the publisher which ensued. In August he and Varina sailed for Europe to get Winnie, and returned in late November. "The Daughter of the Confederacy," born in the Richmond White House while the guns of Kennesaw were booming, was tall and fair, with clear gray eyes and a quiet manner; she spoke, to her father's surprise, with traces of a German accent which she would never lose. Settled again at Beauvoir he looked forward to a peaceful life through whatever years were left him. Then in mid-December came news that Joe Johnston had wondered aloud to a reporter what had become of all the treasury gold Davis had taken along on his flight through Georgia. It came, he heard, to $2,500,000; yet "Mr Davis has never given any satisfactory account of it." In the hue and cry that followed, the general was obliged to run for cover, and letters poured into Beauvoir from all parts of the country, expressing outrage at the slander and admiration for its victim. Davis had won his last skirmish with Johnston, who perhaps was confirmed in his distaste for the offensive.

Still, no amount of adulation North or South could temper the former President's resolution not to ask for pardon; not even pleas from his home-state Legislature that he do so in order to be returned to his old seat in the U. S. Senate. He did however agree to come to Jackson in March, 1884, for a ceremony staged to honor him as "the embodied history of the South." Standing in the high-ceilinged Capitol chamber where he had stood just over two decades ago, near the midpoint of the war, and told the assembled dignitaries, "Our people have only to be true to themselves to behold the Confederate flag among the recognized nations of the earth," he spoke now much as he had then: "It has been said that I should apply to the United States for a pardon. But repentance must precede the right of pardon, and I have not repented. Remembering, as I must, all which has been suffered, all which has been lost — disappointed hopes and crushed aspirations — yet I deliberately say, if it were all to do over again, I would again do just as I did in 1861." His hearers caught their breath at this, then applauded with all their might the fallen leader who represented, almost alone, the undefeat of which they boasted from stumps across the land, now and for years to come. Unforgiving, he was unforgiven, and he preferred it so, for their sake and his own.

Late in the spring of the following year a Boston paper called on Davis for an expression of his views on U. S. Grant, who was dying at Mount McGregor, New York, of cancer of the throat. Bankrupt by a brokerage partner who turned out to be a swindler, the general had lost even his sword as security for an unpaid loan, and was now engaged in a race with death to complete his *Memoirs*, hoping the proceeds would provide for his family after he was gone. He won, but only by the hardest. Reduced by pain to communicating with his doctor on slips of paper — "A verb is anything that signifies to be; to do; to suffer," one

read. "I signify all three" — he managed to finish the book within a week
of his death in July, and royalties approaching half a million dollars went
to Julia and his sons. Davis had declined to comment on the career of
this man whose name, in the course of his two White House terms, had
come to stand for plunder and repression. "General Grant is dying," he
replied to the request from Boston. "Instead of seeking to disturb the
quiet of his closing hours, I would, if it were in my power, contribute to
the peace of his mind and the comfort of his body." Similarly, he had
withheld comment on the passing of other former enemies, beginning
with George Thomas, whose weight rose above three hundred pounds
within five years of the end of the war, when he died on duty of a stroke
in the same year as his fellow Virginian, R. E. Lee. Henry Halleck and
George Meade, who also stayed in the army, followed him two years
later. George McClellan, after serving three years as governor of New
Jersey, died three months after Grant, and was followed in turn by
Winfield Hancock, who had run against Garfield in the presidential
election six years back, just over three months later.

By then it was 1886, the silver anniversary of Sumter. Memorial
services and reunions were being planned throughout the South, and
Davis was pressed to attend most of them as guest of honor. He declined, pleading frailty, until someone thought to point out that Winnie
might never know how dear he was to the hearts of his people unless
he gave them the chance to show their love in public. That persuaded
him. "I'll go; I'll go," he said, and accepted invitations from Montgomery, Atlanta, and Savannah. In late April he sat on the portico of the
Alabama capitol, where he had been inaugurated twenty-five years before, and heard a eulogy pronounced by John B. Gordon, former U. S.
senator and now a candidate for governor of Georgia, who also presented Winnie to the crowd, to wild applause. Next day Davis spoke
briefly at the laying of the cornerstone for a monument to the Confederate dead — repeating once more his contention that the seceded
states had launched no revolution; "Sovereigns never rebel," he said —
then set out for Atlanta, where 50,000 veterans were assembling for a
May Day reunion. He was on the platform, receiving the cheers of all
that host, when he looked out beyond its distant fringes and saw a man
approaching on horseback, portly and white-haired, with cottony
muttonchop whiskers, decked out in Confederate gray with the looped
braid of a lieutenant general on his sleeves. It was Longstreet. Uninvited
because of his postwar views — "The striking feature, the one the
people should keep in view," he had said at the outset of Reconstruction,
"is that we are a conquered people. Recognizing this fact, fairly and
squarely, there is but one course left for wise men to pursue, and that
is to accept the terms that now are offered by the conquerers" — Old
Peter had risen that morning at his home in nearby Gainesville, put on his
full uniform, come down by train, and ridden out to show the throng

that he was of them, whether they wanted him there or not. Dismounting, he walked up the steps of the platform where Davis was seated, and everyone wondered what Davis would do. They soon found out, for he rose and hurried to meet Lee's old warhorse. "When the two came together," a witness declared, "Mr Davis threw his arms around General Longstreet's neck and the two leaders embraced with great emotion. The meaning of the reconciliation was clear and instantly had a profound effect upon the thousands of veterans who saw it. With a great shout they showed their joy."

One occasion of the Atlanta visit was the unveiling of a statue to the late Senator Benjamin Hill, always a loyal friend in times of crisis. "We shall conquer all enemies yet," he had assured his chief within two weeks of Appomattox, but admitted nine years later, looking back: "All physical advantages are insufficient to account for our failure. The truth is, we failed because too many of our people were not determined to win." Davis knew the basic validity of this view, yet he preferred to stress the staunchness of his people and the long odds they had faced. Northern journalists had begun to note the "inflammatory" effect of his appearances, and he tried next week in Savannah to offset this by remarking at a banquet given by the governor in his honor: "There are some who take it for granted that when I allude to State sovereignty I want to bring on another war. I am too old to fight again, and God knows I do not want you to have the necessity of fighting again." He paused to let the reporters take this down, but while he waited he saw the faces of those around him, many of them veterans like himself; with the result that he undid what had gone before. "However, if the necessity *should* arise," he said, "I know you will meet it, as you always have discharged every duty you felt called upon to perform."

Although he returned to Beauvoir near exhaustion, he recovered in time, the following year, to challenge the prohibition movement as still another "monstrous" attempt to limit individual freedom. His words were quoted by the liquor interests and he was denounced by a Methodist bishop for advocating "the barroom and the destruction of virtue." But the fact was he had mellowed, partly under the influence of strong nationalist feelings never far below the surface of his resistance. When he went back to Georgia in October, to meet "perhaps for the last time" with veterans at a reunion staged in Macon — where he had first been taken after his capture near Irwinville, more than twenty-two years ago — he spoke to them of the North and South as indivisibly united. "We are now at peace," he said, "and I trust will ever remain so. . . . In referring therefore to the days of the past and the glorious cause you have served . . . I seek but to revive a memory which should be dear to you and to your children, a memory which teaches the highest lessons of manhood, of truth and adherence to duty — duty to your State, duty to your principles, duty to your buried parents, and duty to your coming children." That was the burden of what he had to say through the time now left him, including his last speech of all, delivered the following spring at Mississippi City, only a six-mile buggy ride from Beauvoir.

Within three months of being eighty years old, he had not thought he would speak again in public; but he did, this once, for a particular reason. The occasion was a convention of young Southerners, and that was why — their youth. He did not mention the war at all, not even as "a memory which should be dear," though he did refer at the outset to the nation he had led. "Friends and fellow citizens," he began, and stopped. "Ah, pardon me," he said. "The laws of the United States no longer permit me to designate you as fellow citizens. I feel no regret that I stand before you a man without a country, for my ambition lies buried in the grave of the Confederacy." Then he went on to tell them what he had come to say. "The faces I see before me are those of young men; had I not known this I would not have appeared before you. Men in whose hands the destinies of our Southland lie, for love of her I break my silence to speak to you a few words of respectful admonition. The past is dead; let it bury its dead, its hopes and its aspirations. Before you lies the future, a future full of golden promise, a future of expanding national glory, before which all the world shall stand amazed. Let me beseech you to lay aside all rancor, all bitter sectional feeling, and to take your places in the ranks of those who will bring about a consummation devoutly to be wished — a reunited country."

Those were his last public words, and they seemed withal to have brought him a new peace, one that fulfilled a hope he had recently expressed to an old friend: "My downs have been so many, and the feeling of injustice so great, that I wish to hold on and see whether the better days may not come." A reporter who came to Beauvoir for his eightieth birthday, June 3, not only found him "immaculately dressed, straight and erect, with traces of his military service still showing in his carriage, and with the flush of health on his pale, refined face," but also observed that he retained "a keen interest in current topics, political, social, religious." He kept busy. In the course of the next year he wrote three magazine articles, a *Short History of the Confederate States*, and even got started on an autobiography, though he soon put this aside. In early November, 1889, he set out for New Orleans to catch a steamer upriver for his annual inspection trip to Brierfield, which he had lost and then recovered by a lawsuit. Usually his wife went along but this time she remained behind with guests. Exposed to a sleety rain, he came down with a cold and was so ill by the time the boat reached Brierfield Landing, late at night, that he continued on to Vicksburg. Going ashore next morning, he rode down to the plantation, only to spend the next four days in bed, sick with bronchitis and a recurrence of the malaria that had killed his bride and nearly killed him, more than fifty years before, at the same place.

Alarmed, for Davis by then was near delirium, the plantation manager got him back to Vicksburg and onto a steamer headed south. Downriver that night the boat was hailed by another coming up with Varina on board. Warned by telegraph of her husband's condition, she had set out to join him, and now she did so, transferring in midstream to claim her place at his bedside. New Orleans doctors pronounced him too ill to be taken to Beauvoir, so he was carried on a stretcher to a private home in the Garden District. He seemed to improve in the course of the next week. "It may seem strange to you," he told an attending physician, "that a man of my years should desire to live; but I do. There are still some things that I have to do in this world." He wanted above all to get back to the autobiography he had set aside. "I have not told what I wish to say of my college-mates Sidney Johnston and Polk. I have much more to say of them. I shall tell a great deal of West Point — and I seem to remember more every day." Presently, though, it was clear that he would do none of these things, including the desired return to Beauvoir. Another week passed; December came in. On December 5, within six months of being eighty-two years old, he woke to find Varina sitting beside him, and he let her know he knew the time was near. "I want to tell you I am not afraid to die," he said, although he seemed no worse than he had been the day before.

That afternoon he slept soundly, but woke at dusk with a violent chill. Frightened, Varina poured out a teaspoon of medicine, only to have him decline it with a meager smile and a faint shake of his head. When she insisted he refused again. "Pray excuse me. I cannot take it," he murmured. These were the last words of a man who had taken most of the knocks a hard world had to offer. He lapsed into a peaceful sleep that continued into the night. Once when his breathing grew labored the doctors turned him gently onto his right side, and he responded childlike by raising his arm to pillow his cheek on his hand, the other resting lightly on his heart. Midnight came and went, and less than an hour later he too obeyed Anaximander's dictum, breathing his last so imperceptibly that Varina and the others at his bedside could scarcely tell the moment of his going.

He died on Friday and was buried on Wednesday, time being needed to allow for the arrival of friends and relatives from distant points. Meanwhile, dressed in a civilian suit of Confederate gray, his body lay in state at City Hall, viewed in the course of the next four days by an estimated hundred thousand mourners. Then the day of the funeral came, December 11, and all the church bells of New Orleans tolled. Eight southern governors served as pallbearers, the Washington Artillery as guard of honor; interment would be at Metairie Cemetery in the tomb of the Army of Northern Virginia, which was crowned with a statue of Stonewall Jackson atop a fifty-foot marble shaft. "The end of a long and lofty life has come. The strange and sudden dignity of death has been added to the fine and resolute dignity of living," the Episcopal bishop of Louisiana declared on the steps of City Hall as the casket was brought out to begin the three-hour march to Metairie. After the service at the tomb, when Taps had sounded, he spoke again. "In the name of God, amen. We here consign the body of Jefferson Davis, a servant of his state and country and a soldier in their armies; sometime member of Congress, Senator from Mississippi, and Secretary of War of the United States; the first and only President of the Confederate States of America; born in Kentucky on the third day of June, 1808, died in Louisiana on the sixth day of December, 1889, and buried here by the reverent hands of his people."

Much else was said in the way of praise across the land that day, and still more would be said four years later, when his body would be removed to its permanent resting place in Hollywood Cemetery, Richmond, to join his son Joe and others who had died nearby in Virginia during the war. Lincoln by now had been a full generation in his Springfield tomb, and all he had said or written would be cherished as an imperishable legacy to the nation, including the words he had spoken in response to a White House serenade on the occasion of his reëlection: "What has occurred in this case must ever recur in similar cases. Human nature will not change. In any future great national trial, compared with the men of this, we shall have as weak and as strong, as silly and as wise, as bad and as good. Let us therefore study the incidents of this, as philosophy to learn wisdom from, and none of them as wrongs to be revenged." Davis could never match that music, or perhaps even catch its tone. His was a different style, though it too had its beauty and its uses: as in his response to a recent Beauvoir visitor, a reporter who hoped to leave with something that would help explain to readers the underlying motivation of those crucial years of bloodshed and division. Davis pondered briefly, then replied.

"Tell them — " He paused as if to sort the words. "Tell the world that I only loved America," he said.

LIST OF MAPS

Maps drawn by Rafael Palacios, from originals
by the author. All are oriented north.

BIBLIOGRAPHICAL NOTE
The following bibliographical note was included with the full text of
THE CIVIL WAR: A Narrative—Red River to Appomattox.

So there now. Twenty years have come and gone and I can say with Chaucer, "Farwel my book and my devocion." All through the second of these two decades—the drawn-out time it took to write this third and final volume—my debt to those who went before me, dead and living, continued to mount even as the Centennial spate diminished to a trickle and then ran dry. Previous obligations were enlarged, and new ones acquired, on both sides of the line defining the limits of the original material: especially on the near side, where the evidence was assembled and presented in general studies, biographies, and secondary accounts of individual campaigns. Chief among these last, to take them in the order of their use, were the following: *Red River Campaign* by Ludwell H. Johnson, *Lee's Last Campaign* by Clifford Dowdey, *Autumn of Glory* by Thomas L. Connelly, *Jubal's Raid* by Frank E. Vandiver, *The Decisive Battle of Nashville* by Stanley F. Horn, *Sherman's March Through the Carolinas* by John G. Barrett, and two recitals of the Appomattox chase, *An End to Valor* by Philip Van Doren Stern and *Nine April Days* by Burke Davis. Similarly, my long-term obligation to works on naval matters was extended by Virgil Carrington Jones's *Civil War at Sea: The Final Effort* and Edward Boykin's *Ghost Ship of the Confederacy.*

No one who has read or even scanned these books can fail to see my debt to them, as well as to the biographies cited earlier, two of which had concluding volumes that came out just as the need for them was sorest: Hudson Strode's *Jefferson Davis: Tragic Hero* and Bruce Catton's *Grant Takes Command.* Having had them, I cannot see how I could have managed without them, and the same applies to J. G. Randall's *Lincoln the President,* completed after his death by Richard N. Current in *Last Full Measure,* and Jim Bishop's *Day Lincoln Was Shot.* Clifford Dowdey's *Lee* brought his subject into sharper focus, and T. Harry Williams filled a sizeable gap with his *Hayes of the Twenty-third,* as E. B. Long did many others with *The Civil War Day by Day: An Almanac.* Nash K. Burger's and John K. Bettersworth's *South of Appomattox* helped get me down to the wire, and Kenneth M. Stampp, who was with me at the start in *And the War Came,* was also with me at the finish in *The Era of Reconstruction,* another old friend among the many I know only through their work.

To all these I am grateful, as I was and am to those mentioned in the end notes to the first two volumes of this iliad, most of whom continued their contribution through the third. Originally I intended to list my obligations in a complete bibliography here at the close of the whole, but even this chore has been spared me—along with a considerable added bulkiness for you—by Ralph G. Newman and E. B. Long, whose 1964 pamphlet, *A Basic Civil War Library,* first published in the *Journal of the Illinois State Historical Society,* enumerates by category the 350-odd books I owe most to, old and new and in and out of print. Other such compilations are readily available, including a much fuller one in Long's own *Almanac,* yet this one is to me the best in its inclusion of the works I mainly relied on, at any rate up to its date of issue. While I hope I have acknowledged my heaviest contemporary debts in this trio of notes, there are two I would like to stress in particular. One is to Bruce Catton, whose *Centennial History of the Civil War* was finished in time for its third volume, *Never Call Retreat,* to be available, together with his earlier *Stillness at Appomattox,* as a source and guide all through the writing of my own third volume. I was, as Stonewall Jackson said in another connection on his deathbed, "the infinite gainer" from having him thus meet his deadline even as I was failing to reach mine. My other chief debt is to the late Allan Nevins, whose close-packed *Organized War to Victory,* the last in his four-volume *War for the Union,* was similarly available during the past two years. Both gave me a wealth of useable material, but at least as valuable was their example of dedication and perseverance, double-barreled proof that such an undertaking could be carried to a finish. In that sense my debt to them is personal, though not as much so, nor as large, as the ones I owe my editor, Robert Loomis, and my wife, Gwyn Rainer Foote, both of whom bore with me all the way.

Perhaps in closing I might add that, although nowhere along the line have I had a "thesis" to argue or maintain—partly no doubt because I never saw one yet that could not be "proved," at least to the satisfaction of the writer who advanced it—I did have one thing I wanted to do, and that was to restore a balance I found lacking in nearly all the histories composed within a hundred years of Sumter. In all too many of these works, long and short, foreign and domestic, the notion prevailed that the War was fought in Virginia, while elsewhere—in an admittedly large but also rather empty region known vaguely as "the West"—a sort of running skirmish wobbled back and forth, presumably as a way for its participants, faceless men with unfamiliar names, to pass the time while waiting for the issue to be settled in the East. I do not claim that the opposite is true, but I do claim that it is perhaps a little closer to the truth; that Vicksburg, for example, was as "decisive" as Gettysburg, if not more so, and that Donelson, with its introduction of Grant and Forrest onto the national scene, may have had more to do with the outcome than either of the others had, for all their greater panoply, numbers, and documentation. In any case, it was my hope to provide what I considered a more fitting balance, East and West, in the course of attempting my aforesaid purpose of re-creating that war and making it live again in the world around us.

So, anyhow, "Farwel my book and my devocion," my rock and my companion through two decades. At the outset of this Gibbon span, plunk in what I hope will be the middle of my writing life, I was two years younger than Grant at Belmont, while at the end I was four months older than Lincoln at his assassination. By way of possible extenuation, in response to complaints that it took me five times longer to write the war than the participants took to fight it, I would point out that there were a good many more of them than there was of me. However that may be, the conflict is behind me now, as it is for you and it was a hundred-odd years ago for them.

—S.F.

INDEX

ABOUT THE AUTHOR

Shelby Foote was born in Greenville, Mississippi, and attended school there until he entered the University of North Carolina. During World War II he served in the European theater as a captain of field artillery. In the period after the war he wrote five novels: *Tournament, Follow Me Down, Love in a Dry Season, Shiloh,* and *Jordan County.* He was twice awarded a Guggenheim fellowship. A longtime resident of Memphis, Tennessee, he died in 2005 at the age of 88.

SHERMAN vs JOHNSTON
Dalton to Peachtree Creek
7 May–17 July

(1) Outflanked via Snake Creek Gap, May 12, Johnston withdraws southward fifteen miles.

(2) Sherman is repulsed, May 14, but Johnston, hearing that the Federals are over the Oostanaula five miles in his rear, begins a thirty-mile displacement.

(3) Bypassing Calhoun and Adairsville, the Confederates occupy Cassville, May 18, while the Federals converge mistakenly on Kingston. Johnston plans, then cancels, an attack; when Sherman comes up, withdraws across the Etowah to Allatoona, May 19, and shifts his base to Marietta.

(4) Sherman cuts loose from the railroad, May 23; heads due south for Burnt Hickory and Dallas.

(5) Johnston conforms; blocks Union advance at New Hope Church, May 25. Both extend lines eastward; clash again, May 28. Johnston cancels planned attack.

(6) Sherman shifts to Acworth; Johnston takes up position, June 4, on Lost Mountain and Pine Top, then sidles eastward to Brush Mountain, covering railroad.

(7) When Sherman advances, June 14–15, Johnston falls back to a new and shorter line next day on Kennesaw.

(8) Skirmishing begins June 19. Hood attacks Federal right, June 22; is repulsed. Thomas attacks Confederate center, June 27; is bloodily repulsed.

(9) Sherman resumes flanking movement, July 2, shifting McPherson westward. Johnston falls back to Smyrna.

(10) Again Sherman advances; Johnston falls back to the north bank of the Chattahoochee. Sherman continues his advance; sends McPherson far to the left, upstream, for a crossing July 8, near Roswell. Johnston falls back across the river next day, then shifts to Peachtree Creek to cover Atlanta, now only six miles in his rear. July 17, still in that position, he receives notice that he is relieved of command.

SHERMAN vs HOOD
Peachtree Creek to the Fall of Atlanta
17 July–2 Sep.

(1) Hood attacks Thomas, July 20, near the Chattahoochee crossing; is repulsed.

(2) Hood attacks Federal left, July 22; is repulsed.

(3) Sherman sidles south around the west side of Atlanta, reaching for the Confederate rail supply lines. Hood strikes him, July 28, at Ezra Church; is repulsed.

(4) Schofield breaks the Macon railroad, Aug. 30, then is joined by Thomas for the march on Jonesboro, wrecking track as they move south.

(5) Hardee attacks Federal concentration; is repulsed; then escapes encirclement, one corps moving south to Lovejoy Station while the other rejoins Hood in Atlanta—in time to assist in the evacuation and act as rear guard on the march to rejoin Hardee at Lovejoy's. The Federals march into the evacuated city next morning, Sep. 2; Sherman notifies Washington, "Atlanta is ours, and fairly won."